Deadlines Past

Deadlines Past

Forty Years of Presidential Campaigning:
A Reporter's Story

Walter R. Mears

**Andrews McMeel
Publishing**

Kansas City

04 05 06 07 FFG 10 9 8 7 6 5 4 3

Library of Congress Cataloging-in-Publication Data

Mears, Walter R. (Walter Robert), 1935–
    Deadlines past : my 40 years of presidential campaigns / Walter Mears.
        p. cm.
    ISBN 0-7407-3852-6
    1. United States—Politics and government—1945–1989. 2. United States—Politics and government—1989– 3. Presidents—United States—Election—History—20th century. 4. Presidential candidates—United States—History—20th century. 5. Political campaigns—United States—History—20th century. 6. Political campaigns—Press coverage—United States—History—20th century. 7. Mears, Walter R. (Walter Robert), 1935– 8. Journalists—United States—Biography. 9. Reporters and reporting—United States—History—20th century. I. Title.

E839.5.M376 2003
324.973'092'092—dc21

                                                        2002043874

Book design by Holly Camerlinck

For Stephanie and Susan,
so that they will know where their dad was all those years,
and for Nathaniel, Madeline, Aidan, and Sean

ACKNOWLEDGMENTS

I am a wire service man, a calling that requires writing news instantly, keeping the copy terse, and keeping yourself out of it. After nearly fifty years of striving for objectivity and avoiding personal judgments, my writing instincts were tuned to the AP wire, not to the pages of a book. Making an author out of a man with those ingrained traits required the patient persuasion of an understanding editor, for which I thank Chris Schillig at Andrews McMeel Publishing. It also required the trust and support of a publisher, in my case John McMeel, whose friendship I treasured long before my deadlines passed. I had an editor at home as well. My wife, Fran, managing editor of Gannett News Service, made my writing better by keeping it down to earth and out of the ether of political jargon. This is a book of memories shared with colleagues and competitors whose names are woven into my experience and into the stories that follow. These experiences are shared in a special way with countless colleagues in the Associated Press, the organization that was my professional home.

My thanks to all of you. Or, in the shorthand of the wire, TNX.

CONTENTS

I lived my professional life on deadline, in the relentless rhythm of my wire service, the Associated Press. Report the story, check the facts, write it, deliver it, and get on with the next one. It is a pressurized world and from the day I entered it in 1955, I knew it was where I wanted to be. The Boston bureau was a noisy, cluttered room, the windows so grimy that the view of Washington Street and what was then Newspaper Row was shaded in gray. None of that mattered. I'd found my element and my vocation.

The dictionary defines a deadline as a line around a prison that an inmate crosses only at the risk of being instantly shot. To reporters and editors, it is the time when a story must be ready for print to make the next edition. Some writers find the modern usage almost as menacing as the old definition. For them, the clock is a threat. Not for me.

I thrived on deadlines for more than forty-six years. I made my reputation as a man who could write and deliver copy almost instantly. The Associated Press is the world's oldest, largest, and finest news-gathering organization. It is a not-for-profit cooperative. (We joked that the description applied to staff salaries, too. In the news business, gripes and wisecracks are part of the language.) The AP is owned by the newspapers it serves, meaning almost every daily newspaper in America. AP people work twenty-four hours a day to deliver them the news as it unfolds, accurately, objectively, and immediately. Somewhere, an AP newspaper is sending an edition to press or a broadcaster is going on the air, which means they need the news on the wire right now. On deadline.

I reported on political campaigns from 1960 until 2000, watching the rise of television and technology, the creation of a new class of permanent political operators for hire, and the last days of the kingmakers as reformers tried to replace smoke-filled with smoke-free rooms. I came to campaign coverage just as the old ways were yielding to the new and covered elections for forty years, reporting on eleven presidential campaigns as the way candidates seek the White House was transformed. Still, despite all the arts of the pollsters and image-makers, the bottom line is still a ballot to be cast for one candidate or another. For a reporter, the task is to get past the managers and spinners to assess the strengths the candidates claim as well as the failures and flaws they try to conceal. Again, on deadline.

The pages that follow are about those eleven presidential campaigns: the changes I saw, the characters I covered, the things I heard, the impressions they left. Stories retold, this time off deadline. When I closed my career after the 2001 presidential inauguration, my deadlines were past.

To recall and write about those campaigns I went to the files of the AP, reading my old stories and those of my colleagues on the cracking, yellow teletype paper of another era, the now antique chronicle of my first twenty years as a political reporter. To find the copy for the next twenty, I could type a command into my computer and call up stories from the electronic archives. It was much more efficient but, to me, less engaging than rummaging through the paper files of the time when teletypes and typewriters were the tools of the trade. They were slow and they clattered, but the din was music to me.

Over all those forty years, I scribbled notes in a personal shorthand even I had trouble decoding a week later. It made no difference, because I didn't save the notebooks. It did not occur to me that what I'd written there could one day be a valuable resource, and if I could pass one lesson on to today's reporters it would be this: Save the notes and when the day's work is over, take ten minutes to jot down the things that didn't make it into the story—the oddities, inside stuff, impressions, and descriptions. It can be a treasury. I wish I had done it back when the only cost would have been a few minutes less time unwinding at the hotel bar at the end of a campaign day.

To reflect about the campaigns of my career, I had to put myself back into them, to relive what I experienced in 1960 or 1980. The work of three old friends and companions on the political road helped me to do it. First, the landmark campaign books of the late Theodore H. White, who reinvented political reporting with his *The Making of the President* books. He wrote those books on the campaigns of 1960, 1964, 1968, and 1972, and they are matchless for his reporting and storytelling. Spend a day with Teddy and you are back in those times. Any political reporter who has not read them all is not fully educated. There's a letter from White in the 1972 book he sent me. He wrote, "I wish that we didn't usually meet only in the turbulence of a campaign every four years when both of us are under the whip of deadlines and the pressure of events." We met again when I reread his books as I tried to immerse myself in the politics of those campaigns.

Jules Witcover and Jack Germond, my contemporaries, were two of the guys on the bus with me all those years and they wrote the history of each campaign from 1976 until 1992. I read their books again as well, to stir my own memories of what we'd witnessed together. Jack and Jules were matchless political reporters, then partners as columnists.

What I have written is not a history but, rather, a personal account of the campaigns of my professional life. The events of those campaigns are the framework for my memories of them. As I recount them now, I am off deadline. Past deadline.

Walter R. Mears
Arlington, Virginia

ONE

First Impressions:
The 1960 Campaign

It was a quiet autumn afternoon in the elegant lobby of the Waldorf-Astoria Hotel in New York, hushed as a library reading room. The only stir was on the side toward Park Avenue, where a cluster of men lounged on a couch and upholstered chairs conversing, sometimes arguing, sometimes a bit loudly. They—we—were reporters, doing what reporters do much of their time. We were waiting, some reading newspapers, one savvy enough to have brought a book. The rest were swapping stories, talking about the 1960 presidential campaign we were assigned to cover, boasting of past exploits, debating who got which story first, who spotted the trend, who wrote it best. I was listening, having no exploits to boast. At twenty-five and new to it all, I was awed to be there, sitting with men I had known only as bylines in their newspapers until I was suddenly sent to join them and report on the campaign for the Associated Press.

A new voice, Boston-accented, put an abrupt stop to the conversation. "How are you?" John F. Kennedy asked us. The accent was on the "are," except that it sounded like "ah." Looking back, the scene was remarkable because it was so ordinary at the time. There was Kennedy, unannounced, a few campaign aides his only escorts. He'd strolled through the lobby without much ado.

New York was a city where Kennedy could draw tens of thousands of people to see and hear him when that was the campaign plan.

It was the city where one day his widow would be stalked to distraction by swarming photographers, where his grown children would be surrounded by onlookers when they walked down the street.

In 1960, as the Democratic nominee for president, John Kennedy could choose to be on- or offstage. On this October day at the height of the campaign, just before the finale of the televised debates between Kennedy and Richard M. Nixon, he chose to be off. That would not be an option for candidates to come, as television moved from the studio to the street. At the Waldorf that day, no crowds attended Kennedy, no broadcast crews pressed around him, no microphones hung over the scene to catch every stray word. The crowds and clamor were for the rallies and the motorcades, with campaign advance men to turn them out. But Kennedy's appeal was not all advance work. He'd drawn more than a million New Yorkers to line a motorcade route two days earlier, a tour timed, as in any street-smart campaign, to coincide with lunch hour, so that the sidewalks would be crowded anyhow.

Kennedy wasn't staying at the Waldorf; Nixon was. Kennedy preferred the uptown Carlyle hotel, and said he'd just come down to get his hair trimmed by a favorite barber. And to just happen upon some of the reporters assigned to cover his rival for the White House, a coincidence we suspected was contrived, although that didn't matter.

We weren't seeing much of Nixon. He was in his suite at the Waldorf Towers, preparing for the fourth TV debate. We were waiting for a briefing by a retired admiral campaigning for Nixon, coming to elaborate on his assertion that Kennedy's positions on defense and foreign policy would risk a new world war. Nixon didn't say such things himself. He left the heavy-handed words and tactics to his subordinates, as he did later, all the way to his untimely presidential end.

Campaign reporting is exciting work, with a touch of glamour about it. You travel the nation, roll into cities in the caravans of candidates who are escorted by police past traffic jams, stand at the front of the crowd, dine out on the company dime, and sometimes close the hotel bar with expense-account nightcaps. The job description does not mention the hours of sitting, watching, and just waiting. It gets boring.

But not that day at the Waldorf when JFK turned up and broke the monotony. He said hello to each reporter by name, flattering them by remembering them. The senator from Massachusetts knew mine because I had covered him as a reporter for the AP bureau in Boston and in Hyannisport when he went to the Kennedy family retreat.

Kennedy made no news that afternoon, said nothing quotable. It was only small talk. In later campaigns, small talk would be recounted as news, but not then. In the code of that simpler era, it went without saying that the chat was off the record, not an interview or an occasion for newsmen to question the candidate. Kennedy did the asking that day.

He wanted to know how his campaign was doing in the eyes of the reporters assigned to the other side, how it looked from their perspective. It seemed to me an awkward question for a reporter to answer without breaching the strictures of impartiality, but my senior colleagues seemed to have no qualms. Fine, they agreed. You're looking good.

It was polite praise, not advice, but I would not have been comfortable offering it to a candidate in a campaign I was covering. So I kept quiet.

In Vermont, early in my career, a Republican running for Congress, who was a friend outside working hours, pressed me to ask the Democratic candidate publicly about his record as a conscientious objector to wartime military service. I refused, saying it was up to him to make an issue of it himself. I probably would have raised it as a reporter if I hadn't been asked by the rival candidate, but to me, that put it out-of-bounds.

The reporters that day in New York knew Kennedy well. He'd cultivated the friendships and they liked him. In defeat, Nixon would say that the campaign reporting of 1960 was unfair to him because newsmen were too cozy with Kennedy. He had a point, but he missed one, too. Nixon put up a shield against reporters because he didn't trust them. The disdain fed on itself and made his problem worse.

That is not to suggest that Kennedy was immune from the frustrations of any politician reading about himself. He was irked at times, too, but he didn't let it show, following the old Democratic rule: Don't get mad, get even. Kennedy observed it by reserving his wrath until he got to the White House. Then he tried to punish coverage he resented, most famously by canceling delivery of the old *New York Herald Tribune,* most hypocritically by trying to get publishers to reassign and thus silence correspondents in Vietnam who wrote that U.S. policy was failing even in those earliest days of American involvement. He didn't succeed. Two of those reporters shared the Pulitzer Prize for their 1963 Vietnam reporting, raising alarms unheeded by the Kennedy administration, which chose instead to believe the optimistic forecasts of the diplomats and generals who said the American cause was winning.

Kennedy the candidate was cordial, using his personal contacts with the people reporting and writing about him as an asset. And there is no more effective way to flatter a political reporter than to ask what he (he and she now, but in 1960 almost exclusively he) thinks about the way the campaign is being run. We reporters tend to believe that we know how to do it better than the people we're covering. That myth persists, despite clear proof that it isn't so. When reporters quit to cross over into political operations, they make the same mistakes they used to snipe at in print. Or worse ones. To me, switching from the straight side to the campaign side is the worst mistake. You lose your license to cover the grandest show in democracy, the campaigns and elections in which Americans decide who will lead them.

For a reporter, a presidential campaign is the Olympics of political coverage, and an assignment to cover it is a front-row ticket from the trial heats to the finals. I had tickets from 1960 until 2000, as a reporter, executive, and columnist for the AP. I watched and knew a parade of candidates, winners, and, often more interesting, losers. Over those eleven campaigns, the system itself was transformed by the rise of television, by reforms in the nominating process and in the financing of candidates. Each step had unintended by-products. In recounting what I saw and thought about it all, I will start at my beginning.

I was born and raised near Boston, and got my first job with the AP in 1955, the year before I graduated from Middlebury College in

Middlebury, Vermont. The job matched my earliest and only ambition. From the time I knew that people worked for a living, I wanted to be a newspaper reporter. Joining the AP meant that I worked for all the newspapers, the member-owners of the news cooperative. Wire service work is different from that of a daily newspaper reporter, who has set times—edition deadlines—to deliver his story. In the AP, the deadline is constant. Once you have done the reporting, you write, or sometimes dictate, a story from your notes, then file, which means delivering your story to the editor to get it onto the wire. In a world-wide wire service, there's always somebody who needs the piece right then. So it is intense, high-pressure reporting and writing that, fortunately, turned out to be my special talent. In the right circumstances, I could produce a story as fast as I could type. When I was part of a team in Washington writing successive updates on the 1962 election, my boss asked a senior colleague to keep an eye on me and report on my performance. He gave me a copy of his memo telling the boss "Mears writes faster than most people think and sometimes faster than he thinks."

Over the years, colleagues marveled that I kept doing it instead of accepting one of the newspaper offers I got, trading instant deadlines for daily ones. I did try it, briefly, as Washington bureau chief of the *Detroit News*. I lasted nine months away from the AP, returning in 1975. There was nothing wrong with the *News* and the pay was better. But I just couldn't take the pace; the immediacy was gone. When Timothy Crouse wrote *The Boys on the Bus* about the 1972 campaign, I was one of them, and he included this sardonically flattering quote from a colleague: "At what he does, Mears is the best in the goddam world. He can get out a coherent story with the right point on top in a minute and thirty seconds, left-handed." It wasn't all flattering. The guy went on to say that it was sort of like a parlor trick. Not to me. I was a wire service man, and speed was part of the job.

I had no seat among the boys on the bus in 1960; I hadn't earned one. That took training and experience. Mine began in the summer of 1955, behind the frosted glass doors of the Boston bureau of the AP, overlooking a narrow sliver of Washington Street, on what was then

Newspaper Row. It was a clattering den of men with cigarettes dangling, the smoke flowing around the green plastic eyeshades of an editor or two, everything stained the blue of carbon paper, including your shirtsleeves as soon as you sat down at a desk. The teletypes chattered as copy came and went over the wires. In a far corner, a Morse code operator, one of the last of the craft, still dispatched news copy to a handful of remote New England newspapers waiting to be wired for teletypes.

My job was to take information over the telephone from correspondents known as stringers, most of them reporters for AP newspapers around New England who got ten cents a line for their copy. I rewrote the stories into AP style and gave them to an editor to be readied for the wire. The pay was $55 a week. At twenty, I thought I'd made it. Not yet, as I quickly learned. My editor was a crusty veteran named Francis R. Murphy and he taught me otherwise in the manner of a drill sergeant, except louder. I would type a story, hand it to him, and watch him turn an angry red. Sometimes he tore my copy to pieces, loudly counseling me that I would never learn. I began to believe it, and figured that my fledgling career was about to crash. Then Frank Murphy looked at a piece I'd written and said, "Okay." From that point on, so was I.

Frank died before I received the Pulitzer Prize in 1977. The veterans in Boston sent me a telegram that said, "Frank Murphy would have been proud." It was a message that brought a tear because he was the teacher who put me on the way to the honor.

In the fall of 1956, I was sent to open a new AP bureau in Montpelier, Vermont. The job was to cover the state government and legislature, in which I had zero experience, and to report on news elsewhere in the state. The job came with no instructions except to go and do it. I took my portable typewriter, drove through an early snowstorm, and found my desk in the attic pressroom of the statehouse, with an AP teletype beside it. I hadn't been trained in operating it, either, but I switched it on and figured it out. It was an education in self-sufficiency that taught me more, faster, about myself and my chosen calling than I could have learned anywhere else. I'd been offered a scholarship to a graduate school of journalism, but Frank Murphy told me I could pay them to teach me or he would teach me and pay me at the same time. So the AP was my journalism school. I was twenty-one when I went to Vermont, at the time the youngest and probably most nervous staffer ever appointed as the correspondent in charge of an AP state bureau. The bureau consisted of me, with long-distance guidance, usually when something went wrong, from my bosses in Boston. At the beginning, I was winging it, but things worked out. Once I got past the wire service version of stage fright, it was fun covering a citizen legislature with a representative from every hamlet in the state. There were 276 members in the House, including one elected by his townspeople because otherwise he would have been eligible for welfare and that would have ruined their record for paying none. I never enjoyed a job more than Montpelier. It was a debut on a small stage. Seven AP newspapers used my in-state coverage. Infrequently, a Vermont story made it to the national wire, as when an encampment of Indians pitched tents on the statehouse lawn and demanded title to land they said was rightly theirs. Or when, in 1958, in what had been a solidly Republican state, a liberal Democrat was elected to the one seat in Congress after a divisive primary saddled the GOP with a rather eccentric nominee who sometimes campaigned in a formal jacket so old it showed traces of mildew on the back. That was a one-term exception; the liberal turn toward Democratic political power in Vermont was a generation away.

There were glitches, most of them my mistakes, each of them a lesson. Although I never did figure out the lesson in one missed story about a murder trial my bosses told me to cover with a stringer instead of reporting myself. I lined up a reporter from the local newspaper at the going rate, a nickel a line. That sufficed for the preliminaries, but not when the state attorney general delivered the opening argument for the prosecution. He said the murder of a farmhand was a lynching by townsmen who didn't like the guy and had roughed him up, killing him after he spilled a pail of milk. "Lynch law justice," the attorney general called it. The rival UPI sent one of its stars to cover the trial, and he delivered a story that won blaring headlines in the

South, where the civil rights era was dawning and lynching was a red flag word. "LYNCHING IN VERMONT," the headlines read, but not in AP newspapers because I didn't get the story until the callbacks poured in, demanding our version. I called the stringer at home. She hadn't been in the courtroom. She took her Scottie dog to the trial each day and the sheriff let her keep the pet in a jail cell, on the condition that she walk him at regular intervals. So she was out walking the dog when the attorney general opened his case. I finally got the story by calling him that night. I also got orders to go cover the trial myself the next day. By then it was routine, with no surprises except that the defendants were acquitted, although everybody in town was sure they'd done it. The judge thought so, too.

In 1960, I was back in Boston, assigned to the statehouse, far from the innocence of Vermont politics. On Beacon Hill, the pay telephone near the attorney general's office was always busy because it was the one informally reserved for bookies and their statehouse customers. The Speaker of the House ran the show at his own whim, ramming through bills the Democratic bosses wanted passed by calling them up for action with his microphone off and whispering them to passage. One noontime, a jealous husband broke the Speaker's jaw at a hotel across Boston Common and he had to have it wired shut. He hid out in his office while his lieutenants did his business for him.

When Senator Kennedy came back from the Democratic convention in Los Angeles as the 1960 presidential nominee, I was sent to Cape Cod to help Washington AP reporters cover him. I walked into the press motel in Hyannis and was greeted by a lanky AP photographer who, I later learned, was double-jointed. He put one foot on the ceiling with the other firmly on the floor, stuck out his hand to shake mine, and said, "Welcome to the big time."

But the big-time stories were for the veterans. I was the rookie and my role was to do their bidding, stand watch while they went to dinner, and write about the lesser events of the day. I also covered things of special interest to New England, as when the Democratic Senate candidate from Rhode Island came to Hyannis for the blessing of the presidential nominee and a campaign photo with JFK. It was a routine campaign endorsement, but I never forgot what Claiborne Pell wore that day. He was clad like a commodore from the waist up—white shirt, complementing tie, blue blazer with polished brass buttons catching the sun. That was for the photo. Waist down, the garb was ragged khaki shorts, no socks, battered tennis shoes. News photographers observed protocol; the photos were head shots of the candidate and the nominee, not the full-length incongruity of his costume. A minor point, but a mark of the time before cynicism erased such unwritten guidelines.

My assignments that fall concentrated on Kennedy when he was in New England. I was sent to join the traveling party as an extra hand for the AP reporters in his entourage. The job involved a lot of waiting because Kennedy was always late, sometimes hours late. The crowds waited, too.

In Connecticut, one Kennedy rally actually was scheduled to begin at midnight, not normally a time for political turnouts. But Kennedy drew thousands anyhow. He was late as usual, and they stood waiting in the autumn chill until he finally got there at 2:00 A.M. In Rhode Island, the most Roman Catholic of states, a crowd too vast to count in the darkness waited at the Providence airport long after midnight for a glimpse of the Catholic candidate. He wasn't coming to speak that night, only to land and drive into the city for an appearance in the morning. But the throng waited anyway, and when the candidate's airplane finally appeared over the runway, they cheered and kept cheering, a roar that rivaled the roar of the propellers at landing.

Over the decades I covered hundreds of airport rallies but I never saw a scene or a response like that one in Providence. In the mob that crowded around the press buses, I couldn't find the national campaign reporters I was there to help. So I pushed my way onto the bus and went into town to catch up there. At the door of the pressroom I asked a reporter to point out Relman Morin, a fabled AP man with two Pulitzer Prizes to his name. He was over in the corner on the telephone, so I went and sat beside him, waiting politely until he was done. "I'm Walter Mears from Boston," I said. "Is there anything I can do to help?" Morin glowered. "Yes," he said, "you can get off my goddam hat because you're sitting on it." I did, he punched it back into shape and forgave me, and we later became friends and traveled together covering national campaigns.

Nixon could draw vast crowds, too, but his were more orderly and organized, less fervent, without the Hollywood flavor that set girls and even grown women to jumping and screaming when Kennedy rolled past them, waving from his top-down convertible. A Nixon rally sometimes looked like a Wall Street lunch break, a businesslike assembly of people in sedate attire, applauding and cheering at the appropriate points.

Kennedy attracted fans like a movie star. Many of them were too young to vote; twenty-one was the voting age then. They swarmed as close to him as they could get, and at times, that was a problem. His shirt cuffs were torn, his hands swollen by people who wouldn't let go. One scratch became an infection by election day.

Nor was everyone friendly. In Milwaukee, a woman threw a glass of whiskey in Kennedy's face as he rode in the motorcade. Then she tossed the glass into his car. Kennedy wiped his face off and picked the tumbler up. "Here's your glass," he said, and handed it to her.

Kennedy was a stylist, quick with a quip. He carried that style and image to the White House, but his brief presidency was not called Camelot while it was happening. People would come to believe that Camelot was the next thing to a sign on the JFK White House, but no one called it that until after he was assassinated. The Camelot legend became part of the Kennedy myth when Theodore H. White interviewed Jacqueline Kennedy and she told him that Kennedy often had listened to the music of the Broadway show as he relaxed at the end of the White House day. White interspersed his story in *Life* magazine with lines from the song—"a fleeting wisp of glory . . . for one brief shining moment that was known as Camelot." And an image was born.

Nixon was methodical, a man who reminded you of the schoolmate who always lugged around his overstuffed book bag. He had some justification for his conviction that many reporters just didn't like him. The good ones kept it out of their copy, but it was an edge against him nonetheless, and Nixon did little to blunt it. Even when he tried he had trouble; casual chats were not in his repertoire. He once dropped in at a reporters' party on the road and described the stewardesses on his chartered plane as the bar girls. "B girls," he said jovially. They took it, but not jovially.

Over the years I covered him, Nixon tried to change the stodgy image and to get rid of the tag that had been hung on him since his wily, no-holds-missed campaigns for Congress in California: "Tricky Dick." He worked to shed the old style and to prove himself "the New Nixon," a phrase that became a cliché as he fine-tuned himself. But whatever the political incarnation, he was still the guy who would be photographed walking the beach in black shoes and business suit.

When the nominees appeared together at a New York charity banquet in 1960, Nixon joked his way into a formal-wear controversy. I watched him take his head table seat in white tie and tails, attire appropriate both to the occasion and to his starchy image. Kennedy wore a tuxedo. The invitation to the Alfred E. Smith Dinner, which raises funds for Roman Catholic charities, said white or black tie; the sponsors didn't care so long as most of the wearers came with money for the archdiocese.

"I guess I'm not very well dressed," Kennedy said when he and Nixon met before taking their head table places. "Well, Jack, I'll make a deal with you," Nixon replied. "Whoever is elected president will abolish white ties. And these shirts ought to have zippers. It's agony." The Nixon campaign then had to make peace with the formalwear industry, which accused him of slander that threatened the jobs of the working people who made the things.

The mismatch in styles also showed onstage that night. Kennedy had considered skipping the dinner because it was sponsored by his church and he was wary of rekindling the issue of his religion, a problem for him because he was only the second man of his faith to be nominated for president. Protestant critics questioned whether a Catholic could obey the commandments of the church and make the independent decisions of the presidency; Kennedy insisted that he could and would. But it was still a lurking problem. The Smith dinner is in the name of the first Roman Catholic nominee, the New York governor defeated by Herbert Hoover in 1928 after a campaign in which religion was an open issue against him.

Kennedy quipped his way through the 1960 dinner. "I assume that shortly I will be invited to a Quaker dinner honoring Herbert Hoover," he said. Nixon looked uncomfortable, ready to make his requisite speech and be done with it. He did, renouncing religion as an issue, and sat down to polite applause.

I traveled with the Nixon campaign for two weeks in 1960 and never exchanged a word with him. Nor did many of the more senior reporters in his entourage, even those who had known him and covered him for years as a senator and congressman.

The Nixon of that campaign viewed reporters as obstacles to be avoided. There was an exception made for the few who displayed their own conservative tendencies. But for the rest, Nixon was convinced that the way to handle political reporters was to go over their heads and try to get the campaign message directly to the voters, unfiltered by the traditional media. That was difficult to impossible in 1960 because television did not yet provide the full, direct—and costly—channel to the voters that would make the medium the predominant one in campaigns to come.

Television spending drove the fund-raising and spending madness of later campaigns and political money became a political issue, but campaign finances were only a minor, side topic in 1960. Nixon said afterward that Kennedy's "unlimited money" was one of the things that beat him. Kennedy once joked that his wealthy father told him not to buy one vote more than necessary because he wasn't going to pay for a landslide. But the Democrats argued that the big money was on Nixon's side. It was an open question. There was no federal campaign finance law to require reports on who spent what.

When Nixon staged a four-hour television call-in session the afternoon before the election, squeezing the soap operas off 157 stations on the ABC network, the Democrats said he was the one trying to buy votes, spending at least $300,000 for the TV time. Big money in 1960; petty cash in campaigns to come. The Nixon telethon also set an endurance record: more time on the air at one sitting than any candidate had ever spent before, or would afterward. Kennedy bought his own TV time to reply, a half hour on the same network, with his three sisters reading him questions called in by listeners. Neither program made campaign waves or scored many political points.

Kennedy had invested more time and money campaigning to get his nomination than Nixon, who, as vice president, was the next man in Republican line and was spared what could have been a formidable challenge when New York Governor Nelson A. Rockefeller stood aside. The Democratic campaign of 1960 began the rise of the presidential primaries as the arenas in which nominees for president are chosen. Primaries were not new; the first one was held in 1903. But until 1960 they were more often ignored than influential. Presidential nominees were determined by party leaders and power brokers— political bosses. Kennedy's tactics began changing that. Kennedy used the primaries to convince the party, and the bosses, that a junior senator from Massachusetts, not only little known but also a Roman Catholic, could win the presidency. His first evidence was in the primary election victories that proved he could get votes in states far from home and, crucially, that he could carry Protestant regions despite his Catholic faith. When Kennedy won in West Virginia—95 percent Protestant, Bible Belt country—his only active rival, Senator Hubert H. Humphrey of Minnesota, quit the campaign, leaving only sideline candidates, Senator Lyndon B. Johnson of Texas among them. But they couldn't stop Kennedy after those primary victories. He had not won enough delegates to clinch the nominating majority; the reform system that enabled candidates to do that was a dozen years away. Kennedy's winning strategy was to use the primaries to make his national name, prove his ability to win, and establish himself as a leader the party bosses could neither ignore nor snub at the national convention.

So it was Kennedy, the new face, against the more familiar one of Vice President Nixon. The Kennedy game plan was to sell youth and vigor against the two-term vice president who seemed part of an older establishment, even though the rival nominees were contemporaries.

Nixon was only four years older; both were Navy veterans of World War II and both had been elected to Congress the year after the war ended. With either man the torch would have been passed to a new generation, in the words of JFK's inaugural address. But Kennedy seemed new, Nixon somehow worn.

Nixon had an expert, affable press secretary, Herbert G. Klein, as his go-between with reporters. But the gossip was that even Klein, long his aide and adviser, was suspect to some of the Republican inner circle. After all, he'd been a newspaperman himself at the *San Diego Union* (and would be again after Nixon was defeated). Reporters liked Klein, and the mistrustful Nixonites, who couldn't see that those friendships made him a more effective advocate for the nominee, marked him as a man to be watched.

Pierre Salinger had an easier job in speaking for Kennedy. He'd been a newsman, too, and had worked on Capitol Hill. He blended that experience with a breezy, outgoing personality that made him fit nicely as press secretary to JFK in the campaign and the White House. The Democrats valued the kind of press friendships that Republicans found suspect. Salinger did me a favor in 1960, although I didn't find out about it until years later. He saw my Hyannisport copy on the AP wire and told my senior colleagues that they should pay attention to me because I seemed to know the moves. It was a generous gesture, especially in view of the fact that given my junior level there wasn't anything to be gained in return.

In 1960, chartered campaign jets were the exception. I still remember the sensation of my first jet takeoff, with Nixon, in a Boeing 707, on the way south from Buffalo. It felt like taking an elevator when I was used to the stairs. But that was only one hop. Lumbering propeller-driven airliners were the rule. Nixon traveled the East Coast in one, designed with the luxury compartment near the front, by the one door. Nixon and his wife, Pat, would board first, take their first-class seats, and sit silently, eyes usually straight ahead, as the pool reporters traveling with them boarded and headed down the aisle to the rear of the plane. I filed aboard with them in my first experience with the campaign road show because an AP reporter always got a seat on the

Nixon plane. Getting on and off was always the same. We walked past the Nixons, who rarely offered a nod, almost never a smile or a word of greeting as their obligatory traveling companions went by. We were the pool, meaning that we represented the other campaign reporters who wouldn't fit on the candidate's plane and traveled on a separate press charter. The pool reporters shared with them whatever we learned on the Nixon charter. In my experience that year, there never was anything to share because Nixon shunned us.

It was as though we were aliens, not fellow passengers on the weary, relentless journey of a presidential campaign. We were paid passengers, our organizations billed for first-class-plus travel at rates that enabled the candidate and his entourage to fly free, or close to it, in the era before campaign finance laws.

That wasn't the mood on the Kennedy plane. JFK often strolled the aisle, chatting with reporters, commenting on the day's campaigning. Flying into the night after the first TV debate, Kennedy told reporters he'd found it useful—the understatement of the season since the joint appearance burdened Nixon with a dour image he never really erased. After the debate, even Nixon's mother called to see if he was all right because he hadn't looked well. Nixon's forlorn appearance under the TV lights in Chicago was a product of illness—he'd lost weight because of a knee infection and hospitalization—and a primitive makeup job. After the first debate, Nixon began drinking four milkshakes a day to get his weight back and he paid attention to the makeup experts when he went on camera.

The candidates' differences in that debate, like those to follow, were largely predictable replays of the arguments they voiced daily from campaign platforms. Even Quemoy and Matsu, two island specks off the coast of China, had come up before. The islands and the question of defending them against the Communist mainland became the buzzwords of the season. Basically, Nixon said yes and Kennedy said no. After the election, Quemoy and Matsu buzzed back to obscurity, where they had been before. But not before Kennedy had issued an easily kept campaign promise. "I intend to see to it that not a single American dies on those islands," he vowed. None did.

I helped cover the final Kennedy-Nixon debate, in New York two weeks before the election, writing running accounts in front of a TV set at AP headquarters. Working from television was and is the only way to deliver the story as it happens. That debate stirred an ironically prophetic argument about Cuba policy. Kennedy advocated a U.S. policy of fomenting revolution against Fidel Castro, saying that as president he would help foes of the Communist regime invade to overthrow it. The Eisenhower administration was already preparing for just such an invasion and Nixon said later that he assumed Kennedy knew about it because of CIA briefings he had received as a nominee. Nixon wrote that he had to protect the planned operation, so his only option was to oppose Kennedy on the issue. He certainly did that, saying in debate that the idea was dangerously irresponsible. Nixon had that right, even though his administration was planning to do it. When the Bay of Pigs invasion failed, in 1961, Kennedy was president.

The debates were a landmark change, the breakthrough of the 1960 campaign. There were four between Kennedy and Nixon, the most ever conducted between presidential nominees. Kennedy wanted a fifth just before the election but Nixon wasn't interested, which was understandable because he'd suffered in the first debate and the other three were standoffs.

Congress had cleared the legal path to the debates by suspending equal broadcast time requirements as a one-time-only experiment, so that the major party nominees could meet on TV without including minor candidates, of whom there were 104 in 1960.

Nixon agreed to the debates against the advice of some Republicans, who saw no advantage for the better-known vice president. But Nixon believed himself the stronger debater, figuring that the man who'd stood up for the American way in an argument against Soviet Premier Nikita S. Khrushchev in Moscow could easily put away a novice like Kennedy. But pure debate points did not count as much as points for appearance and delivery, and Kennedy swept those in the opening debate. The debates also closed the recognition gap and established JFK on an equal, face-to-face footing with the vice president.

After the first debate in Chicago, Kennedy remarked on the major change it had wrought, saying that it would take a month to talk to 500,000 people on the road but that "this way, in one evening on television, we talked to millions." It was an opening installment in the rise of television to center stage of presidential campaigning. Nixon left that debate weary; Kennedy was energized. He flew half the night to be in position for rallies the next morning. A colleague passed word that on the way, Kennedy ate a hot dog, followed by beef tenderloin with wild rice. Then a salad, two glasses of milk, and tomato soup with cream.

Kennedy said after the election that he wouldn't have won it without the debates. Nixon always insisted there were too many factors in an election as close as 1960 to pick one as decisive. The evidence is that he regretted his decision to debate. He ducked debating in his two subsequent presidential campaigns. He even rejected entreaties to participate from retirement in a television history of the debates. In 1960, he said debates would be inevitable in future campaigns. He changed his mind, and there were none in the next three presidential contests. In his memoirs, Nixon wrote that too much style and too little substance made debates a dubious forum. "I doubt that they can ever serve a responsible role," he wrote.

While access to the nominee was not so guarded in the Kennedy campaign as in Nixon's, dignity was. The Kennedy campaign imposed a rule against news photographs of him while he was eating. And when Chief Hollow Horn Bear made him an honorary Sioux at a stop in South Dakota and put a feathered headdress on him, Kennedy instantly whipped it off. "They'll never get a picture of me in those feathers," he said later. "I still remember that picture of Calvin Coolidge in the Indian headdress and those shiny black patent leather shoes."

In the 1960 campaign a reporter could travel with Nixon for ten days and never meet him. I didn't, until five years later. By then he had lost the presidential election and foundered in a comeback attempt for governor of California in 1962. He moved to Wall Street, to the law firm that was his base until he rose from the political grave, ran again for president, and won in 1968.

I interviewed him in his law office in 1965. His secretary, Rose Mary Woods, ushered me in and introduced us. Nixon said nothing at first, only looked at me intently. Then he said my name, Walter Mears, slowly, and repeated it, slowly. It was as though he was recording it on a memory bank. Perhaps so; he never failed to use it when we met afterward, although not always precisely. I had a crew cut in those years and so did an AP State Department reporter. After Nixon became president, the diplomatic writer covered him on a foreign trip and was introduced to an assortment of world leaders as Walter Mears. Recognition by the cut of our hair.

Years after, when I was appointed executive editor of the Associated Press, Nixon wrote me from the political exile that followed Watergate. "Congratulations on reaching 'the top of that greasy pole,' as Disraeli would have put it," he wrote. By then he had reached the top of the pole he'd struggled so long to climb, and it had been greasy indeed as he'd slid to the depths of forced resignation.

The 1960 campaign was a starting point for many of the changes that would remodel the process of choosing candidates and presidents. It was the last campaign in which neither candidate was guarded by the Secret Service, protection that unavoidably changed the system.

So there would never again be a situation in which an overenthusiastic supporter could jump into Kennedy's open car and try to shake his hand, as a man did in Willow Grove, Pennsylvania, one campaign day. Police pulled him out and charged him with disorderly conduct and he was fined one dollar. In later campaigns, after the assassinations, anyone who tried that would have been in peril. Armed bodyguards would have intervened.

Nor would a presidential nominee again promise to go everywhere, as Nixon did unwisely in 1960. He pledged that he would campaign in each of the fifty states that fall and stuck to the promise. The mileage was wearing and the toll was made worse by the knee infection that took him out of action for nearly two weeks around the traditional Labor Day start of the campaign. It was a perfect excuse for dropping the all-state pledge, and Nixon's advisers wanted him to take that way out, but he refused. He completed the fifty-state circuit with a wearing and essentially pointless round-trip flight to Alaska just before the election, a day in the air for a two-hour campaign stop in a state with three electoral votes. Nixon won them, but Alaska was going to his column anyhow. Meeting the all-state pledge cost Nixon far more than it earned him.

Lesson learned. For the rest of his career, as campaigner and later as onlooker, Nixon based election strategy and forecasts on the ten biggest states, with their decisive share of the electoral votes. In 1960, Kennedy led the popular vote by less than one-tenth of one percentage point. But the electoral college vote was decisive: Kennedy 303, Nixon 219. And those are the votes that count.

There were stirrings in 1960 of the civil rights issue that soon after would become a major one in American politics and government. Kennedy was celebrated by black leaders for telephoning the pregnant wife of the Reverend Martin Luther King Jr. when King was jailed in Georgia on the pretext of a traffic violation. Kennedy's political advisers would have told him not to place the call, for fear of alienating the white South, but he didn't ask them. Still, he did not make a major point of it at the time, commenting offhandedly that he had been concerned about a friend. It looked better later. The Democrats distributed leaflets about the call outside black churches in the North.

Jackie Robinson and Joe Louis were for Nixon that year, but a ballplayer and a boxer were no match for King.

Nixon was confounded when Henry Cabot Lodge Jr., his running mate, said in Harlem that "there should be a Negro in the Cabinet," and made it sound like a pledge. Lodge had become United Nations ambassador after Kennedy won away his Senate seat in Massachusetts in 1952. A Negro in the Cabinet would have been a striking appointment in 1960; Kennedy made no such promise. As president, he appointed Robert C. Weaver, a black man, to head the federal housing agency in 1961, but the job didn't have Cabinet rank at the time. Kennedy did elevate more black men and women in the government and the judiciary than any president before him, and he tried to get Weaver's housing job upped to Cabinet rank, but southern Democrats blocked the proposal in Congress. That change did not come until 1966, when President Lyndon B. Johnson made Weaver the first black Cabinet officer.

Lodge's promise of "a Negro in the Cabinet" was venturesome, and he kept repeating it, although he finally acknowledged that as vice presidential nominee he was not in a position to make such a commitment. Still, Lodge said it would be a wonderful thing. Nixon and his people didn't think it was wonderful, especially coming without notice from a running mate freelancing, which is not what vice presidential candidates are supposed to do. The Nixon Republicans did not expect to win significant support among black voters. Racial barriers were still the law in southern states where whites would decide who won, in large measure because many blacks weren't allowed even to cast ballots. Poll taxes, literacy tests, and plain threats barred their way. Those who voted, especially in the cities of the North, were a Democratic constituency. Nixon campaigned to crack what was still the solid Democratic South—conservative but not Republican. Much of the region stayed that way in the 1960 election, the last in which the old party line held.

Nixon's southern standing sagged when Lodge made the unauthorized Cabinet promise. Nixon ducked as best he could, saying that he would appoint "the best men" regardless of race or creed. That's what Kennedy was saying, too. In that era, nobody talked as Bill Clinton would three decades later about creating a Cabinet that looked like America.

For Nixon, Lodge's Cabinet venture created a no-way-out situation. He couldn't say no without sounding racist, and he couldn't say yes without undermining his attempt to win in the South. So he had to pretend the question wasn't there. He and Lodge met with the campaign high command at a Hartford, Connecticut, hotel on a dreary, rainy Sunday in mid-October. The Cabinet pledge was on the agenda, along with broader campaign strategy planning. The session went on all day. We reporters waited outside the conference room until Nixon finally emerged to say that he would make Cabinet choices on merit, without regard to race or to political party. He also said that he and Lodge didn't differ on the matter.

They obviously did, but Nixon couldn't say so. Reporters had speculated that it would be a woodshed meeting for the vice presidential nominee, which was what Nixon advisers wanted in order to avoid further damage in the South. Whatever was said inside, Lodge wasn't chastened. The faded clipping of the story I wrote that day shows that he said again that he favored the appointment of a Negro to the Cabinet.

The stir over that difference between Republican running mates was surprisingly brief. The campaign soon moved on to other topics. There was no television megaphone, no chorus of talk shows to turn up the volume and keep it going. In campaigns to come, those echo chambers would put far less significant topics on the agenda for days and weeks.

Technology was a ponderous obstacle to close-in television coverage of the 1960 campaign. The cameras were immobile, not portable. Set pieces—a national political convention, a major address, or a debate—could be televised because they were covered from fixed camera positions. But the clamor and movement of a presidential campaign defied TV coverage. It took a giant motion picture camera, a bank of glaring lights, and hours to deliver and develop film in order to report a campaign appearance on the TV news.

When I covered a Kennedy foreign policy speech in New York shortly after his nomination, TV was there with bulky cameras set on tripods in the back of the room. Reporters stood in front of them. One of the cameramen tried to nudge a cantankerous *New York Times* man out of the way and the correspondent told him in terms not fit to print that if it happened again, he would kick out the camera legs. I recalled that episode as I watched the TV cameras move toward the front of the campaign halls over the years, pushing the print reporters to the rear.

In time, the camera platforms gained the prime locations when a candidate or a president faced an audience, often blocking the view from the press tables and from a good many of the spectator seats. Television was the medium. Audiences were part of the show. Writing reporters would write, even if they couldn't see the stage. We were left to scramble for position.

Today, technology puts TV everywhere, and almost every moment a candidate spends in public is a moment on camera. Transplant JFK's casual Waldorf visit to 2000 and he could not have driven downtown without a Secret Service motorcade and a trailing crowd of reporters with cameras, tape recorders, and an overlay of microphones to pick up and record each word. No offhand chats; crowds beget crowds, and Kennedy would have been at the center of a moving throng.

In 1960, the Secret Service deployed after a candidate was elected president, not while he was running. Indeed, its protection was the first certification from the federal government that a candidate had become president-elect.

It took all night and part of the next day to determine that Kennedy had won the 1960 election in the closest count of the century. It was closer in popular votes than the overtime election of 2000. The sun was just rising when the order came from Washington for the Secret Service to protect President-elect Kennedy at the family compound in Hyannisport. When waiting reporters spotted the agents, they filed bulletins on the signal that the government deemed Kennedy the winner. Even then the protection order was premature. Kennedy's victory was not sealed by electoral votes for another five hours.

The Secret Service didn't guard presidential candidates until June 1968, when President Johnson ordered them protected after the assassination of Robert F. Kennedy as he campaigned for president. In the living of it, 1960 did not seem a tranquil time but in retrospect, it was, the simpler season before the assassinations, before the trauma of Vietnam, before the changing standards that eventually made everything and anything fair for the news media. In time, every word, no matter how informal or offhand, would be treated as news, whether it was newsworthy or not. There would be microphones everywhere to catch a candidate's blurted blunder or off-color remark. Or to record an internationally awkward aside, as when President Ronald

Reagan joked in a sound test about bombing Moscow in five minutes. Or to put politically embarrassing words on the record, as in George W. Bush's open-microphone slur against a *New York Times* reporter in 2000.

Bizarre moments often passed unnoted in earlier campaigns, before the advent of miniature tape recorders that easily pick up every syllable. Sometimes odd or awkward incidents or words were recorded in print, sometimes not at all.

Take, for example, the way Prince Stanislaus Radziwill, brother-in-law of John Kennedy, demonstrated his odd, patrician contempt for both American political ways and family furnishings one day in 1960. In the crowded reception room of Joseph P. Kennedy's mansion in Hyannisport, as JFK and LBJ made their first appearance together as running mates, I watched Radziwill imperiously flip his spent cigarette from its holder to the floor. He ground it out into the Oriental carpet with the heel of his polished boot. I was standing beside another newsman, who remarked that the Kennedys probably would blame reporters for the burned spot. Nothing was written about it. It didn't fit the news formula of the time, would have been denied, and couldn't have been proved.

Over time, the wise candidate learned never to be too candid, not to risk a word that wouldn't look good in print. Items that once would have been relegated to gossip columns—beneath the attention of the lordly political reporters of 1960—became part of the story.

The relationship between political candidates and the reporters who cover them never was truly unguarded. Friction is inevitable because the objectives of the candidates always collide with the efforts of the reporters to learn and tell more than the campaigners want told, especially since Watergate and the Clinton sex scandal.

Personal conduct and misconduct that might have passed unwritten is no longer out-of-bounds in the tell-all age. That change came gradually, too.

Franklin D. Roosevelt's wheelchair was unreported, as was his relationship with Lucy Mercer, an affair his wife, Eleanor, discovered in 1918. It was a tie FDR never severed and it was never reported. By the standards of the time, it was not a fit subject for the news. Mrs. Mercer, often FDR's companion in his final years, was with him when he died in 1945.

Harry Truman could play poker with reporters half the night and nobody wrote about it or about his salty words when the cards went bad. Dwight Eisenhower's relationship with a World War II WAC aide was a topic of gossip but no more, and not even the gossip saw print until years later. No word of Kennedy's affairs was published until long after his death.

The easy explanation today is that the reporters of those times followed an unwritten code of silence about such intimate personal matters. There is something to that, but it also misses a point. There is a gap between gossip and suspicion and reportable fact. A story is no story unless you can prove it.

As a young reporter during the Kennedy campaign and presidency, I never missed an opportunity to sit with the veteran journalists covering JFK, to hear their stories and insider banter.

In that kind of setting, late at night before last call at the hotel bar, reporters gossip constantly, about politics, about absent friends, and often about sexual affairs supposedly involving political figures. It is only gossip, nothing a reporter can write because it cannot be proven as fact. Talking about the purported sex lives of politicians is another matter, fair game. And in all those nights in 1960, I never heard any talk about the Kennedy liaisons that would become known long afterward. I believe that it was not a matter of reporters protecting Kennedy, but of Kennedy taking care to protect himself against disclosure. His affairs were secret because he saw to it.

Even in that simpler era, I do not think any reporter who had a reportable hint that Marilyn Monroe was the president's mistress would have failed to write about it. To put the superstar of American politics in bed with the superstar of Hollywood would have been more than a bombshell. It would have been nuclear.

Later candidates who fell because of sexual flings would complain that the rules had been changed. That was true because society had changed and the coverage of it, including political coverage, had followed. What once was unprintable language no longer was off-limits. Sex scenes that once would have gotten a movie theater shut down became standard fare, in print and on television. Language coarsened. Barriers came down and the level of cynicism about politics and politicians went up, often for cause. The level of trust that prevailed in 1960 eroded over the years that followed, inviting intrusive, unfettered, and sometimes downright hostile coverage of candidates and presidents, too many of whom earned it.

Sometimes politicians do lie and misbehave, although probably no more often than people in business or lawyers or, for that matter, journalists.

But most of the politicians I covered ran for office because they thought they could achieve change for the better, not purely for power and surely not for money, although wealth came to some of them because they held or had held office. That's not to say they did not relish power. Power translates into the ability to do what a candidate believes should be done, and politicians are an ego-driven lot, out to sell themselves on the public stage in ways that would embarrass most of us.

Still, in the years since JFK, trust and confidence in national leaders has suffered because of the misconduct of too many of them. After a century in which impeachment sometimes was a threat but always a sheathed weapon against presidents, it was used twice within twenty-five years.

As all of this unfolded, there was an explosion in the corps of journalists, quasi journalists, and hangers-on purporting to cover campaigns and the federal government. The multiplying number, from the hundreds into the thousands in Washington, has smothered stories behind a media crowd that often gets between a candidate and the average American.

In theory, more voices, more outlets, and the unlimited time and space of cable television and the Internet should deliver more information and encourage more interest. Instead, imitation news, shouted opinions, and plain rumor have flowed in to fill the time and space. Instead of attracting people, the news noise level distracts them. The throngs who waited for Kennedy and Nixon in 1960, the fathers who held a small child aloft to see the man who might be president are fewer and rarer now. The familiarity of TV may have bred disinterest instead of engagement. People can see and effectively be at a campaign rally without going there.

At the same time, the reporters who once were messengers have become part of the message. Some of them are known for what they discover and what they write. Too many are known for their emergence as television performers on the shout shows or as commentators on the affairs they cover. That draws attention and it can be rewarding in the lucrative lecture market a reporter with TV credits can tap.

A news generation ago, elected officials were the sounding board for reaction and commentary on national events, policies, and crises. The Senate was peopled with figures of national standing, and they were the first line of reaction—an Everett Dirksen, a Mike Mansfield, a Hubert Humphrey, or a J. William Fulbright. There were fewer known names in the House, but Tip O'Neill became a familiar and formidable figure as Speaker and Democratic counter to President Ronald Reagan.

They were partisans. That was known and stated when their viewpoints were reported. Some were more expert than others, but all had the standing of elected officials. Not so with the commentators who have taken over that role. The initial response to a White House decision or a crisis abroad comes from people who also cover the events. They take positions, sometimes overtly, sometimes subtly. Either way, the clamor of voices and vehement views does more to confuse than to inform. A reporter who doesn't know the facts of the story can't write it or broadcast it, but a journalist on a TV talk show can improvise.

Fortunately, they weren't at it on election night 1960. It was the first election in which the television networks used selected sample precincts and computers to project the outcome. It also was the first in which the experts read the trend inaccurately while the votes were being counted. At first, the computer called it a Nixon landslide. By midevening, the projection was of an easy Kennedy victory. After midnight, it was close to even, too close to call until the next morning, when Kennedy won the final electoral votes that made him president. Long afterward, Nixon wrote that Kennedy told him after the election that they would never know which of them really got more popular votes.

There were Republicans who demanded a challenge to the 1960 outcome, but Nixon would not do it, saying recounts would lead to turmoil and uncertainty—and fearing without saying that to try and fail would brand him a sore loser and finish him as a national politician.

Kennedy was president. Nixon would be back.

TWO

Odyssey of a Loser:
On the Road with Goldwater
in 1964

Presidential nominees are driven men. With rare exceptions, they are impelled by lasers of ambition aimed at the greatest political prize, the White House. Barry Goldwater was an exception. Some days he wanted to be president, some days he didn't seem to care. To flinch in a presidential campaign is usually enough to undo a candidate long before he can win nomination. Again, Goldwater was the exception. He didn't stop at second thoughts about what he was doing; he had third, fourth, and fifth thoughts. And he talked about them. In a mismatch against the unbeatable President Lyndon B. Johnson in 1964, Goldwater told me he didn't expect to win. I came to believe that he didn't really want to, that he thought his mission was accomplished when his conservative Republicans seized party power.

During his campaign that spring, Goldwater told me of visiting John F. Kennedy at the White House in 1961. He'd been invited to talk with the president, and he got to the Oval Office first. When Kennedy walked through the open door, puffing a small cigar, Goldwater was sitting in the president's rocking chair, the one prescribed for the back pain they both suffered. Goldwater stood to greet Kennedy.

The president jabbed a finger toward him.

"Do you want this fucking job?" he asked the Arizona conservative, whose supporters were already preparing a challenge for it.

"No," said Goldwater, "not in my right mind."

Kennedy laughed humorlessly.

"Well," he said, "I thought I had a good thing going. Up until this morning." It was the day the Bay of Pigs invasion against Cuba's Fidel Castro began collapsing into disaster.

I wasn't the first to hear Goldwater recount that story, and certainly not the last. He told it with variations over the rest of his political career, and by the time he wrote his memoirs, what began as an ironic anecdote had become a turning point in his own thinking about the presidency.

Goldwater seldom told quite the same story twice. His variations made him a political reporter's dream and a manager's nightmare. Campaign handlers want their candidates to sell themselves and their proposals by repetition. That bored Goldwater, and he balked at it. We talked about it early in his campaign and he said that if he had to make the same speech over and over again every day, he'd go nuts before the election. The senator said what he thought, which sometimes changed. No hobgoblin consistency worried him. He was accused of shooting from the hip, but he wasn't always that careful.

Goldwater tried to follow instructions and avoid making off-the-cuff headlines, but he never really managed. I listened as he outlined his Cuba policy one day during the primary campaign and already was framing the story in my mind when he topped himself. Somebody asked him about Cuban interference with water lines into the Guantanamo Bay Naval Base. Goldwater said that if Castro didn't keep the water on, he'd send the Marines into Cuban territory to turn it on.

Forget the details of foreign policy. That was the story.

I learned one lasting, if painful, lesson early in that campaign by blowing the lead on Goldwater's first primary season news conference in New Hampshire. He said that intercontinental ballistic missiles were not reliable, that if he became president he wouldn't trust ICBMs, and that manned bombers were the only certain way to guarantee nuclear deterrence against the Soviet Union.

Prepping for the Goldwater assignment, I'd read his views on such topics, and that included his disdain for the ICBM. He'd said the same thing months before so it was old stuff, and I didn't include it in my story. My lead was on a new and, I thought, far more inflammatory statement he had made, accusing Johnson of trying to make the assassination of Kennedy into a political issue to ride in the 1964 campaign. Bad choice. The Pentagon turned the ICBM into the issue— and the story of the day—by denouncing and denying what Goldwater had said. I got an irate call from a Washington editor demanding to know why I hadn't reported the ICBM story that had the Pentagon in an uproar. I'd figured there was no hurry because it was stuff he'd said the year before, but I learned better. After that I followed a simple rule. My lead was the most interesting thing I learned or heard that day. It was my job to know everything possible about the candidate and his philosophy and background, and to write for readers who did not and who wanted to know what Barry Goldwater had said and done today, regardless of what he'd said the year before. The background was valuable when a candidate reversed himself and that became part of the story. But getting bogged down in it was a mistake.

I spent thirteen months covering Goldwater's campaign for the Republican presidential nomination and the White House. In an odd way, I owe the assignment to the candidate. When he met Wes Gallagher, the chief executive of the AP, at a cocktail reception in New York in 1963, Goldwater complained that we didn't seem to be paying much attention to him. Gallagher, who could be as impetuous as Goldwater, called my boss in Washington the next day and ordered me assigned to cover the senator. Presto, I was a full-time presidential campaign reporter. Right place, right time beats career planning any day.

I'd been in that right place in Hyannisport when Kennedy was nominated and elected, getting assignments to go to the Cape and work as junior partner with the reporters who covered politics and the White House for the AP. By then, I knew that I wanted to make my career in Washington, and the JFK stories gave me a boost toward that goal. I was working among the men whose bylines I'd admired, and envied. They were reporters of skill, experience, and, I learned, stamina I could not match. One Friday night, I stayed up with them until the motel bar closed at 2:00 A.M., then staggered to bed with a wakeup call for 6:00 because I had to go back to my Boston assignments and cover a football game at Harvard that afternoon. The Harvard Band boasted the world's biggest bass drum. I believed it that day; I felt as though it was booming inside my hungover head. The press box was atop the stadium, up flight after flight of concrete steps, with no elevator. I finally got to my place, opened my portable typewriter, and set about my game day duties. It wasn't much of a game so the story was routine—until the Harvard quarterback, touted as an All-America prospect, broke his leg in the second quarter. Suddenly, instead of a nothing game it was a major sports story. That meant I had to trudge down all those stairs to the field and get to the locker room to find out what had happened, then climb all the way back up to write the story and send it to the bureau. And the band was back at it with that drum. I made it, did my job, and learned not to act as though there was no tomorrow when the drinks were flowing in the hotel bar.

One Saturday in Hyannisport, Marv Arrowsmith, the AP White House correspondent, told me that I could write the main JFK story for the Sunday newspapers. I'd usually been relegated to stakeouts and side pieces, so that was a plum. I wrote the story, filed it by Western Union, and went into the restaurant where Arrowsmith was having lunch. He started chewing me out, saying that Sunday papers had early deadlines and that I was supposed to be writing the story instead of delaying it for a lunch break. "I've already done the story," I told him rather timidly. He didn't see how I could have written and filed a solid story in so little time, and he went back to the pressroom to make sure it was okay. He came back shaking his head with a wry smile, told me the story was fine, and said I was faster than he'd thought. High praise for a wire service man, especially one as green as I was.

Contacts like that got me onto the list of prospects for the Washington bureau. And it didn't hurt that Arrowsmith was promoted to the No. 2 job in Washington the next year.

I was transferred from the Boston bureau to Washington in October 1961. I worked the late-night shift for more than a year, a job that involved answering queries and complaints from newspapers dissatisfied with the stories they'd received from us, and trying to match stories other news outfits had beaten us on. That often meant waking up an official or a government spokesman in the middle of the night and trying to get the information from someone who was annoyed or angry at the call. It was Washington, but it was inside work; a desk job with no time for reporting and not much for writing. I was liberated from the night desk and assigned to cover the House of Representatives in 1963.

The House was a fascinating place of party rivalries and conflicting personalities, with leaders trying to orchestrate action out of the dissonance. Seniority ruled, usually southern Democratic seniority. The committee chairmen were the lords, ruling lesser congressmen with their monopoly on information and preferential treatment. One of them was Clarence Cannon of Missouri, chairman of the Appropriations Committee, master of the money. He didn't talk to reporters, and when he talked to the House you seldom could understand him. It was English uttered incomprehensibly, on purpose I thought, so that nobody would challenge him in debate. Even the *Congressional Record* transcribers couldn't make it out. When he spoke, the next day's record would read, "Mr. Cannon addressed the House. His remarks will appear hereafter." They never came. I was covering the debate on a defense appropriations bill one day when Cannon uttered several quotable sentences that I actually understood. I put them in the lead of my story and had an exclusive; my competitors hadn't been paying attention, figuring it would be unintelligible. I can't remember the words in detail, but he was talking about putting more money into the already bristling missile arsenal of the Cold War.

The titans of the House scorned the Senate and chafed at the attention senators got in the press. When Representative Emmanuel Celler of New York was chairman of the Judiciary Committee, he complained about it graphically. "If I took a leak off the Capitol steps, you'd write a sentence," he told a group of reporters one day. "If a senator did it, you'd write paragraphs describing the beauty of the arc."

Cannon and an equally superannuated Senate counterpart, Senator Carl Hayden of Arizona, made the rivalry between the chambers part of the Capitol architecture when they were chairmen of the two appropriations committees. After each house had passed its version of an appropriations bill, delegations representing the House and Senate met to negotiate final terms to be passed and sent to the White House. But Cannon balked at even stepping across the line between the House side of the Capitol and the Senate side, where the room numbers carried the S prefix. And Hayden wouldn't agree to meet on the House side. That blocked final action on appropriations bills until wiser, younger leaders agreed that a room in the middle designated neither H nor S was the way out. The east side of the Capitol was being renovated at the time and one of the new rooms was numbered EF—east front—100. They could confer there without bruising either chairman's ego, and they did.

My boss at the House was a veteran congressional reporter named Bill Arbogast. He knew everything and everybody up there. His vantage was the press gallery, usually the card table, where idling reporters and staffers played nonstop games of hearts and gin rummy. The office of the Foreign Affairs Committee was just outside the gallery door, and when a member keeled over and died of a heart attack in the hallway, Arbogast was close by. Legend has it that he said, "Hold the hand," got the story, filed it, and went back to the card table.

I spent less than a year covering the House before I was sent out with Goldwater. It was a dream job for a twenty-nine-year-old reporter. In a way, the AP became part of my name. I marked my press badge "Mears AP" and before long, people on the campaign were calling me "Mearsap."

At an icy street rally in Concord, New Hampshire, I wrote with a shivering hand when Goldwater began his primary campaign in

January 1964 by declaring that the Bay of Pigs invasion would have succeeded in overthrowing Castro had the Cuban refugee force gotten the U.S. air cover they thought was coming. Elect him president, Goldwater said, and he would try it again and get it right, training a new force to invade, arming them, and sending U.S. warplanes to back them. He wouldn't say why he thought a second try would do any better in convincing Cubans to overthrow the Castro regime, only that more force would succeed. That was typical Goldwater, always angered at the warmonger tag his rivals applied, always ready with a hard-line proposal to help them make the label stick.

Goldwater was an opponent, not an advocate. His proposals were few, his solutions fewer. He ran to take conservative command of the Republican Party, his target since 1960. When Goldwater endorsed Nixon at the Republican convention that year, he told his followers, "Let's grow up, conservatives . . . if we want to take this party back, and I think we can someday."

Someday was supposed to be 1964. But there was a familiar obstacle in the way of the conservative movement: the eastern Republican establishment that long had dominated party councils. It was personified in New York Governor Nelson A. Rockefeller, old line, old money, old power, initially the 1964 favorite over Goldwater, the conservative frontier upstart.

"Sometimes I think the country would be better off if we could just saw off the eastern seaboard and let it float out to sea," Goldwater once said. The line was replayed by his opponents as an example of his divisiveness, although he uttered it not as a politician but as a Phoenix businessman dealing with balky New York investors. Which is not to say that he wouldn't have preferred to see Rockefeller's New York put to sea.

The conservatives couldn't manage that, but Rockefeller's personal life boosted Goldwater's political stock before the campaign for the nomination began. The governor had divorced his wife of twenty-three years and was remarried in the spring of 1963 to a woman who had just split with her husband. Her nickname was Happy, now Happy Rockefeller. The political impact was not happy for the governor, who slipped behind Goldwater in the precampaign polls on the next year's nomination.

The political show in the first half of 1964 was all Republican, a bitter intramural struggle between Goldwater and Rockefeller. It began in New Hampshire, where the senator and the governor each spent the better part of a month campaigning for the first primary. Rockefeller came with money and skilled managers. Goldwater came without a game plan. At first he held almost constant news conferences, a bad idea given his tendency to ad-lib his way into controversy. He'd had foot surgery and he campaigned with his right shoe cut open to ease the pain. He limped through eighteen speeches in one day I spent with him. In the lakeside town of Moultonboro, we pulled up to an elementary school, where Goldwater found his audience to be third- and fourth-grade students. He gave them a grandfatherly talk, then chewed out the aide who'd sent him to talk to kids who wouldn't be voting for years. It turned out that the local campaign chairman had set up the appearance for her own advancement in town politics.

Rockefeller had to cope with the attacks of the *Manchester Union Leader,* the state's dominant and ardently conservative newspaper, which featured almost daily front-page editorials against "the wife swapper."

Rockefeller was a glad-handing candidate, throwing an arm around any voter in reach. "Hi ya, fella," he would say, sometimes to women. He campaigned in platitudes; reporters devised an acronym based on one of Rocky's recurring lines and used it to describe the message of his everyday set speech: "BOMFOG." That meant "brotherhood of man, fatherhood of God."

Goldwater was not into such homilies and he didn't like the hands-on style. When his campaign sent him to the Puritan Restaurant in Concord to shake hands, he balked. "If somebody walked up to me while I was eating and stuck out his hand, I'd put my hamburger in it," he said.

"I'm not one of those baby-kissing, handshaking, blintzel-eating candidates," he said on the steps of the Hanover Inn, shortly after Rockefeller had breezed through town doing all of the above. "I don't like to insult the American intelligence by thinking that slapping people on the back is going to get you votes." Goldwater was the first presidential candidate of Jewish ancestry, and he couldn't say "blintz" correctly.

But Rockefeller wasn't his real rival in the New Hampshire primary. Improbably, Henry Cabot Lodge was, the sleeper candidate, ambassador in far-off Saigon, silent on politics back home. A self-starting team of young political operatives came north from Boston, set up shop on less than a shoestring, and began a campaign for write-in votes for Lodge.

In a primary day blizzard, campaigners Goldwater and Rockefeller were beaten and absentee Lodge won easily, on what I described in my story that night as a snowslide of write-in ballots.

As it turned out, that primary made no lasting difference. Another vote on election day did: New Hampshire approved the first modern state lottery, legalizing a form of gambling that later would spread across most of the nation.

The permanent political imprint of the primary had nothing to do with the outcome but, rather, with the way it was reported. Eighteen minutes after the polls closed, before anyone had a chance to count and tabulate ballots the old-fashioned way, Walter Cronkite was on CBS reporting the Lodge write-in victory. I was working in an AP election-night office in a rambling, wooden hotel in Concord, surroundings as antique as our vote-counting operation turned out to be. We were set up for a standard counting operation, prepared for the familiar succession of reports on who led and by how much. It had always been done that way—first the suspense of the count, then the verdict of the votes. It would not be done that way again. The CBS report was based on instant calls from an army of vote watchers and on the outcome in selected sample precincts, and it was the future.

So began the 1964 contest among the networks to call elections first and boast about the scoop, even though it was measured in a minute or two. The networks hired legions of election night stringers to call in the vote. By the end of the primary season, the cost of getting all those people to get all those votes instantly was making the competition ruinous. And so was born the News Election Service, in which the networks, the Associated Press, and United Press International pooled their resources to count votes. For the first time, and in every national election after 1964, all the major news outlets reported the same vote numbers instead of competing to get them first.

Eventually, the pooled effort would be expanded to project outcomes on the basis of voter interviews before the ballots were counted. That seemed to be a reliable science until it proved not to be in Florida, in the 2000 election that was and will forever be too close to call with statistical certainty.

Lodge had his moment in New Hampshire; he won no more and stayed in Saigon. Goldwater and Rockefeller struggled and maneuvered all spring, to their last and decisive match in the California primary. It was an intense campaign. After an exhausting motorcade in southern California with stops for twenty-one speeches, Goldwater said, "If it's going to be like this, I quit."

There were legions of Goldwater girls in gold and brilliant blue outfits to brighten the rallies. One day in Los Angeles, a network colleague told me to watch and he'd prove the power of television. He summoned about thirty Goldwater girls and got them to form a circle. On his command they circled left, then right, while a cameraman focused on them. There was no film in the camera.

In solidly conservative Orange County, south of Los Angeles, John Wayne introduced Goldwater at an outdoor rally by denouncing the reporters he said were writing lies about the senator. "They're right down there," Wayne said, pointing at us in the press section beside the stage. Some in the crowd pushed forward, literally growling at us. There were no casualties.

But for all the campaign intensity, Rockefeller's personal life may have tipped the outcome to Goldwater's hard-line victory. Three days before the primary, Rockefeller went home to New York for the birth of his son. The baby pictures revived the personal issue and certainly cost Rockefeller votes in a California election he barely lost.

Even with Rockefeller finished, there were pockets of Republican resistance bent on stopping Goldwater. In an odd way, the "stop

Goldwater" movement included former President Eisenhower, although he said vehemently that he wasn't part of it. Eisenhower said he wanted an open Republican convention, which meant other candidates would stand a chance, while insisting that he did not oppose the nomination of Goldwater. That was contradictory because Goldwater had more than enough delegate votes to win, closing the choice of the convention before it began. There could not be an open convention unless Goldwater was stopped.

That was obvious, but Ike didn't see it, or at least wouldn't admit it. I went with Marv Arrowsmith, who had covered the Eisenhower White House, to interview the former president at his home in Gettysburg, Pennsylvania, and he stuck to his contradictory position. He wasn't against Goldwater, he was just for an open convention. When I persisted in pointing out the inconsistency, he got angry and Arrowsmith changed the subject. The only time I ever met Dwight Eisenhower I made him mad.

The Republican convention in San Francisco was bitter and divided. The conservatives booed and jeered to drown out Rockefeller when he tried to deliver his convention speech. They cheered, wildly, when Goldwater essentially read moderates out of the campaign, saying that he didn't expect support from "those who do not believe in our cause." A united Republican front couldn't have defeated Lyndon Johnson. A bitterly divided one wasn't even competitive.

Through it all, Johnson and his Democrats just watched, which was all they needed to do. No need to tear at the Republicans when they were tearing themselves apart, to nominate a man more bent on taking control of the party than of the White House.

Goldwater varied the story a bit in his retellings of the 1961 White House visit with a fuming President Kennedy as the Bay of Pigs operation unraveled, but one part of the recollection stood: The JFK expletive about the lousy job of being president never was deleted.

Yet, in his 1988 memoir, Goldwater described the episode as a turning point in his own thinking about the presidency because, he said, Kennedy had asked for his advice and he'd given it—get tougher against Castro. For the first time, he wrote, he came to believe "that I had the toughness of mind and will to lead the country."

That doesn't fit with his other ruminations about the office. Before he ran, Goldwater said, "I'm not even sure that I've got the brains to be president of the United States." He won the Republican presidential nomination shortly after saying publicly that he couldn't win the election.

When Goldwater invited a newcomer to his staff to his home in Phoenix, he told the astonished presidential campaign recruit, "You're looking at the one man in the United States who doesn't want to be president." The guy had to wonder what kind of a campaign he'd joined.

The official period of mourning for Kennedy had just ended when Goldwater began his campaign. President Johnson was the third man to hold the office within three years and the voters were not about to change leaders again. Goldwater knew that and told me so, although off the record.

After the trauma of assassination, people wanted stability, not change, especially change so abrupt as Goldwater advocated. He was pushing for a sharp turn to the right. He wanted to repeal social programs dating from the New Deal. He brandished U.S. nuclear power in careless words that enabled the Democrats to depict him as a warmonger. He described battlefield atomic artillery as "conventional nuclear weapons," and what he said scared people.

He wasn't scary in person. When I wrote his obituary in 1998, I described him as cantankerously cordial. Like many of the conservative politicians I knew over the years, he was generous when he saw somebody in trouble or need. He wanted to help individuals when he saw their plight one-on-one, perhaps as much as he wanted to stop government programs to assist masses of people in need.

No candidate is truly drafted to run for president, but Goldwater was pushed to the task by conservative activists who saw him as their one hope of dominating the Republican Party. It irked him when he had to campaign hard.

Johnson was the opposite; he thrived on campaigning, couldn't seem to get enough of the cheers and adulation of the crowds. Kennedy had chosen Johnson for vice president after defeating him for the 1960 Democratic presidential nomination. I was at Hyannisport when Johnson arrived there for the first postconvention meeting between the 1960 running mates. "Ah've come to see mah friend and leader," Johnson said, accentuating the Texan amid the clipped accents of Cape Cod. But the suspicion persisted that he thought the ticket was backward, that he belonged on top. Now he was determined to put the LBJ brand on a White House he'd inherited. He wanted a mountainous mandate in 1964, a landslide to contrast with the razor thin margin of Kennedy's victory in 1960. He wasn't only running against Goldwater; he was running to eclipse the JFK legend with his own.

Vice presidents have to submerge their egos and that was no easy task for Johnson, who had dominated the Senate as majority leader before he joined the 1960 ticket. After he won the White House for himself, his Texas ego thrived. A colleague recalled an off-the-record session over drinks on Air Force One in which Johnson delivered his version of modern history. No note taking was permitted, so he could only paraphrase the president from memory. Look at the world today, Johnson said. Churchill, dead. Stalin, Kennedy, all dead. And—his voice rising now—I'm the king.

Goldwater said he had decided to run against Kennedy in the fall of 1963. He told me it would have been a clear test of conservative versus liberal in a race with civil rules. He said later that he and Kennedy had agreed on an unprecedented arrangement in which the two nominees would conduct regular debates, not only appearing together but also traveling together, all to dramatize the clear choice awaiting the voters. No one ever confirmed that story and I always wondered whether such an unlikely campaign deal was real, but Goldwater told it often in the years after his presidential defeat, and it became part of the lore. Al Gore cited the supposed Goldwater-Kennedy plan as precedent when he dared his challenger to constant debates in the 2000 primary campaign.

Goldwater said that after Kennedy was assassinated, he decided "to heck with the president thing." He always said he'd liked and respected Kennedy, although the rhetoric didn't sound that way. He had, for example, accused Kennedy of running the worst foreign policy in American history, "wall-eyed . . . cross-eyed . . . and blind."

Kennedy, in turn, thought Goldwater was the weakest Republican he might face for reelection in 1964. He was far more worried about Rockefeller, the liberal Republican who could take centrist votes away from the Democratic ticket.

But Kennedy did not live to run, and Goldwater, oddly, claimed that he then decided not to run himself because he despised and distrusted Johnson. That seemed to me to be all the more reason to challenge the man, but Goldwater said he didn't want to be involved in a nasty campaign and Johnson would wage one. When he campaigned against Johnson, Goldwater wasn't sparing with his own nastiness. He called the president a treacherous hypocrite and the phoniest man he knew. The senator could be nasty, too.

Long afterward, Goldwater wrote that Johnson made him sick. The contempt was mutual. "He's just as nutty as a fruitcake," Johnson said in a telephone conversation early in 1964, recorded on the LBJ tapes. He pretended he wasn't campaigning at that point, just being president—which is, of course, the most effective campaign a president can wage. When he got around to campaigning openly, Johnson called Goldwater heartless, extreme, and dangerous.

It was a campaign with the election outcome never really in doubt, even though Johnson was given to wailing privately that it was and that Democrats who disputed him risked turning the presidency over to Goldwater. Even so, the 1964 campaign left lasting landmarks.

One was the beginning of the marathon presidential campaign. The conservatives who captured the Republican nomination for Goldwater worked at it for more than two years, operating below the political radar to take over the party in a quiet revolution. Their operation foretold the years-long campaigns that would become standard.

The 1964 conservative takeover was fashioned in a sort of political guerrilla war. The Goldwater Republicans began it by capturing control in neighborhood GOP meetings, the caucuses that are the first step in choosing the delegates who vote on presidential nominations. A handful of activists could win at that level. Party veterans suddenly found themselves outnumbered by conservatives who hadn't shown up before. A New York political tactician named F. Clinton White managed the operation, building a pyramid from neighborhood caucuses to county and state conventions to the Republican National Convention. The primaries against Rockefeller were political theater, but conservative command was won offstage. By the time the party's old guard figured out the takeover strategy, they couldn't stop it.

Before national convention time, Goldwater had the delegate commitments he needed to win the nomination and was unstoppable unless liberal and centrist Republicans could pry loose enough convention votes to deny him. They couldn't, because the Goldwater delegates were not sometime supporters, they were conservative true believers, unmoving and unmovable. In time, conventions would become TV pageants, celebrations, and political reunions. The 1964 Republican convention wasn't a reunion; it was a divisive show of conservative brawn. At earlier conventions, delegates were usually the same faces every four years, many of them the old-line Republican power brokers of New York and the East Coast. But three-quarters of the 1964 Republican delegates at the Cow Palace in San Francisco were strangers, people who had not been at the 1960 convention.

So the party fractured, with Goldwater and his supporters on one side and the old moderate GOP establishment on the other. Goldwater seemed to revel in the disintegration. After he was nominated he told his Republican opponents he didn't care about their support in the fall. He made the obligatory rounds of state caucuses during the convention, but preferred to spend his time talking on a ham radio installed at his Mark Hopkins Hotel suite. "This is K7UGA portable six, from the top of the Mark Hopkins Hotel," he'd say. "The handle is Barry—Baker Able Robert Robert Yankee." He talked with ham operators from as far off as Australia. He still felt cooped up, so he slipped out of the hotel, eluding reporters and the convention crowds by using a cobwebbed tunnel that led from the hotel to a secluded exit atop Nob Hill, where an unmarked police car waited to take him to San Mateo County airport and a rented plane. Goldwater went flying three times that week and told me later that he had buzzed the Cow Palace while the convention there was getting ready to nominate him for president.

Wes Gallagher, the top man at AP, was convinced that Goldwater was going to be a troublesome candidate to cover, one who would try to deny things he said when they turned out to be damaging. In fact, he didn't do that. He'd talk his way off the reservation but he lived with what he said, although he sometimes tried to ignore troublesome statements that were on the record, or claimed that he had been misinterpreted by reporters. Since Gallagher thought the AP was going to be arguing with him over quotes, he ordered me at the San Francisco convention to carry a tape recorder during the campaign, get everything Goldwater said on tape, and keep it for proof when an AP story was challenged. But the small, handy cassette recorders that would become standard equipment for reporters in later campaigns had not yet been invented. The recorder Gallagher wanted me to carry was bulky and hard to handle. You couldn't take notes and run it at the same time. Besides, you had to thread each reel of tape into it, which defied my less than minimal technical ability. AP reporter Rob Wood, who worked with me on the Goldwater convention story, showed up at the Mark Hopkins Hotel with the thing. I called the convention bureau, which was at the foot of Nob Hill, and said I wouldn't use it because I couldn't be a reporter and a sound man at the same time. I was told that I had to because Gallagher wanted it. When I tried to protest to Gallagher, I was told he was on his way back to New York. So I could not lodge an appeal. Instead, I sent Wood back down Nob Hill to the AP convention bureau with the hated tape recorder, figuring that it was like a subpoena; if it hadn't been served it didn't count. Wood trudged back down the hill with it. He was ordered to deliver it to me again. He was smart enough to know I'd only balk again, so I saw no more of the recorder until I got on Goldwater's chartered campaign plane. It was in my seat. I surrendered and carried it around for a while, but I never did figure out how to use it to any good purpose. The truth is that I never recorded a word on the thing.

Goldwater had long since riveted himself into positions that guaranteed all but like-minded conservatives would shun his ticket. Civil rights was a major one. Goldwater said his aim was neither to establish a segregated society nor to establish an integrated one but "to preserve a free society." The message was clearer than the logic. Goldwater cast one of the twenty-seven Senate votes against the 1964 civil rights act barring racial discrimination in hiring and segregation in restaurants and hotels. (In his memoir, he wrote that his was the only vote against it, but then, he was given to exaggeration.) He was a states' rights conservative, and that was music to the Old South holdouts against civil rights laws. The Goldwater ticket opened the first cracks in what had been the solid South of white, conservative Democrats since the era of Reconstruction after the Civil War. Five of the six states Goldwater carried against Johnson were in the South, foretelling the realignment of party power that would make the region a Republican base in elections to come.

Earlier in 1964, Governor George C. Wallace, who had cried, "Segregation forever" as an Alabama campaigner, took his message north into three Democratic primaries and "white backlash" became part of the political lexicon. Wallace peaked at 43 percent of the primary vote in Maryland. Interviewing Wallace later in his Montgomery office, I listened to his boasts about his 1964 campaign, which came with visual aids. At least it was supposed to be an interview. Wallace did monologues; a question asked usually was a question ignored. He pulled out a sheaf of photos of campaign rallies in the territory he'd invaded, and bragged about all the people he'd drawn to hear him. He claimed to remember the size of the crowd at the major rallies, but he saw a lot more people in the photographs than I did. "Looka this," he'd say. "This is in Milwaukee, looka all those people come to hear me."

In Maryland, Wallace was leading midway through the primary night vote. Afterward, he told of the lead that vanished. First, he said, those TV people said he was winning. But then they announced that they were going to recapitulate the vote, and he lost. "I don't know what re . . . cap . . . it . . . u . . . late means," he'd drawl, dragging out the syllables, "but if anybody ever tells you they fixin' to recapitulate on you, watch out."

While Wallace and Goldwater demonstrated the holdout power of the right, the 1964 election turned the government to the left, delivering Johnson's Great Society social programs as Democrats took overwhelming command of Congress.

But even while that was happening, Ronald Reagan emerged from Hollywood and television as a champion Republican fund-raiser, beginning the political rise that would one day deliver in his name the conservative presidency Goldwater could only talk about.

Reagan the movie actor had become Reagan the television host and performer on the rubber chicken lecture circuit. In the final days of the campaign, the Goldwater organization bought thirty minutes of national television time for a fund-raising address, intending to have the nominee use it for a Reagan-style speech to rally conservative troops and money.

But Goldwater told them a speech like that wasn't his style, overruling the advisers who wanted him on camera and saying Reagan could deliver it more effectively. "You're more eloquent than I am," he told Reagan. That was an understatement. Goldwater's speechmaking style was as bland as his words were fiery. Reagan was the performer, and the Goldwater speech was his debut as a national political figure.

When he was elected governor of California in 1966, Reagan telephoned Goldwater to say that it wouldn't have happened without his 1964 sendoff. But the conservative tie didn't bind when Reagan challenged President Gerald R. Ford for renomination in 1976 and Goldwater supported the president. Nancy Reagan had a long memory and Goldwater, back in the Senate, never made the list for White House social affairs after Reagan became president in 1981.

The Vietnam War was threaded through the 1964 campaign, a shadowy issue begetting the deceptions that would tear the Democrats apart four years later. The war was escalating, and Johnson got his franchise to intensify it with the almost unanimous vote of Congress, Goldwater included, for retaliation against purported North Vietnamese torpedo firings on U.S. destroyers in the Gulf of Tonkin.

Nevertheless, Johnson promised, "We are not going to send American boys nine or ten thousand miles away from home to do what Asian boys ought to be doing for themselves." Within months of Johnson's reelection, he did so. It led later to a Goldwater story about a supporter of his saying, "They told me that if I voted for Barry there would be a half-million American troops in Vietnam. I did, and there are."

But Vietnam did not become a major issue in Johnson's campaign with Goldwater, who seemed to have two minds about the subject. At one point he said it was too divisive to be made a political topic, at others he accused Johnson of lying about Vietnam and demanded an accounting.

I remember the incongruity of scene and subject the day Goldwater and we reporters covering him flew in light planes to the unpaved airstrip of an orchard town in northern California. While a warm spring breeze blew across acres of peach blossoms, the scent perfuming the air, Goldwater told townspeople that the United States was risking disaster and stalemate in Vietnam. He said it would become another Korean War or worse unless heavier American weapons were unsheathed and U.S. bombers struck the Communists. Frightening prospects, told in a mild, almost singsong style, no raised voice, no sound of alarm. An awful war was escalating, but in the election of 1964 Vietnam was all but irrelevant.

The war the Democrats wanted to talk about wasn't Vietnam. It was the imaginary war they conjured by charging that as president Goldwater would be so reckless as to risk nuclear conflict. Goldwater's loose-cannon talk helped them draw the image. The Democrats reinforced it with television attack ads linking Goldwater to mushroom clouds and nuclear fallout, the first of the negative TV commercials that would become lamentable fixtures in later campaigns. None were more adroit or more devastating than the 1964 Democratic ads implying that Goldwater would risk nuclear war.

Goldwater's was the last of the freestyle presidential campaigns. There was no map. Literally, at times. On one of those light plane campaign flights, the pilot lost his bearings and had to find a highway he recognized to show him the route to the airfield. I got an early lesson in Goldwater's habits aloft when I flew from Phoenix to California with him in a twin-engine plane, and the clouds closed in as we headed through a mountain pass. He nudged me and pointed out the window at a snowy mountain crag that pierced the cloud bank above us and, it seemed to me, distressingly close. I paled. He laughed.

Goldwater relied on strategists and advisers short on national campaign experience but long on personal friendship, loyalty, and conservative ideology. It was an operation innocent of the hired consultants who would come to guide the decisions of nominees and would become the permanent establishment of presidential campaigns.

Nor did Goldwater worry much about polls. He might have stayed home if he had. He was down to Johnson by two to one or worse all year. He told me the polls didn't make any difference; he was going to speak his piece and run his party.

Goldwater later claimed that he had made campaign proposals even though he knew they would be unpopular, such as when he advocated making Social Security voluntary, to the distress of retirees, and when he called in Nashville for the sale of TVA power plants to private investors. But he set those political traps for himself long before he ran for president, in his speeches and writings as Mr. Conservative. As Mr. Candidate, he actually tried to temper them, saying that he did not believe in changing contracts like Social Security and that, besides, Congress would not let any president do things like making the system voluntary or selling off TVA. Over the decades, versions of both notions became less radical and more acceptable, at least for debate. But in 1964, they were sitting targets for Johnson and the Democrats.

So were Goldwater's observations about nuclear weapons. He said in 1963 that U.S. NATO commanders should have the authority to use tactical nuclear weapons in Europe in case of Communist attack. Scary talk, which he had to defend and try to explain. Eventually, he said he meant only the Supreme Allied Commander, not his subordinates. Later still, he said that Johnson and his predecessors already had delegated that authority to the commander—singular—and that his statement reflected what already had been done without public notice.

Explanations aside, raising the nuclear prospect only added to qualms and outright fears about the candidate on the right, handing political ammunition to the Democrats. In a television interview that spring, Goldwater talked of blocking Communist supply lines in Vietnam with nuclear weapons. "There have been several suggestions made, I don't think we would use any of them, but defoliation of the forests by low-yield atomic weapons could well be done." That was inaccurately reported as a Goldwater proposal for the use of nuclear weapons in Vietnam. He hadn't proposed it, he protested. No, he had not. He'd speculated about it, which was problem enough. Careless words about nuclear weapons only dug the political hole deeper for the senator who had once talked about lobbing one into the men's room at the Kremlin.

He was a dangerous radical, Johnson would say. "Whose thumb do you want on that button?" became a regular question in Democratic campaign speeches.

Personally, the menacing zealot the Democrats depicted was an engaging, friendly man, a talented amateur photographer, a tinkerer who delighted in gadgets like his automatic sunup flag-raising device in Phoenix. When a colleague went to Goldwater's house to interview him, he was directed to the swimming pool but saw no sign of the senator, who liked to use underwater breathing gear to lounge at the bottom. He finally surfaced and the interview proceeded.

Goldwater was at home in and around airplanes, a pilot since World War II. He delighted in his campaign-chartered American Airlines 727, christened *Yai-Bi-Kin*, which is Navajo for "House in the Sky." But even the cockpit veteran was startled by one maneuver, on takeoff from Bristol, Tennessee. The jet began climbing and suddenly turned sharply, roaring back and down toward the runway. It was unnerving, even when the plane leveled just off above the runway. By

then the more devout passengers were deep in prayer. I told my terri-
fied seatmate that we probably weren't going to crash because they
hadn't turned on the No Smoking sign, and if we were really in trouble, they would have denied us a last cigarette. Goldwater got up from
his seat near the cockpit and braced himself to walk the few steps to
the door. He came out laughing. The pilot had buzzed the runway on
a dare from a friend in the control tower. "That was to separate the
men from the boys," Goldwater said on the loudspeaker. Most of us
sided with the boys.

The myth is that there was at least a cold war between Goldwater
and the reporters who covered him. There was not. To the regulars, a
half dozen of us who reported his campaign from the beginning, he
was as friendly as Nixon had been aloof. He entertained us in his
home in Phoenix. He arranged a trip to Nogales, Sonora, for dinner
at the Cave, his favorite Mexican restaurant, once a Pancho Villa
hideout. That excursion wound up in the middle of the night at the
Phoenix airport with Goldwater and his wife sharing swigs from a
bottle of tequila with four reporters.

After his landslide defeat, Goldwater told those of us who had
traveled with him and reported on his campaign that we had treated
him fairly, even though he thought, correctly, that most of us disagreed with much of what he said. To a professional political reporter,
disagreement makes no difference. You keep your personal views out
of the coverage and out of the story if you're any good at the job.
Goldwater said it was the columnists and commentators, "that end of
the press," who had misrepresented him. "I have never seen or heard
in my life such vitriolic, unbased attacks on one man as have been
directed to me," he said.

There is a special camaraderie among the reporters who share the
rigors, rewards, and plain fun of traveling with the candidates. It's the
only work I know in which the boss gives you a credit card and some
cash and sends you roaming around the country to write stories that
are all but guaranteed to be on front pages every day. It becomes a
lifestyle that is hard to let go when the election is over. I remember
a sort of depression after my first full-bore experience at campaign

coverage. Suddenly the show that had been central to my life and work for months or longer was over and it was time to go back to the real world, covering stories, in my case on the Senate, that seemed routine compared with where I'd been. I experienced the same letdown feeling after later campaigns and elections, but by then I understood it and knew that the way to handle it was to plunge into the next story, not mope about the end of the last one.

We reporters were close friends, but no less competitive for the friendships. When you come up with a story the others don't have, you write it hard and let them try to catch up. There's no greater compliment for a political reporter than to have your friends show up late for dinner and cuss you out for beating them. Next time, almost certainly, one of your competitors will have the beat and you're going to be chasing the story. But on the daily routine—checking quotes for accuracy, getting filled in on what's happened while you've been off filing, for example—we took care of each other. The protective code applied when a reporter had a drink or two too many at the end of a travel day and needed a bit of help writing that night. I'd had a couple, maybe more, one night in Kentucky before I went to the pressroom to write what we called an overnight, a story summing up the day and looking ahead to tomorrow, for afternoon papers. I must have been staring at the typewriter a bit longer than usual. David Broder, the great political reporter and columnist, then with the evening *Washington Star,* was at work on his story across the room. Broder, who honestly fits the description of gentleman and scholar, finished his overnight piece, filed it Western Union, and then, without a word, dropped a carbon copy—we called them blacksheets—of his overnight on my desk. Just in case I needed some help in writing my own. I glanced at his copy as he left and jerked myself out of my reverie. I got to work writing my own overnight, cranked it out and filed it, and walked into the hotel bar with a copy, which I dropped on the table where Broder was relaxing. "I can write better drunk than you can sober," I told him, laughing. He laughed, too. It wasn't so, but it was one of my better lines. In pressroom lore, there is the story of a New York reporter who got too drunk to write while covering Harry

Truman in Key West, Florida, and slumped over his typewriter. Colleagues covered for him. Three or maybe four revised their stories, put his byline on them, and filed them to his newspaper, until his editor sent back a message saying, Okay, enough.

There also were feuds among certain reporters, some dating back years. Merriman Smith, the UPI White House man who won the Pulitzer Prize for coverage of the Kennedy assassination in Dallas in 1963, grabbed the one radio telephone in the press car and dictated his bulletin after the shots were fired, then hogged the phone to prevent the AP's Jack Bell from filing his story. They wrestled over it; by the time Bell got to file we already had our story on the wire, from a staff photographer who had seen Kennedy shot in the head, which was more than Smith knew. Smith said later that he wouldn't have done it to another AP man, but with Bell, it was a grudge match. He said Bell had done a number on him years before when Smith was sent to cover Dwight Eisenhower's presidential campaign. Smith claimed that Bell had told Ike's press secretary not to trust him because he wasn't a reliable reporter. I never thought that was so; I never knew whether Bell had said it was. Whatever the gossip, it didn't slow Smith's career; he became the best known of White House reporters. Bell was my boss at the Senate and I traveled with him for years on political stories. He didn't talk about what happened that day in Dallas but it haunted him. I realized that one night when the two of us were having dinner on the road, discussing the campaign we were covering and suddenly, as though talking to himself, he said, "I should have torn out that goddamned phone." Then he went back to the conversation we'd been having.

Goldwater was a westerner who liked his guns, which would have been a Secret Service nightmare when government guards were assigned to candidates four years later. Once, when he and Peggy Goldwater entertained a few of us for lunch at their home, he got to talking about handguns with the *New York Times* man, Charles Mohr. While the rest of us chatted with Mrs. Goldwater over sandwiches, shots sounded at the front door, one room away. We jolted out of our chairs.

"That's just Barry with his pistol," Mrs. Goldwater said reassuringly. But she made him cease fire. He and Mohr had been shooting at a metal box target, a bullet trap across the driveway from his house. Goldwater acknowledged that some of his shots missed and strayed into the valley beyond. He said that seemed to bother the people at the church down there even though they were out of range, so he didn't shoot on Sundays.

One day in Dallas, Goldwater told a veterans' convention that the *New York Times* was no better than *Izvestia*, the Soviet newspaper. The veterans cheered and afterward, Mohr asked Goldwater what he'd meant by that slap. "Oh, I wasn't talking about you, Charlie," Goldwater said, and dropped it. But their relationship was fractured after the election when Mohr wrote a magazine piece titled "Requiem for a Lightweight," about Goldwater, his campaign, and his failings. Goldwater considered it a slur and never forgave Mohr or his newspaper. When he returned to the Senate in 1969, he would not speak to *Times* reporters and that was his rule until he retired, three terms later.

Still, for all the conservative complaints about the "Eastern Liberal Press," a label we reporters had put onto lapel pins as a sarcastic inside joke, Goldwater got a more than even break in his coverage. The reporters who knew him and his tendency to blurt words he didn't intend would ask him to slow down and say what he meant. He wasn't absolved of major missteps that way, but he got a chance to try to make himself clear in the day-to-day fare of campaigning. That could not happen now, with every public statement recorded on tape. Nor would it, given the journalistic ground rules enforced by an era of scandal and purposeful political lies. Indeed, as Goldwater climbed past the nomination into the general election campaign, the coverage intensified, and he was held to every word.

"Write what he means, not what he says," asked Paul F. Wagner, who became Goldwater's last, best campaign press secretary that summer. He used to call me "the damned quoter," who just wrote things down and put them on the AP wire. That was my job, of course, and he was joking. Or at least half joking.

Wagner was the operations man when the Goldwater high command decided on an odd, and futile, policy meant to protect him from his own words. He decreed that the nominee could not be quoted directly when speaking off-the-cuff and answering questions. His news conferences would be under background rules, meaning that what he said could not be attributed to him, only to sources familiar with his thinking or other such terms of art. That way the Goldwater campaign could disown words that would have created problems. It was dishonest and it also was impossible, given the campaign setting. I challenged the rule, telling Goldwater that the AP would not report campaign statements that could not be attributed to him by name. I said that in my reporting, he'd have to run for president under his own name, not as a source. My bosses backed me up and the AP skipped some stories our competitors used.

The attempt to protect Goldwater from his own words was a failure. No candidate could run under cover in a plane full of reporters. The campaign dropped the device, but not before it produced such anomalies as a *New York Times* story quoting sources close to Goldwater, beside a photograph of Goldwater answering questions from reporters in his campaign plane.

Presidents and politicians still try at times to immunize themselves with background-only rules when they want to say or leak something but don't want it attributed to them. It doesn't work in a crowd, only when the word is whispered to one reporter or a handful of them. Even then, background strictures, meaning no name attribution, or the more restrictive off-the-record, meaning no use at all, have become fragile and often transparent in a wired political environment. The only way to be really off-the-record is to be silent and that is not what politicians do for a living.

When Goldwater began his 1964 campaign, he promised, "A choice, not an echo." His campaign certainly offered that. Seldom, perhaps never, have two men so diametrically different in philosophy, style, and ambition as Goldwater and Johnson been rival nominees for the White House. Johnson wanted total victory—a shutout if possible. Goldwater was just running. "I don't know if any man has a burning desire for this job," he told me a month before his nomination. "It's the worst job you can have."

LBJ didn't think so, although he, like Goldwater, sometimes threatened to quit the whole business. Goldwater didn't like the work of running or the workload heaped upon him. Johnson reveled in both but he couldn't stand Democratic dissent against him. When a dispute over a black challenge to the all-white Mississippi delegation threatened to disrupt the Democratic National Convention, Johnson threatened to quit the campaign. "This will throw the nation into quite an uproar, sir," George Reedy, his press secretary, said, mildly understating the political upheaval that would have ensued had Johnson really meant it. Johnson was outraged by Democratic disputes. "Why in the living hell do they want to hand—shovel—Goldwater fifteen states? . . . If they want to elect Goldwater, that's not going to make me cry one bit," he cried. It made no difference that he was overwhelmingly ahead in the polls, on his way to a November landslide. He wanted unanimity.

"They think I want great power," he told Reedy in a recorded Oval Office telephone conversation reported in Michael R. Beschloss's book *Taking Charge*. "And what I want is great solace and a little love. That's all I want."

For a politician, the greatest solace is votes. He had more than enough of those and everybody knew it. The White House was going to remain Democratic against any Republican challenger. Goldwater's nomination guaranteed it. Johnson wanted unity and harmony. Goldwater didn't worry about either. Nominated, he told his Republican opponents they could just go sit out the campaign. Then came the defiant declaration that guaranteed the left-right split would be a chasm: "I would remind you that extremism in the defense of liberty is no vice. And let me remind you also that moderation in the pursuit of justice is no virtue."

"Extremism in pursuit of the presidency" Johnson called it.

The Vietnam question never quite went away but it never became the issue it should have been. In a more perfect political world, 1964 would have been the campaign and election in which to debate the war, before instead of after U.S. forces were fully committed, before intervention expanded into the agonizing conflict of the late 1960s and early 1970s.

At the Republican convention, Goldwater said Vietnam should be a campaign issue. "Don't try to sweep this under the rug," he challenged Johnson. But the president did just that, and, strangely, Goldwater helped him.

When the war did come up, Johnson denounced Goldwater as belligerent. He said it was easier to start wars than to end them and that a policy of bombing North Vietnam would cost American lives and lead to ground warfare. It did, of course, but by then it was Johnson's policy.

Despite Goldwater's convention rhetoric, shortly after his nomination he told the president that he believed neither of them should heighten divisions about the conflict "by making Vietnam an issue in the campaign." Goldwater said he would not do so, a mystifying commitment he didn't really keep. Johnson obviously was delighted at the offer to keep Vietnam out of the campaign. It played to his strength by letting him hammer on concerns at home while depicting Goldwater as the potential warmaker. Goldwater let him do it, although he periodically denounced administration policy as incompetent and derelict.

Just as oddly, Goldwater announced that fall that if elected he would send Eisenhower to Vietnam to help decide U.S. policy—an echo of the former president's own 1952 campaign pledge that he would go to Korea to deal with that war. When a Goldwater aide called me at home to tell me of the send-Ike-to-Vietnam proposal, I thought he was joking. Finally convinced that he was serious, I asked what Eisenhower thought of the idea. Oops. No answer. Typically in their haphazard operation, nobody had thought to mention the Vietnam idea to Eisenhower first.

Goldwater said he had his personal talk with Johnson about Vietnam as an issue when he went to the White House in late July to pledge that he would not make civil rights a campaign issue, either. His Senate vote against the civil rights act that spring had made it one.

Even Goldwater's own advisers, no fans of the civil rights movement, wanted him to vote for it because enactment was inevitable and a "no" vote would hurt his campaign.

Johnson had proposed the legislation and signed the law, overriding the last stand of the old Democratic South in the Senate. But George Wallace had demonstrated the power of the backlash vote, and despite the advance of civil rights measures, there was racial violence in American cities that summer. The whole subject was explosive.

Goldwater would claim later that he had decided the civil rights issue should be calmed and that he had planned to go see Johnson and work out a joint pledge to keep racial questions out of their campaigns. Actually, Goldwater walked into the situation inadvertently and, again, played to Johnson's strength. The idea of a meeting between the Republican challenger and the president grew out of a reporter's question at an airport news conference in Chicago. After Goldwater said he would do nothing as a candidate to risk worsening racial tensions, the reporter asked whether the senator thought the nominees should have a summit meeting on the issue. Goldwater answered that he would welcome the chance to discuss it with Johnson because civil rights should be "a completely quiet question" in the campaign. My story got to Washington before Goldwater did, and Johnson preempted the topic by announcing he'd be meeting his opponent at the White House. He'd even set the date.

It was an LBJ show, a sixteen-minute meeting with Goldwater after the senator had been kept waiting twice that long in the Cabinet Room. The White House issued the only report on what was said: Johnson had "reviewed the steps he had taken to avoid the incitement of racial tensions," and the two had agreed that they were to be avoided. Goldwater was ushered out a side entrance without giving his version of the meeting that day.

Not that he could have said much anyhow. He'd gone into Johnson's arena, and the president had shown his command. That was the image LBJ wanted: Action Johnson, the man who got things done. Johnson reveled in his campaigning. "If the president gets out of his car and talks to a colored boy in New Orleans or a widow woman in Kentucky or a banker in New England, they feel pretty important," Johnson said after striding into the crowds to touch hands, to the constant dismay of his Secret Service guards.

Goldwater wouldn't have worried them. He kept his distance. When Goldwater drew unexpected crowds, which was not often, they seemed to annoy him. We flew into a southern airport late one campaign night and there was a spontaneous crowd waiting to see the senator. Goldwater was handed a portable loudspeaker to address them, but instead of using it he thrust it into the hands of his startled wife. End of rally. When he found a small but noisy hometown crowd waiting one night at the Phoenix airport, he waved, shook a few hands, managed a thin smile, and left. As he did, I heard him hiss at an aide, "Who's responsible for this?"

Until fall, Johnson maintained a transparent pretext of political virginity: He was too busy being the president to be a politician. He went to dedications, inspections, universities. He proposed his Great Society with its array of social programs, among them Medicare, which he won the next year. After his nomination, that pretense was over. At the Atlantic City convention, the president said America needed a man who would "build a house instead of a ranting, raving demagogue who wants to tear one down."

He was his own cheerleader, exhorting the street crowds to join his rallies: "Come on down and hear the speakin'." Sometimes they didn't have to because he would grab the bullhorn and do some speakin' right there. On his one foray into Goldwater's Arizona, Johnson went to Phoenix on a Sunday saying he was going to church there because "this is a day for God, not politics." Sure it was. He got to the church service two hours late after a tumultuous motorcade with nineteen stops on the way from the airport.

There seldom were crowds big enough to delay Goldwater. He did draw an unexpected turnout at the airport in Charleston, West Virginia, leading his lieutenants to boast that he was showing his appeal in heavily Democratic territory. When I talked with some of the people in the crowd, they said they'd come to see Goldwater's chartered Boeing 727 jet because they hadn't seen one there before.

Besides, a man added morbidly, they wondered whether the plane would be able to land on the relatively short runway of the mountaintop airport.

It did, and Goldwater went into the city to say that Johnson's war on poverty was phony and to advocate that welfare recipients work for their checks. Asked what they should do, Goldwater said that in Phoenix they trimmed the dead fronds off the palm trees. There were no palm trees, no fronds, and not enough jobs in West Virginia. Johnson got 68 percent of the vote.

While Goldwater campaigned by chartered jet, sometimes taking the controls himself against federal aviation rules, his running mate, a little-noted congressman named William E. Miller, traveled by turbo-prop, which took longer and gave him more time to play cards. Goldwater said he picked Miller, an upstate New York representative who had been party chairman, because the man drove Johnson nuts. That wasn't the case in 1964, when the LBJ Democrats welcomed the nomination of a candidate so anonymous then and later that he wound up appearing in American Express commercials about the power of the card even in the hands of the obscure.

The Miller campaign became a nonstop card game. The plane would taxi to a stop and he'd tell the aides and reporters in the game to put the cards down while he went to make his speech. When he got back they would pick up the hands and resume the game. One stop was in Phoenix, where he met with Goldwater at the airport, returned to the cards, and said, "Poor guy thinks he's going to win." Late in the campaign, a reporter offered him long odds on a bet for the Republican ticket. "I may be a gambler, but I'm not crazy enough to bet on this election," Miller said.

Typically, Johnson made a public display of his choice of a running mate, calling decoy candidates to the White House, circling the building for ninety minutes in the August heat one day in a walking news conference at which he talked much but said little about his deliberations. His running mate was the obvious choice, Senator Hubert H. Humphrey of Minnesota. Humphrey was a relentless campaigner, loyal to the point of subservience in the campaign and as vice president. He would suffer for it when he ran for president himself in 1968. Goldwater said Humphrey talked in gusts, which he did. His campaign was one long gust, day and night for the LBJ cause.

By late summer, Goldwater was getting negative ratings of 70 percent and worse in the public opinion polls. And the Democrats would soon be piling on with those devastating television attack ads, the mushroom cloud commercials. "Those bomb commercials were the start of dirty political ads on television," Goldwater wrote. "It was the beginning of what I call electronic dirt."

The first was the daisy petal ad, which the Democrats broadcast only once, on September 7, during a commercial break in a Gregory Peck movie on NBC. It showed a little girl picking the petals from a daisy, her childish count yielding to a menacing voice counting backward from ten, to a nuclear explosion. Then Johnson's voice, warning that the election stakes were life or death. No mention of Goldwater. None needed; the target was that clear.

The Johnson campaign did not have to sponsor it again. The television networks rebroadcast it repeatedly as news, the pictures and text were printed in newspapers. Another anti-Goldwater ad showed a little girl licking an ice-cream cone, described as polluted by nuclear fallout. A third simply showed two hands tearing up a Social Security card.

Goldwater had no ammunition with which to strike back. Johnson had seen to it that there would be no television debates, no replay of the Kennedy-Nixon series that had seemed likely to become part of the campaign process after 1960. Johnson's Democrats blocked any possibility of 1964 debates by seeing to it that Congress did not pass legislation to again suspend equal time requirements. Goldwater said he wanted to debate Johnson, but he'd already undercut himself even on that. He had said earlier that he did not think an incumbent president should debate on TV because "I'm fearful that a president in the heat of debate might disclose something that shouldn't be disclosed."

So he played out his quirky campaign against "Lyndon Johnson and his curious crew," a line he started using after what seemed to be a mid-October break for his side. That came when Johnson's closest personal aide was arrested for disorderly conduct in a homosexual encounter in a men's room of the Washington YMCA. Word of it soon circulated to the Goldwater camp, but there were no news accounts for five days after the arrest, until the Republicans accused the White House of trying to suppress it. Walter Jenkins resigned and the episode seemed to fit Goldwater's prior complaints of "moral decay" under Democratic rule. Goldwater said he wouldn't make an issue of Jenkins's personal trouble. He raised it by inference but never directly. I asked him what he meant by "curious crew" and he told me I'd have to figure it out myself.

The Jenkins episode came and went quickly; the day after he quit the White House major world events eclipsed it, taking over the front pages. Nikita S. Khrushchev was ousted as leader of the Soviet Union, Communist China announced it had successfully tested a nuclear bomb, and Great Britain changed governments. Even when he wasn't creating his own misfortunes, Goldwater's luck was bad.

On election eve, Johnson played his campaign finale to Texas-sized throngs in Houston and Austin. Goldwater's last campaign stop was in remote Fredonia, Arizona, the good luck town, he said, where he'd concluded his Senate campaigns. He spoke there at dusk, to a crowd that outnumbered the three hundred people who lived in the desert hamlet. He thanked them for coming, especially the Indians, the Hopi and the Navajo. The last words of his campaign: "If there are any Paiutes out there, I want to thank you, too."

Then he went home to await the inevitable. The Goldwater believers set up an election night headquarters at a resort hotel with a giant blackboard listing the fifty states, to record the unfolding returns. From the time the first ballots were counted, Johnson's 61 percent landslide was evident. Chalk never touched the blackboard. The numbers were too devastating for the Republicans to post.

I was there to write about Goldwater's election night, but we never saw him and could only report that he'd taken a walk in the desert before dinner and wasn't coming out again. It was a short election but a long night for a political reporter surrounded by increas-

ingly angry conservatives who were still capable of ignoring the numbers and shouting that if we hadn't lied about Goldwater, he would
have won. I finally retreated to my room when I heard some
Goldwater fans making plans to throw reporters into the swimming
pool.

By election night in my first full campaign season, I was starting
to gain a reputation as a political reporter, especially inside the AP. I
didn't realize it until the Phoenix bureau sent a reporter to help me at
Goldwater headquarters. I'd been on the road for a week, wearing the
same threadbare, black, double-knit suit, which by then was so
bedraggled and soup-stained that it wasn't worth the price of getting
it dry-cleaned. My helper aimed to please. There wasn't much going
on, but I had to keep the story updated with new leads, based on comments from Goldwater aides, on the mood and scene, on whatever I
could find to report. I'd write them and give them to the local guy to
dictate for me while I looked for more information. I wrote five leads
and each time I did, he'd tell me how great the writing had been, the
adjectives getting more effusive as the night went on. By the last of
them, he'd run out of superlatives for my copy. He looked at me for a
moment and then he said, "That's a nice suit you're wearing." I had
to choke down the laugh; it hadn't been that long since I was the local
bureau guy trying to impress the national reporter.

Goldwater stayed at home and did not emerge to issue his redundant concession until the next day. After a brief break he flew back to
Washington, one last trip on his chartered jet. One last chance to
break the rules, take the controls, and land the 727, which he did. The
plane banged into the runway at Dulles International Airport and
bounced back into the air. Another bang as the tires hit and the plane
jumped again. Then it settled back down on the runway. I spotted
Goldwater in the cockpit and caught him before we left. "That first
landing was exciting but the third one was pretty smooth," I said. He
smiled and growled at the same time.

THREE

The Grim Year: Nixon, Humphrey, and the Chaos of 1968

The night Lyndon Johnson surrendered to the war he could not end or win, Senator Eugene McCarthy was on a college stage in Wisconsin, in his element, cheered by a youthful antiwar crowd as he declared that America must change course, stop the bombs, and negotiate peace with the Communists in Vietnam.

I'd heard his speech often enough to repeat the lines from memory, so I listened with one ear for anything new and found a television set in an office just outside the hall to tune in President Johnson's address on war policy. It was March 31, 1968, the Sunday night before the Tuesday presidential primary election in Wisconsin, where both sides knew Johnson would lose to McCarthy. Hours before, on another campus, the Minnesota senator had boasted that the presidential choice awaiting voters in the fall was down to two men, him or Republican Richard M. Nixon. He had it half right.

In his TV address, Johnson offered a gesture to Hanoi, limiting the bombing to the area of the sadly misnamed demilitarized zone between North and South, and stopping it if the Communist regime would negotiate productively. But he also announced that he would send more U.S. troops to the South and more money to strengthen the government in Saigon. It was not a drastic departure from his policy texts, not until the ending. Then, in one stroke, Johnson abruptly, startlingly changed the course of the 1968 presidential campaign by declaring that he would no longer be a part of it. In a divided nation, he said, the president must not be diverted by political concerns. So, Johnson said, "I shall not seek, and I will not accept, the nomination of my party for another term as your President."

McCarthy was still talking, about to invite questions from the student crowd at Carroll College, in the Milwaukee suburbs. I rushed down the aisle toward the stage, stopped, and waved at him to come over. He saw my gesture and dismissed it. I waited a moment, then climbed the steps to the stage with a cluster of reporters following me, walked over to McCarthy at the microphone, and told him Johnson had just announced he was not running. For an instant, McCarthy froze. Then he flinched, as though the news had hit him physically. He had challenged the power of a president in his own Democratic Party and the president had quit. LBJ had been the target and the target was gone. In a way, it seemed, McCarthy's mission was, too. Among Democrats, it would be McCarthy versus Senator Robert F. Kennedy and, obviously, Vice President Hubert H. Humphrey for the nomination to run against what could only be a Nixon ticket.

The audience was stirring, confused by the strange scene on the stage. McCarthy turned to the microphone and told them that the president had just announced he would not run again. The 1,500 or so burst into a bedlam of cheers. "I think that this is a surprise to me," McCarthy told them when he could be heard again. "Things have gotten rather complicated.

"He's not running," he repeated, as though convincing himself.

Robert Kennedy, who had entered the race only fifteen days before, wondered aloud that night whether Johnson would have quit had he stayed out. The answer, I thought, was a clear yes—the Wisconsin polls showed McCarthy was going to beat the president in the primary, a humiliation LBJ avoided by quitting. Nixon called it the year of the dropouts, first two of his Republican rivals, then Johnson.

After the din ebbed in the college hall, we reporters wanted McCarthy's instant reaction to what Johnson had done. He would not

offer one, would answer no questions as he made his way to his limousine to head back to Milwaukee, until a novice reporter asked
where he was going. "I'm going to the White House," he replied. It
was political hyperbole; McCarthy was boasting that he would win
the election, but the reporter took him literally and filed a bulletin saying that the senator was planning to go to Washington to see Johnson.
He was not, of course, although I had to convince one of my editors
that the rival story wasn't so. He was going back to his hotel to consider what had happened and what he should say about it. He waited
far into the night, long past most deadlines. When his press secretary
told him the reporters were getting impatient, McCarthy told him,
"Go play them some music."

Finally, in an overheated hotel hall, he said the obvious. Things
had changed. "This change in American politics began among the
people." McCarthy also called Johnson's decision a "generous judgment" that cleared the path for national reconciliation.

There was none, then or long after that transforming moment in
a transforming presidential campaign. Johnson was a casualty in 1968
and Humphrey was a political prisoner of war. Kennedy was murdered. McCarthy could not fill the void; the man who began by daring to become the symbol of Democratic resistance to the president
and the war was in the end only a diffident bystander.

The day I got back to Washington after covering the Wisconsin
primary election was the day the Reverend Martin Luther King Jr. was
assassinated, igniting the street riots that raged within two blocks of
the White House. Johnson called in the Army on Friday as the looting
and fires spread from black neighborhoods to the city's business and
government center. I drove back into Washington from the Virginia
suburbs to help handle the story. It was a strange trip. Early that afternoon, the outbound traffic was stacked bumper-to-bumper with people rushing away from town and I was among a handful of drivers
going the other way, into the city. Clouds of black smoke from torched
stores and buildings rose over the skyline, shrouding the Washington
Monument. Army troops and Marines took up positions around the
Capitol and the White House, with sandbagged machine gun

emplacements on the Capitol Plaza. In time, heightened security would make those buildings guarded bastions, but that wasn't routine in 1968. The Capitol was an open building, where nobody even checked your press card and tourists strolled at will. So the incongruity was all the more jarring. A colleague and I drove down Pennsylvania Avenue around dawn. The smoke was almost choking and a glance down the side streets showed the looters dragging goods from the shattered store windows, a capital under siege. That wasn't supposed to be happening amid the marble monuments and grand buildings of Washington, although big city riots had been erupting for more than a year. The King assassination led to violent outbursts of black rage in more than one hundred cities. I'd been covering an upheaval in the American political order. Now order itself was yielding to tumult, with more chaos to come. And there was Nixon, the buttoned-down beneficiary of the disarray. He was for law and order, which translated to stop the rioting, whatever it takes.

From what had seemed to be political bankruptcy, Nixon rebuilt his political fortune amid the Democratic wreckage to win the presidential election, narrowly, by a margin that was shrinking in the final days, in part because LBJ did stop the bombing and announce peace talks.

Amid the turmoil and tear gas that beset the Democratic National Convention in Chicago, the beginning of reforms that would reshape future presidential campaigns drew scant notice. The furies of the Chicago convention would fade; the campaign changes the Democrats began there would not.

The savagery of the assassinations, of King in Memphis, then of Robert Kennedy in Los Angeles, led to Secret Service protection of presidential candidates and that, too, changed the process permanently.

Nixon's unmeasured campaign spending, far more than double that of any candidate before 1968, prompted a finance reform law. That led his money men to an aggressive fund-raising drive early in 1972, before the law could take effect and force them to name their donors, and the excesses of their conduct would become part of the undoing scandal of Watergate. In 1968, I put together a story estimating what Nixon was raising and spending on his campaign. There were no federal campaign finance reports in those days, so I had to compile the numbers from a variety of unofficial sources. I came up with a total of at least $28 million, a level no candidate had approached before Nixon. The *New York Times* published my story and the Nixon people read it before we all got into the motorcade for a day's campaigning. None of them argued with it. But Bill Safire, now a *Times* columnist, who then was a speechwriter and spokesman for Nixon, needled me about the story. "Twenty-eight million, haw," he sneered, suggesting without saying that my accounting was off. It was. The Nixon campaign spent about $43 million, which would be about $219 million in today's dollars.

While maintaining the façade of an old-fashioned personal campaign, Nixon demonstrated that a candidate could run most effectively on television, using the techniques of commercial advertising and the pretense of sham question-and-answer panel programs. "I am not going to barricade myself into a television studio and make this an antiseptic campaign," Nixon told us as he declared his candidacy in New Hampshire that winter, but he did.

The racial unrest that had burst into rioting in American cities long before the King assassination was an unanswered issue in the 1968 campaign. Democrats promised to deal with city blight and minority grievances, but quelling the violence in the name of law and order was the more salable political response. Alabama's George Wallace was a third-party candidate, and when he drawled about law'norder it was his code for repressing black unrest. Nixon was not so brazen, but he saw the opening and styled himself the candidate who would restore law and order. So, while Vietnam dominated the Democratic debate, peace on America's streets was the companion issue.

McCarthy insisted he was more than the antiwar candidate, that he had ideas about dealing with city and racial problems at home as well. He did little to show it. In Wisconsin, where the blue-collar ethnic vote would be crucial in the primary, too direct an appeal to black Democrats carried a risk of backlash. McCarthy said little to or about minorities and their problems. A *New York Times* reporter wrote that McCarthy was avoiding the black precincts of Milwaukee. So on a quiet Saturday, the word went out to reporters that McCarthy would be leaving the hotel in an hour for a walking tour of black neighborhoods. I went with him. A party of twenty or so, the candidate in the lead, walked briskly from downtown under a railroad bridge to begin the march. A dozen black teenagers playing basketball on a playground court saw the white crowd coming. One of them pointed and shouted. All of them ran from what must have looked like threatening invaders. By the time we got to the playground, there wasn't one kid there.

McCarthy walked for nearly two hours in black wards to prove he wasn't shunning them. But even while he was there, he did. He saw few voters and talked with almost none. The black man at his side on the ghetto march was from Washington, a former Capitol barber who had joined his campaign entourage.

As it turned out, the reporter whose story prompted the eight-mile hike had the weekend off and missed it. I got blisters so painful that I had to buy new shoes, which McCarthy thought hilarious. On the far side of the black district, McCarthy hailed a cab and went back to his hotel.

The problems of the cities were central issues for Kennedy and he stirred black voters on his course through the primaries, losing to McCarthy only in Oregon, where there were few minority votes to be had. Kennedy was an antiwar candidate, too, but with a difference: I heard him challenge college crowds about the privileges and student deferments that kept them on campus while poor and minority youths were being drafted and sent to combat.

Still, even Kennedy was not entirely above the backlash. In the California campaign, McCarthy advocated housing programs that would include relocating some people from the inner cities to the suburbs. In their one campaign debate, Kennedy twisted the idea against him, saying McCarthy proposed "to take ten thousand black people and move them into Orange County," the conservative, affluent area south of Los Angeles. McCarthy hadn't said that, but he did not rebut what seemed to me to be a cheap shot. When I asked him why he hadn't countered in the debate, he just shrugged. By then, it seemed to me, his campaign was mostly a shrug, the winter's fire of his challenge to Johnson long past.

The Vietnam issues Johnson had evaded four years before fractured the Democrats, first with McCarthy's challenge, then Kennedy's. In the fall campaign, with Johnson out but not really gone, the LBJ war policy burdened and probably beat Humphrey. And, ironically, it nourished Nixon, the old cold warrior who said there must be no surrender to communism.

Humphrey's ticket suffered the wrath of the war protesters while Nixon, curiously, was spared their disruptions. He wasn't identified with the Johnson war policy. He ventured none of his own and so found political shelter. Humphrey told us he couldn't understand why the protesters were hounding him but not the more hawkish Republican. I thought it was because the antiwar people figured Nixon wouldn't pay any attention to them; indeed, when they did show up in his campaign neighborhood, he used them as a foil for more law and order talk.

Nixon's stance on the war in 1968 was as evasive as Johnson's in 1964. Campaigning in the meeting hall of a red brick factory in Hampton, New Hampshire, Nixon went beyond the calculations of his advisers with a flat declaration that as president he would end the war and win the peace "in the far Pacific," meaning Vietnam. It was a rare fissure in the careful control of his message. Nixon was only making his expected rounds of New Hampshire in a presidential primary campaign he had already won by default; he planned no major policy pronouncements, just the set speech rehearsed on scores of platforms before. But this time he went a fraction beyond, from vague promises of peace with honor to a specific commitment to end the conflict. Now there was a story to report, a measurable promise to be kept, from the candidate who usually avoided commitments to which he might one day be held.

So was created Nixon's "secret plan to end the war" in Vietnam, a phrase he never uttered, a promise he didn't intend to make in any but the most general terms. He had no secret plan, no plan at all, but he was in a box. He couldn't deny that he had one without admitting that he didn't know what he would do as president. It became a celebrated issue, a question Nixon would talk around.

Those of us reporting on Nixon's campaign that day near the New Hampshire seacoast hurried to the stage when he finished his talk to ask the obvious question: How did he intend to win the war and win peace as he had just promised? Nixon would not say. Wily even when a bit off stride, he made his silence seem a virtue. Nixon told us that it would not be proper or patriotic for a man running for president to prescribe policy. There could be only one president at a time and no candidate should undercut him by saying exactly what a new administration would do about the war, he said. I could only marvel at his craft in deflecting a problem he had just created. We pressed for an answer as Nixon left the stage; we followed him out of the hall into the thin winter sun, still trying. He would not say.

Before the election that fall, Nixon's supposed qualms about undercutting President Johnson vanished when a glimmer of progress toward peace threatened his election prospects against Humphrey. But in the interim, it was a way around the issue that tormented the Democrats. An alibi for avoiding the major issue of the time, I thought.

I remember, ruefully, dictating my story to the Associated Press that day in Hampton, New Hampshire, shivering in an outdoor telephone booth. I quoted Nixon's promise to end the war and win the peace, and reported that he refused to say how he would do it. It is a rueful recollection because a rival reporter eclipsed my lead with one that announced: "Richard M. Nixon said today he has a secret plan to end the war in Vietnam." He didn't, but no matter; it was the invented phrase that stuck. When I wrote about that years later, a television producer called me to say he wished he had known the real story before his boss on a Vietnam documentary sent him on a long and costly expedition through TV archives looking for film or tape of Nixon saying that he had a secret plan.

In 1964, Johnson had run as the peace candidate, denouncing Republican talk of bombing the North—action he ordered within a month of his 1965 inauguration—and of risking the use of U.S. combat troops—forces he sent to Vietnam before the year was half gone. By 1968, it was Johnson's war.

I had watched that happen as a Senate reporter during the Great Society years of the mid-1960s, when Johnson was riding the political crest with lopsided Democratic command of Congress, pushing through his array of domestic programs, waging war on poverty, winning momentous civil rights legislation. I covered the shaping, drafting, passage, and signing of the Voting Rights Act of 1965, from the marches and street-blocking sitdowns outside the White House to the day Johnson made it law. "President Johnson signed his monumental Negro voting rights bill today, treading the century-old path of Abraham Lincoln and declaring the new law is a triumph for freedom as great as any won on the battlefield," I wrote. He signed the act in the ornate President's Room, just off the Senate floor, using the desk on which Lincoln signed an order freeing slaves impressed into Civil War service by the Confederacy. In such signings, presidents use multiple pens, etching a fragment of a signature with each, then handing them out as souvenirs. Johnson had fifty in a rack, and ran out. "We need several more, boys," he told his aides. But pens weren't enough for an LBJ-sized ego. I learned later that the White House had ordered replicas of the antique Lincoln desk so that Johnson could give them to congressional and civil rights leaders. It was a tip I could not prove but did not doubt; my sources were solid. When I called the White House, a spokesman denied it. One of my sources told me later that they already had eight or ten of the replicas but weren't going to give them out because public reaction would have been adverse, and the president had forgotten about his idea anyhow. So the desks, I was told, were locked away in a warehouse at an Army depot in Alexandria, Virginia.

I traveled with Johnson to Independence, Missouri, where he went to sign the Medicare bill at the Truman Library, with the former president who had first proposed it. I learned that day why there is a war between editors and reporters. I wrote this lead: "President Johnson journeyed 1,000 miles today to sign the bill beginning government medical care for the aged and share 'this moment of triumph' with Harry S. Truman." A literalist on the AP desk in New York checked the atlas for the distance between Washington and Independence and changed it to say 996 miles. My poetic license obviously had been revoked.

But even during Johnson's days of dominance, dissent against the escalating war in Vietnam was building. I covered Senator J. William Fulbright's hearings on war policy and saw the policy split opening, enraging Johnson, who privately threatened to punish dissenting senators by blocking projects and spending they wanted in their home states.

The Senate was the ideal assignment for a political reporter between elections. It was the arena—the cave of the winds, we called it—in which political issues were debated and sometimes even settled. And at least a quorum of the Senate's members thought they should become president someday. I'd proven myself in the 1964 campaign. When the 1968 campaign buildup began, I was on the story for the AP.

Nixon, the master political plotter, was well cast for center stage in the 1968 campaign. With guile and incredible luck, he had come back from the hairline defeat of 1960 and the abject embarrassment of defeat for governor of California in 1962 to flirt, briefly, with what would have been a futile candidacy for president in 1964. But Nixon stepped back into party line to become a working loyalist for the doomed Republican ticket, while avoiding blame for the election disaster. Within weeks he was planning his way back. When I interviewed him in his New York law office, he talked about how it could be done almost as though he were foretelling another man's campaign instead of his own. Nixon said a candidate getting ready to run in 1968 would first assemble a small team and go on the road for Republicans, knowing that the party would inevitably come back in 1966. Nixon said he could rebuild his own standing with a leading role, campaigning for Republican House and Senate candidates in the off-year elections. I wrote about it in January 1965, reporting that Nixon was already planning a way back, setting the foundation for a 1968 presidential campaign. That story had scant impact, which reveals something about the workings of political journalism. Even with my 1964 credits, I was still a relative newcomer, and my byline did not yet sell a story. So my report that Nixon was setting up a 1968 campaign for president went virtually unnoted, published in a handful of newspapers and forgotten. Later in my career, that kind of story under my byline commanded attention and set other political writers to matching it for their own publications. Not then, though.

While Nixon was wily about strategy and policy, he sometimes lapsed into candor when talking politics. It was his profession and his hobby. He once described to reporters the way he could modulate his message without markedly changing his words, so as to appeal to moderate Republicans in the North and then to the conservatives in the South. He couldn't resist boasting to us how cleverly he operated, even when it added to the "Tricky Dick" image.

Nixon put it all into practice in the off-year campaign, setting up an organization called Congress '66. He traveled thirty thousand miles to eighty-two congressional districts, accompanied on much of the journey by a recruit named Patrick J. Buchanan, a St. Louis editorial writer before he joined Nixon, as blunt and harshly conservative then as when he became a presidential candidate himself a generation later. The party's comeback succeeded and so did Nixon's, although he couldn't have done it by himself. He got unintended help from President Johnson.

Nixon attacked Johnson on Vietnam three weeks before the 1966 elections, accusing him of offering peace terms that would amount to communist victory. The president blew up. "I do not want to get into a debate on a foreign policy meeting . . . with a chronic campaigner like Mr. Nixon," the president said. Johnson said Nixon found fault with his country at campaign time every election year. Suddenly Nixon the loser was Nixon the leader of the opposition.

Nixon feigned dismay at what he called a shocking display of presidential temper and said he was surprised. Surprised perhaps, but certainly delighted that the Democratic president had taken his bait and made him the Republicans' chief national campaigner. The party made Nixon its TV spokesman. He was news again. He campaigned through election eve, then watched the Republican revival, gains of forty-seven House seats, three senators, eight governors. After two election defeats, nationally in 1960 and in California in 1962, Nixon was identified with Republican victory. He was not yet "the one," as his 1968 campaign motto would have it, but he was on his way.

His first move was to wait. Nixon announced a personal moratorium on politics. That kept him out of the line of precampaign fire while the 1967 leader in the Republican opinion polls, Michigan Governor George W. Romney, began running—and stumbling.

At the same time, liberal Democratic insurgents were organizing rebellion against Johnson over Vietnam. They wanted Kennedy to challenge him but the answer was no, he didn't think Johnson could be stopped. While McCarthy realistically rated Kennedy the strongest prospective challenger, he was listening. If Kennedy wouldn't run, McCarthy would. Those of us who had covered him as a senator listened as he announced what we thought would be the longest of long shots late in 1967, saying he hoped that his challenge would be a vehicle to ease the "sense of political helplessness" afflicting Americans, especially young Americans.

Declaring his improbable presidential candidacy, McCarthy said he'd waited a decent period to see whether others would run and that if Kennedy had, he wouldn't have needed to do anything. McCarthy was the poet politician, quick with a quip but also given to musing, even as he began the great campaign of his life. Would he yield should Kennedy become a candidate later? It might not be voluntary, he replied. At the time, it seemed quixotic, a futile gesture against a dominating president. I told him so over coffee in the Senate restaurant one day, and he said he'd prove otherwise. He did.

While he came to disdain many of the political reporters who covered his presidential campaign, once likening us to blackbirds who all flew together and lit on the same wire, as a senator McCarthy sought and enjoyed the company of Capitol Hill reporters. He'd stop by the press table of the Senate dining room most mornings to have a cup of coffee, to chat and comment, often acidly, on the people and proceedings of the place, and on politics in general. That included

Kennedys, even before Robert became his rival. Too privileged, he suggested. He didn't spare JFK because, he said, "You had to worry when a guy cut the crust off his Wonder Bread." Sardonic poetic license, and envy as well. McCarthy was a devout Roman Catholic who could only watch as Kennedy became the first of their faith elected president. He grumbled that he was more Catholic and more qualified than Kennedy.

Campaigning in New Hampshire in 1968, McCarthy stopped at a Concord arena, put on skates, and played in a pickup hockey game. The Kennedys play touch football, he said, suggesting that was sissy stuff.

When he became a candidate, McCarthy was written down if not off by those who thought, as Kennedy had, that Johnson could not be denied the Democratic nomination. But McCarthy said from the start that he believed somebody other than the president, not necessarily he, would be the Democratic nominee.

Johnson's allies in New Hampshire told us McCarthy would be lucky to get 10 percent of the vote in the opening presidential primary, an estimate they would regret. It served to magnify McCarthy's showing when he more than quadrupled their forecast.

Slowly at first, then with a force of volunteer campaigners that swelled into an army of thousands, the antiwar movement was changing the political arithmetic. McCarthy was not a galvanizing campaigner; there was nothing memorable about his speeches or the way he delivered them. The issue mobilized the movement. It was a different kind of politics. McCarthy was the candidate and symbolic leader of the insurrection but, especially in those first weeks, he sometimes seemed like a passenger, not a pilot. He'd take a break when he wanted, write a poem about a hardened wood baseball bat—in his prime he'd been good enough at the game to impress some professional scouts. McCarthy the poet said baseball was the best game because it responded to no clock, only to the final out of an inning that could last forever. When the conversation was compelling, often with his friend, the poet Robert Lowell, McCarthy would linger and let the campaign crowds wait.

The fervor was in the college recruits who rallied to the antiwar candidate. McCarthy himself roamed the state like a political tourist. To me, he seemed to be an onlooker on the route of the parade he was supposed to be leading. When he went AWOL one campaign day, reporters spotted him in his hotel dining room having a long dinner with Lowell, unwilling to be interrupted. He was not a man to immerse himself in crowds.

When McCarthy pointlessly ran for president again in 1976, he talked about political lives as though he had not led one. "You know what a Benedictine monk once said about a man who was a very good football coach?" McCarthy asked. " 'He's just smart enough to understand the game and not smart enough to lose interest in it.' That sort of applies to most politicians."

In 1968, the McCarthy insurgents played the campaign game in a different way. The movement did not begin with a candidate; it embraced McCarthy because he was the only one available. He could denounce the Vietnam War as a moral outrage without raising his voice. He said sardonically that he would know how to deal with the Pentagon as president: either go there personally or try to get diplomatic representation. Once a professor, McCarthy now campaigned on campuses and sounded like one. He lectured. His was no strident summons to rally against the war. None was needed. Youthful McCarthy volunteers trimmed their long hair, tidied up their dress and their manners, and came to New Hampshire "clean for Gene" to work door-to-door, campaign on wintry street corners, stuff envelopes, and try to stop a war.

Johnson was not on the New Hampshire primary ballot. A cadre of party leaders worked and spoke for him, seeking write-in votes with tactics that offended some New Hampshire Democrats. They sent out numbered pledge cards to be signed by voters promising to write in Johnson's name, with a notation saying that a copy would go to the White House. It suggested that LBJ was watching every voter, and McCarthy said it was an intrusion on the secret ballot.

We watched McCarthy's newcomers operate with more discipline than Johnson's Democratic establishment. McCarthy's popular vote in the New Hampshire primary beat the odds but not the president, threatening but trailing the Johnson write-in. But McCarthy won almost all the nominating delegates, elected separately, because his camp ran one candidate for each delegate slot. The Johnson side couldn't control entries in his name. There were too many ambitious and jealous Democrats who insisted on trying to get themselves elected to go to the national convention. So there were nearly twice as many would-be Johnson delegates as there were openings. That divided the Johnson vote and gave McCarthy the delegation.

McCarthy came within seven percentage points of Johnson in the popular vote. For an insurgent against an incumbent president, that amounted to winning, and McCarthy said it convinced him that he could get the nomination. He told his young volunteers that if they could go to the national convention in Chicago with such strength there would be "no violence and no demonstrations," but celebration. Offstage, he crowed a told-you-so at those of us who had considered his challenge hopeless when he began it.

More telling words of change were spoken by Robert Kennedy the next day. Kennedy said he was reconsidering the possibility of running. He'd stayed out rather than risk dividing the party in what would be seen as a personal grudge match with Johnson but now, he said, the split was clear and a campaign could be about issues he had raised long before: the war and the crisis in the cities. Reconsidering meant running, of that there was no question, so Kennedy's move to candidacy instantly eclipsed McCarthy's New Hampshire showing. McCarthy never forgot what he considered Kennedy's political bad manners. He thought his people were entitled to at least a day to revel in what they'd accomplished.

McCarthy responded to Kennedy's emergence by saying that a lot of political figures were afraid to take the field against Johnson until he risked it and challenged the power of the White House. "They were willing to stay up on the mountains and light signal fires and dance to the light of the moon," he said. "But none of them came down." A reporter asked McCarthy where he'd found that image. "*The Book of Druids,*" the senator replied. Not certain he'd heard correctly, the reporter asked again. What book? "Book Five," McCarthy said smugly.

While new wave Democrats were trying to overthrow their party establishment, the Republican campaign began turning in the opposite direction, to the old guard, Nixon.

Michigan's Romney started as the front-runner, elected by increasing margins to three terms as governor of a major industrial state. He was a moderate untainted by the rightward lurch of 1964, a man with a résumé of success. He was an automobile executive who put American-made compact cars on the market and saved American Motors Company. He had the support of Nelson Rockefeller, who said that he did not want to be president. Incredulous, we asked him whether he really meant that he did not want the office he had sought so long. Yes, he said. The disinterest turned out to be temporary.

Romney comfortably led in early public opinion polls, which reported him leading President Johnson. But that was in 1967, before he had been tried as a national campaigner. He was no good at it, misspeaking, fumbling questions, his square jaw jutting angrily when reporters pressed for answers about his policies, especially toward Vietnam. Romney had supported the administration on Vietnam but by 1967 he was doubtful and saying so, seeking another way, although he hadn't figured out a policy proposal.

He'd gone to Vietnam two years earlier with a delegation of governors, he said on a Detroit TV talk show in September 1967, and had heard the administration line from the military and the diplomats, all claiming they were on a course to victory. "I just had the greatest brainwashing that anybody can get when you go over to Vietnam," Romney said.

It was the word that symbolized his political fall. Brainwashed. When he died nearly thirty years later, obituaries still tagged him with it, subordinating a lifetime of successes. I thought Romney's description of the way the Johnson White House was trying to sell its Vietnam policy was accurate. Trying to explain, Romney said he'd been talking about "LBJ-style brainwashing." Anyone who had seen Johnson in operation knew what he meant. The heavy-handed LBJ style of persuasion was called "the Johnson treatment." But "brain-washing" became shorthand for the growing impression that Romney was a fuzzy, foundering candidate. McCarthy put in that he didn't think brainwashing was needed in Romney's case when "a light rinse would have done it."

A more adroit campaigner might have talked his way around the brainwashing flap, but political footwork was not Romney's talent; it was his problem. "I'm glad I used that word that went around the world," Romney said after his campaign foundered and he quit the race. "Nobody will forget it. This country has been brainwashed on Vietnam."

By the end of 1967, Romney had gone from leader to obvious loser. Trailing Nixon by widening margins in New Hampshire opinion polls, he campaigned doggedly through the state for two months while everything went wrong. His campaign billboards proclaimed: "Romney's Right—We must stop moral decay." It sounded as though he wanted to take the voters to the dentist.

On his first campaign day there, before dawn on a below-zero morning, he stood hatless at a Nashua plant gate, stopping workers to shake hands and ask for a vote. Reporters took turns watching him, sharing their notes so that most could go inside and get warm. Jack Germond, the rotund sage of our political writing fraternity, remarked that Romney must have plastic ears. He stood at the gate for well over an hour, oblivious to the fact that the workers were more interested in getting inside, where it was warm, than in stopping to see a candidate. Afteward, Romney was asked how he'd stood the cold and he said he was wearing long jeans. He meant long johns, of course, and that made the *New York Times,* cited as another example of his tendency to misspeak. While I thought that was overreaching for a jab, Romney did have a pattern of saying things he didn't mean. His spokesmen would catch us after he'd fumbled a line and try to fix it. Germond, who became a *Baltimore Sun* columnist and the sardonic realist of television talk shows, said he needed a special key on his typewriter that would put in the phrase "Romney later explained."

The dogged Romney style was displayed when he stopped at a bowling alley in Franklin and tried his hand at candlepins, in which the bowler gets three balls a turn. Romney wasn't good at that, either. He knocked down three pins with his three rolls, but he wouldn't stop. After eight tries one pin was standing. The square jaw jutted and he kept going until he got that last pin—on his thirty-fourth attempt. Then he was satisfied, and the fact that everybody in the place was laughing at his performance didn't bother him.

Romney had been campaigning and sinking for a month when Nixon came to New Hampshire, declaring his candidacy in letters to 150,000 homes in the state and at a press conference on February 2. "Gentlemen, this is not my last news conference," he began, in what passed for humor from the man who had said in 1962 that reporters wouldn't have him to kick around anymore. He still had to deal with the loser image, but he said that other candidates had come from defeat and that he was better qualified than before to deal with the problems of the presidency.

To take questions did not mean he had to answer them. Communist forces had just launched the Tet offensive in Vietnam, but Nixon would not comment on those attacks or discuss what he would do about the war. He said he would be "spelling out ways and means" as he campaigned, but never did.

Every move was planned. The Nixon operation was an ordered contrast to the unscripted, wandering Romney campaign. The night he began in New Hampshire, Nixon threw a cocktail party for reporters, telling us that he would be accessible and open about what he was doing as a candidate. The next morning he went unannounced to Hillsboro for the television taping of a session with selected townspeople, eluding the same reporters. Pat Buchanan, the tough guy even then, said no apologies were due because had reporters been allowed, the invited participants would have been inhibited. Never mind what Nixon had promised only the night before. It was the prototype for the closed and controlled TV shows that were central in Nixon's national campaign.

The new Nixon was not so remote as the old, but his campaign exposure was rationed, not to be overdone. The fifty-state candidate was no more; Nixon's 1968 plan was to concentrate on seven big ones that, together with the electoral votes of safely Republican states, would add up to the presidency. Nor would he weary himself with a marathon schedule of appearances when one or two a day would do. Covering him that fall was a rest cure, especially for survivors of the dawn-to-midnight Humphrey campaign. When the two campaigns crossed paths, the Humphrey reporters might make it to the hotel bar for last call. Those of us traveling with Nixon would have enjoyed a leisurely dinner by that hour.

Nixon's was a marketing campaign with the candidate as the product to be sold, not oversold. It was tested in New Hampshire and it worked, his lead widening to a landslide. He could run safely and slowly, letting the crowds come to him, drawn by his celebrity and the advance work of his organization.

While Romney ran a living room campaign, negotiating icy side streets and pathways to speak to twelve or twenty people at a time, Nixon drew 1,500 for his opening speech at a rambling wooden hotel just off the interstate in Concord. It became the set speech; he'd later say he had delivered it well over 115 times. I heard it so often I thought that was an undercount.

"The real crisis of America today is a crisis of the spirit," Nixon would say, blaming Democratic leadership. He said the voters had reason to change leaders when America was tied down in a war with no end in sight, when crime and lawlessness were rampant at home.

The law and order issue became a Nixon staple, especially with Wallace threatening his southern flank. "I believe that some of our courts, including the Supreme Court, have gone too far in weakening the peace forces as against the criminal forces in this country," Nixon would say. I interviewed him in his limousine one day near Indianapolis in a motorcade led by a phalanx of motorcycle police. I told him the criminal forces must be having a field day because all the peace forces seemed to be out guarding his motorcade. He didn't see the humor.

Romney, hopelessly behind, quit the campaign twelve days before the New Hampshire primary. Nixon swept it, with Rockefeller write-in votes outnumbering Romney's share. Even against the inevitable landslide, quitting had not come easily to Romney, ineffectual in the campaign but a man of grit and determination. He died at the age of eighty-eight while working out on his treadmill.

When Kennedy barged into the Democratic campaign after the New Hampshire primary, McCarthy loyalists called the move opportunistic, ruthless politics. Kennedy was called ruthless so often that he sometimes joked he was trying to be ruthful.

He said he would not direct his campaign against McCarthy and believed they could work in harmony for change, which sounded nice but was impossible in a two-candidate campaign. After he'd won two primaries, Kennedy suggested again that they could work together. McCarthy said no, there would be no deals. There could be none unless one or the other effectively conceded the nomination. Whatever partnership Kennedy envisioned, he certainly did not mean to be the junior partner.

To me, his campaign is a blur of crowds, motorcades, so many hands grasping for his that Kennedy's were sore and sometimes bloodied. He stirred audiences as the understated McCarthy did not. On campuses, they cheered even his criticism of their student deferments. Kennedy favored a lottery draft with no exemptions. He wanted action on civil rights, the use of government funds to draw investment and jobs to needy neighborhoods to fight crime there.

His parting line in every speech was a liberal rendering of George Bernard Shaw: "Some men see things as they are and say, 'Why?' I dream things that never were and say, 'Why not?'" For reporters, that was the signal to get moving or miss the press bus. He skipped it at one whistle-stop and left a handful of newsmen behind. When they caught up, he promised gravely not to omit the ending again.

In high winds one day, his twin-engine chartered airplane aborted a takeoff, made it on a second try, and flew into gusts that made for a jolting flight. I remember that even John Glenn, the astronaut who became a senator and was campaigning for Kennedy, looked queasy.

The flight was still bumpy when Kennedy ignored the Fasten Seat Belt sign and strolled back to the press section to needle white-knuckled reporters that if the plane didn't make it, he would be the lead story, and we would all be in the fine print.

Kennedy won two midwestern primaries but faltered in Oregon, where he lost to McCarthy, the first family defeat in twenty-seven elections. He came back in California and won, before everything changed in a murderous instant. Kennedy had just celebrated his California primary victory in Los Angeles when the assassin shot, eight times, mortally wounding him and injuring five other people. He was kept alive for more than twenty-five hours, dying at 1:44 A.M. on June 6.

The night he was shot in a kitchen corridor at the Ambassador Hotel, my assignment was to write the story of the election he was winning, reporting the returns. So I was downtown at a special election bureau, writing a lead that covered Kennedy's victory rally. The only missing pieces were McCarthy's concession and the latest returns, and the night's work would be done. When Kennedy was shot, McCarthy was with his aides, trying to decide how effusive to be in congratulating the victor. Not very, the thinking went, before it became irrelevant. Suddenly, just after midnight, the concession and the numbers were pointless. Kennedy had won by about four percentage points over McCarthy. But the winner had been shot.

My first impression of the shooting was of a television report with no form to it, an announcer crying out that something had happened to Kennedy. There was a TV picture of chaos. The crowd with Kennedy turned into a crush of bodies as reporters and photographers jammed in from the adjacent press room. The phone rang in our election bureau. It was Bob Thomas, AP's Hollywood reporter, on political duty for a night. Kennedy has been shot, he said. The editor wanted attribution, a source. He had one on the phone. "I saw it," Thomas said, and dictated the story while the TV commentator learned and reported what the chaotic images meant.

What they meant was that Kennedy was dying without a political heir to take command of the Democrats bent on overthrowing the party establishment and striving to end the war. McCarthy's strength was as messenger and symbol. But he seemed distracted, almost aimless, after the assassination, a political actor who couldn't figure out his role. After Humphrey was nominated, McCarthy opted out of the campaign. He took a vacation abroad and signed up to write about the World Series for *Life* magazine. When he did get around to endorsing the Democratic ticket, it was with a backhand slap at Humphrey. McCarthy said he supported Humphrey's running mate, Senator Edmund S. Muskie, for vice president. Finally he said he would vote for Humphrey, but by then nobody much cared.

My memories of the Kennedy assassination are from the distance of a rewrite man, assigned to write the accounts of a team of reporters into one comprehensive roundup story. The night he died I had gone back to my room at the Ambassador to try to sleep for a few hours after a day and most of a night at the typewriter. The phone summoned me back shortly after midnight. I'd had two hours of restless sleep. There would be a briefing at the hospital in about an hour. We knew what that meant. I found a taxi and was headed down the long driveway of the hotel toward Wilshire Boulevard when I saw an AP colleague who had covered Kennedy's campaign wandering dazedly on the broad hotel lawn. I told the cabbie to stop, went over and took the reporter's arm, and led him to the taxi. Suddenly he was alert, a reporter again. The enervating emotion of what was happening had overcome his instinct as a newsman. A man we both knew and liked had been shot, murdered. Kennedy had not been pronounced dead but we knew he soon would be. I dropped my colleague near the hospital, where he covered the announcement of Kennedy's death. I went on to the bureau to write the lead: "Robert F. Kennedy died of gunshot wounds early today, prey like his president brother to the savagery of an assassin."

The assassination of President Kennedy in 1963 stiffened the Secret Service line around presidents; Johnson's bodyguards did not like his crowd-roaming ways in 1964. But for candidates, unless and until they got to office, campaign security was up to the campaign organizations.

After King was assassinated on April 4, Johnson asked Congress to approve Secret Service protection for candidates as well as for presidents, but no action was taken. When Robert Kennedy was killed, Johnson ordered the protection himself and Congress approved funds for it the next day. So ended the era of wide-open campaigns, in which the motorcade could take an unexpected turn and even get lost on the way to the next stop. Protective details were deployed around all the candidates, even the lonely, perennial Harold Stassen.

Inevitably, there were points of friction between the political people and the security people. Nixon wrote that when he was campaigning as president in 1972 and the Secret Service tried to speed his motorcade past a crowd of demonstrators, "I told them to slow down." He wanted to defiantly wave his V for victory signal at the protesters.

The political mission is to get the candidate as close to as many voters as possible. Security comes between them, and the balance has to be negotiated. The art form is to be protective and unobtrusive at the same time. Even when that balance worked, Secret Service protection caused subtle but real changes in the ways of campaigning. The motorcades that sometimes had wandered off course now would be planned and often traveled in advance by security details. Schedules would not always be kept, but at least they would mean something. Crowd control was part of the security package coordinated with local police.

In my Hyannisport days, off-duty Secret Service agents socialized with the reporters covering JFK after the workday was done, over dinner or a drink. I was in the lounge one night with an agent named Clint Hill and I ordered a cocktail of whiskey and ginger ale. Bad choice, he told me. It's the mix that gives you headaches. Drink Jack Daniel's Black Label straight, over ice, and you'll never have another hangover. So I tried it that night and it's been my drink of choice for more than forty years since. But Hill was wrong about hangovers—too many Jack Daniel's will give you one as surely as any other drink. Hill was in Dallas when Kennedy was shot. He was the agent who climbed up the back of the moving convertible to guard Jacqueline

Kennedy moments after the fatal bullets hit the president. After the assassination, the line between agents and reporters hardened; no more socializing after the workday. The Secret Service men weren't unfriendly, unless one of us got in the way. They did their job and we did ours.

No security could have capped or controlled the war protests that burst upon the Democrats at their 1968 Chicago convention. There was rioting when the Republicans convened, too, but at a distance, across Biscayne Bay from the sanctuary of Miami Beach. Three people were killed in riots in the black ghetto of Miami. In the antiwar protests and police attacks on demonstrators in Chicago, the tumult was at the doorstep of the Democrats and the image of violence sent a picture of a political party in trauma. Protesters and youthful campaign volunteers were bloodied in what would be assessed as a police riot. Tear gas fumes drifted up to the suites of the candidates in the Conrad Hilton Hotel. Protesters triggered stink bombs. I was staying at the hotel in a closet-sized room and often was teary from the gas, nauseous from the smell.

"We knew this was going to happen," Humphrey said, blaming the trouble on plotting troublemakers. "It was all programmed." But neither the Democrats nor the city had programmed a way to deal with the mass demonstrations without violence.

The 1968 Democratic convention was one of reform as well as turmoil. It changed the rules and began what would become the remodeling of future campaigns for candidates of both parties. The Democrats voted to overhaul their delegate selection system before the next campaign, to make it more representative of the party in each state. That would mean more blacks, more women, and fewer organization-installed delegates. It would also mean a proliferation of presidential primaries that would affect Republican candidates as well because state primary election laws apply to both parties, not just one. The primary elections, not party establishments, would dominate the choice of future nominees. John Kennedy had used the primaries to show his vote-pulling ability in order to persuade party bosses to back him. After the 1968 reforms took effect, candidates could, and did, win nominations outright by capturing a majority of the delegates in the primaries, with binding commitments. Humphrey was nominated in 1968 without entering a primary. The reforms would make that next to impossible in future campaigns.

But the protests and violence of the moment, not reforms for the future, were the image of the Chicago convention. The convention hall was the International Amphitheatre, next door to the Chicago stockyards. With black slums on one side and the downtown avenues where demonstrators thronged on the other, the city and the Democrats put the hall under unprecedented security. A chain-link fence topped with barbed wire surrounded the convention site. We waited in long lines to get through one of the few gates that hadn't been locked. One delegate was grabbed and briefly handcuffed when he used an ID card instead of his official credential to get through the automatic entrance gate. Getting there from downtown was a challenge even before the demonstrations made it impossible because Chicago cabdrivers were on strike. We had AP vans to go back and forth, but the only way to be sure of getting there in time to cover the sessions was to go in the morning and spend the day and night in the cavelike basement space that served as our workroom. Under normal circumstances we would have worked in town at the hotel except during the convention sessions, but that wasn't an option in Chicago because there was a telephone strike, too.

Republicans dispatched a team of observers to Chicago to watch and comment on the Democratic convention. It is standard for the opposition to set up an outpost at the other party's convention, calling it a truth squad although that seldom is the product. Donald Rumsfeld, then an Illinois congressman, and John Love, the governor of Colorado, led the Republican team in Chicago. They took a suite on the seventeenth floor at the Conrad Hilton. But there wasn't much for an opposition "truth squad" to say or do. The protests and internal Democratic strife needed no rebuttal from them. They invited me to the suite for a drink one night, and we stood by an open window listening as thousands of protesters in Grant Park chanted, "Dump the Hump," and then switched to "Fuck you, LBJ." All the Republicans had to do was watch. One of them asked me what I thought the GOP observers should do and I suggested they might as well have another drink.

At week's end, Rumsfeld and Love did issue one Republican slap, saying that Humphrey and his ticket were inextricably tied to Johnson and his war policy. That was true, although Humphrey inched away from the administration line later in the campaign. Nixon was simply evading the issue. Since the "secret plan" episode in New Hampshire, he had claimed it was his duty not to say what he would do about the war as president. Talk about future policy, he said, and "the enemy will wait for the next man" in the White House. Or, as it would turn out, the ally would wait, since South Vietnam balked at peace negotiations just before the election—and Democrats had evidence that a woman in the Nixon camp had told Saigon a new Republican administration would demand settlement terms more to their liking.

While "Stop the war" was the chant of the peace demonstrators, not even the antiwar candidates proposed to quit the conflict outright. McCarthy said he wanted "some kind of settlement" but did not advocate unilateral U.S. withdrawal. The signal issue was halting the bombing of North Vietnam. At the Chicago convention, the war policy contest was over the party platform, with a "peace plank" that advocated an end to the bombing, mutual withdrawal of both U.S. and North Vietnamese forces from the South, and negotiations between Saigon and Hanoi on a coalition government. Humphrey tried to get Johnson's agreement to those terms, but the president rejected them, saying that for the party to adopt them would undercut his policy. His version, written into the platform, was for a bombing halt when it would not endanger U.S. troops. That would be contingent on a response from Hanoi. In other words, the war would go on as he had ordered it waged, with settlement talks in Paris but no concessions to North Vietnam on the bargaining table there. The Republicans already had adopted a platform advocating "progressive de-Americanization of the war," which suggested gradual withdrawal, the course Nixon would take as president and bequeath to Gerald R. Ford, in office when the last Americans fled Saigon on 1975.

The Democrats' split on war policy was part of the legacy that saddled Humphrey from the day he began campaigning to succeed Johnson, seeking the nomination the old-style way—the last time any candidate would be able to do it. He came to the race too late for the major presidential primaries, and looked to the political chieftains of the Democratic establishment for the votes he needed to be nominated. He got them, as the heir of an increasingly unpopular administration.

"Here we are the way politics ought to be in America, the politics of happiness, the politics of purpose and the politics of joy," he said when he declared his candidacy. Incongruous words after the political fall of the president and the King assassination, even more jarring when Humphrey stuck to his slogan that summer, with Kennedy dead and Chicago torn by convention violence while the Democrats met behind barricades and barbed wire. The night he was nominated I wrote: "Hubert H. Humphrey, apostle of the politics of joy, won the Democratic presidential nomination tonight under armed guard."

Humphrey was neither naïve nor immune to the jagged political edges around him. But there was an innocent optimism about the man despite it all. He ran, and talked, at top speed. "The policies of tomorrow need not be limited by the policies of yesterday," Humphrey said in accepting the nomination, but his options were limited by those very policies. Johnson would yield him no running room, and Humphrey would not openly dispute his president. Three liberal Democratic governors told us of going to Humphrey after the convention and urging him to resign the vice presidency so that he could run as his own man and improve his prospects of overtaking Nixon. Humphrey said no, he would not quit his job, would not put the aging Speaker of the House, seventy-six-year-old John W. McCormack, next in the line of succession to the presidency.

The LBJ reins were tight. When Humphrey said he thought the United States would be able to withdraw some troops from Vietnam late in 1968 or early in 1969, Johnson countered that "no man can predict when that day will come." In his memoir, Humphrey wondered "why Johnson shot me down" on a prediction he said had originally come from the White House. "Ruined my credibility," Humphrey wrote. "Made me look like a damn fool. It hurt."

It all hurt. Hecklers disrupted his rallies. When Humphrey campaigned in Boston with Senator Edward M. Kennedy, demonstrators shouted down both the nominee and their own senator. Muskie, the vice presidential nominee who became the star of the Democratic ticket, handled hecklers by letting them speak their piece, sometimes turning over the microphone with their commitment that they would yield it back and let him speak. It worked for him. Nothing seemed to be working for Humphrey.

The protesters hassled him and left Nixon alone, which confounded Humphrey, who mused that they didn't seem to understand that the chance of peace would be far better with him than in a Republican administration. There were some demonstrators as Nixon campaigned, but not so many that Republican retainers couldn't crowd or push them out. The antiwar activists concentrated on Democrats, figuring there was at least a chance of changing minds there.

The protests quieted in midcampaign when Humphrey declared a degree of independence on war policy. He edged away from Johnson by saying that as president he would stop bombing North Vietnam "as an acceptable risk for peace," but that he would reserve the right to resume it if Hanoi pressed the war south anyhow. He also advocated "de-Americanization" of the ground war, as did the Republican platform. Humphrey told Johnson what he would say before delivering his speech in Salt Lake City on September 30, but this time, he did not ask for an okay. Johnson resented it, although what Humphrey said was only a minor turn from administration policy.

Nixon was campaigning in Detroit that night, and it was the first time I saw cracks in the haughty confidence of his team. They were leading the public opinion polls comfortably and wanted to campaign placidly for five more weeks while time ran out on Humphrey. Suddenly, it seemed the vice president might be breaking free on Vietnam. The next day, Nixon was ready with a written retort: Humphrey was giving away the best card American negotiators had to play in Paris by offering a concession Hanoi might get only after the election. Nixon said Humphrey should clarify his remarks "and say that he is not undercutting the U.S. position."

But Humphrey had not only taken his stand, he had underlined it by taking the vice presidential seal off his campaign lecterns. The message, he said, was that he was not running as Johnson's vice president but as his own man, "the candidate and the leader of my party."

The art of campaigning as vice president is to promise more of what people liked best about the outgoing administration while pledging change to make things even better. It helps when the candidate can lean on the popularity of the departing president, as Nixon tried to do with Dwight D. Eisenhower in 1960 and as George Bush did in running to succeed Ronald Reagan in 1988. For Humphrey in 1968, the situation was the opposite. He had to put room between himself and his boss of four years, and Johnson made it difficult.

So Humphrey's mini-step away from LBJ war policy was a breakthrough. It gained him a measure of trust from the antiwar side, energized his campaign, and broke the dour Democratic mood. With that and the rallying of labor and other Democratic factions, Humphrey began narrowing Nixon's lead in the opinion polls.

As he got closer, near the end, the controlled marketing of the Nixon campaign was shaken. Until then, the Nixon product was selling. A presidential campaign is inherently exciting—the crowds, the cheers, the travel, the stakes. In 1968, Nixon and his organization tried to keep that as a façade while playing a guarded game more in keeping with commercial advertising than with traditional campaign tactics.

What Nixon said and did today and would do tomorrow was essentially what he said and did yesterday. The political drama was for Democrats, not the Nixon operation of practiced, passionless politics. His traditional, traveling campaign was largely a cover for the one waged on paid television. The rallies were timed for TV, the crowds often invitation-only. He did have an advance man who specialized in balloon drops, and there were a lot of balloons. Nixon had said it would not be an antiseptic campaign but it was, from the primary season until his assurance was shaken and Humphrey almost caught him in the final days, when Johnson stopped the bombing of North Vietnam to seek a peace settlement.

While Nixon avoided policy surprises, he sprung one in choosing his running mate. In an odd way, Nelson Rockefeller had a role in that. Rockefeller had ruled himself out of the campaign, then into it. In the process he so angered Spiro T. Agnew that the governor of Maryland became a Nixon man, and ultimately vice president. Agnew led a movement to draft Rockefeller early in 1968 and was so confident the New York governor was going to run that he invited an audience to his statehouse office to watch what he assumed would be a declaration of candidacy in late March. The *New York Times* said so. Instead, Rockefeller announced he would not run, embarrassing and angering Agnew, who got no advance word. He signed on with the Nixon campaign. Agnew was still "Spiro Who?" when Nixon put him on the ticket that summer. "This guy has got it," Nixon said. "If he doesn't, Nixon has made a bum choice." He had.

Forty days after saying no, Rockefeller decided to run after all. He said he could do better than Nixon against Humphrey and that the polls showed it. Some did, some didn't. Nixon was more concerned about a challenge on the right from Reagan, who had been governor of California for two years. Reagan ran initially as a favorite son, meaning he would hold his own state delegates, then declared himself a national candidate. It was too soon for Reagan, too late for Rockefeller.

Nixon was on script. His entourage included longtime advisers and friends, but a new team was in charge of the backstage operation that ran the real show, men skilled in the ways of advertising, marketing, and television. It was a step toward the coming of campaigns dominated by professional managers and consultants for whom presidential politics was a matter of business, not personal loyalties. In time, the pros would largely take over presidential campaign management. The era of personal campaign crews—Kennedy's Irish Mafia, Goldwater's Arizona crowd—was yielding. The loyalists would still be there, sometimes in power, as with Jimmy Carter's Georgians and

George W. Bush's Texans. But they were exceptions. Hired specialists would become the rule, most of them tied to one party or the other but few with long-standing commitments to candidates.

The Nixon operation was tuned to television. The medium that had shown him at a disadvantage in the first 1960 debate with Kennedy became his campaign vehicle, but not in debates; there would be none in 1968 or in 1972. For the leader, they offered no advantage and could mean trouble. Humphrey wanted debates, but Nixon had an easy out: George Wallace. He said it was a two-man contest and he was not getting involved in anything that included Wallace because that would build up the Alabama governor and get him more votes. That could only hurt Nixon, who didn't want to debate Humphrey anyhow.

Controlled television was Nixon's choice. He'd tested the invitation-only panel format at the start, in New Hampshire, and he used a more practiced version ten times in regional television programs during the campaign against Humphrey. It was show business. The studio audience was invited and no reporters were allowed lest they see and hear the warm-up instructions and applause signals. The no-reporter rule was rigid. When Nixon performed in Boston, I arranged to have my parents invited to be in the audience. When the show was over, and we were leaving town, I tried to get into the studio to say good-bye to them. Campaign security men wouldn't let me in. I spotted John Ehrlichman, one of Nixon's senior aides, and he got me through, whispering to the nominee, who came over to say hello and shake hands with my parents.

The one-hour Nixon campaign shows were imitations of the old *Meet the Press* panel programs. A half dozen people selected by the campaign would question Nixon, usually predictably. Bud Wilkinson, the former University of Oklahoma football coach, was the moderator. Most of the questions were friendly because most of the questioners were. Nixon responded to them by simply repeating a paragraph or two from the set speech. We reporters knew it was boilerplate Nixon, but to the television audience it looked spontaneous.

Occasionally, Nixon got an uncomfortable question and seemed to bristle at the intrusion into his pattern.

That was the case when a panelist asked Nixon whether he changed his positions when it was politically expedient. The question drew a ripple of applause from reporters isolated in the pressroom because he did exactly that, as we had reported more than once. "I suppose what you are referring to is, is there a new Nixon or is there an old Nixon?" he replied curtly. "I suppose I could counter by saying, 'Which Humphrey shall we listen to today?' " The audience applauded as if on cue and that gave Nixon a moment to get back on message. "My answer is yes, there is a new Nixon, if you are talking in terms of new ideas for the new world and the America we live in."

Nixon's campaign days were built around television schedules, which made them leisurely. His two or three public appearances were timed so that the TV crews could film them and ship the film to meet local or network deadlines. He stayed on script and on schedule.

The candidate who controlled his message became a president who limited his news conferences and contacts so that he could speak on his own terms and choose his own subjects. Flying to Key Biscayne, Florida, after the 1968 election, Nixon invited three members of the press pool—me, Merriman Smith of UPI, and Garnet (Jack) Horner of the *Washington Star*—to his cabin to talk about press relations in the new administration. He said he especially wanted advice "from Smitty and from Jack. Walter, you're a bit younger and newer." I was thirty-three. "That's true, Mr. Nixon," I said, "but I'm older than Ron Ziegler and he's your press secretary."

So I got to offer my bit when the elders said they wanted more background briefings, including some with the president, in which stories could be attributed only to well-placed or White House sources. That practice can make reporters sound like important people in the know, but I consider it deceptive and was appalled to hear two senior correspondents inviting it. So I disagreed and said that officials, especially presidents, should speak for themselves, on the record.

Not that it made any difference, since Nixon disregarded all of us, old or young, and did things his own guarded way, as he did in the campaign.

I remember one long day, whistle-stopping across rural Ohio as Nixon preached law and order from small-town depots, striking because of the dissonance between his peaceful surroundings and his message. "In the forty-five minutes it takes to ride from Lima to Deshler," he said after rolling through the peaceful farm fields from one town to the other, "this is what has happened in America: There has been one murder, two rapes, forty-five major crimes of violence, countless robberies and auto thefts." Then his standard promise to strengthen "the peace forces" against crime.

The Nixon campaign controls were overdone at a rally in Cleveland. It was by invitation only, no one admitted without a ticket, and the local organizers guarded the doors against people they thought looked like potential hecklers. In the attempt to get a safe, reliably Republican crowd, they miscalculated. When Nixon spoke, only about half of the ten thousand seats were filled. The balcony was empty except for the "Nixon's the One" signs propped on each seat there. We called it the "Beau Geste" rally after the phantom soldiers on the ramparts in the Rudyard Kipling tale. We heard later that Nixon had raised hell with his aides about it.

With Humphrey catching him in the polls as the election approached, Nixon worried about an "October surprise" in which a White House concession in Vietnam policy might yet beat him after all the months of serene confidence. On October 25, he couldn't take it any longer. The new Nixon stepped aside for the old Nixon, crafty in doublespeak. He said he had been told that the administration was driving for a bombing halt agreement possibly accompanied by a cease-fire. "I have since learned that these reports are true," Nixon said. "I am also told that this spurt of activity is a cynical last-minute attempt by President Johnson to salvage the candidacy of Mr. Humphrey. This I do not believe." He went on to say that Americans would welcome a bombing halt that would save and not cost

American lives, and that he'd do what he could to help Johnson pursue a just peace.

Nixon's people wouldn't say who had told him of all this, or that it was cynical politics. That way he could make the accusation and posture himself above it. I thought Nixon was playing the very cynical, last-minute politics he had suggested the Democrats were up to, but my job was not to say what I thought, it was to report what the candidate thought, said, and did. The judgments were for the reader to make.

On October 31, Johnson announced that he was ordering a halt to the bombing "in the belief that this action can lead to progress toward a peaceful settlement of the war" at peace talks in Paris. The election was five days away, a new round of peace negotiations were to begin the day after the voting, and the administration had indeed taken a step certain to boost Humphrey. I was covering the Nixon campaign in New York, and his people were in a bind, bitter at the political impact of a step they could not risk criticizing. So they told us it had come too late to turn the election to Humphrey. At a rally at Madison Square Garden, Nixon said he hoped there would be progress in the talks. "We want peace," he said.

But the peace venture already had been undermined. The next day, the South Vietnamese government balked at joining the Paris talks. "The prospects for peace are not as bright as we would have hoped a few days ago," Nixon said, feigning dismay. He thought it had been a political setup.

The question was whether, as the Democrats suspected, Nixon had known in advance that Saigon would not bargain. Mrs. Anna Chennault, widow of the Flying Tiger general of World War II, a fund-raiser and women's organizer for Nixon, had been telling South Vietnamese officials that their interests would be better served by waiting for a Nixon administration.

Johnson had evidence of what she'd done, because the administration had wiretaps on the South Vietnamese embassy. Nixon denied any involvement and sent word to the White House that he was surprised and shocked. Even the accusation of diplomatic sabotage would have been explosive, possibly the undoing of the candidate who had claimed his own policy of silence was to avoid undercutting Johnson on the war. Humphrey knew about the Chennault affair, but said nothing, wary of making an explosive accusation he was not certain he could prove.

Nixon won by less than one percentage point over Humphrey, becoming a president without a majority with 43 percent of the popular vote. Wallace got 13.5 percent.

"To lose to Nixon, ye gods," Humphrey wrote in his memoir. "No warmth, no strength, no emotion, no spirit."

Humphrey also wrote of the blocked peace effort. "I wonder if I should have blown the whistle on Anna Chennault and Nixon. He must have known about her call . . . I wish I could have been sure . . . Maybe I should have blasted them anyway."

Celebrating his victory, Nixon recalled that whistle-stop day in Deshler, Ohio, and a sign he'd seen a girl carrying there: "Bring us together." He said that was his great objective.

It was his great failure.

FOUR

Nixon's Lonely Landslide: The Dishonored Campaign of 1972

R ichard Nixon's last election was the one he couldn't lose. The men who might have been the president's most threatening Democratic challengers in 1972 toppled one by one. By that spring, Nixon was in comfortable command of the campaign. So it was incredible that he and his henchmen would try to steal what they were winning anyhow. They did, and made themselves into losers after Nixon's overwhelming reelection.

To travel with Nixon in that campaign was to watch a sort of political minuet. It was controlled, contrived, and, we would discover too late, as corrupt as the intrigues of a medieval court. On the road with Senator George McGovern, the doomed Democratic nominee, you got the hectic, often improvised air of a disco dance.

I never met so many people who later wound up in prison as when I covered the Nixon campaign. Among the convicts were the arrogant White House bosses, self-righteous political lieutenants, and a handful of sadly ruined young men who had simply done what presidential aides were expected to do—what the president wanted. The young lawyer who signed Nixon's fraudulent income tax return without checking its accuracy, a 1968 campaign volunteer who had been rewarded with a job in the Treasury, was indicted, jailed, lost his law license, and wound up working as a hotel detective.

Another young lawyer, John Sears, masterfully engineered Nixon's campaign for the 1968 nomination in the presidential primaries but was squeezed out of the top echelon by senior rivals who resented his influence and blunt advice to the president-elect. It was his good fortune, he told me after Watergate, because he wasn't certain he could have resisted the kind of presidential instructions that proved the undoing of his former colleagues.

That was the cauldron of dirty tricks and Watergate, the more mystifying because it was more than stupid—it was pointless. They were going to win and didn't need to cheat. I'd covered Nixon long enough to know that he was always watching his back, checking over his shoulder, wary that somebody was gaining on him. He practiced the politics of suspicion. His palace guard was just that, an array of unquestioning loyalists. Over drinks after a campaign day, we'd joke with political aides about their candidates' foibles. We called McGovern "McGoo," and some of his people joined the sardonic shorthand. Nixon's campaigners called him "The Boss," or "R.N.," and you had the impression they might stand and salute at the mention.

After covering Nixon's campaign of 1968 and his transition to power, I was assigned to the White House at the start of his presidency. I spent about five months there, the only time in my career I covered the White House full-time. I never wanted to; it was a narrow, confining kind of job. Reporters work in the isolation of the pressroom, get briefings there, and work the telephone in often frustrating efforts to get something more than the doled-out information. The assignment is to cover a man surrounded by armed guards, inaccessible except when he wants to be seen, silent except when, and on what topics, he chooses to speak. I always preferred the Capitol, especially the Senate, and got back there as quickly as I could, late in the spring of 1969. Reporting on Congress, you can talk to the people you cover, call a senator off the floor for an interview or catch him in the hallway or the elevator. White House news coverage was programmed; Senate reporting was not.

Still, White House coverage had its advantages. Travel was one. Until I covered Nixon, I'd never been farther abroad than Montreal. I was assigned to the presidential grand tour of Europe early in 1969: Brussels, Paris, Rome, Berlin, and London. Traveling with a president you don't get much time to see the landmarks because the schedule is too tight and the work too intense. But there is compensation in the things you do see—the glittering dining hall at Versailles, the reception room at Buckingham Palace. There was an hour long after midnight for a quick cab trip to Notre Dame. It had rained and the cathedral was mirrored in the wet, deserted streets. The great square was empty except for us. It was a scene I never forgot. Jack Germond was with me. For a few moments, we cynics stood in speechless awe. Germond broke the silence. "Jesus Christ," he marveled, irreverently but appropriately. I said I thought that was supposed to be the point.

By late spring, the advantage of my Nixon campaign contacts was about up—the people I knew had become White House aides and officials, and 1968 was history. So I happily returned to the Senate, became chief of the AP staff of five reporters covering that side of the Capitol, and got back to congressional and political reporting, on the 1970 off-year elections and then on the skirmishing for the 1972 Democratic presidential nomination.

Before the campaign year, public opinion polls showed Senator Edmund S. Muskie preferred over Nixon, enough to make the president nervous because, he said privately, the Maine senator had "a fair chance of beating me." So the Committee for the Re-election of the President, aptly acronymed CREEP, set out to see to it that there would be no fair chance.

I knew the buttoned-down, slickly combed cadre at CREEP. I didn't know what they were up to until the Watergate scandal burst into public view the year after the campaign, the misconduct magnified by the Nixon cover-up attempt. The *Washington Post* began reporting White House and campaign ties to the burglary and dirty tricks before the election, but the disclosures by Bob Woodward and Carl Bernstein didn't became a significant issue despite McGovern's effort to put Watergate on the political agenda before Americans voted.

We campaign reporters wrote what McGovern said about it all: that Nixon was the most corrupt president in American history, the sponsor of burglars and political buggings. We then reported the White House denials, a balancing act that was and is the habit of American political journalism. The balance struck an average between valid accusations and dishonest denials, but charge and response is the flawed ritual of political reporting, even though the average between a lie and the truth is still a lie.

Nixon's CREEP campaign command post had the atmosphere of a bank. McGovern headquarters had the clamor of a supermarket. McGovern campaigned aggressively, Nixon hardly at all. The president logged just over three weeks of campaign travel all year, and those were short workdays of a stop or two, usually to invited audiences, with few open rallies. It was an invitation-only campaign. Often, Nixon spoke to leaders of his own vote-hunting organizations, purposely preaching to the committed. "Against McGovern it was clear that the less I did the better I would do," Nixon wrote in his memoirs.

But I always sensed a political paranoia about his operation. Nixon claimed he had set up CREEP because he wanted to keep politics out of the White House. That sounded statesmanlike, but Nixon was the ultimate pol, a man obsessed with political maneuvering. He ordered a White House aide to hire a private investigator to look into Chappaquiddick in 1971, just in case Ted Kennedy surfaced as a candidate. The private eye came up with nothing new but rumors about the accident that killed Kennedy's passenger, a young woman campaign volunteer. Kennedy wasn't running anyhow.

Pat Buchanan even recommended that the Nixon operation try to disrupt the campaign of Pete McCloskey, a liberal California congressman running as a protest candidate in the Republican primaries. McCloskey was a negligible annoyance, but the Nixon people didn't want to be annoyed. Nothing came of the Buchanan memo.

The dirty tricks operation against the Democrats was paid for with CREEP money but it was coordinated out of the White House by Dwight Chapin, Nixon's young, carefully combed appointments secretary. We used to joke that Chapin's hair was all one piece because there never was a strand out of place.

Days before the Watergate burglary of Democratic Party headquarters on June 17, 1972, Nixon dashed off a memo: "McGovern is more clever and less principled than Goldwater and will say anything in order to win." Two days after the break-in, Nixon learned that somebody on the CREEP payroll was involved. "My confidence in CRP was undermined more by the stupidity of the DNC bugging attempt than by its illegality," Nixon wrote later. That mind-set was the undoing of his presidency. Instead of denouncing the stupidity of it all and cleaning house in his campaign, Nixon reacted by having his own offices checked constantly to make sure that he wasn't being bugged as the Democrats had been, and by trying to cover it up behind a CIA cloak, the lie that finally forced him to resign.

Trying to erase the stain, Nixon wrote, lectured, and, in 1986, addressed an Associated Press publishers convention in San Francisco, where I wrote questions to be put to him, one of which was what he had learned from Watergate. "Just destroy all the tapes," he said. No thought of any apology or the lesson his disaster might send to future generations of politicians. Burn the tapes, he thought. That way the cover-up might have worked. He had asked me in advance for suggestions on what he should talk about and I'd answered the obvious, that foreign policy and politics were his specialties. He autographed his next book in appreciation for my "wise counsel," and told the publishers that day how much I had helped him prepare for his address. I told Nixon afterward that I wasn't convinced being described as his speechwriter was a good career move for an AP man. By then he could laugh about it.

I think Nixon would have won reelection in 1972 even had he confessed that his campaign's fingerprints were on the Watergate break-in. He might have come in short of the 61 percent and the forty-nine states he carried, but he would have won with votes to burn. Had he admitted the role of his campaign, Congress probably would not have sent investigators in pursuit of the facts all the way to the smoking gun tape—the attempt to use the CIA for cover-up purposes—that forced his resignation.

In the primaries, McGovern had been marginalized by rivals in his own party who argued that he was far left of the Democratic mainstream, a sort of liberal counterpart to the Goldwater of 1964. That crippled McGovern even before the fiasco in which he chose, then dropped, Senator Thomas F. Eagleton as his running mate. McGovern had embraced Eagleton "one thousand percent" after the disclosure that he had been hospitalized for depression, a mental illness more damning to a politician then than now, but prodded him from the ticket when the reaction was too adverse to accept.

McGovern knew how to cut his losses, although he did so too late in that case. He wasn't quite the naïve straight arrow he sometimes seemed. He was a veteran of deadly combat in World War II, a decorated bomber pilot. McGovern was the peace candidate but he knew how to fight.

Purity doesn't pay in politics. I saw McGovern cut a campaign corner here and there, reneging on promised commitments, dumping staff aides when it served a political purpose, sometimes misrepresenting what he had said or done. Nothing scandalous, but not in keeping with the image his campaign tried to project of the trustworthy heartland Democrat up against the trickiest of presidents. Besides, McGovern always seemed to get caught, as when he asked Pierre Salinger, the former Kennedy press secretary and briefly senator from California, to meet with North Vietnamese peace negotiators in Paris to see whether they would release any American prisoners. They would not. When word of the errand leaked out, McGovern first denied any involvement, saying he hadn't given the slightest instruction to Salinger. He had, and within hours he had to admit it. While McGovern couldn't get away with anything, Nixon got away with Watergate during the campaign. "The White House had no involvement whatsoever in this particular Watergate incident," he said to every report that it had. The serial denials got him through 1972, past the election, and into the scarred second term he had to quit. That was the ultimate humiliation for Nixon, who coveted the presidency so long and then sacrificed it to his own strange, insecure, incredible misconduct. He was the most fascinating figure I encountered as a reporter, a political genius with a conscience of clay, a fearful man but at times a belligerent one, a public figure who could orate but couldn't chat.

The *Washington Post* began reporting Watergate links to the Nixon campaign two days after the burglary on June 17, with more damning disclosures in the fall, at the height of the campaign season. Even before that, the Associated Press reported that one of the names involved, E. Howard Hunt, had ties to the White House. McGovern sharpened his corruption accusations but the issue had no bite. He kept demanding that somebody call Nixon to account, but nobody did until later.

The White House again denied involvement, and the elusive president weathered the issue with the denials. That summer, at his first campaign news conference, Nixon told us that overzealous people sometimes do things that are wrong in a campaign and added an unforgettable line that seemed a throwaway at the time. "What really hurts is if you try to cover it up."

His standard line was that he was too busy being president to be diverted by mere politics. Campaigning presidents usually say that since there is no political platform to match the White House. Nixon's breakthrough journey to China, ending a nearly quarter-century freeze on U.S. contacts, began just before the year's voting opened in the New Hampshire primary. He called it "the week that changed the world." No mere candidate could compete with that.

I was shivering with McGovern in New Hampshire the day Nixon arrived in Beijing to begin dismantling America's great wall against the communist government there. McGovern was campaigning to sparse crowds and trying to get gloved passersby to pause and shake hands on icy street corners. "Who is that?" one woman asked me.

Muskie, still the Democratic front-runner by far, was in Chicago paying court to Mayor Richard J. Daley, the last of the old-line political bosses. Muskie figured he could spare the time away from New Hampshire, next door to his Maine home. We hadn't yet learned that

New England loyalties were not going to be the vote magnet Muskie thought they would be.

Nixon was riding a wave: He had the troubled economy stabilized, he had the world stage for his China and Moscow summits, and he seemed to have the Vietnam War under control, although it ravaged on and Americans still were dying in combat. More than 400,000 U.S. troops had been withdrawn during his first term, and Nixon said he had cut American casualties by 98 percent. He had campaign money to squander, and did.

Watergate became the landmark of the 1972 campaign, but it was a time of indelible changes, among them:

- The first political finance reform law in nearly fifty years, a disclosure measure that Nixon signed for show and then arranged to evade. Watergate led to more stringent reforms and to the public financing of presidential campaigns.

- The increasing number and impact of state presidential primary elections, making them into the arenas in which all future nominees would have to win the delegates to control their conventions. While that was a product of Democratic reform rules, it applied to Republicans, too, because when the states enacted presidential primary election laws, they covered both parties. In 1972, there were twenty-three state primaries and they chose 63 percent of the Democratic nominating delegates, the first time a majority was selected by the voters.

- The final nail in the coffin of the old boss system, symbolized when Daley was evicted from the Democratic National Convention with his Illinois delegation. Daley's slate had been elected in a presidential primary, but the reformers said the primary election itself was tainted because only the boss-chosen could get on the ballot. So the delegation was kicked out of the convention in favor of one the reformers deemed more representative of the party in Illinois, with more women and more black delegates. It wasn't quite a quota system but it came close.

- The rise of what would be called "the expectations game," in which commentators and onlookers went into odds-making in the primaries, deciding what would constitute a solid enough margin to represent a victory for the leader or an upset for the long shot. Preprimary public opinion poll margins were one test, and we always tried to goad candidates and their managers into setting targets themselves. The wise ones wouldn't do it.

But a Muskie manager did in New Hampshire in 1972, and the gaming was the beginning of the front-runner's undoing. Muskie lost to expectations when he won the primary, and McGovern won there by losing. From that election day on, candidates have tried to lower their own expectations and raise those for their rivals, the better to claim victory whatever the outcome.

Ed Muskie beat McGovern by nine percentage points—and never recovered from the victory. The Maine senator had made his name and reputation as the vice presidential nominee of 1968, the New England voice of reason in a strident season. The wisecrack of that campaign was that Hubert Humphrey's best chance of defeating Nixon would be to promise that upon inauguration, he would resign and let Vice President Muskie take over.

Muskie was the Democrats' spokesman on television on election eve 1970, getting the last word after a harsh Nixon speech and adding to his reputation as a calming voice in a political storm, saying that the president peddled fear while he spoke for "the politics of trust."

That helped install him as the towering leader among Democrats who wanted the nomination to challenge Nixon; a dozen more or less serious candidates would enter the contest. Once Kennedy stood aside, Muskie was more than a front-runner. He looked like a sure thing. Mark Shields, a skilled, sought-after campaign strategist before he became a political commentator, had offers from all significant Democratic candidates that year and asked my off-the-record advice as a friend. I told him to be practical and sign on with Muskie. He never let me forget it.

When Muskie started campaigning for the 1972 nomination, the calm, craggy, trust-inspiring candidate turned out to be cranky, impatient, and directionless. He asked the voters for their trust but never really said what they should trust him to do.

He started with the traditional moves, calling on party leaders, lining up support, touring world capitals. When he visited Israel, one of the reporters who went with him was Dick Stewart of the *Boston Globe,* a man of irrepressible wit who later became Muskie's press secretary. At lunch by the Sea of Galilee, Stewart told the waiter he wanted bottled water because he didn't want to be drinking water people had been walking on. It wasn't Muskie's kind of humor; his middle initial was S for Sixtus, after a pope, and his jokes tended to be New England–accented set pieces, not quips. He'd shake his head at Stewart's wisecracks, but he always got a laugh out of them, until the campaign collapsed into no laughing matter.

I knew Muskie socially and as a Senate reporter, and played golf with him in Miami the day of the Florida presidential primary, in which he would run a faltering fourth and effectively fall from contention. There's not much to do on an election day except wait until the polls close, and a Miami golf course is an ideal place for waiting. So our foursome went out, with Muskie my partner in a two-dollar bet against the other guys. On the ninth hole, our opponents both got into trouble. Muskie's was the high handicap so he had a one-stroke advantage. He slashed his second shot into the rough and called me over to ask for advice. His ball was in a tangled downhill lie, just visible in the gnarl of grass. He wanted to know what club to hit, and I said he should take a wedge and just get the ball back into the fairway. "Like hell," he said. "I can hit this onto the green." Arnold Palmer couldn't have hit it there. Muskie took a mighty swing and managed only to top the ball deeper into the rough. Now he was getting angry. He looked down the fairway toward the green, a good 180 yards away, and spotted a Miami television crew setting up there. "Damn them," he snarled. "You can't even play golf without having TV people screw up your shot." That was candidate Muskie: stubborn, cantankerous, often angry, and convinced that what went wrong was somebody else's fault.

In other settings he was a talented, usually gracious, gentle man. He was just a lousy candidate for president.

McGovern, improbably, turned out to be good at it. He'd run briefly at the 1968 convention. He declared his 1972 candidacy a full year in advance, methodically organizing in chosen primary states and brushing aside the questions we asked him about his inability to break past single digits in the Democratic preference polls. He knew what he was about. Ten days before he announced he was running for president, McGovern resigned as chairman of the party reform commission that had written the rules of competition for the 1972 Democratic nomination, rules he said guaranteed the "least boss-ridden and most democratic" campaign ever conducted. After presiding over the writing of guidelines to open the process to the grass roots, McGovern would now run on them.

His campaign was led by the same people who had worked on the reform rules. Gary Hart—breezy, deceptively casual, handsome, and driven at thirty-four—was one of them, managing the McGovern campaign and beginning the political course that would take him to the Senate from Colorado and eventually into a presidential bid of his own.

It didn't take a genius to see that the new system put a premium on organizing support from the bottom up. That was obvious, but Muskie's people seemed oblivious. They set up a pricey campaign bureaucracy at a showy Washington headquarters near the White House and looked to party leaders for support. Muskie campaigners scrimping in state outposts called it the Taj Mahal. The rent and the staff cost more in a month than the McGovern campaign spent on its entire national operation. Muskie gained endorsements like no candidate before him, lining up senators, governors, and House leaders for what we called the endorsement-a-day show. But party leaders had lost control, and their endorsements were all but irrelevant. When we asked Muskie about the endorsement strategy, he always claimed to be organizing his grassroots base at the same time. He'd illustrate with the story of the two Polish builders trying to put up a house by building the roof before digging the foundation. Given his ancestry, Muskie could tell Polish jokes with impunity. But Muskie and his people kept building a roof-down campaign.

He was the Democrat every potential rival, including Nixon, was watching. He didn't take to the rigors of the road, but he worked at the campaign buildup in thirty-two states before the election year began. Locals kept asking him whether he was running for president, which he obviously was. It finally got to him. "What the hell do they think I'm doing here?" he snapped at us over a drink one night in San Mateo, California. As though he'd suffer being in such a place except as a presidential candidate.

Muskie had a habit of complaining about the rigors of running for president. In Los Angeles, he told a women's luncheon that he wanted to work for positive policies, a conviction without which "I would not be wandering around the country putting up with the inconveniences of time changes and physical difficulties, including the runs." He was nothing if not candid.

At times, the candor was admirable. After he'd met with black leaders in Watts, word leaked out that he had told them he would not consider a black running mate because the country wasn't ready for it; such a ticket would lose and the result would set back the cause of equal rights. That was true, but impolitic. Muskie said he "chose what I thought was the honest answer," not the safe one. McGovern and the rest of his rivals all reacted by saying that race or sex would not rule anyone off their tickets, the standard line in such situations even though it wasn't so and they knew it.

Muskie said he was going to campaign slowly and methodically. Part of his method was to collect those big name endorsements. "If you're going out on a limb, take a lot of people with you," he told us. He did that, and the limb snapped.

At first, McGovern traveled with no entourage and scant notice. His was one face in a crowd of Democrats looking toward the 1972 nomination. He was the antiwar candidate, promising immediate American withdrawal from Vietnam. But by 1972, the Democratic ballot was full of antiwar candidates—Muskie and Hubert Humphrey were for withdrawal, too.

Muskie had been running for months by the time he declared his candidacy early in January 1972, on a paid national television hookup. McGovern had pronounced himself a candidate with no such fanfare a full year before. At the time, his was the earliest formal declaration of candidacy since Andrew Jackson.

Muskie said he would campaign everywhere and might enter all the Democratic primaries, certainly the first eight. That meant spreading his efforts thin, but he told me he already was a national candidate so he had no alternative.

McGovern did. He picked his spots, beginning with New Hampshire, where the public opinion polls put Muskie so far ahead that McGovern could run against the odds instead of against the front-runner. Muskie was, after all, the next thing to a favorite son. One of his state campaign managers said that any showing short of an outright majority over the other four candidates in the primary there would be grounds for suicide. "If my neighbors don't think well of me, how do I go to the rest of the country?" Muskie asked.

The early polls showed Muskie the favorite of two-thirds of New Hampshire Democrats, with McGovern in single digits. Muskie could only come down and McGovern could only go up. As the voting neared, that is exactly what happened. Muskie complained that we were putting him up against a phantom candidate—those expectations. He was going to win. The question was of the margin. And we political reporters would judge that.

One night in the hotel bar we wrote a "Rock of Ages" parody about the role of the political press—especially the lead reporters for the *Washington Post* and the *New York Times*—in judging how much of a margin would be enough for Muskie:

David Broder, write for me.
Tell me what is victory.
Johnny Apple we'll recruit,
And the rest will follow suit.
David Broder, write for me.
Tell me what is victory.

McGovern had more than expectations going for him. He was the liberal against Muskie the centrist, and the left usually is the push in a Democratic primary, where constituencies are more liberal than in the electorate at large. He had the young activists at work for him. He adroitly used the issue of campaign finance disclosure, as popular a cause in New Hampshire then as it was for John McCain in 2000. He made public his finances and donors, which was not required at the time, and demanded that Muskie do the same thing. Muskie said no, that he had complied with the law and need not go beyond. He told me later that he might have done it but for contributions he'd gotten from Republicans who didn't like Nixon but didn't want it known that they were donating to the other side. The issue dented his image as the man to trust. For McGovern, campaigning on a shoestring, telling all was easy because there wasn't much to tell.

Muskie took another image dent, this one self-inflicted, when he staged a challenge to the *Manchester Union Leader* and rightist publisher William Loeb, ten days before the primary, and choked on his own anger and emotion. It was snowing that Saturday as he stood on a flatbed truck outside the newspaper and called Loeb a "gutless coward." The story that ignited his public wrath was about Jane Muskie and her unladylike language when talking with a group of women reporters, one of whom put it into print. I don't know whether Muskie cried that day or not. Dick Stewart, by then Muskie's spokesman, was standing close to him and always said the moisture was melting snow running down his face. But tears or snow, he certainly was choked up, and not, as he later conceded, the solid, steady figure he'd tried to present. Anything but. He was emotional, and he was angry.

Curiously, the story that supposedly enraged him wasn't a *Union Leader* story at all, but a reprint of a reprint, picked up from a newsmagazine that had, in turn, picked it up from *Women's Wear Daily*. So it was old stuff by the time Muskie denounced it, although that fact didn't make the stories about his meltdown.

He had another grievance that day, a letter the *Union Leader* published saying that Muskie had laughed when he heard people of

French-Canadian descent derisively described as "Canucks." Muskie denied it and the letter turned out to be a Nixon campaign dirty trick. I found that one curious, given that "Canucks" was not so insulting a term as to prevent its becoming the name of the Vancouver team in the National Hockey League.

McGovern had tried to goad Muskie into a campaign debate in New Hampshire but the front-runner ducked until his poll numbers started to slip. Then he agreed to a forum with all five primary candidates just before the election. Muskie the debater did not look like the dominant figure he was supposed to be. Not that McGovern distinguished himself, either. The only memorable debater was a man named Ned Coll, a social worker from Hartford, Connecticut, a fringe candidate who wasn't even old enough to be president. Coll came with a prop to dramatize the plight of the poor. Every time it came his turn to speak he would dangle a rubber rat by the tail. "This is what it's all about," he would say.

Muskie carried New Hampshire with 46 percent to McGovern's 37, then angrily tried to fend off our questions about why he hadn't done as well as expected. He snapped that we were the ones who set the expectations and then wrote about them. The mood around Muskie only got testier. There was the night in Green Bay, Wisconsin, when reporters gave Muskie a fifty-eighth-birthday cake and Jane Muskie pushed a piece of it into the face of the *Newsweek* correspondent. McGovern won that primary and the stock question to Muskie became when he'd concede and quit. He stopped campaigning on April 27 but said he was still a candidate. As his campaign had foundered, Muskie was asked whether he was in trouble; the answer was obvious but journalistic convention required the question. He replied with a New England joke about the guy whose car wheels were spinning in the mud. Somebody asked the man whether he was stuck and he replied that you could say that, "if I was going anywhere." That April, I was summoned to New York to address the AP Board of Directors about the campaign, a command performance I dreaded. To make it worse, the forum was a cocktail reception, no place for a talk on politics. But the boss insisted, so at the appointed time, he banged a spoon on a glass and announced that I was about to speak. Adding to my discomfort, the wife of the chairman of the board stopped me as I went to the lectern and said, "Keep it brief, please. We've been having fun." I did, avoided forecasting the Democratic nominee, and said thank you. The boss decreed that I would answer questions. There was only one, repeated: Who would the Democrats run against Nixon? "I don't know," I answered. Muskie was sinking but McGovern still seemed the unlikeliest of choices. The board chairman commanded that I pick a name. "I don't know," I said. "Muskie might come back." He quit campaigning within the week, and I was still being needled about it thirty years later.

Muskie retreated to Hilton Head, South Carolina, and invited me to interview him on the condition that I did not announce his whereabouts. He didn't want any more TV cameras around. He told me he'd stay in as a candidate because the party might need a compromise nominee and he would be available. He was, but there would be no compromise, no alternative to McGovern by the time the convention voted. Even then, McGovern seemed an improbable nominee. To the old guard Democrats, the new crowd looked like a collection of hippies. "We got beat by the cast of *Hair*," Representative Tip O'Neill lamented after McGovern was nominated that summer.

There were familiar faces available—Humphrey's, for example. He was trying one last time, picking his spots, beginning with the Florida primary. But there wasn't much joy left in his politics. I traveled with him in Florida, and we arrived at the Miami airport late one night, the terminal all but deserted except for the cleaning crews. The drivers who were supposed to have met the candidate were late. As the nominee four years before, he had campaigned with all the trappings and privileges, along with all the political burdens, of the vice presidency. Not now; his entourage was stranded. Humphrey wearily surveyed the empty airport. "Shit," he summed up, to no one in particular but for all of us to hear.

That Democratic primary in Florida was dominated by one issue, mandatory busing of schoolchildren for racial integration. George Wallace rode busing to 42 percent of the vote; Humphrey limped in with 19 percent despite an uncharacteristic attempt to cater to the antibusing mood by saying that he'd approve the practice only to improve education, not for desegregation. Senator Henry M. Jackson of Washington was a candidate, too, and he tried to ride the issue by advocating a constitutional amendment against mandatory busing. Jackson knew that was close to the edge on a racial issue. As an antidote, he singled out a black TV reporter covering his campaign, draping an arm around the guy's shoulder and repeatedly calling him "my little buddy," since he was not only black but short. The reporter didn't like it and we commiserated, but short of slugging the candidate he couldn't see a way out. Jackson flunked the sensitivity test and the primary, too, running third. He stuck around but never was a real contender.

Humphrey battled McGovern for the rest of the primary season, until the finale in California, which, he told us, would be the ball game. By that time, McGovern was the leading Democrat but a wounded candidate. Humphrey had campaigned against him as a man out of tune with most of the party, a fringe candidate with unreliable ideas. It puzzled McGovern, since they had been midwestern friends and colleagues in the Senate. He told us that Humphrey seemed to him to be uneasy with the tactic, which he found a somewhat comforting thought about a man who once had been a mentor. McGovern said that in a birthday telephone conversation, Humphrey told him he didn't like being mean. Perhaps not, but he didn't ease the pressure. He ridiculed McGovern's idea about giving everybody in the country $1,000, to be taxed back from the rich and to help the poor, setting up a target for Republicans. The proposal came with no numbers and not even an estimate of the price, although McGovern dreamed one up: zero. He said the tax-back plan would cover the cost, which defied both political and mathematical reason. McGovern eventually dropped the proposal, but the Republicans didn't. Humphrey said McGovern was proposing spending cuts that would undermine national defense; the Republicans grabbed that line, too.

In California, Humphrey counted on organized labor support while McGovern mobilized a McCarthy-style army of volunteers and activists, thousands of them canvassing the state door-to-door. Humphrey and McGovern met twice in one-on-one television debates. I came away with a slogan not of my making, but one that stuck for the rest of my career. It came out of Tim Crouse's description of the debate pressroom in his campaign book *The Boys on the Bus*. There were about thirty of us watching the debate on television. As a wire service reporter, I had to write a running story as the two candidates argued. My copy would be in first; everybody else's editor would see it before their own reporters had delivered their versions of what happened. So in situations like that one, colleagues used to ask me what I'd chosen as the lead. They did that day in Los Angeles, and Crouse took note, covering the coverage. I'd written a lead saying that both Humphrey and McGovern had said they would not accept George Wallace as a vice presidential nominee, but that Democrats needed to consider his views. Wallace, who had been shot and partially paralyzed in Laurel, Maryland, on May 15 had won three Democratic primaries and was second in delegate strength.

"Walter, what's our lead?" asked Marty Nolan of the *Boston Globe*, half serious, half needling. I told him mine; he wrote his own. But ever after, people said to me, "What's the lead, Walter?" It got to be a campaign junkie's cliché among people who didn't even know me. At the end of the 2000 campaign, the National Association of Manufacturers' PR people sent out what was labeled a Campaign Survival Kit: a canvas shopping bag containing small packs of headache pills, snacks, toothpaste, and the like, along with a list of the spokesmen and officials they hoped reporters would call for comments on election night. On the other side of the bag was a drawing of a press plane and a question: "What's the lead, Walter?" A bonus on my fifteen minutes of fame.

Nolan was a talented, insightful political reporter, as good as they came. After Crouse's account, *Boston Magazine* ran a column questioning why the *Globe* would send out a fancy reporter when the guy could do no more than copy the lead of some wire service drone. Nolan sent me a copy of the magazine with a hint that I might want to set them straight. So I wrote a letter to the editor saying Marty

Nolan never copied my leads because he wasn't smart enough to use them.

Tim Crouse captured the fraternity house atmosphere of the press buses and workrooms of those campaign times. *The Boys on the Bus* eventually made reading lists at journalism schools, although a student who reads it now will find a different world out there. The boys have been joined, sometimes outnumbered, by the girls on the bus. Laptop computers have supplanted the blue-cased Olivetti typewriters all of us toted in the '60s and '70s. With a laptop, reporters can keep working between stops, save the copy in memory, and file at the next stop—sooner, with a cell phone to plug into the computer and deliver it en route. I remember being the first reporter to board a campaign jet years ago, settling into my seat when a newly assigned stewardess asked me if I could suggest what she should do to prepare for the press crowd. I told her to get started on about two hundred Bloody Marys. Nowadays, she'd have to start popping Perriers.

We used to work hard, compete hard, and unwind hard. We had our own tribal rules, named for the inventors. The Weaver rule, for example, under which the last man into the taxicab sits in front and pays the whole fare. Warren Weaver of the *New York Times* devised that one, and it led to some athletic cab entries. The Germond rule was Jack's contribution: No matter what you eat for dinner, everybody at the table pays an equal share of the tab. Jules Witcover and I added a corollary one night after getting saddled with a bill inflated by the multiple martinis a colleague drank like water. Our two-word rule: "Drink defensively."

Germond and Witcover, whose double byline would grace political columns for a generation in the *Washington Star* and the *Baltimore Sun*, were my close friends, but I tested them to the limit one night in Milwaukee. It was getting late, I was hungry, and I could see the flashing neon of a steak house outside the hotel pressroom. "Fazio's," it blinked. No need to take a cab somewhere, I said; why don't we just go over there and get a steak. They agreed and some other reporters joined us. We got a table that stuck out into the aisle so far that Witcover, seated at the end, had to stand up when other diners wanted to pass us. The steaks were okay, but just. Neither food nor ambience worked for Germond, the gourmet of the crowd. Before we left, Jack and Jules required me to sign a note. It said, "I promise I will never again choose the restaurant." Witcover carried it in his wallet until the paper disintegrated from age. I never again chose the restaurant.

Germond was dedicated to fine dining, but his profession came first. He went to lunch with George Wallace one day in Montgomery. Wallace had a habit of dousing every meal in catsup, but he didn't like it called to attention because it added to the impression that he was a Deep South redneck with dubious manners. (He was, but never mind.) Germond knew all that, so before Wallace could pick up the catsup bottle, he did, and poured it all over his own lunch. Wallace beamed, had his catsup, and always answered Jack's telephone calls.

McGovern won California, 44 percent to Humphrey's 39 percent. That won him all 271 delegates from the biggest state, which was ironic because his reform commission had wanted to do away with winner-take-all primaries in favor of a rule that would award delegates in proportion to shares of the popular vote. The reformers couldn't get it approved, and now it served the purpose of the chief reformer. Then the reformers and the old guard suddenly switched roles.

The establishment—labor, Humphrey, conservative southern Democrats, and what was left of the Muskie and Jackson campaigns—still were trying to stop McGovern by denying him the entire California delegation, letting him have only 120 nominating votes to reflect his 44 percent of the popular vote. They argued that would fit the spirit of reform. To which McGovern retorted that the game was over, and changing the rules after the fact was no reform but a hijack attempt. The convention credentials committee voted to split the California delegates, the McGovern side went to federal court, the Supreme Court opted out and sent the issue back to the national convention, and the California challenge became the whole show.

Finally, McGovern won back his California sweep, clinching his nomination in a boisterous, all-night session that set the pattern for convention week.

The convention was a clamor of interest groups shouting for attention. Gay rights came out of the political closet. Traditionalists complained that the convention was all about acid, amnesty, and abortion. At the convention hall in Miami Beach, old-line Democratic leaders were among strangers. Daley was ousted in the name of reform, although McGovern was pragmatic enough to go to Chicago after he was nominated and claim that he'd tried to keep the mayor in the convention, which wasn't so. But Daley still knew how to deliver Democratic voters in Illinois.

The Democratic platform demanded complete, immediate U.S. withdrawal from Indochina, with postwar amnesty for Vietnam draft evaders. The Democrats embraced school busing, advocated freedom "of lifestyles and private habits" for homosexuals.

It was a televised turnoff for middle America, at least for those who still were watching the show from Miami Beach. Much of what the Democrats decided was settled so late at night that the audience had tuned out. McGovern didn't deliver his acceptance speech until 2:48 A.M., and by the time he got to his "Come Home America" closing, it was 3:25 in the morning, and most everyone was at home asleep.

That closing would be part of his everyday campaign speech, and it touched on a war record he seldom mentioned. Barely into his twenties, McGovern served heroically in World War II, logging thirty-five combat missions, 230 hours at the controls of his B-24 bomber, named *Dakota Queen* for his wife, Eleanor. McGovern named his chartered campaign jet *Dakota Queen II*. He ran for president under fire from within his own party and from the Republicans as a man weak on defense, unmindful of the need for military strength, a naïve peacenik type on Vietnam. But this was a man who knew more about war than his critics did. At one point he had to defend his war record against false accusations by the rightist John Birch Society that he had shirked combat. In fact, he had piloted his full share of bombing missions and had seen more than his share of perilous skies over Nazi targets.

There was an air of midwestern reserve about McGovern. He seldom talked about himself. He wasn't a shouting, demonstrative campaigner, even when his accusations were unrestrained. He said, for example, that Nixon's Vietnam bombing was "the most barbaric action that any country has committed since Hitler's effort to exterminate the Jews," but in a voice as nasally bland as the assertion was inflammatory.

His "come home" theme recalled his military service. "I was a bomber pilot in World War II," he told a Labor Day rally. "I still remember the day when we were hit so hard over Germany that we were all ready to bail out. So I gave this order to the crew: 'Resume your stations. We're going to bring this plane home.' I say to you and to people everywhere who share our cause: 'Resume your stations. We're going to bring America home.' "

It became the set closing to his set speech.

Nixon's Republican convention in the same Miami Beach hall was as tightly controlled as the Democrats were unruly and unmanageable. No postmidnight sessions for them, only prime TV time. It was so closely supervised that even the opening prayer had to be submitted to party officials for approval in advance. It was the first convention run on a script and timed to the minute. A Republican contact slipped me a copy of the schedule the day before the opening gavel sounded. It told in minute detail what would happen at every moment of every session all week. "Begin spontaneous demonstration," it would say, giving the time for the delegates to cheer and parade. When time was up, it decreed, "End spontaneous demonstration." It told the presiding officers how to announce the outcome of votes on convention business—the ayes had it, long before the votes were taken. The script ruled every session, almost exactly on time, although the fourteen-minute floor demonstration after the roll call vote that nominated Nixon did run two minutes over the allotted time slot. Nothing was improvised. The Nixon people wanted a television show and they produced one.

The Democrats' rowdy, run-on performance was a factor in McGovern's most damaging decision of the campaign, his tortured choice of a running mate. He was weary, his advisers were exhausted, and because these were the liberal reformers, there would be no select, inner circle council to decide on a vice presidential nominee. Instead, McGovern had more than twenty advisers and campaign allies assemble in a conference room at the Doral Hotel to talk about prospects. It was a reflection of the interests that had dominated the convention, with scant room for the advice of traditional Democratic powers, including organized labor, which wasn't going to endorse the McGovern ticket anyway. Names bounced on and off the table, and the hastily assembled vice presidential screeners took votes on scraps of paper like some odd jury. The list they finally sent McGovern was headed by Boston Mayor Kevin White, but that had to be cleared with the senator from Massachusetts and Ted Kennedy blocked it. The fallback: Senator Eagleton of Missouri.

There is something to be said for smoke-filled rooms. At least they imposed order on political decision-making. In the end, only one vote for vice president counts in setting the ticket, the one cast by the presidential nominee. The way nominees pick their partners was changed forever because of what happened to McGovern and his fractured ticket.

Nobody bothered to do a background check on Eagleton before he was chosen; there wasn't the time or the inclination. A McGovern lieutenant asked Eagleton whether he had any skeletons rattling in his closet and the senator said no. That was it. But Eagleton had been hospitalized three times for psychiatric treatment, and twice had undergone electroshock therapy for depression, most recently in 1966. Cover stories had kept that quiet as he ran in Missouri, but this was a different league.

After Eagleton, nominees would be more careful, meticulous, about checking the records of their vice presidential prospects. There would be preselection questionnaires, interviews, and vetting by aides commissioned to conduct vice presidential talent hunts well before the conventions.

The Eagleton nominating session was a circus. It was entertaining for a while, then it got tiresome. I had to wait out the convention silliness before writing my story about the serious business that got pushed well past midnight by the vice presidential follies. The Democrats wasted prime time by putting up an assortment of seven other vice presidential candidates, with pointless speeches for each, followed by a roll call in which thirty-nine names got votes. One was cast for Archie Bunker, one for Mao Tse-tung.

When the Democrats broke camp in Miami Beach, the story of Eagleton's mental health treatments was breaking out. Reporters Bob Boyd and Clark Hoyt of Knight Newspapers won the Pulitzer Prize for disclosing it, although Eagleton, knowing that the story was about to break, announced it himself before they got into print.

By then, McGovern was taking a break at a Black Hills resort in Custer, South Dakota, and making a bad situation worse. Eagleton joined him and McGovern said the senator would stay on the ticket, adding the "thousand percent" endorsement he soon had to swallow. The reaction in the party and on editorial pages was adverse to hostile, and it was obvious Eagleton had to go. McGovern tried hints, then long-distance prodding, and finally met with Eagleton in Washington and got him to withdraw.

Now the problem was getting a candidate to replace him on a ticket that obviously was going nowhere. McGovern hadn't had much of a chance before, and he had none after the Eagleton episode. So he went shopping for a new vice president and kept getting turndowns. The joke around the Capitol was that there was a signup sheet in the Senate Democratic cloakroom for anyone willing to run with McGovern. He finally got Sargent Shriver, the Kennedy brother-in-law who had run the Peace Corps and the war on poverty and who said he didn't mind being seventh choice. Actually, we figured he was No. 6. At least the vacancy was filled, and McGovern could get on with his futile campaign. Shriver made no waves.

The Democrats were the only show we political reporters had. Nixon was just watching their soap opera and staying close to the White House. For every Watergate disclosure, there was a vehement White House denial. Nixon had the high hand. McGovern could denounce the war; Nixon could announce just before Labor Day that he was going to end the draft within the year.

McGovern used to come back to the press section of his campaign plane and complain to us that while we kept cross-examining him on every proposal he made, we never held Nixon accountable. That was so; we couldn't get at Nixon. Since only one candidate was campaigning, he got all the coverage, good and bad. McGovern traveled with an entourage that sometimes took three airplanes: his, the press plane, and what we called "the Zoo Plane," home to overflow reporters, TV technicians, and assorted others. It was a noisy, unkempt charter, but the bar was always open and there were spare seats.

McGovern's frustration only grew as the Watergate disclosures appeared in the *Washington Post*. Based on the *Post* reports, he said that Nixon was abusing power in a fashion that threatened a constitutional crisis, prophetic but widely ignored despite our stories about it. Nobody seemed to care.

"The men who collected millions in secret money, who passed out special favors, who ordered political sabotage, who invaded our offices in the dead of night, all of these men work for Mr. Nixon," McGovern said. They did, of course, but the accusations were not registering. Nixon wouldn't reply to McGovern. "I have been charged with being the most deceitful president in history," he said. "I am not going to dignify such comments."

The *Post* reports on Watergate and campaign sabotage pointed ever higher in the Nixon operation, then directly into the White House, and McGovern kept trying to make an issue of it. But it never took hold. Nixon and his spokesmen simply kept denying involvement—and arguing that their denials were more credible than the reporting of Woodward and Bernstein because the news accounts were based on unidentified sources. The Nixon camp succeeded in making damning disclosures into a matter of political argument.

McGovern complained to us that people were treating it like politics as usual when it was not; it was abuse of presidential power. But that did McGovern little good in the campaign. The White House stonewall stood, well beyond election day.

Nixon postured above it all. He had the presidential stage. Like all presidents he was guaranteed a crowd when he wanted one, he could make news with whatever he did, and he could travel under the guise of official business. He used those advantages and a limited campaign itinerary to sell his "four more years." He set up a grandly named operation in which other Republican figures represented him in campaigning. They were called the Surrogates. Officially there were thirty-five of them traveling for the Nixon ticket, including Cabinet members, senators, governors, and White House officials. Stand-ins for the candidate had always been part of presidential campaigns, but until Nixon, they had no fancy title. Now they were the Surrogates. Nixon was big on pomp.

McGovern was like a frustrated prizefighter who gets a title bout only to see the champion send sparring partners to face him. McGovern told me it was galling to see his hard day's campaigning boiled into ninety seconds on network television, followed by "equal time for those lackeys of Nixon's." He said he was running against a vacuum. "I'd like him to get out here and mix it up."

That was the opposite of the Nixon plan. He was a landslide ahead in the polls. The Wallace shooting in the spring had eliminated the threat of another third-party challenge like the one that plagued him in 1968, and McGovern was going nowhere. Nixon said that as president it was "necessary to stay in the White House to do the job the people elected me to do." He ducked TV debates again and made it sound like presidential patriotism. Nixon said it would not be in the national interest for him to debate McGovern because a president "makes national policy every time he opens his mouth" and a debate wasn't the place to do it.

McGovern kept trying. I watched on a cold late-autumn afternoon in Cleveland as a chill wind off Lake Erie whipped away hundreds of colored balloons that were supposed to have risen over a campaign rally as he forlornly renewed his debate demand. "Nixon knows the kind of questions he would be asked if he once came out on a public platform in face-to-face debate instead of hiding behind the surrogates and spies and saboteurs that seem to be running his campaign," McGovern said. So Nixon didn't come out.

The Vietnam issue was a pale shadow of what it had been four years before, when the war was the undoing of Johnson and then Humphrey. There was still a war on, but Americans were coming out, casualties were shrinking, and Nixon got overwhelming support in the polls that spring when he ordered the mining of North Vietnamese harbors and intensified U.S. bombing, which McGovern said risked World War III. The White House announced an outpouring of cards and telegrams supporting the Nixon orders. We dutifully reported that, and found out long after that the letters and telegrams of support had been arranged at CREEP and the Nixon people were essentially sending the messages to themselves.

At least the Democrats were colorful. Shirley MacLaine, the actress, had campaigned with McGovern off and on since spring. They walked through a ward at a veterans hospital on Long Island, shaking hands and pausing to chat, and after they had passed, one codger cackled to Jules Witcover that he'd once had an affair with the actress. When Jules told her, she laughed and said he might well have.

Earlier, her brother, actor Warren Beatty, had turned up in the McGovern entourage in Florida. One night I drove my rented car up to the valet parking stand at the Four Ambassadors Hotel in Miami, got out, and flipped the keys to a guy in denims who was standing there. When I got into the lobby, a colleague was choking with laughter. He said I'd just tossed my car keys to Warren Beatty. I doubt that he parked my car, but it was ready when I called for it the next day.

McGovern slugged on to the inevitable election burial. What could go wrong did. When he and Kennedy went out to shake hands with shoppers in a suburban Detroit mall, the amateur advance men hadn't figured out a route, and they couldn't move through the crowd. So they decided they'd give speeches instead, although there was no platform and no microphone. They wound up standing on a display table at the Barna-Bee Children's Shop trying to shout over the static of a faulty bullhorn. When McGovern dipped into his meager treasury to buy time for a dozen televised call-in sessions near the end of the campaign, the callers got hostile. "Why do you find it necessary to find so many things wrong with Mr. Nixon when he doesn't say anything against you?" a woman asked him in Seattle. He said that as the opposition candidate he had every right to challenge the president. "Instead of accusing me of mudslinging I wish you would use whatever influence you have to get Mr. Nixon to come out of the White House, to come out of hiding," he said.

McGovern's strategy wasn't working but he stuck to it as his campaign sank, concentrating on nine major states where he claimed he stood a chance (he lost them all). He went regularly to Ohio, prompting us to put new lyrics to a tune from *Wonderful Town*.

> Why, oh why, oh why, oh,
> Do we keep going to Ohio?
> Why must you humblus with so much Columbus,
> We'd rather see Athens or Nome.

McGovern laughed at our rendition and then seriously lectured us on the importance of Ohio's twenty-six electoral votes.

Near the end of his futile 200,000-mile campaign route, McGovern finally had enough one day in Battle Creek, Michigan. A portly young man festooned with Nixon buttons heckled him as he shook hands along the airport fence. "Nixon will beat you so bad you'll wish you'd never left South Dakota," the man said. McGovern stopped and leaned toward the guy's ear. "I've got a secret for you," he said in a whisper loud enough for a reporter to hear. "Kiss my ass."

The election ran to form, a Nixon runaway. McGovern carried only Massachusetts, plus the District of Columbia. Nixon was a winner doomed by his own tainted tactics, at the head of a Republican ticket he did not help. He didn't try. CREEP claimed all the money it could get for the presidential campaign, leaving other GOP candidates short of campaign funds. The Democrats actually gained two seats in the Senate plus a governor, and lost only a dozen House seats to the Republicans despite the presidential landslide. The morning after,

Nixon issued a call for the resignations of his entire Cabinet and staff, not intending to accept many of them, but sending the strangest of victory signals to the people who had campaigned for him, Surrogates and all.

I wrote that it was a lonely landslide.

When Nixon wrote his memoirs, he said that he had been reelected with a toothache, the result of a broken cap. "I am at a loss to explain the melancholy that settled over me on that victorious night," he wrote. "Perhaps it was caused by the toothache." The ache was going to get a lot worse. Within six months he would have to force the resignations of his two senior aides, H. R. Haldeman and John Ehrlichman, trying to cut his own losses in Watergate. In 1974, he'd have to resign himself.

William P. Rogers, then the secretary of state, told me years later that Nixon had tried to get him to tell Haldeman and Ehrlichman to resign in April 1973. Rogers said he replied that they were Nixon's men and he'd have to do it. "Well then," he said, "will you come up to Camp David while I tell them?" Rogers agreed. When he got to the presidential retreat he was ushered to his cabin and found instructions to join the president and the other two at another lodge. Rogers said he started out the door and then stopped himself. He said it occurred to him that Nixon was just tricky enough to leave him alone with Haldeman and Ehrlichman, effectively forcing him to carry the resignation message. He called the other cabin and found out that the president had done it when Nixon's butler, Manolo, answered the phone. "Is the president there?" Rogers asked. "Yes, and so are Mr. Haldeman and Mr. Ehrlichman and they're all crying."

One more Watergate postscript: As the scandal and impeachment unfolded it became a badge of honor among journalists to have been included on the "enemies list" the Nixon crowd put together. It was the mark of a tough political reporter. I always thought I was a fair one. But I must confess that I wound up on another list. In a 1969 White House memo, Haldeman told Herb Klein that the president wanted "a list of all his good personal friends in the working press."

"I don't know exactly what he has in mind on this," Haldeman wrote.

So Klein put together a list of forty-nine names, which surfaced years later in the Nixon archives. My name was on it. I don't know what he had in mind, either.

FIVE

Jimmy Who, Plain Old Jerry, and the Pulitzer Prize: The 1976 Campaign

G erald R. Ford was a bland, balding Republican congressman from Michigan, a political nice guy, the House minority leader but no political star. Nobody ever envisioned him as a president, certainly not Richard Nixon, who once told insiders that appointing Ford his vice president in 1973 was his insurance against being forced out of office in Watergate. Bad guess, because Ford not only became president, his plain talk rallied Americans past the nightmare scandal Nixon and his henchmen had visited upon them.

Jimmy Carter was a former Georgia governor and as unlikely a candidate when he began his campaign from Democratic obscurity. Carter got started early, long before Ford was summoned from Congress to become vice president in 1973, the only man ever to take that office and then the presidency itself without election to either job.

In the end, the improbable Democrat beat the unelected Republican, but only narrowly. It was not surprising that Ford lost the 1976 election. That he came close to winning it was a political miracle for a humdrum Republican who had never before run in an election outside his Michigan congressional district, who came to the presidency because of his own party's scandal, and worsened his situation by pardoning Nixon for Watergate crimes.

The 1976 presidential campaign was a political show no scriptwriter could have invented. It was the first campaign subsidized by the government, with candidates who could prove significant public support for their party nominations entitled to have their contributions matched by Washington. That was a magnet for candidates, as were the thirty primary elections in which Democratic rules required that even far-back losers who managed at least 15 percent of the vote get shares of a state's nominating delegates in proportion to their popular votes.

So the prospects and pretenders lined up, with Carter first, at the start as at the end. When he began, Carter was a former governor of Georgia with no national standing. Carter said he was so obscure that he couldn't even get anybody to rake his muck, although he always insisted there was none to rake. Carter said he never misrepresented or lied, never would, and had never in his life made a promise he didn't keep. That in itself defied belief, but he kept saying it. Think of it—the first president since George Washington who never told a lie, and Carter hadn't even chopped down a cherry tree. But there was a tough politician behind the façade, and if he didn't lie, he certainly bent the record when it suited his campaign purposes.

Ford had to fend off the challenge of Ronald Reagan for the Republican nomination, and barely did. He wouldn't have but for the Republican protocol of going by the pecking order, which meant renominating the sitting president even though they would have preferred the more conservative, more polished performer from California.

For a reporter, it was great political theater and I got a bonus along with my front row seat. I received the 1977 Pulitzer Prize for national reporting for my coverage of that campaign. Gene McCarthy used to say that you knew you were over the hill when you started quoting yourself, but that didn't stop him from doing so, and I will risk it. One of the stories in my Pulitzer entry described the candidates as "Gerald R. Ford, who never sought the presidency until he held it, and Jimmy Carter, the driving, self-started Democratic challenger." I wrote before the election that Carter led narrowly by standard measurements.

"However, this is not a standard election, this contest to restore the seal of voter approval to a White House that has lacked it for 27 months."

The Pulitzer Prizes are awarded in the spring and most winners, being reporters themselves, find out about it in advance. With a clue, you could wear your best suit to work for the celebration. I had no hint. I didn't even know the date the Pulitzers were being awarded that year, although I certainly remember it now, April 18, 1977. I was going out of town that week, so I went to get my hair cut and to buy a new pair of shoes. The AP bureau couldn't figure out where I was when word of my prize hit the wire. I did my errands and was headed back to the office when I met two colleagues carrying cases of champagne. Before I could ask what that was all about, Ann Blackman told me, "You just won the Pulitzer Prize." I was stunned. We walked into the bureau and all of my colleagues stood up and started applauding. At first I was too dazed to say anything except "Let me see the bulletin." I wanted to see on paper that I really had received the highest honor in my profession. I read it, took a few minutes to settle down, thanked people, and shook hands. The moment I remember best was on the telephone a few minutes later. I called my father, retired in New Hampshire. "Dad, I just won the Pulitzer Prize," I told him. He didn't say anything for a few moments, and when he did speak, his voice was too choked with emotion to be understood. At that point, mine was, too. By my desk I have an unabridged dictionary my parents gave me that spring, inscribed with "a deep sense of pride for which we cannot find the words."

When you get a Pulitzer, everybody you know calls, and so do some people you don't. My friend Jules Witcover called to congratulate me and added, "I suppose you're wearing those awful pants." He knew my fashion taste, or lack of it, too well. I had on checked, bell-bottom double-knit pants, which I now know should not have been worn on my worst day at the office let alone my best. The AP photo that moved on the wire that day shows me standing with one foot on the desk, one checked pantleg all too prominent, on the telephone with a cigar in my mouth. When newspapers published the lineup of Pulitzer winners the next day, it was a row of serious journalists with an oddball AP guy in the middle. I'm still stuck with that awful photo. It is the one selected by the Newseum, the museum of journalism, to go with my biography in their display.

One of my calls that day came from an agent who wanted to represent me on the speaking circuit. I never was comfortable making speeches for a fee, wary of anything that might seem to conflict with my work. So I told the agent no. I also said I thought it was amusing to be called a few hours after I won the Pulitzer. "I'm not any smarter than I was yesterday," I said. But at age forty-two, I did know the lead on my obituary: "Pulitzer Prize–winning journalist," or some variation of those words.

After the 1972 election, I accepted a management job, becoming assistant chief of the Washington bureau of the AP. The job was to help manage a bureau of more than one hundred reporters and photographers, satisfying work when it dealt with the news, frustrating when it involved complaints from headquarters in New York and from dissatisfied newspapers. There was too much of the latter for my taste. I spent too many hours researching and explaining last week's slipup, not enough working on next week's stories. I dealt with it but I didn't like it. When Ford became president in 1974, he hired an old friend, Jerald ter Horst of the *Detroit News,* to become White House press secretary. Jerry resigned as bureau chief of the *News* to take the job, and the editor called me, offering half again the salary I was getting at the AP, with a company car for good measure. It added up, and I left the AP to take the *News* offer. (By the time I did, Jerry had quit the White House in protest at the Nixon pardon, becoming a columnist.) My new job was cushy and relaxed by AP standards. I hated it. I was used to the pressure and urgency of the wire, not the more leisurely pace I found. It was a good bureau and a good paper, with good people. It just wasn't my place, and I hadn't been there a month before I knew that I wanted to go back to my professional home. In less than a year, I did, returning to the AP after Labor Day 1975 as a special correspondent. I was a reporter again and there was a campaign beginning again. I took a pay cut to go back. No company car, either. I never regretted it.

Carter had rewritten the calendar for presidential candidates by starting his campaign earlier than anyone before. That was the only way up for the man who began as "Jimmy Who?" He spent twenty-two months campaigning actively, toting his trademark garment bag over his shoulder from airports to Holiday Inns or borrowed beds in the homes of supporters. He began his first address as the Democratic nominee with the line he had uttered from a thousand platforms: "My name is Jimmy Carter and I'm running for president." It was part nostalgia, part told-you-so to the Democratic establishment that would have preferred somebody else—Ted Kennedy if he would have run, or Hubert Humphrey if he hadn't been so shopworn, or Walter Mondale if he'd had the stomach for the rigors of the campaign. Fourteen Democrats did try, some so pointlessly that they had to get out shortly after they got started.

The most persistent of the losers was Representative Morris K. Udall of Arizona, "old second-place Mo" as he came to call himself after chasing Carter in almost every presidential primary. Udall was a man with a serious program to offer and a serious campaign to run, but he didn't let that make him pompous. He used to tell his campaign audiences about the day he introduced himself at a barbershop in Keene, New Hampshire:

" 'Hi. I'm Mo Udall and I'm running for president,' I said. And he said to me, 'Yeah, I know, we were just laughing about it.' " Udall said he was at least distinctive because, as he liked to observe, except for him there were no six-foot-five, one-eyed Mormons who had played pro basketball running for president that year. The campaign wore on him, but it never wore out his humor.

One night he draped himself over a threadbare blue chair in what passed for a fancy suite at a hotel in New Hampshire and mused on the lifestyle of the candidate. "There goes the imperial presidency bit," he said, sipping his Scotch and water. "Who the hell reserved this one?"

The 1976 campaign sequence began, inevitably, with Richard Nixon, who shaped it when he resigned the presidency to avoid impeachment for Watergate. Agnew, his vice president, had been forced to resign in 1973 to escape jail for tax evasion on bribes he'd taken from Maryland contractors since his days as county executive. For the first time, the president chose the vice president, subject to approval by Congress. Nixon nominated Ford, the House minority leader, a man with the seniority and congressional standing for easy confirmation. No superstar, just a plain-vanilla congressman, which was fine with Nixon, who didn't want any long shadows cast by the man standing behind him.

So it was Vice President Ford and then President Ford when, on August 9, 1974, Nixon became the first president ever to resign the office. Ford said at first that he might not run for a term in his own right in 1976, but he got over that after eleven months as president by appointment.

So the president who quit was the effective kingmaker and king slayer of the Republican campaign of 1976. Nixon's Watergate crimes haunted the party and the Ford ticket. The Nixon pardon made the burden heavier for Ford. Then, instead of gratefully getting out of the way in 1976, Nixon persisted in claiming attention from his political exile.

But for Nixon, Ford would not have been running. But for the baggage Nixon left, he might well have been elected.

Nixon wouldn't shut up. He wouldn't go away. Just before the New Hampshire primary, with Ford struggling to hold off Ronald Reagan, Nixon emerged from exile for his first public venture since his resignation—a high-profile visit to China. The Chinese sent a jetliner to pick him up in California. The skeleton was out of the closet. New Hampshire voters started asking Ford again about the unconditional pardon he had granted the resigned president in September 1974. It had to hurt in a primary election Ford won by only 1,317 votes. I never figured out why Ford didn't renounce Nixon as a bothersome ingrate meddling in foreign policy. Instead, Ford said he'd asked Nixon to relay his greetings to Mao Tse-tung.

Lyndon Johnson once called Nixon a chronic campaigner. Carter became one in his quest for the Democratic nomination. He began planning his 1976 campaign before McGovern's drubbing in the 1972 election. He'd been interested in joining the McGovern ticket and had let the nominee know he was available for vice president. Fortunately for Carter, McGovern never called.

Carter waged the prototype nonstop campaign, planning and preparing for the better part of two years even before his marathon run for the nomination, which he began with his support in public opinion polls barely above the 3 percent margin of error, which meant, statistically, that he could have been near zero. He made about 1,500 speeches, in about one thousand cities. He went to all fifty states. He traveled nearly a half million miles. It was told that after a wearying campaign day, a bleary-eyed Carter inadvertently grabbed the hand of a department store mannequin. Hubert Humphrey once remarked that after enough campaigning, a candidate's hand becomes a frozen stump and the handshake itself becomes an act of hostility, not friendship.

When strategist Hamilton Jordan set out the campaign plan to Carter, he told the candidate it would be vital to cultivate the right political reporters in order to get national attention. Jordan figured there were about forty worth knowing, but at first he could only come up with eighteen names. Carter followed instructions. I saw him in New Hampshire early on, and he said, "I've heard good things about you." I didn't know why. In those precampaign days, I hadn't heard much about him.

With that garment bag, he looked like a salesman, and he was one, pitching himself. Another point in the Jordan blueprint was that stories about a candidate in the *New York Times* and the *Washington Post* don't just happen; they have to be planned. Which meant that he had to get somebody to pay attention to him. The Carter folks figured that one way was to compete in some straw polls early on, when just showing up would be enough to lead them. So they organized to get votes in window-dressing straw polls before any of the other candidates bothered or paid attention. All it took was a handful of votes to beat the rest of the field, and Carter did. Suddenly, the meaningless straw poll at a Democratic dinner in Iowa had meaning—it got Carter's name in the newspaper and on television. I had colleagues who boasted at the time that they had discovered Jimmy Carter in Iowa. I think he discovered them first, engineering stories that billed him as a formidable candidate in the state where the first Democratic votes of the campaign would be registered in neighborhood caucuses. No candidate before had devoted the kind of attention and effort Carter invested in Iowa, and it paid dividends. He led the precinct caucuses, the first voting of 1976, with 28 percent of the vote. That made him the winner among candidates, although the real winner, nearly 10 percent stronger, was the vote to remain uncommitted. Even so, Iowa was the send-off Carter needed and he arrived in New Hampshire a made man.

There was a crowd waiting—fourteen candidates, five of them with broad enough backing to have qualified for federal campaign aid, in which donations were matched after a candidate proved himself by raising $5,000 in small contributions in each of twenty states.

Mo Udall was there, joking as usual. He said he'd adopted the platform of the sheriff of Tombstone, Arizona: "Ladies and gentlemen, them is my views, and if you don't like 'em, I'll change 'em." Only joking, he told his rallies, presenting himself as the real Democrat, the dedicated liberal who would pursue the traditional objectives of the party. Later in the campaign, Udall went out to shake hands at dawn at a Pittsburgh plant gate. "Here's Mo Udall," a union host announced. "Come over here and tell him our problems." One steelworker shook Udall's hand, eyed the weary campaigner, and walked away. "He's got more problems than I do," the man told the union guy. I have an age-yellowed note to myself, saved for unremembered reasons, on an interview with Udall in his Boston hotel room. We're both tired. I ask, he answers, questions about the coming primaries, about Carter, about what happens next. But as he talks, Udall starts rubbing his eyes, including the glass one. And suddenly my attention is off the interview and on his left eye. He's rubbing it hard. I conjure up a scene in which that glass eye is going to pop out and it is going to roll across the room. It will be like the football game when the player loses his contact lens. Referees, linesmen, everybody on his hands and knees, pawing the football field for the contact lens.

Except we'll be looking for an eye, not a lens, and it probably will roll under the couch and be hell to find. My notes are becoming decidedly eccentric. That's enough interviewing. Thanks, Mo. Good night.

Carter was a center-right Democrat, but he didn't concentrate on philosophy. His secret was to play it both ways. At a rally in Dallas, the band brought him onstage with an appropriate medley: "Dixie" and "The Battle Hymn of the Republic." Carter ran as the anti-Nixon, the trust-me candidate. He went to church every Sunday, read the Bible; the religious dedication was part of the image. "I'll never tell a lie. I'll never make a misleading statement. I've never made a promise in my life that I didn't keep," he said in speech after speech. And if that claim wasn't a lie, he was a saint. One way not to make political promises he didn't keep was to make promises so vague that he could not be held to specific commitments. He said, for example, that he would cut the federal government from 1,900 to 200 agencies, but he would not say which ones would go. No matter; nothing of the sort ever happened.

Nor did he jettison the entire tax code, "a disgrace to the human race." One of my images of candidate Carter is of a man standing at a lectern with thick law books piled so high he had to peer around them, not over them. That's the disgraceful tax code, he would explain, then promise that he would erase it in favor of a simpler, fairer system. That, of course, did not happen either.

It angered him when people complained that he was indefinite and imprecise. When he heard that Ted Kennedy had said so, Carter snapped to an *Atlanta Journal* reporter, "I'm glad that I don't have to depend on Kennedy or Hubert Humphrey or anyone like that to put me in office. I don't have to kiss his ass." That didn't sound much like Jimmy the Baptist, but he would periodically step out of that character, usually because he was angry.

To get to the nomination, Carter had to climb through a crowd of Democratic candidates, a roster of political pilgrims who didn't yet know they were going nowhere.

Sargent Shriver, for example, was trying to prove himself more than a Kennedy brother-in-law. It didn't help that his plan to seek the nomination had been leaked into print by Senator Kennedy, who had opened the whole field in the first place by announcing he would not be a candidate. Jules Witcover went to see Kennedy to check the story about Shriver's plans. In his book *Marathon*, Witcover reported Kennedy's account: "He told me he was going to run and I wished him well." That seemed the faintest of praise. So Witcover needled the senator about it. " 'Well,' I asked him, 'if Benito Mussolini walked in here and told you he was going to run, would you wish him well?' Kennedy laughed and then, grinning broadly this time, said, 'If he was married to my sister.' " Shriver staggered through the early primaries and quit after spending more than $800,000, saying that he had achieved remarkable success in view of all his handicaps, not least the idea that he was just trading on family connections. At that price, success had to be in the eye of the candidate with a family fortune.

The story went that before he quit the campaign, Shriver walked into a bar near the Boston waterfront and cried heartily, "Beer for the house. And I'll have a Courvoisier." Shriver insisted it never happened. He said Tip O'Neill made it up. Perhaps he did, but Shriver's problem was that people believe it could have happened, whether it did or not.

Birch Bayh, a senator from Indiana, was running in place, too. He lasted two primaries. Bayh was all hands; he liked the politics of touch. He punched people playfully in the arm. It was said that Bobby Kennedy once threatened that if Bayh punched him in the arm one more time, he'd punch him in the nose. In Concord, New Hampshire, Bayh walked up to a man, stuck out his hand, and said, "Hi. Birch Bayh of Indiana." "Hi. Chris Wells of New Hampshire," the man said, and walked away. One day Bayh talked about the horror of nuclear war. "If I'm president, and I'm kind of horrified to think about it," he began, and paused. Somebody started laughing and then everybody did.

Fred Harris, a senator from Oklahoma, was never going to be president, but he was going to not do it with a touch of class. When his turn came to speak in a droning, ninety-minute campaign debate, Harris suggested that the TV audience would appreciate it if they'd agree to play a tape of Muhammad Ali's last fight instead. He'd run briefly in 1972 and didn't get anywhere then, either. He was deadly serious about his issues but not about himself. His last campaign words bear retelling:

"You couldn't call it victory because we didn't run that well. But we ran just well enough to keep going. So it wasn't really defeat. So we didn't know what to call it and we just decided to call it quits."

Then he told about the guy who was defeated for sheriff but showed up the next day wearing his pistol anyhow. "Somebody said, 'Well, Willie, what are you doing with that pistol? You didn't get elected sheriff.' He said, 'Listen, anybody who doesn't have more friends than I do needs protection.' " Udall's variation was the crack he made in conceding one in his succession of primary defeats: "The people have spoken, the bastards."

Senator Henry Jackson of Washington was running again. Since 1972, he'd had surgery to correct a drooping eyelid and create a new, alert look. We used to joke that his audiences needed an alertness booster more than he did. Jackson, a senator of substance and achievement, was no orator although he'd been instructed to try to be demonstrative. He overdid it. On the platform, Jackson looked as though he were demonstrating karate. Chop, point, wave, slash. He won two primaries, including Massachusetts, where court-ordered school busing had the voters inflamed. In one of his more bizarre boasts, Jackson used to tell people how he had courageously confronted that issue: "I laid it on the line. I took on the bigots . . . I told them I was against forced busing." That was some ultimatum—what Jackson told them was, obviously, exactly what they wanted to hear.

George Wallace was telling them what they wanted to hear, too. In three campaigns, the Alabaman had become a national political force, despite the 1972 assassination attempt that had cost the use of his legs. Now he was campaigning again, in pain and in fear, running when he could not walk, and without a chance of winning. "When I was taken out of the primaries," he would say, meaning when he was shot and partially paralyzed. The boisterous Wallace rallies of earlier campaigns were shadows now; people were searched for weapons at the door, and the former governor who used to glory in wading through crowds now spoke from behind a bulletproof plastic shield. Getting there was trying, too, because Wallace was afraid of flying. But he kept going. "Some folks in government are paralyzed in the head," he told his crowds. "At least I'm not paralyzed in the head, I'm paralyzed in the legs." If this were any other candidate, you would assume that ambitious men were using him, forcing him to run despite the torment. But this was George Wallace, and campaigning was what he did.

In Boston, where tempers were heated over school busing for racial desegregation, I watched him play the Orpheum Theater. Vaudeville was back on the old stage in new, political trappings. First the warm-up man, barker and cheerleader in one, to get things started, and then the country-and-western music folks, pickin' and singin' for George. Then the candidate, wheeled to the stage, lifted into position behind his bulletproof lectern. The body was broken but the voice still strong against those unelected bureaucrats and judges, those "social experimenters" who wanted to bus children away from their neighborhood schools. The Wallace theme was "Send them a message," and this time it would be a message from liberal Massachusetts if he got any kind of support in the Democratic primary. (He ran fourth.) All right, Wallace said that night at the Orpheum, he wouldn't win the primary tomorrow, but he'd do better than expected. Under Wallace rules, any votes at all should count as more than expected.

I'd seen the Wallace shows in three campaigns. This was a sad reprise in a fitting setting. The Orpheum was long past its prime, but a majestic relic. The blue paint was peeling from the balcony, the vast maroon curtain looked worn, seedy. The murals over the stage were faded; the columned loges and vast lobbies were mementos of another era. After vaudeville, the theater went to screen and stage acts, then to movies, then to whoever wanted to hire a hall for a night. Last night it was the Black Muslims. Tonight, Wallace Campaign Inc. Tomorrow, dark.

Along with the name candidates there were, as always, fringe entries. The Reverend Arthur O. Blessitt, for example, who sometimes campaigned carrying a big cross, later found to have had a small wheel at the bottom making it easier to maneuver. With the Federal Election Commission in business, there was now a government agency to which the token and oddball candidates could report that they were running for president, so that they could at least seem to be official. I got the FEC list and wrote a story about the more than forty names on it. One of them was a man who called himself Joe America and I put him in my story. His widow called after it appeared to say he had killed himself some time after he filed, an awkward development I decided I could only make worse by doing a follow-up to report why he wasn't running.

After leading the field in Iowa and winning the New Hampshire primary, Carter was the Democrat to beat. He had the organization, he had the campaign contacts, and he was not going to be stopped. He also got the breaks. In the Wisconsin primary, Udall seemed to have upset the favored Carter, holding his first and only victory rally of the primary season before it turned out he'd lost. ABC and NBC both declared that Udall had won. The AP did not. Dion Henderson, our Milwaukee bureau chief, knew his state too well to get it wrong. Too many precincts are still out in the Janesville area, he said. It's conservative Democratic country, and Carter is going to catch up there. He did. The newsman knew better than the network computers.

But the *Milwaukee Sentinel* went to press with a banner headline: "CARTER UPSET BY UDALL." And the bare survival that would have been an embarrassment to the front-running Carter became instead a Harry Truman moment. The next day's news photographs were of the beaming Carter holding up the front page, as Truman had displayed the *Chicago Tribune* that incorrectly announced his defeat by Thomas E. Dewey in 1948.

Udall took it with wry, painful humor. "You may amend my statement of last night and insert the word 'Loser' where I had 'Winner,' " he told us at his morning-after news conference. He kept running second to Carter. "I'm old second-place Mo," he told us. "We'll get the nomination on the second ballot." Except that there would not be a second ballot because Carter won on the first one, as had every convention nominee, in both parties, since 1952.

The stop-Carter movement—an alliance of the Jackson campaign, proxies for Humphrey, and organized labor—tried to peak in Pennsylvania. Carter peaked instead. When he won that primary, his seventh victory, the contest was effectively settled, the nomination his, even though two more rivals came off the Democratic bench and beat him more often than they lost to him.

Carter made his mistakes. For example, he used a line that might have crippled a candidate in more politically correct times. He defended "ethnic purity" in American neighborhoods. He said he saw nothing wrong with it and would not force racial integration of a neighborhood by government action.

Questioned about it later, he repeated the phrase and said he resented any suggestion that it was racist. He finally admitted he'd made a serious mistake and apologized for it. While he was trying to live it down, a campaign invitation came in from the Family of Leaders, a group of middle-class blacks in Philadelphia. He figured it was a drop-by appearance; instead he was stuck for three hours. Before Carter was introduced to the audience, the audience was introduced to him, one at a time, about 180 people. A man in a blue jacket with the odd label "Ducky's Dashery" passed among them with a microphone so that every member of the audience could do a self-introduction by name and organization. And some of them were real joiners, with long lists of affiliations to tell Carter about. "I won't be any better president than I am a candidate. I'm going to make some mistakes," he said when he finally got to speak. One of which clearly was not going to be a return engagement before the Family of Leaders.

The new Democratic rivals awaiting Carter in the closing month of the primaries were Senator Frank Church of Idaho and Governor Edmund G. Brown Jr. of California, Reagan's free-form successor. Each won four states but it was too late to stop Carter. He won when and where it counted. Carter lost two out of three primaries to Brown on the last day of the season, but he won big in Ohio, closing in the delegate majority he needed, and convincing the party's powers that he was their man, like him or not.

Carter liked to say that he had no need of political big shots or bosses in his campaign. Maybe he didn't need them, but he certainly used their services. He kept in regular contact, privately, with Chicago's Mayor Daley. After the primaries, the mayor returned the favor, saluting Carter's eighteen victories and telling the party there was no reason to hesitate in lining up behind the inevitable nominee. "Carter's victory in Ohio is the ball game," Daley said. Favor for favor, when nominee Carter got to Chicago he called Daley "the greatest mayor in the world."

In the Republican primary campaign, the only president never elected started fast but then stumbled against Reagan, the former California governor who had his own celebrity as a movie actor and television host. They were mostly B movies, but Reagan was an A performer on the campaign stage. He would easily have won the 1976 nomination had Ford not reversed his early disclaimer of candidacy and run for the office he held by appointment. Reagan came close to winning the nomination anyhow, despite Ford's presidential pulpit and his efforts to placate the Republican right. The major one was the campaign sacrifice of Vice President Nelson A. Rockefeller. Ford had nominated Rockefeller his vice president and Congress had concurred, but the conservatives never had liked the New Yorker and never would. So the Ford political people began sending signals that Rockefeller should renounce his candidacy. When the Ford campaign committee opened, the signs and banners bore his name only, no mention of Rockefeller.

At an outdoor presidential news conference that summer, where the legs of the folding chairs sank into the mud of the overwatered South Lawn of the White House, I joined the clamor for recognition to ask a question. I wanted to ask Ford whether the absence of his vice president's name at his newly opened campaign headquarters meant that Rockefeller was going to be replaced on the ticket. The answer was obvious—he was out—but Ford almost certainly would have ducked the question somehow. I never got to ask it. Another reporter jumped up in the row in front of me and shouted his question instead. Washington was hot and humid in the summer, this guy asked incisively, so would Ford be prepared to absolve men from wearing neckties to work? Sure, said Ford, after which somebody shouted, "Thank you, Mr. President," and the news conference was over. Vice President Rockefeller yielded that fall and said he did not want to run again, quitting before he could be fired from the 1976 ticket. Ford operatives thought maybe they could get Reagan onto the ticket. But Reagan didn't want to run with Ford; he wanted to run over him.

So it would be Reagan the showman against the solid, stolid Ford. "I have been called an unelected president, an accidental president," Ford would say later in the campaign. "We may even hear that again." Actually, it went without saying. It was so. Then, too, Ford was charismatically-challenged. "Gerry Ford gave a fireside chat and the fire went to sleep," said Mark Russell, Washington's resident comedian.

Ford's plain, everyman beginning as president, "a Ford, not a Lincoln," the guy who got up and made his own breakfast, was in winning contrast to the wily pomposity of the Nixon White House. But Reagan was a performer, showing the style he would patent when he did become president. He was the master of the unassailable statistic. "Did you know that there is more than three-fourths as much forest in America today as there was when Washington was at Valley Forge?" he asked one crowd. "Do you know that there are more white-tailed deer?" No, on both counts. I didn't know that. When I asked Reagan how he knew it, he said he'd read it somewhere. He also had read or heard somewhere that the paperwork generated by the bureaucracy in Washington in a year would make a pile one hundred feet high, one hundred feet wide, and 4,500 feet long. Prove that wrong. Or right. "I think it would make a great annual bonfire," he said.

One frigid day he climbed on top of a pile of feed sacks in front of a country store in Cornish Flats, New Hampshire, and warmed to the numbers game, complaining about the obstacles the government put in the path of new nuclear power plants. Reagan said it took eleven years to get one built because of all the "fairy tales" about risks, which he claimed were infinitesimal. "The odds against a fatality are one in three hundred million," he declared. "Your odds against having a fatal automobile accident are only one in four thousand . . . of getting struck by lightning one in two million, a hurricane or tornado one in two and a half million, your odds of drowning one in thirty thousand." He had more odds, but I didn't write them down.

I did ask Reagan's campaign aides where all those numbers had come from. One said the National Safety Council. Another said Jimmy the Greek. A third said he didn't care. A week later, the campaign sent me a memo, saying the odds were taken from the report of a task force that studied nuclear risk ratios for the government.

So informed, I covered what the Reagan campaign called a Citizens Press Conference. Those were fake Reagan news conferences at which only ordinary citizens, not reporters, were allowed to ask questions. That way the questions were almost always the same and easy to answer. But at Dartmouth College, a young man who had seen Reagan's nuclear risk numbers had a trick question for the candidate: "Do you know what the odds would be for a horse to drown in molasses?" Reagan didn't know but he said that didn't affect all the research that proved nukes safe. Nobody knew. There were no odds for what happened to the horse in Boston's North End in the Great Molasses Flood of 1916, when the streets flowed in the stuff from a factory disaster. The questioner was a student who had been riding the campaign press bus as a reporter for his college newspaper. The Reagan people kicked him off, saying that he was no longer entitled to ride the bus because he had disqualified himself as a reporter by asking a question at a Citizens Press Conference. That taught him. Play by their rules or walk home.

Reagan was the government minimalist. One New Hampshire campaign day I heard him ponder what would happen if the government just quit for a while. "I wonder if we were to close the doors and sneak away for a few weeks, I wonder how long it would take the American people to miss us," he said, drawing a ripple of laughter from a confused audience that had come to hear him tell what he wanted to do as president, not that the job was irrelevant.

"What is wrong is that an intellectual elite living on the shores of the Potomac has taken over our decision-making," Reagan said that day, a line that could have come from a George Wallace dissertation on pointy-headed bureaucrats.

Those were bits from the Speech, the set piece Reagan delivered as he campaigned, little changed from the text he had used when he was in the lecture and broadcast business before he ran. He always had been a one-speech man. I covered him during his first campaign for governor of California in 1966 and flew with him one day in a four-seat plane for an appearance in the San Joaquin valley, farm country. The use of migrant Mexicans, then called *braceros,* as farm laborers was an issue in that campaign. Reagan opposed federal plans to cut back the number of migrants admitted to work the fields, arguing that the Mexicans would do jobs Americans would not take. Stooping to cut asparagus, for example. He made the asparagus-cutting part of his set speech, as unvaried a dissertation as any theatrical script. Flying up to the valley that morning it got hot and Reagan got thirsty. He asked the pilot for a cold drink but there wasn't any, except for a bottle of champagne in a cooler under the seat. So the campaign hop became a 10:00 A.M. champagne flight. We sipped, chatted, and looked down at the checkerboard of farm fields below. I jokingly asked Reagan whether that was asparagus growing down there. He solemnly delivered the *bracero* speech, word for word.

Reagan's 1976 campaign did one thing for late night television. It knocked *Bedtime for Bonzo* off the air. That was one of Reagan's fifty-one movies, the one in which his costar was a chimpanzee. Dartmouth students showed it one night to needle him while he was campaigning in Hanover, but Reagan wasn't bothered. "That was a good movie," he said. It was off the rerun air because the Federal Communications Commission had ruled that equal time rules would apply to any TV station that broadcast Reagan movies. Equal time for what was not clear, since Ford didn't make movies.

Things kept happening to Ford. He stumbled down the steps of Air Force One. He bumped his head on the helicopter door. He tumbled on a ski slope. No matter that he was the most athletic president since Theodore Roosevelt. He was accident prone, to be kind. To be cruel, he looked like a klutz. At a rally in North Carolina, a Ford supporter introduced the president defensively, as "a man who has proved he can win elections and chew gum at the same time." He lost the primary there. Ford went to California to campaign for S. I. Hayakawa for senator and called him Hayakama. It was alleged that Ford had said Hiawatha, which wasn't true but made print anyhow. Hayakawa won.

In Walnut Creek, California, he was dedicating a replica of the Liberty Bell and was supposed to ring it. When he reached for the clapper it came unhooked and fell out of the bell.

When the Nashua, New Hampshire, chamber of commerce honored its man of the year, President Ford was there for a perfect photo opportunity. Or nearly perfect. The winner was the chief fund-raiser for the Reagan primary campaign against Ford.

Then there was the dairy tour in Cambellsport, Wisconsin, when Ford got too close to a cow, which soiled the presidential pants. They hustled out to the motorcade for another suit and Ford changed in the farmhouse.

Both parties had cow problems. In Omaha, Nebraska, the Carter campaign staged a mock cattle auction as a fund-raising gimmick. A cow was supposed to be led down the street to publicize the event. But it went berserk and had to be hauled off to the stockyards. "It was not a committed cow," Carter said.

In Concord, New Hampshire, Ford met Tommy Boyd, fourteen, who had a cast on his left arm.

"How did you get that?" the president asked.

"I fell," Tommy replied.

"I fall a lot, too," Ford said.

By then, Ford's press secretary, Ron Nessen, was sporting a "Ski New Hampshire" button at every public appearance, atonement for his politically regrettable remark that the president found the slopes there too icy for his skiing. And his campaign spokesman, Peter Kaye, was trying to get over a gaffe of his own. The Ford campaign had dropped a plan to canvass door-to-door, walking the state, in political parlance. They would use telephone canvassing instead. More effective, Kaye said, although we reporters knew the real reason was a shortage of volunteer canvassers.

"New Hampshire is a difficult state to organize," Kaye said. "It's a helluva state to walk in because if you get forty miles outside the city, there's nothing but trees and bears." Not a smart start in an effort to get primary votes. "I put my paw in my mouth," Kaye confessed.

Reagan had his own set of problems. There was the Social Security hangover, a touchy issue in New Hampshire, where elderly voters were a powerful constituency. As a Goldwater champion, Reagan had joined in promoting the idea that the system should be voluntary, a proposal he now disowned. When he stirred a controversy by suggesting that Social Security funds might be invested in the stock market, Reagan got out of it with a ploy he would use as president, saying it wasn't a proposal from him, just an idea he had read about. He finally ducked the Social Security issue with the cop-out politicians always use, saying a commission should study the system and its future financing.

In New Hampshire, Reagan's best friends were at times his worst headaches. Governor Meldrim Thomson, for example, the textbook publisher who became a textbook right-wing Republican and cultivated state conservatives for Reagan. The trouble was that he insisted Reagan was going to beat Ford outright in the primary. The Reagan people wanted him to be quiet; they were trying to play down expectations, saying that 40 or 45 percent of the vote would be a victory against a sitting president. Thomson wouldn't stop. Just before the voting he said on national television that Reagan would beat Ford by at least five percentage points. With Thomson's unintentional help, Ford won the expectations game.

The Republican primary vote was close to a tie, Ford winning by less than 1 percent. Reagan claimed a moral victory, pointing to the way McCarthy in 1968 and McGovern in 1972 had been judged winners in defeat. Not this time. Ford had won his first election outside his Grand Rapids, Michigan, House district, after trailing in the early polls and in Thomson's late forecasts of a Reagan victory. In different circumstances, a standoff would have been an embarrassing setback for a sitting president. But for Ford, any victory was victory enough.

Reagan was the glamour candidate, although it didn't do him much good at the beginning of the primary campaign. Ford plodded past him in the first three primaries and the question became when Reagan would throw in the hand. Even John Sears, Nixon's 1968 primary genius, then the Reagan manager, talked privately about withdrawal after a Ford landslide in Illinois. But Reagan wasn't quitting; he still had cards to play. And Ford was misplaying his. His people were overconfident, counting on a North Carolina primary victory that would end the Reagan threat. Actually, the Reagan people expected to lose, too. They were planning a last try, an address on national television, hoping for a performance as igniting as the one he had given for Goldwater in 1964. But Reagan himself was not writing off North Carolina. He was running hard there, denouncing Secretary of State Henry Kissinger and the very idea of détente with the Soviet Union, the policy Ford had inherited from Nixon. He found headway in the Panama Canal issue, saying that negotiations to turn it over to Panamanian control at the end of the century were a giveaway he wouldn't tolerate. "We built it, we paid for it, it's ours, and we're going to keep it," he said in a line that became so standard that we reporters and then some people in his crowds began reciting it with him. The Reagan campaign made more adroit use of television than before, an obvious tactic when the candidate was a TV pro, but one oddly ignored in the earlier states. They simply put the old TV performer on TV, talking to the camera in taped speeches, a format Reagan's managers had shelved out of concern that it would call attention to the fact that the candidate was an actor. He was, but the voters didn't worry about it.

It worked, not least because Ford was bumbling through his campaign with so-what speeches. The Ford people spent their efforts lining up Republican leaders to demand that Reagan get out of the president's way. "Tell *him* to quit," Reagan retorted.

Reagan said that the pressure for him to withdraw was coming from the same White House that had tried to keep him from running in the first place. When Ford had said earlier that Reagan was too far right to win the election, the challenger had a ready comeback: "It does come rather strange since he tried on two different occasions to persuade me to accept any of several Cabinet positions in his administration. I didn't want to be in the Cabinet."

Was Ford trying to take him out of the 1976 campaign?

"No." Reagan smiled. "I just thought he recognized my administrative ability."

Ford had to confirm the offers, and said he had made them in an effort to unify the party. But he couldn't appoint Reagan out of the way and now he couldn't force his challenger out, either. Reagan upset the president with 52 percent of the vote in the North Carolina primary, a turnaround so surprising that he'd flown out of the state and couldn't even claim his victory on election night. He'd left behind his state campaign chairman, Senator Jesse Helms, but the senator didn't want to be around to take the blame. Helms flew to Washington before the polls closed, saying he had to tend to Senate business, although there wasn't any. By the time the Reagan upset and revival became evident, it was too late for him to get back to celebrate.

Reagan was in La Crosse, Wisconsin, that night, speaking to a hunters' group called Ducks Unlimited and ducking requests for his reaction to the North Carolina returns, even when they showed him leading. He was in the air on the way to Los Angeles when word came that he really had won. By then, the Reagan campaign had announced that he was canceling campaign appearances for the following week to put together a national TV address. His half-hour speech was a reprise of what he'd been saying to primary state audiences. In it, Reagan escalated his Kissinger attack. He quoted Kissinger as having said, "My job as secretary of state is to negotiate the most acceptable second-best position available." Quite a quote, but he didn't cite a source. A spokesman said he got it from Admiral Elmo Zumwalt, who had feuded with Kissinger as chief of naval operations. The State Department said the quote was invented and irresponsible. But it was fodder for the Reagan set speech from then on. "The evidence mounts that we are number two in a world where it is dangerous if not fatal to be second best."

From that point, the Republican campaign became a war in the political trenches, with neither candidate able to advance past the other. Overall, Ford won fifteen primaries, Reagan twelve, on the way to the most closely contested national convention of the era. Ford's strength was still his office; he could flatter uncommitted Republicans with White House invitations while his campaign lieutenants pressed for commitments.

But in a party dominated by conservatives, Reagan was the conservative preference. He was an unrivaled political performer—even when he wasn't trying, as on the misty morning in Flint, Michigan, when Reagan boarded his motorcade outside the three-tiered motel where he'd spent the night. I glanced up at the third floor and there was a man at the window, which was open wide, gawking down at the Ronmobile. He was naked, and clutching the drapery around his middle like a towel after a shower. On the other side of the window stood a woman and she also appeared to be wearing nothing but the wraparound drapery. They watched intently as the caravan pulled out. Adam and Eve in the garden of presidential politics.

When Ford got awkward questions he tended to answer awkwardly. For Reagan, the aw shucks, look at your shoes, smile wanly response was an art form. He actually told one audience that he was embarrassed to ask for votes for president. "I wonder what you think of God?" a man asked him one day. "I wonder if you will let Him direct your life." Reagan did the modesty number. "I've always had a little difficulty talking about my own faith and my own beliefs," he replied. Only a little, though. "I don't know how any man could ever seek the position I seek or hold the position that I held for eight years and think that he could do it without being able to call on God for help." Years later, I was told, President Reagan and his wife, Nancy, were taking communion at a church where the practice was to take a piece of the bread, dip it in the wine, and then partake. She went first and the bread slipped from her fingers and dropped, irretrievably, into the wine cup. Reagan seemed puzzled. He took the bread and paused. Then he dropped it into the wine and walked away.

While Ford and Reagan were wrestling for Republican delegates until and into the Republican National Convention, Carter was strolling to his Democratic nomination. He already had set about a methodical talent hunt for a vice presidential nominee, personally delivering the most significant and lasting reform of the 1976 campaign. In time, the studied search for a running mate would become standard in both parties. McGovern's Eagleton disaster had shown the flaws of the hurried, haphazard way of choosing. Agnew had resigned the vice presidency for misconduct a careful screening might have spotted.

Carter put his staff to work on vice presidential possibilities in the spring as he campaigned for his own nomination. Before the convention he winnowed the list to seven names, had his lawyer friend Charles Kirbo check them out, and broke tradition by announcing the names he was considering. Each of the finalists got a questionnaire about his personal and political life, his medical history, finances, and tax returns. Then Carter personally interviewed them, some at his home in Plains, Georgia, some at the convention in New York. It was a new way of picking a vice president, a sort of public auditioning. But there was still only one vote that counted: the presidential nominee's.

Senator Walter F. Mondale of Minnesota was one of the men Carter interviewed, and he obviously made a winning impression, despite early misgivings about him as a campaigner. He had, after all, run a fledgling presidential campaign himself, exploring the possibility of candidacy and observing during a visit to Atlanta that Jimmy Carter was just the kind of running mate he might want. Mondale dropped his presidential campaign notions in 1974, saying he didn't have the overwhelming desire it would take to make the race and didn't want to spend two years sleeping in Holiday Inns. But he told Carter in the vice presidential interview that he'd really quit after concluding he wouldn't be able to line up enough support to win. Now he was ready to run for No. 2.

Outside, Carter said he had had no doubt that Mondale would be a vigorous campaigner despite his presidential dropout. "What I said at the time was that I did not want to spend most of my life in Holiday Inns," Mondale said. "But I've checked and found they've all been redecorated. They're marvelous places to stay and I've thought it over and that's where I'd like to be." There were others to be interviewed, but he would be the man. He had hit it off with Carter, and he had passed what another of the Plains interviewees called the real test. He'd stood answering questions with Carter without raising a hand to try to shoo away the swarms of gnats that buzzed around your face when you stood still there.

Carter kept his choice to himself until the morning after he was nominated at the New York convention. Then he called Mondale. That had at least kept a bit of suspense alive at a foregone convention. In his convention speech, Carter praised the Democrats for their on-time decorum, "without any fights or free-for-alls" like those in Chicago in 1968 and Miami Beach in 1972. I wrote at the time that it was "an affair without passion, a marriage without romance, performed with all the precision of a prearranged royal wedding. But after their flings, their spats, their divorces of the past decade, Democrats were ready for Jimmy Carter, the outsider who barged into the party and became the bridegroom." And Carter began with a runaway lead in the public opinion polls over either potential Republican nominee, Ford or Reagan.

In the Republican struggle, Reagan broke the old rules on the vice presidency in an attempt to pry nominating votes away from Ford. It wasn't Reagan's idea; it was a ploy designed by Republican strategist John Sears, who sold it to the candidate. Three weeks before the convention, Reagan announced his prospective running mate, reaching left to say he'd run with Senator Richard Schweiker of Pennsylvania, a liberal but, according to Reagan, a man whose "independent thought and action" set him apart from the Washington buddy system. They certainly set him apart from Reagan's political buddies. The idea was to persuade moderate and liberal Republicans aligned with Ford that they should take another look at Reagan. The problem with the odd political pairing was that the Reagan people had to placate their own conservative allies. Schweiker said he certainly could support Reagan's policies, although he didn't seem very familiar with them. Organized labor gave Schweiker's Senate voting record a 100 percent rating, which put him on their side more reliably than Mondale.

Reagan, who didn't know Schweiker before he signed on, slipped now and then and called him Weicker, which was the name of another liberal Republican, Senator Lowell P. Weicker. That was fair enough since Schweiker had trouble pronouncing Reagan's name at first, not knowing whether to accent the *e* or the *a*.

No matter: They were a ticket—an odd ticket, but a ticket. The Sears game plan went beyond that, though. He engineered a rules proposal to force all candidates, meaning Ford, to name their vice presidential selections before being nominated. It was to be a test of convention strength in which the nominating commitments Ford had won in the primaries and caucuses for votes on the nomination would not be binding on the delegates, and Reagan might show the muscle to prove that they really wanted him for president. He couldn't do it. The rule change was narrowly rejected and the game was up. Reagan's managers tried one more maneuver, winning a platform plank that effectively rejected the administration's foreign policy of détente with Moscow. Ford's managers said fine, they didn't care. They wanted no more procedural tests, only the climactic vote on the nomination. Nobody read platforms anyway. Ford was nominated with a margin of 117 votes, the closest contest of modern convention times, and then called on Reagan at his hotel in the middle of the night. It was a gesture of political détente because people customarily go to see the president, not the other way around.

Ford made his vice presidential selection the old-fashioned way. Reagan would have been the ideal running mate, but he'd insisted that he not even be asked. So the president batted names around with his inner circle in the small hours before dawn, settling on Senator Bob Dole of Kansas, who had Reagan's blessing, which meant he was fine with the restive conservatives. Besides, Dole was a tough, acid campaigner, the kind of candidate who could run a road show while the president stayed close to the White House. Too tough and too acid for his ticket's own good, it would turn out later.

Trailing by a pollster's landslide as he began his campaign against Carter, Ford issued the challenge that would revive televised debates between presidential nominees, making them a part of every campaign to come. "I am ready and eager to go before the American people and debate the real issues face-to-face with Jimmy Carter," the president said in his convention closing speech. Within minutes, Carter had issued a statement accepting debates and saying the candidates should face tough examination of their proposals. I wrote it that way and got a complaint from the Carter camp saying that they hadn't accepted the Ford challenge, they had issued a counterchallenge and had intended to seek debates before the president did. The pettiness got pettier when the two camps negotiated debate terms. The Carter people demanded sit-down debates or adjustable podiums so that Ford's height advantage wouldn't show—he was three inches taller than Carter. They finally agreed on lecterns approximately forty-two inches high, based on a formula that averaged the distance between the top of each candidate's belt buckle and the floor. By then the Carter people had figured out that the candidates would be standing so far apart that the height distance wouldn't show, but neither side would yield a point that might conceivably be to the other's advantage. Trivia like that keeps campaign consultants in business.

Carter campaigned as he had in the primaries, on a platform that consisted largely of not being Nixon, promising never to lie, and snapping at anyone who suggested that his proposals were lacking in specifics. They were lacking, but he didn't like hearing it. One dull weekend in Americus, Georgia, where reporters stayed when Carter was in Plains, I did some research on Carter's statements about the Democratic record on the economy and wrote a piece saying that the story he told wasn't the whole story. I didn't think what I wrote was hostile or harsh; it just filled in some blanks with facts. Past Democrats hadn't done quite as well as Carter claimed on inflation and economic growth. He'd gone back to Harry Truman for the inflation numbers, for example, without including the fact that wage and price controls had been in effect at the time. It was not the kind of story to make waves, but it arrived on a quiet news day and the *Macon Telegraph* put my piece on the front page, where Carter read it. He then told his staff to rebut it. On the campaign plane that week, press secretary Jody Powell came by my seat and handed me what looked like a college term paper. It was about twenty pages long, in a blue binder. "Read this," he said. It was the Carter staff rebuttal. It argued with my story, but it didn't contradict my facts. Indeed, it ended with a concession that his figures on past budget deficits were wrong. I read it and took it back to Jody. "Have you read this?" I asked. He had not. He did, and that seemed to be the end of it. But a week or so later, Carter met with AP reporters and executives in Washington in a session I had arranged and told my bosses he couldn't understand how "a good reporter like Walter" could have written such a story. They didn't know what he was talking about. I defended my story. They didn't know what I was talking about. So we dropped it. After the session, Powell called me over to make peace with Carter. We shook hands. "Truce?" I asked. "Truce," Carter agreed. Then he turned to the president of the AP and complained to my boss that I certainly had written an awful story.

Carter was a master of having it both ways. He said he was against outright amnesty for Vietnam draft evaders—but he would offer them all unconditional pardons. He would cut defense funds by at least $5 billion, but he wouldn't say whether the cuts would be from actual current spending or from some undefined future budget projection. Pressed for details on his promise to slash hundreds of agencies out of the government, Carter was asked again, Which ones? Can't say yet. So how could voters judge him on that promise?

"Well, whether they can or not, they'll have to, because there is no way I can take off from campaigning to do a complete and definitive study of what the federal government is and what it's going to be three or four years in the future," he retorted. Nevertheless, he did promise that he would balance the federal budget within one term as president. "You can count on it," he said. Actually, you couldn't. Ford made the same balanced budget pledge when we asked him about Carter's. "I guarantee it," he said. In Ford's flat accent, it came out "gorontee." No matter how it was said, it wasn't going to happen, no matter which man became president. Reagan chimed in with an identical pledge in 1976 and in 1980 when he won, but he couldn't accomplish a balanced budget either.

Carter had a guaranteed applause line for every audience. "I owe the special interests nothing," he would say. "I owe people like you everything." He used it in odd circumstances, as when thanking labor unions, which certainly are special interests, for the money they were putting into his campaign.

He was a born-again Christian with an odd outreach plan aimed at people who weren't. That showed up in his interview with *Playboy*, not usually a forum for devout Southern Baptists. In it, Carter volunteered that he wasn't all that pure. "I've looked on a lot of women with lust," he said. "I've committed adultery in my heart many times . . . and God forgives me for it." Carter said forgiveness extended beyond a man who looks with lust but to one who leaves his wife "and shacks up with somebody out of wedlock. Christ says don't consider yourself better than someone else because one guy screws a whole bunch of women while the other guy is loyal to his wife." This strange campaign fare was published just before the first Ford-Carter debate, but it wasn't mentioned. None of the panelists asked a question about the interview and Ford could hardly raise it himself, although he had criticized Carter's exposition as "poor judgment and lacking in good taste." Later, the Ford campaign bought ads in 352 newspapers, reproducing a *Playboy* cover that promoted the interview. "Now, the real Jimmy Carter," the promo read.

Carter might have done better to borrow a line Udall had used "about the minister who had a sign outside his church and it said, 'If you're tired of sin come in,' and underneath, somebody had written, 'If you're not, call 836-.' " At least that left them laughing at the joke, not joking about the candidate.

That first debate didn't change much. No breakthroughs on the issues, no mistakes to mark either candidate. It would have been memorable only as the first presidential campaign debate in sixteen years except that the sound system failed, leaving the candidates and panelists on the Philadelphia stage in strained silence for twenty-seven minutes while technicians fixed the problem. Since nobody knew for sure when the microphones would be live again, Ford and Carter stayed at them, saying nothing, neither looking at the other, both perspiring in the blaze of the television lights. The TV people finally got the sound hooked up again, the moderator apologized for the breakdown, and the candidates picked up where they'd left off, as though nothing had happened.

By late September and early October, Ford was gaining on Carter. The polls were narrowing and the president seemed to have things moving his way. Then he made the great blunder of the great debates, in the second of the series, when he declared that "there is no Soviet domination of eastern Europe and there never will be under a Ford administration." Astounded at the misstatement, Max Frankel of the *New York Times* followed up by asking whether he'd understood Ford to say that the Russians had not made eastern Europe their sphere of influence and occupied most of the countries there. It was a way out for Ford but instead he dug in deeper, saying people of nations like Romania, Yugoslavia, and Poland did not consider themselves dominated by the Soviet Union. "Each of these countries is independent, autonomous, it has its own territorial integrity, and the United States does not concede that those countries are under the domination of the Soviet Union," the president said, as though he could erase the Iron Curtain. I thought Ford blundered into that misstatement because as a congressman and House Republican leader he was attuned to the annual "captive nation resolutions" declaring freedom in the states Moscow actually controlled. Whatever the reasoning, or lack of it, Ford couldn't see that he'd erred. He came out of the San Francisco debate thinking he'd done fine, and resentfully resisted advice to back off the eastern Europe statement. He got angry at campaign advisers who wanted him to recant. Hadn't they told him back at the debate hall that he'd been great? He preferred to believe that. He got angrier at reporters who kept questioning him about the debate gaffe, but he wound up defending himself and finally apologizing for what he called a misunderstanding. It took him two days and five attempts before he finally said "what I meant to say," which was that he did not accept or recognize Soviet domination of eastern Europe. Carter was reveling in it. Maybe Ford had been brainwashed like George Romney on Vietnam, he suggested. "I understand Polish-Americans for Ford is disbanding," Carter sniped. Later, he said he had been shocked by Ford's insensitivity and lack of knowledge. "He disgraced our country," Carter said, an overstatement but one made for political cause, since the flap was carving into Ford's support, especially among ethnic voters. There had been a sense of momentum about the Ford campaign but now it stalled.

After the *Playboy* and eastern Europe episodes, I addressed an editors' conference and summed up the choice awaiting the voters: "It's either the Walter Mitty of adultery or the man who freed Poland." It had to be my best line because a gossip columnist picked it up and attributed it to Mark Russell, the master of political comedy.

Carter's challenge was that he was a relatively conservative man with a business background, leading a relatively liberal party accustomed to leaders with congressional, academic, or labor résumés. That also was part of his strength. The voters were quite content in the center. They just didn't like what Nixon had done, and Ford still bore the taint of the man he stopped identifying by name, calling him "my predecessor" or "Lyndon Johnson's successor."

Ford usually was a placid campaigner, but he bristled when pressed about the Nixon connection. Earlier in the campaign a college questioner ran the list: Ford's support of Nixon in Congress, his defense of the ex-president against impeachment, the Nixon pardon. "We have a new team," Ford snapped back. "We have followed a very middle-of-the-road to conservative view in economic policy. It has been a policy decided by me. I don't go back and look at what the former president did because he didn't have the hard decisions like we had in 1975. If there is a similarity, it is pure happenstance." But he could not exorcise the ghost, especially the pardon he granted Nixon a month after the resignation in 1974, saying he did so to end "an American tragedy in which we have all played a part." He had been in a no-win spot. Let the threat of prosecution linger over the exiled ex-president, and the scandal would linger, too. Let Nixon be indicted and put on trial, and the spectacle would dominate national attention. Pardon him for Watergate crimes and the new administration would pay. The honeymoon would be over after a month. Ford did and it was.

Two years later Ford was still trying to get past the pardon. He said he'd done it for the good of the nation and was glad he had.

"Now, the political ramifications . . . it is up to the public in the general election, but I am convinced it was right in the national interest, and I would do it again." The political ramifications were obvious, but he couldn't admit that. The Nixon pardon hurt. It cost him votes, perhaps enough votes to have made the difference in what turned out to be a close-count election.

Carter could have that one both ways, too. "I still think the action he took was improper and ill-advised, and I would not have done it, but I honor his right to make that decision," he said. Nor, said Carter, would he try to make an issue of it. He didn't need to. But just in case, he added, "The American people know who pardoned President Nixon."

The Nixon pardon was the question that got Bob Dole into trouble when he debated Mondale. I asked it. I was a panelist at the Houston debate, held ten days after Dole had accused Mondale of mudslinging for raising the Watergate and pardon issues. I reminded Dole that he'd said during his 1974 Senate campaign in Kansas that the pardon was premature and mistaken, and asked him why it wasn't an equally appropriate topic for the Democrats in 1976.

"Well," Dole said, and coughed a bit nervously, "it is an appropriate topic, I guess, but it's not a very good issue any more than the war in Vietnam would be or World War II or World War I or the war in Korea, all Democrat wars, all in this century." He wasn't finished. He said he had added up all the casualties "in Democrat wars in this century," and it came to about 1.6 million, equal to the population of Detroit.

For Mondale, Dole's claim that they were "Democrat wars" was a can't-miss pitch and he hit it. "I think Senator Dole has richly earned his reputation as a hatchet man tonight," Mondale said. It was an image that stuck to Dole in that campaign and beyond. He later backed off the "Democrat wars" line and effectively apologized, but it stuck, a liability in 1976, revived by his critics twenty years later when he ran and lost as the Republican presidential nominee himself.

In 1976, Dole played the role of the Republican heavy, and he also did the hefty lifting of the campaign. He traveled for the ticket while

Ford stayed home at the White House to accentuate his incumbency, as though being there was his best argument for staying there. It may have been. It almost worked.

I not only reported the 1976 campaign, I was reported on, in a *Wall Street Journal* profile. Flattering stuff. The headline read, "AMONG THE BOYS ON THE BUS, WALTER MEARS IS IN THE DRIVER'S SEAT." The *Journal* assigned Ron Shafer to report the piece, and he traveled with me as I traveled with Carter. He was a fine reporter and good company on the press bus, but I found it a bit odd and awkward to be covered while I did my job of covering the candidate. Shafer found it a frustrating assignment because I wasn't doing anything out of the ordinary and he needed a lead. "Do something colorful," he pleaded. Finally, at a campaign stop in Eau Claire, Wisconsin, he found his material, although I thought it told more about how skilled he was than how colorful I was. His lead:

"During a recent campaign stop here, reporters traveling with Jimmy Carter rushed to an auditorium room where phones were set up for their use and found that the door was locked. As they pounded on the door, they didn't notice a pay phone on the wall behind them— or the man who was calmly striding toward it. At the sound of a phone being dialed, the group turned to see Walter Mears of the Associated Press dictating a news story to his office. Mr. Mears flashed a Jimmy Carter grin, waved to his pals, and kept on transmitting the news."

That election night was a long one. Once lagging by thirty points in the public opinion polls, Ford almost overtook Carter. It took most of the night to cement Carter's victory, by what turned out to be a two-point edge, with only twenty-seven more electoral votes than he needed. There hadn't been a presidential election that close in sixty years. I wrote the AP's running story on the election, updating it as the situation and the numbers changed. In our parlance, each updated story is a lead. I wrote eighteen that night and early morning, the last of them timed off at 4:19 A.M. "Democrat Jimmy Carter defeated President Ford and won the White House early Wednesday, ending eight years of Republican rule and crowning his long, often lonely campaign out of the political wilderness. He rejoiced in Atlanta at 4 o'clock in the morning after the tension of a long count and a close race." When I won the Pulitzer, the *Los Angeles Times* said it was for "the volume of his copy." A colleague said that made me the first reporter ever to win one for overfiling.

Even a near miss was a miracle for Ford. He was the nominee of the party of Watergate and Nixon. The liabilities Nixon had snidely cited after nominating him for vice president had not gone away. Fairly or unfairly, he had the image of a bumbler. His own campaign polls showed that going in, a majority of Americans did not consider him a strong leader, and a significant minority did not think he was particularly smart. He had barely survived the Reagan challenge in a wearing campaign for the nomination.

Looking at that pile of troubles, the smart political money would have been on an easy Democratic victory, perhaps a landslide, certainly not the 50 percent Carter got to Ford's 48. In defeat, Ford said he thought that history would treat his brief presidency kindly. It has. His special gift was that he was an ordinary American. A better politician would have made a worse president in his time. Inaugurated, Carter thanked Ford "for all that he has done to heal our land." Carter also said that no defeated president had ever done as much as Ford to help the victor prepare to take over the White House.

"I wanted the new president to have an easier start than I had," Ford said.

SIX

The Winning Act: Reagan Beats Carter in 1980

R onald Reagan never really stopped running for president after his near-miss 1976 campaign for the Republican nomination. Jimmy Carter might have been better off if he'd just kept campaigning, too. But he was president, and he never was as good at that as he'd been at running for the job. He'd campaigned as an outsider, promising a different kind of presidency. He also had run as a loner, outside and often against the Democratic establishment. He'd been elected without coattails to work with a Democratic Congress, where most of the members were elected by margins wider than his in their states and districts. Carter was a virtuoso candidate, but he proved to be a politically tone-deaf president. He'd promised a government as good as the people; cynics said he was accomplishing that and the government wasn't very good. Campaigning against Washington worked. Governing that way did not, and halfway through his term, Carter looked like a lame duck in the making.

Reagan didn't have to concern himself with governing. He traveled the nation, preaching the conservative Republican gospel at every stop on what he called "the mashed potato circuit." That's what Reagan did for a living between presidential election years. Then he stopped doing it for money and started doing it for votes. He'd already set up the functional equivalent of a campaign committee early in 1977, taking a leftover million dollars to bankroll Citizens for the Republic to help conservative Republican candidates in the midterm campaign. The Reagan message didn't change much nor did the cheers from the Republican right. His conservative devotees were loyal and sometimes loud.

I learned a lesson about their devotion in the spring of 1977, and a lesson in humility at the same time. Shortly after I received the Pulitzer Prize, I got a call from a radio talk show hostess in St. Louis. She asked me to be on her program and answer listener questions about the campaign and election. All I'd need to do was get plugged in by telephone from Washington and share my obviously vast knowledge with her listeners. Sure, I said. I figured I owed my Pulitzer-certified wit and wisdom to the radio world. What's more, they were going to pay me fifty bucks. So we set it up. I listened to her ego-massaging introduction, and then it was time for the call-in questions. The trouble was nobody called. Zero. So the two of us talked a bit, and then she said, "Okay, all of you listeners, we're ready for your questions for Walter Mears." Silence. This went on for most of an agonizing hour. She kept pleading for questions from the folks out there in radioland. They kept not calling. I welcomed the commercial breaks.

Our dialogue went awkwardly on and on. Then she asked me whether I thought Reagan would have done better than Ford against Jimmy Carter in the 1976 election. No, I said, he would have done much worse because he couldn't have carried states like Michigan and Illinois, where Ford won, and he couldn't have cracked Carter's hold on the South. Finally, we had callers, outraged Reagan fans who wanted to argue. For the rest of the program every call-in line was busy with more listeners on hold waiting to tell me what a jerk I was. And waiting to vote for Ronald Reagan in 1980.

Carter dropped politics from his agenda when he got to the White House. He'd be president, not a politician. He didn't even make time for routine political niceties. His political advisers grumbled that they had trouble getting in to see him. But a president is not only commander in chief, he is also politician in chief. Scrapping politics sounds like the presidential thing to do. But keeping political lines out and open puts the cloistered leaders in the White House in touch with the trends beyond the Washington Beltway. Carter tried to do it with what were styled as town meetings, answering questions in sessions away from Washington and also in telephone call-ins. He tried to revive the fireside chat, and talked about the energy crisis on television, logs blazing by his chair, wearing a cardigan sweater to make his point about turning down thermostats. He got more ridicule than real contact.

There is a place for the political parties and their leaders as intermediaries between official Washington and the voters between elections. Using them doesn't mean yielding to them. In the Carter White House their calls usually went unanswered. Congressional Democrats found the new people aloof and often uninterested in them. That was no help to a president who had to cope with gasoline shortages and service station lines, inflation, and double-digit interest rates. The wisecrack in Washington was that Carter would really be in trouble when his approval ratings in the polls went lower than the 20 percent interest rates. He made solid proposals, notably on energy, but Congress would give him only a short ration of what he sought. His White House neglected the simple favors and customary courtesies that usually lubricate relations between presidents and Congress. The missteps became legendary.

They neglected to consult Tip O'Neill before Carter appointed a Massachusetts Republican as U.S. representative to a relatively minor but nonetheless noticeable international conference. That clumsy snub would have been trouble enough if it had only involved appointing someone from the home state of the Speaker of the House without telling him. Worse, the man Carter appointed was a potential political rival to O'Neill's son back in Massachusetts. The episode was a symptom of the trouble Carter and his Georgians had getting along in Washington. Tip already was unhappy with the Carter crowd because his family and guests got lousy seats at the 1977 inauguration. He took to calling Carter's top aide, Hamilton Jordan, Hannibal Jerkin.

When Carter held a state dinner for the prime minister of Japan, the White House left Representative Norman Mineta of California off the guest list despite his Japanese ancestry. The Carter arrangements people thought he was Italian.

Campaigning as an outsider against the Washington establishment was an effective way to win an election, but ignoring the amenities of the capital was not an effective way to govern. Carter once joked about his campaign for a second term: "A lot of people ask me if I'm running, and I ask them, 'Running what?' " The line was an unintentional preview of the questions about his effectiveness that dogged him going into the 1980 campaign. Whatever could go wrong did. For example, one of his media advisers devised a plan to improve his image. Jerry Rafshoon set up a series of small dinners in the White House family dining room, just Jimmy and Rosalynn with a presumably impressionable group of news executives and newspaper publishers, about a dozen people at each affair. We called it being Rafshooned. I was Washington bureau chief of the AP at the time, so I got my turn at the Carter table, along with the UPI brass and wives. During the dinner conversation, Carter discussed his position on relations with Iran, worsening at the time because the ailing, deposed Shah had been admitted into the United States. Mrs. Carter interrupted. "Jimmy, that's not our policy," she said, and described what she thought it was. So, I thought, he's not only second-guessed by Congress but at home, too. Henpecked was not the image the White House was trying to promote.

After dinner, while Mrs. Carter gave the women a tour of the family quarters, Carter and the news executives—all men—had drinks and talked in a sitting room. Carter had suffered the most renowned case of hemorrhoids of the era and somebody asked whether he was okay now. Carter said he was, although still uncomfortable at times, and added that one of his doctors had talked about surgery for the condition. I'd had the problem and the operation myself, and I told him he ought to say no because it would hurt like hell and if my experience was any guide, he'd get no sympathy, only bad jokes. Then, having had more than one nightcap, I ventured one myself. I told Carter that presidents are always taking up the cause of foundations trying to find cures for rare diseases with unpronounceable names. I said he ought to change that and take up a campaign against the hemorrhoid because if science really worked on the problem, there had to be a painless way to fix them. Think of the payoff for finding a cure for piles, I said, which had to be a pain to countless voters. I envisioned volunteers going door-to-door with collection canisters, seeking money to cure the common hemorrhoid. "The president sent me," they'd say. Carter never smiled. I shut up.

I became Washington bureau chief of the AP in September 1977, two years after returning from what I called my sabbatical with the *Detroit News*, the only break in my AP service from the day after I graduated from college until the day I retired, forty-six years later. As bureau chief I could call my own shots, and one of them was to keep writing news copy, usually analytical pieces. With Carter in the White House, there was no shortage of grist for it.

He had to confront an energy crisis of gasoline lines and soaring prices, driven by the oil imports on which the nation was increasingly dependent. Dealing with those problems took the courage to advocate politically distasteful steps, and Carter did it. He said he was declaring the moral equivalent of war, but got ridicule instead of credit. The acronym was MEOW. His proposals foundered in Congress. Carter backed off, revised his programs, and confessed in jest that he had taken to sending Congress his energy plan of the month. Still, at least he tried, daring to recommend voter-unfriendly gasoline consumption taxes and other steps most politicians shunned for fear of punishment at the polls.

Carter's presidential attainments, notably the Camp David accords for peace between Israel and Egypt, were eclipsed by the persistent energy problem, rising prices and interest rates, his ragged relations with Congress, and the disdain of Democratic leaders. All of that became political ammunition against him, not only for Republican snipers but for dissatisfied Democrats, among them the name that counted most—Kennedy, Edward M.

By late 1978, opinion polls showed that Democrats preferred Kennedy over Carter for president in 1980, and the margin kept increasing. The wisecrack went that Carter couldn't have done worse in the polls if he'd been the one driving the car at Chappaquiddick. Carter was getting a Jerry Ford problem. Every stumble was magnified, every proposal the butt of political jokers. Carter had advocated ending tax-deductible business lunches, an old Democratic target. He called them three-martini lunches. Barry Goldwater said that until Carter got to be president, people didn't need three martinis at lunch.

Kennedy called a Carter energy proposal a fig leaf. Carter said, "That's a lot of baloney." Kennedy countered that they weren't arguing, they were just getting ready to open a delicatessen together. Not likely. Let Kennedy run, Carter told a group of Democratic congressmen at the White House in 1979, and "I'll whip his ass." One congressman asked whether he had heard the president correctly. Carter replied that he had. When that word got to Kennedy, he said he always knew Carter would stand behind him but didn't know how close.

Kennedy's mother, Rose, famously disclosed that she had no objection to her last son running for president in 1980. He had shunned three prior opportunities when there was no Democratic incumbent in the way. Now he had his mother's permission, which turned into the wisecrack of the season in Washington. I was chatting with Bob Dole, the Republicans' senior sardonic wit, at a cocktail party and we talked about the Rose Kennedy okay. Joking, I told Dole that my mother didn't think he ought to run in 1980. That's when I learned that Dole was sure to be running. He whipped out a piece of paper and asked for my mother's name and address so he could write to her and see why she objected. He was serious. I convinced him that I was only kidding.

Carter entered a road race and collapsed after running three miles, instant material for TV comedy. Nobody mentioned that Kennedy would have had trouble running three hundred yards. He wasn't the only looming challenger. Jerry Brown was getting ready to run, too. First, though, he traveled to Africa with a lady friend, singer Linda Ronstadt, prompting a poll on the question of whether a presidential candidate should go on safari and share a tent with a rock star. Two to one, people said it was okay. Twelve percent said they thought more highly of Brown because of it. Brown said the people who objected were just envious. Not that it made any difference; he ran but he faded fast.

With Carter's policies and his political standing both sinking, the president came up with a curiously counterproductive way to deal with his problems. He retreated to Camp David in July 1979, spent eight days there, and called in a succession of politicians, academics, members of Congress, governors, economists, labor leaders—about 150 people—to talk about the national situation and why it was so sour.

He then delivered what would forever be known as the "malaise" speech, a nationally televised address diagnosing "a crisis of confidence . . . that strikes at the very heart and soul and spirit of our national will." He said that when Americans looked to Washington to chart a way out, they got inaction, "paralysis, and stagnation, and drift." That was a strange complaint, coming from the man who was supposed to be in charge. He'd won in 1976 as the outsider running against Washington, but that wouldn't work again because to most people the president is Washington personified. Carter shook up his Cabinet, replacing five of its members, and reorganized his White House staff. His detractors said all he was doing was blaming the country for his own mess. "Malaise" stuck, a troublesome label, although Carter didn't utter the word in his speech. Clark Clifford, the venerable adviser to Democratic presidents, used it to describe the mood, and it became shorthand for what ailed the Carter presidency.

And that was before the mood got a mascot, when the tale of the "killer rabbit" surfaced. Brooks Jackson, then an AP White House reporter, broke the story of the rabbit versus the president. He reported it sensibly, as an oddity and not a big deal, including it in a weekly column of White House lore. An irate newspaper editor called me demanding to know why my bureau was burying major news, namely, the rabbit yarn. I had no idea what he was talking about, but calmed him down and said I'd find out. Up bobbed the rabbit, submerged in the gossipy column.

Jackson's story was about an episode four months earlier, recounted to him by a White House assistant. It seemed that while Carter was fishing near Plains, Georgia, a crazed rabbit, hissing, with teeth flashing, suddenly swam toward his canoe. Carter beat it back with a canoe paddle and "the banzai bunny," in Jackson's inspired phrase, swam away.

Carter told aides about it, but they were skeptical. It turned out there was a photograph, which he got enlarged to prove that he had resisted a real rabbit. "It was a killer rabbit," a bemused staffer reported. "The president was swinging for his life."

The tale got out of hand, the cartoonists had a frolic with it, and Carter tried to play down the episode. "It was just a nice, quiet, typical Georgia rabbit," he said, smiling. But the story stuck. Now even rabbits wanted a piece of the faltering president. Carter clarified. He didn't think the rabbit was trying to attack; it probably was fleeing some predator, and swam back to shore when he splashed water at it with the canoe paddle. Carter said he didn't want the beast climbing into his canoe. "I determined this would be an unpleasant situation for me and the rabbit," he said. By then it was open season for rabbit jokes. Dole, for example, said he was sure the rabbit meant no harm but was swimming against the tide to get into the canoe with Carter because "everyone else seems to be leaving the ship."

It went that way much of the fall. Kennedy was readying his candidacy, the polls were weighing ever more heavily against Carter, and some big name Democrats were defecting openly to the Massachusetts senator. Then it was Kennedy's turn to fumble. He did it in a taped television interview with Roger Mudd of CBS, broadcast two days before he formally declared his challenge to Carter on November 7. Kennedy struggled through the hard questions about Chappaquiddick, his personal life and strained marriage, his answers evasive but not memorable. Then Mudd, his toughest questions asked, lobbed Kennedy one softball. "Why do you want to be president?" he asked. It sounded as though Kennedy had no notion of why. He went on for 243 rambling, ungrammatical, impenetrable words. "And I would basically feel that, that it's imperative for this country to either move forward, that it can't stand still, or otherwise it moves back," Kennedy concluded. That last sentence was about as clear as he managed to make it.

The movie *Jaws* was on ABC against the CBS Kennedy interview. Dole said people who watched the movie and those who watched

Mudd question Kennedy couldn't tell the difference. But the teeth were not in the question; the wound was in Kennedy's befuddled response on a subject you'd hope a presidential candidate would have clearly in mind before running for the office. Kennedy had a script to read on his reasons for running when he declared his candidacy. He said Americans were pessimistic because the government seemed paralyzed and he'd change that and restore faith that "the system can be made to work." That sounded better, but his challenge already had been undermined, by an event neither he nor Carter could control. On November 4, 1979, one year before the presidential election day, an Iranian mob invaded the American embassy in Teheran, incited by their ayatollah to violently protest the admission of the deposed Shah into the United States for medical treatment. They held fifty-two Americans hostage.

Suddenly the hapless president was no longer a target of derision, he was Mr. President, the leader in a storm. In times of crisis, Americans turn to the only president they have. The poll ratings that had beset Carter turned upward as Americans rallied to him and he overtook Kennedy. Carter would pay heavy political dues for the Iran hostage crisis later; what helped at the beginning of the campaign undermined him at the end.

While Carter had been struggling, Reagan had been cruising, the Republicans' leading man acting the part. He said two years in advance that only something unforeseen would keep him from seeking the presidency in 1980. He was the front-runner and he was in no rush to tell Americans what anyone interested already knew, that he was a candidate again. He had seven Republican rivals, all clamoring against him while he ignored them.

Dole was one. He ran briefly and not well in 1980. When he quit the race, Dole said, "It may well be necessary for a man or woman to work full time for four years to launch a serious campaign." Reagan had been doing exactly that when he coasted into 1980, promising Americans he would get the government off their backs, cut taxes 30 percent over three years, balance the federal budget, and sharply increase defense spending. The other Republican candidates, predictably, were eager to get Reagan into televised debates. He wasn't interested, saying that Republicans shouldn't be arguing with one another because it was too divisive. Reagan's campaign pace was leisurely on the way to the first voting of the season, the Iowa Republican caucuses. The other six Republicans met in a two-hour tele-vised debate in Des Moines that January and spent more time gunning for the man who wasn't there, Reagan, than disputing each other. I was one of the questioners and I asked them how any president could bal-ance the budget while cutting taxes and increasing defense spending, as Reagan was promising. "It's very simple," said Representative John B. Anderson of Illinois. "You do it with mirrors." The rest of them wanted to knock Reagan but not the idea of a tax cut, so they hedged, even George Bush, who later delivered the campaign's most memorable tag for the Reagan plan: "voodoo economics."

Reagan's above-it-all game plan didn't work in Iowa. Bush, the résumé candidate—former United Nations ambassador, envoy to China, Republican Party chairman, and CIA director—upset Reagan in the caucuses, getting 31 percent to Reagan's 29. It wasn't much of a margin but it was victory enough, because he had beaten the front-runner. Bush promptly oversold it, claiming that the rest of the Republican field would be "howling and yelling at my heels."

"What we will have is momentum," he told us. "We will look for-ward to Big Mo being on our side, as they say in athletics." What they say in politics is that Big Mo is fickle. Bush's expectations were up but his momentum didn't last a month.

Reagan reclaimed full command in New Hampshire, where he campaigned more intensively and changed tactics to face the field in debate. "I can't be the only one concerned with unity," he said with a theatrical shrug, the pretense being that he had ducked debating to avoid party discord. His strategy had been to avoid sharing a stage with rivals when he figured it could only help them, not him. So he debated, first in a seven-man forum that didn't prove a thing, then head-on against Bush, who never got over his hapless performance before the debate even began. That was the night Reagan comman-deered the microphone and left Bush looking like a wimp.

It was an artful double cross in which the Reagan campaign pulled a switch on Bush and then managed to cast him as the villain. When Bush looked like a threat, the Reagan camp dared him to debate one-on-one. But Reagan gained strength after the all-comers debate, and decided that a crowded stage was to his benefit. By then, the *Nashua Telegraph* had asked Reagan and Bush to a debate it would sponsor, and they had agreed. But Dole got a Federal Election Commission ruling that the newspaper would be making an illegal campaign contribution by paying for a debate between only two of the candidates, so the *Telegraph* dropped its financing. The Reagan campaign then proposed to split the cost with Bush, no big deal because the whole bill was only $3,500 to hire a hall and a sound system. But Bush refused. So Reagan said fine, he'd pay. Then, without telling Bush, the Reagan organization invited the other Republican candidates to the debate. Four of them came, and Reagan's campaign manager told the Bush side that they were going to open up the debate to make it a six-candidate forum. Bush wasn't playing. His people said they hadn't made the rules, the *Telegraph* had.

So with more than two thousand people sweltering in folding chairs in the high school gym, Reagan talked with the other candidates about getting them into the debate. Bush took his seat on the debate stage at the appointed hour; no Reagan. Time passed with Bush still solo on stage. I kept waiting for him to say something. Instead, he sat there, mute and uncomfortable. That's where he blew it. The hall was hot, the folding chairs were uncomfortable, the crowd was getting bored, and if Bush had said something, almost anything, he could have had the audience on his side before Reagan even got there. He didn't. He sat silent. Not Reagan. He led the other four candidates onto the debate stage. The crowd cheered. At least something was happening. J. Herman Puliot, the publisher of the *Telegraph*, said the four extras were not invited. "This is getting to sound more like a boxing match," he said.

Bush sat and stared. Reagan took a microphone and started to argue for opening the debate to all the candidates. Jon Breen, the editor of the newspaper and the debate moderator, turned to the man running the speaker system and ordered: "Turn Mr. Reagan's microphone off."

"I'm paying for this microphone, Mr. Green," Reagan snapped, misnaming the moderator and winning the debate before it started. The four unseated candidates finally stalked off the stage to hold fuming, anti-Bush press conferences in the high school hallway. Reagan and Bush debated, but what they said was predictable and forgettable. The memorable moment was Reagan's, taped and replayed on TV again and again in the three days before the primary. It beat any campaign commercial, and it added to his landslide. Reagan won the New Hampshire primary more than two to one over Bush, with the rest of the field lagging even further behind. Bush kept running for another three months while the other candidates dropped out, but Reagan was unstoppable. He wound up winning twenty-nine primaries to Bush's six. Reagan finally put Bush on his ticket, but with reservations, not least his feeling that Bush had looked weak and hapless that night in Nashua.

Reagan's route to the nomination was not without potholes, but he dug most of them himself. There was, for example, the joke on the campaign bus in New Hampshire. "How do you know the Polish guy at the cock fight?" Reagan asked. "He's the one with the duck. How do you tell the Italian guy? He's the one who bets on the duck. How do you know the Mafia was there? The duck wins." It was not a very good joke, but that wasn't Reagan's problem. It was an ethnic joke and bad form for a candidate. Reagan said he'd thought it was just for the people on the campaign bus, and that it was a "cheap shot" when the duck joke was reported, first by ABC. In the mini-flap that followed, Reagan apologized and then invented a way out. He had told the ethnic joke, he claimed, only to illustrate the kind of humor he didn't like. "From now on I'm going to look over both shoulders and then I'm going to tell stories about Irishmen, because I'm Irish," he said.

Nothing came of the episode, but it was a lesson for any candidate in the ways of the modern campaign: Don't say anything you don't want to see in the newspaper or on TV.

Reagan also ran afoul with a habit he never broke, not as a candidate and not in eight years as president. He recounted as facts things he'd seen in print or heard somewhere—the sourcing usually was that vague when he was asked about it. He said things that just weren't so. "This is an energy-rich nation," he declaimed one day. "Alaska alone has more oil reserves than Saudi Arabia." Wrong. He had an assortment of bureaucratic horror stories—the welfare queen of Chicago, getting rich on false claims for benefits; the number of pages of paperwork it took a corporation to keep Washington placated; the number of people who had to be hired to produce all those reports. His yarns didn't check out, but that didn't bother him. He'd always done it that way when he was on the lecture circuit.

Then there was the question of age. Reagan was sixty-nine when he ran in 1980, seventy shortly after he was inaugurated in 1981. Dwight Eisenhower's second term ended when he was seventy. The oldest man elected president until Reagan was William Henry Harrison, who took office at sixty-eight in 1841 and died a month later. Reagan handled the age issue with one-liners, joking that he could remember things because he'd been there—things like the Roman Empire and the Constitutional Convention. He said people asked him why he always looked younger when he rode horseback. "I keep riding older horses," he said. When it got serious, he'd respond that his health was excellent and that the other side of the age coin is experience. Carter, who once had said that Hubert Humphrey was too old to run at sixty-four, said it would be up to the voters to decide whether Reagan was too old in 1980, and that he wouldn't try to make an issue of it. He then took every opportunity to say that he wouldn't make an issue of Reagan's age, in case anybody forgot how old the Republican was.

Bush kept plugging, upsetting Reagan in Pennsylvania and then trouncing him in the Michigan primary. It nettled Bush that his biggest victory came the night Reagan finished him off, collecting enough delegates to guarantee a nominating majority. Bush's managers knew the game was up, and so was the campaign treasury. They started shutting down before the candidate admitted he was beaten. Jim Baker, Bush's closest adviser, persuaded him—or, rumor had it, just told him—that his campaign was over. Bush didn't like it at the time, but it was true, and it also was an important step toward his eventual spot on the Reagan ticket. Baker later served in the Reagan and Bush Cabinets. Bush finally conceded at the end of May, but even then he said the news media had forced him out. He was quitting because of "the perception that the campaign is over." The perception was reality, but getting out gracefully is more difficult than any grueling, sleepless campaign tour for a presidential candidate forced to surrender ambition to defeat. To run in the first place takes a mind-set and a driving ambition alien to the rest of us. Campaigning is costly and exhausting. At times, self-delusion takes over and candidates keep running past the point of hopelessness. At the extreme, that gives you a Harold Stassen, a serious candidate in 1948, a Republican fixture in campaigns ever after.

There are beaten candidates who keep running because they want to champion their causes to the end and beyond. Kennedy did so against Carter. The Kennedy challenge never was so potent during the real campaign of 1980 as it had appeared the year before. Only a political miracle worker could deny a sitting president the nomination of his party, and Ted Kennedy was not a miracle man. While Carter had a sour economy to defend, crises abroad worked initially to his advantage, first the hostage-taking in Teheran, then, at the end of 1979, the Soviet invasion of Afghanistan.

With dual foreign crises to confront at the White House, Carter had a good explanation for staying there, out of the campaign cross fire. He had agreed, improbably, to debate Kennedy and Brown in Des Moines before the Iowa caucuses. When his fortunes looked up, Carter pulled out of the debate, which would have been the only instance of an incumbent president according an equal platform to challengers for his party's nomination. The Carter camp had agreed to it with the president far behind Kennedy in the polls. When he caught up, Carter decided that to share the debate stage with Kennedy and Brown would make him just another candidate, yielding the advantage of the presidential pulpit. That wasn't his explanation, of course. Carter said he had a job to do as president, and no time for campaign debates or, indeed, campaigning. With that standard presidential line he adopted the Rose Garden strategy: Try to keep the White House by keeping to the White House as his campaign platform.

To punish Moscow for the invasion of Afghanistan, Carter ordered an embargo of U.S. grain shipments to the Soviet Union, not a promising campaign step in Iowa, the farm state where Democrats would register the first votes of the election year. I went to Kelley, Iowa, to look at the real world impact of the Carter order. "In the gnawing cold outside Dan Froning's grain warehouse there is nothing abstract about the issues raised by President Carter's embargo of shipments to the Soviet Union," my story began. "They are as real as the snow-dusted mounds of corn heaped on the pavement because the grain elevator is full; as real as the thirty railroad cars waiting to be loaded with corn that may go nowhere."

The Carter campaign passed out forms to farmers seeking their endorsements of what the administration called a suspension of shipments, not an embargo. In farm country, they didn't see the difference and there weren't many signers. But on the street and at Democratic affairs, you got a sense of grudging admiration that the president had acted against the Soviets despite the political risk. Carter's rival candidates chorused opposition to the embargo. Kennedy advocated a military buildup and pressure at the United Nations, saying all the embargo would do was hurt farmers and taxpayers, not the Russians. Among the Republican candidates, only Anderson approved the embargo. Reagan, the Cold War hard-liner, said with inexplicable logic that the grain embargo was unfair to farmers because the invaders were Russians, not "pigs, cows or chickens." Vice President Mondale accused Kennedy of playing politics over the national interest by opposing an embargo he called "the patriotic thing to do." We asked him whether he was questioning Kennedy's patriotism, and he said no, although it sounded that way. "I don't think I or the members of my family need a lecture from Mr. Mondale or anyone else about patriotism," Kennedy snapped back.

The embargo, which also covered high-tech exports, didn't accomplish anything. It was symbolic action, no more a deterrent than the U.S. boycott of the Moscow Olympic games that summer. But it was something. At least it was action, and by a president who had sometimes seemed immobilized. He wasn't now. He had acted against Iran over the hostages, freezing assets, expelling diplomats, blocking oil imports, seeking international sanctions; and he had slapped Moscow in spite of the campaign risk in Iowa.

It worked politically. The president easily won the caucuses over Kennedy, the challenger who had looked so formidable before the campaign. Now Kennedy was limping home to New England, seeking to rehabilitate his challenge in the next states up, Maine and New Hampshire. Along with his regional advantage in Maine, Kennedy had the governor campaigning for him. No way he could lose Maine. But he did, narrowly. Upset in his backyard, the senator from Massachusetts said he and Brown together had gotten more caucus votes than Carter, and claimed that proved a majority of Democrats wanted the president to come out of the Rose Garden and debate his rivals. Governor Joseph Brennan, Kennedy's Maine man, came up with an even more inventive claim of victory in defeat. "It's clear that the momentum is with Senator Kennedy," Brennan said at a morning-after news conference at which even he couldn't suppress a laugh or two at what he was claiming. "In the unlikely event that Senator Kennedy ever does lose an election, how will we know?" I asked Brennan. "I'll tell you," he assured me.

The New Hampshire primary was next, and it came with another example of the way the White House stage works for a president. This time it was a diversion from the headaches abroad. Four days before the primary, a team of American amateur and college hockey players scored the greatest upset in Olympic hockey, then or ever, defeating the mighty Red Army team from the Soviet Union in the Miracle on Ice. Then the Americans beat powerful Finland for the gold medal. Mondale was in the arena as an administration cheerleader. The U.S. players, with a roster dominated by New Englanders, became instant national heroes. On the eve of the primary, Carter greeted the gold medal winners at the White House with hugs and handshakes. No challenger could match that picture.

It was Carter's primary anyway. He won easily, in a state where a year before there had been opinion polls suggesting that Kennedy was popular enough to beat the president on write-in votes without entering the campaign. After the season in which it had seemed nothing could go right for the president, everything was breaking his way. He kept winning.

By late March, Kennedy was a primary away from having to quit the challenge, and he was behind in the polls in New York. But in that primary, Kennedy upset Carter, in part because Jewish voters were angry at the administration over a United Nations resolution offensive to Israel, although Carter tried to avoid the blame by saying his ambassador had voted for it by mistake. By then, the mood of rallying to the president was wearing thin with the American hostages still captive, daily reminders on the network television news, and no sign Carter had any way out for them. As that happened, the sagging economy that had been Carter's weak point in the first place gained impact as an issue. Now Kennedy was back, the winner in New York and Connecticut, and it was Carter's turn to counterpunch.

That led to one of the strangest primary election performances I ever saw. I was in Milwaukee, sleeping in as the Wisconsin primary election polls opened. I'd left no wake-up call, but I got one. Carter was having a press conference in Washington, and I'd better get to work, now. Fortunately, the AP bureau wasn't far and I got there, unshaven and unkempt, as Carter went on television at 7:13 A.M. to report a "positive step" in U.S. efforts to get the hostages out. He didn't quite say they were coming home. "I presume that we will know more about that as the circumstances develop," Carter said. "We do not know the exact time schedule at this moment." Carter's people always insisted that the poll-opening press conference was not a politically calculated move but an honest effort to keep America informed. Misinformed, it turned out, since the optimism was unfounded, and the hostages remained captive. I did get back to shave and shower before the polls closed. Carter swamped Kennedy in the Wisconsin primary. He would have won without the hostage announcement, but it probably inflated his margin. There was something of a replay just before the November election when the Iranian parliament set terms, unacceptable but potentially negotiable, for release of the Americans. Carter, campaigning in Chicago that weekend, flew home to the White House at dawn. No go. "I wish I could predict when our hostages will return," he said that Sunday night. "I cannot." They returned only when Reagan was inaugurated president.

To keep going, Kennedy had to win the next major primary, in Pennsylvania. He did, barely. I never had a more difficult night as an election writer. In the AP system, the bureau chief in the election state makes the decision on when to declare the outcome in favor of one candidate or the other, based on the size of his lead, knowledge of the territory, and patterns in prior elections. So the Philadelphia bureau chief was in charge that primary night. I was writing the story as the returns came in, and it was close. But after midnight, Kennedy opened a lead, with a bloc of votes yet to be counted but most of them in city precincts where he was running strong. So my colleague checked the patterns and declared Kennedy the winner. I wrote the story, and the telephone began ringing with calls from other political reporters who weren't so sure and wanted to know that my piece was solid. Sure, I said, since I couldn't admit I was nervous about it, too. I'd been reluctant to have us call Kennedy the winner, wanting to wait for more votes to be counted, but the guy in charge said Kennedy's win was a certainty. He then went home to bed. At about 4:00 A.M., I did, too. For an hour. At 5:00, I got a call from our New York headquarters. Carter was gaining on Kennedy, the editor said, and I'd better get back to the bureau. I did, and waited. I called the bureau chief. Don't worry, he said. He'd be in later. I worried. Precinct by precinct. Carter was gaining on Kennedy, not many votes, only a handful. But a handful might be enough. We might be wrong. Which meant I might be wrong, because my byline was on the stories people were reading over breakfast. I worked all day as the late returns trickled in. Kennedy was still ahead, but it was too close to call, certainly too close to have called the night before. The bureau chief breezed in at midafternoon. We finally got the last precincts. Kennedy won—holding on by three-tenths of 1 percent. "I told you not to worry," the expert said smugly.

I was too exhausted to retaliate. I also had nervous hiccups, and it took two days to get rid of them.

By midspring, with the Iran hostage crisis dragging on and his poll ratings slipping, especially after the failed and fatal attempt at a helicopter rescue raid, Carter dropped his no-campaign rule. He ventured out of the White House to hunt votes, saying his challenges as president were manageable enough for him to do some campaigning away from Washington. I didn't see that the challenges had changed, only the campaign, which was souring on him. His emergence didn't make a lot of difference at first; most people didn't notice the change. He was winning primaries but Kennedy wasn't quitting. On the last day of Democratic voting, Kennedy won five primaries; Carter won three, and gained enough delegates to clinch his nomination. He'd won twenty-four primaries, Kennedy ten. Carter's delegate commitments guaranteed him the nomination unless his challengers could change the reform rules they once had forced upon the old Democratic establishment. So they tried. They weren't going to be hobbled by consistency or principle. Since Carter had won and the liberals preferred Kennedy, the sometime reformers tried to erase their own rules, and declare that they were not bound to the candidate who had won their commitments in the primaries. George McGovern, who engineered the rules reforms, tried to undo them to release delegates "who are trapped in the time capsule of decisions made months ago." It was some reversal by a man who had threatened to bolt the party unless his primary-won delegate commitments were honored at the 1972 convention. Carter kept his delegates in 1980.

The Kennedy Democrats were not alone in their inconsistency. John Anderson claimed he had a realistic shot at the Republican nomination when no one else thought so. He learned that the skeptics were right so he ran as an independent. Anderson was a liberal Republican before that became self-contradictory and he was campaigning for his last House election, in 1978, when he started talking about running for president. I was seated with him at a dinner party that spring. We had two drinks, maybe three, and chatted about politics. He told me he might run for president in 1980. He was an improbable candidate at best, third in the House Republican leadership, but treated there as the obligatory liberal in a conservative lineup, and unknown beyond Congress and his Illinois House district. He was not without assets, not the least of which was the look and sound of a candidate sent by central casting, with his mane of white hair and his gifts as an orator. Over wine he told me he was serious about running in 1980. I called him the next day and said that if he really meant it, we needed to talk, because I didn't write stories about the things people told me after the third drink. He laughed and said come on over.

So I did, and wrote the first story about not-quite-candidate Anderson in the spring of 1978. "I'm obviously thinking about it," he said. After all, Carter had come out of nowhere. "You could suddenly blossom the way he did," he said. He ran but didn't blossom. With Reagan headed toward the nomination, Anderson decided he could do better outside the GOP than in its primaries. He said his independent campaign wasn't an attack on the two-party system but on the nominating process, which sounded to me like the same thing. When I asked him the difference, he just laughed.

Switching to independent candidacy that April after ten months as a candidate for the Republican nomination, he said he did not intend to be a spoiler. Third candidates always say that, but to get anywhere they have to take votes from one major party nominee or the other. Usually, the third entry does not get enough votes to make the difference between the major parties. Anderson certainly took votes from Carter in November, but even with all those votes switched to his column, the president would have lost. Still, significant third candidates change the campaign. Anderson did.

After Anderson turned independent, he held a press conference with Kennedy and hinted that he'd quit the race if the Democrats nominated the challenger instead of Carter. He also said he would quit if he thought he was helping to elect Reagan. Although his chances were worse than slim to none, Anderson was an attention-getter. He was different, a bit of seasoning in the mix of routine campaign politics. The polls late in the spring and through the summer showed that he was gaining strength and that he was cutting into Carter's constituency. The

John F. Kennedy and Jacqueline Kennedy at the family compound in Hyannisport, with newsmen watching. I'm the one with the crew cut, standing beside the cameraman. *(AP/Wide World Photos)*

Senator Barry Goldwater hobbles onto the patio of his home outside Phoenix to declare his presidential candidacy in January 1964. *(AP/Wide World Photos)*

After a two-hour hike through black neighborhoods in Milwaukee in March 1968, Senator Eugene J. McCarthy breaks into a trot, while gasping reporters struggle to keep up with him. I'm trying—fourth from the right, over McCarthy's shoulder. *(AP/Wide World Photos)*

Richard M. Nixon turns his back on one campaign crowd to wave toward people on the steps behind the platform in Columbus, Ohio, in 1968. In the press stands, to the left, we joked that it looked as though he was trying to levitate. *(AP/Wide World Photos)*

Vice President Hubert H. Humphrey tells TV technicians to move the boom microphone out of his way so that he could see the TelePrompTer text of the speech in which he would edge away from President Johnson's Vietnam War policy. He did not use the vice presidential seal on his lectern that night or for the rest of the 1968 campaign, a symbolic gesture of political independence from LBJ. *(AP/Wide World Photos)*

Senator George McGovern arrives in Little Rock to campaign for the 1972 Democratic presidential nomination, with campaign volunteer Bill Clinton beside him. Joe Purcell, the state Democratic chairman, is at McGovern's left. *(AP/Wide World Photos)*

McGovern delivers his speech accepting the 1972 nomination at the Democratic convention in Miami Beach—at 2:48 A.M., the television audience long lost. Images of Robert and John Kennedy and Adlai Stevenson tower over the candidate. *(AP/Wide World Photos)*

I'm talking with Jimmy Carter at a coffee shop in Concord, New Hampshire, as the 1976 primary campaign begins. *(AP/Wide World Photos)*

Senator Walter F. Mondale rebuts Senator Bob Dole at their vice presidential campaign debate in Houston. As a panelist, I had asked Dole about Watergate and he had tried to dodge by saying that all Twentieth Century wars were "Democrat wars." Mondale said that proved Dole deserved his reputation as the Republican hatchet man. *(AP/Wide World Photos)*

President Gerald R. Ford in the Oval Office, answering questions in an interview with me (at the left) and AP White House Correspondent Frank Cormier. *(White House Photo)*

I'm accepting congratulations on the 1977 Pulitzer Prize, on a day I wish I'd chosen to wear plain pants instead of the checked double-knits that proved I would not be winning any fashion awards. *(AP/Wide World Photos)*

I am a questioner and George Bush is one of the debaters, as Republican presidential candidates meet in Des Moines before the 1980 Iowa caucuses. Ronald Reagan skipped that debate and Bush upset him in Iowa. *(AP/Wide World Photos)*

Ronald Reagan bristles as the moderator orders his microphone turned off because he is demanding that four unseated Republican candidates be included in a campaign debate with George Bush, who is at the right. Reagan wanted Representative John B. Anderson, Senators Howard H. Baker and Bob Dole, and Representative Phil Crane to join the debate but the sponsoring *Nashua Telegraph* said it was to be between him and Bush. Before the others walked out, Reagan snapped that he'd paid for the microphone, a winning performance that helped him trounce Bush in the New Hampshire presidential primary. *(AP/Wide World Photos)*

Reagan answers questions at an AP interview in New York during the 1980 campaign. To Reagan's left, beside me, is Rupert Murdoch, publisher of *The New York Post*. Taking notes across the table is Louis D. Boccardi, president of the AP from 1985 until 2003. *(AP/Wide World Photos)*

Governor Michael Dukakis, in shirtsleeves, waves at the flag wavers in Bakersfield, California. The Democrats turned out the flags at their rallies in 1988 to counter Republican complaints about his veto of a bill to require that Massachusetts schoolchildren recite the Pledge of Allegiance every morning. *(AP/Wide World Photos)*

I'm interviewing Dan Quayle in his vice presidential office in 1990, with AP Political Reporter Don Rothberg. *(White House Photo)*

Campaigning in Pembroke, New Hampshire, in 1992, Pat Buchanan is confronted with a white supremacist newsletter that had printed one of his conservative columns. He said he couldn't always control who published his stuff. *(AP/Wide World Photos)*

The first President Bush talks with a dairy farmer as a cow named Holiday looks on, during the campaign for the 1992 New Hampshire presidential primary. *(AP/Wide World Photos)*

Interviewing President Bill Clinton on Air Force One, with AP White House Correspondent Terry Hunt. Clinton was on his way to Vietnam, the first president to go there after the war. *(White House Photo)*

George W. Bush makes sure I'm photographed with him while wearing a cap with a W on it. We'd been given the minor-league baseball caps at a campaign rally. Bush claimed the initial as his 2000 campaign symbol, although I told him I'd been a W before he was born. *(AP/Wide World Photos)*

president said he was a creation of the media and there was some truth to that. We paid attention to him because he was interesting and often fun. "I am not just a fad," he said, but he was.

He'd gained a sort of cult status when he was still competing for the Republican nomination. Cartoonist Garry Trudeau featured him in a two-week sequence in his comic strip, "Doonesbury." Anderson was losing, but colorfully. He quoted Ralph Waldo Emerson to campaign rallies: "There is nothing that astonishes men so much as common sense and plain dealing."

I even made "Doonesbury," in a strip that showed an Anderson aide on the telephone at campaign headquarters.

A diversion in the spring, Anderson would be a factor in the fall.

With the primaries over and his nomination commitments in hand, Carter was still trying to cope with Kennedy. Carter called his challenger twice the night of the final primaries, but he had to leave messages. Kennedy didn't get back to him until the next day—lèse-majesté with a message. Carter said they should meet. Fine, said Kennedy, make it tomorrow. The president had figured on a few cooling-off days, but he couldn't say no. So Kennedy went to the White House accompanied by eight aides, three of them press spokesmen, plus the reporters assigned to his campaign. Carter and Kennedy talked for an hour and eight minutes, the president seeking peace, the senator seeking points. Kennedy emerged beaming, declared that he was still a candidate, and said he expected to win, all on Carter's White House turf. Carter had beaten Kennedy's challenge for the nomination but the president looked like the supplicant. In a way, he was. Carter needed Kennedy's help against Reagan. If Kennedy and his liberal allies walked away from the ticket, the president's prospects would go from worsening to awful. Carter couldn't afford to be heavy-handed against his challenger. It wouldn't have worked anyhow. Kennedy could get along just fine without him.

So Carter was publicly polite while he and his aides fumed in private at Kennedy's refusal to get out of the way. Carter had clinched the Democratic nomination but before turning to the campaign against Reagan his people had to spend the summer dealing with Kennedy, first resisting the "open convention" attempt to grab his delegates, then negotiating on the Democratic platform. The platform was Kennedy's last stand, and he forced Carter to accept provisions that collided with administration policy, notably a $12 billion job creation program the president opposed because he thought it would worsen inflation. With Madison Square Garden as the arena, Kennedy played his final campaign cards, and the political theatrics could have earned a stage on Broadway, a few blocks uptown. The nominating votes were Carter's but the star that night was Kennedy.

He set the place roaring when he took the convention stage to argue his cause even though his candidacy was defeated. It was an hour of high emotion at a businesslike convention, I wrote that night as Kennedy spoke. The hall erupted into cheers for the man the Democrats would not nominate. Blue-and-white Kennedy campaign signs waved across the floor and balconies above, eclipsing the green Carter placards of the winner. "For me, a few hours ago, this campaign came to an end," Kennedy said. "For all those whose cares have been our concern, the work goes on, the cause endures, the hope still lives, and the dream shall never die."

When Kennedy finished, the convention burst into a demonstration that roared on, oblivious to the gavel-banging of Chairman Tip O'Neill. Staged ovations are standard convention fare, but from where I sat, this one seemed real. I never saw one to match it. O'Neill was trying to begin a convention roll call vote on the disputed platform provisions, but nobody could hear the proceedings. It wasn't going to happen anyhow. The Carter camp, wary that the president might well lose, decided to make a deal with Kennedy. O'Neill announced that there wasn't going to be any roll call. The platform would be settled by voice vote. Nobody could have heard a voice vote in the tumult, but Tip could take care of that. He asked for ayes or nays, got an unintelligible response, and announced the prearranged outcome. "In the opinion of the chair, the ayes have it." So it went until the deal was ratified.

Carter was stuck with an economic platform he didn't want and a Democratic rule requiring that he endorse it or say where he differed. So he kept it vague, saying he supported the intent, spirit, and aims of the platform. That didn't placate the liberals. Representative Shirley Chisholm of New York said Carter's words were "nebulous poop." But then, so are most political platforms.

Carter was duly renominated, but the energy and emotion of the convention were spent on the loser. When Carter paid his ritual respects to past Democratic leaders he included among them "Hubert Horatio Hornblower—er—Humphrey." The band struck up and the balloons were supposed to shower down, but one big basket got stuck and wouldn't open. And the loudest roar of the night came when Kennedy turned up, belatedly, for a ritual encore, the loser's unity appearance with the nominee before the final gavel. They shook hands and Kennedy moved on. Watching from the press stand beside the platform, I got the impression that Carter was trying to catch him and drag him up front for a more effusive display of solidarity. But Kennedy, minimal duty done, wasn't playing.

While Carter was fending off Kennedy, Reagan had the better part of two months to get ready for his campaign against the president. His one distraction was a brief fling with the notion that Jerry Ford might do what no former president ever had and take the vice presidential nomination. While the Reagan camp and some old Ford pals had speculated about it, the improbable ticket sprouted—and wilted—in the hothouse of the Republican convention, on television, and in the press, including the AP, to my embarrassment.

Reagan had plenty of time to put his ticket together. He didn't lack for willing prospects, among them rivals he had beaten for the nomination. Bush was the logical name, but Reagan wasn't a fan. For one thing, Bush was the guy who had frozen at that debate in Nashua, and Reagan wondered to aides whether he'd be tough enough under pressure. Besides, conservatives didn't like him much, and Bush had etched the voodoo label on Reagan's centerpiece issue, the tax cut that was supposed to prime the economy and put more money into the treasury to balance the budget.

The Ford possibility put Reagan's vice presidential quest on hold. Ford's was the only name that added points to Reagan's ticket in campaign polling. Ford already had said no, but maybe he'd change his mind.

Reagan got to the Republican National Convention in Detroit with Ford on his mind and no decision on a running mate. Ford came with an opening night speech to deliver: "Some call me an elder statesman. I don't know. I don't mind telling you all that I am not ready to quit yet . . . I've never been much for sitting." The word was around by then, although still only gossip and rumor, that Reagan might try to enlist Ford. The next day, Reagan dropped Ford's name at a meeting with congressional Republicans, and the rumors got real. Then he talked with Ford and asked him to reconsider the role. Ford declined, and Reagan asked him to think it over. By then, the

Reagan-Ford ticket was the talk of the convention, a sure thing according to more than a few Republican leaders, who said they knew it was set but wouldn't be quoted by name. And that was before Ford started talking about it on television. "Honestly, if I thought the situation would work, if all the other questions could be resolved, the problem of pride would not bother me in any way," Ford said Wednesday morning on NBC. That evening it was CBS, where he told Walter Cronkite it would be difficult to decline a vice presidential draft, but that he wouldn't run to be a figurehead. Ford said he would have to believe "that I will play a meaningful role across the board in the basic and the crucial and the important decisions that have to be made."

Cronkite said that sounded "something like a co-presidency." Ford said that would be for Reagan to decide. When Reagan heard that description, he decided. He wanted a vice president, not a co-president. This might not work out. But by that time, Republican leaders on the convention floor were telling anyone in range that the dream ticket was a done deal, that they'd heard it from somebody so close to Ford, or perhaps Reagan, that it had to be set. Reagan's managers controlled the convention and could pass instructions to every delegation with the flip of a telephone switch but, strangely, they did nothing to stop the roaring and supposedly authoritative speculation. They'd tell you that the talk was premature, but when politicians say that they usually mean that something is about to happen. By midevening, it was no trick to find a party leader who would say on the record—some on the air— that it was going to happen. "Informed sources" said Reagan had made the offer and that Ford had accepted. Not well informed, it turned out. One of those informed sources told an AP reporter Ford was running, and a second confirmed it. The AP reported that it was set. We were not alone in getting burned with a bad story by the combination of wishful Republican rumor repeated as fact and the intense competitive pressure to be first with the news of it. It wasn't my reporting, but it was my fault. I was the Washington bureau chief.

What we did not know was that the Reagan and Ford people still were trying to work out terms under which the two men could work together if they were elected, and they weren't finding a formula. Without one, Ford wasn't running. Reagan was getting impatient. Late Wednesday night, Ford took the elevator from his Detroit hotel suite on the seventieth floor down one level to Reagan's, and told him he had decided against running for vice president. He thought Reagan seemed relieved. Before midnight, Reagan called Bush. Then Reagan made an unprecedented midnight appearance at the convention to announce his choice of a running mate. It wouldn't be "the dream ticket" and he wanted to take the edge off the letdown. Reagan told the convention, and thus the nation by television, that it was true he and Ford had been going over the idea, but they had decided not to go ahead with it. Ford's price for taking second place on the Reagan ticket had been a share of presidential power and Reagan wasn't going to pay that much for a running mate. Bush was free and ready to pass any loyalty test. He even tried to pretend he'd never said "voodoo economics," but wound up having to swallow the words instead. "God, I wish I hadn't said that," we heard him mutter that fall.

Reagan still was given to straying from his campaign script. His managers wanted him to stick to the memorized lines instead of wandering off into his funny numbers about the bureaucracy or the environment, or venturing impromptu thoughts that took the campaign off message. When he told a convention of Christian evangelicals that he saw great flaws in the theory of evolution, that became the story of the day. Vice President Mondale said Reagan's roster of supporters included "the Flat Earth Society, the Committee to Stamp Out Dancing, and Americans United Against Charles Darwin." Digressions are an occupational hazard for an everyday campaigner, because we reporters are listening for anything new and different, anything to break the boredom of hearing the set speech at stop after stop after stop. Reagan's managers wanted him to stay on script; an actor ought to be able to do that. But those oddball additions kept coming. In his speech circuit days he had made it a habit to jot down an index card entry when he spotted an item that might be handy, never bothering to check for accuracy. His after-dinner audiences liked the stuff and nobody argued. His sometime gaffes in the primary election campaign were not major ones. As the nominee, he was in a different league. His purported facts were being checked and shown to be wrong, sometimes drawing ridicule. The "killer trees" theory, for example. That was the sarcastic shorthand for his claim that "growing and decaying vegetation" was causing air pollution. When Reagan appeared in a California college town, students strung a banner between two trees. "Chop me down before I kill again," it read. When we asked Reagan about his flawed facts he'd just shrug, smile, and say that he was only passing along knowledge he'd picked up here and there. In the end, the distractions didn't damage Reagan, and the managers got his habits largely under control. Their on-message strategy became the rule in the Reagan White House. Decide what they wanted imparted and stick to it, no matter what. It would lead to the routine in which the president hurried to the helicopter so that the roar drowned out questions and he could avoid topics he didn't want to discuss.

Reagan turned one of his campaign slips to advantage, making it part of his standard speech. He had inadvertently used the word "depression" to describe the foundering economy, a scare term to Americans who remembered the great one. He'd meant to say "recession." Carter tried to make an issue of it. "I was speaking in human terms," Reagan countered. "A recession is when your neighbor loses his job. A depression is when you lose your job. And recovery is when Jimmy Carter loses his."

Carter never had mastered campaign humor. He was a detail man, the nitpicking president who kept an eye on reservations for the White House tennis court. I went to the Oval Office to see him one day, shortly after I'd had gum surgery. My cheeks were still swollen. Carter asked what had happened to me and I explained. "I need your teeth," I said. Carter's prominent, perfectly aligned front teeth were a trademark feature, the cartoonists' delight. I managed a sore smile. Carter stayed serious. He told me his teeth weren't that good and then he showed me. I found myself looking into the yawning mouth of the president of the United States while he pointed to a back tooth and said he was going to need dental work on it. He was not much for kidding. He tried humor, but his jokes were not very funny. One was that a Reagan presidency would "Hollywoodize" the White House and foreign visitors would be leaving their imprints in cement on the South Lawn. Then again, when presidents try to be funny, audiences laugh. A newspaper publisher who accompanied Carter on a trip to Tokyo told me the president had recited a joke to a Japanese audience through a translator. The Japanese roared with laughter. My friend said he later asked the translator how he had put Carter's humor into Japanese to draw that response to a bad joke. "I didn't," the translator replied. "I told them, 'The president has just told a joke.' "

Reagan was the raconteur, sometimes too glib for his own political good. The first stop of his fall campaign was in Jersey City, with New York Harbor and the Statue of Liberty as his backdrop at a carefully staged Labor Day rally meant to demonstrate his appeal to ethnic groups and blue-collar Democrats. There were Reagan campaign buttons for every ethnic bloc—Poles, Lithuanians, you name it. I saved one emblazoned "Byelorussians for Ronald Reagan." He had hot dogs and beer with steelworkers at a backyard cookout. It was made for television, all taped without a snag. Then he stepped on his own lines at the next stop.

We were standing in the rain at the Michigan State Fair as Reagan delivered the familiar set-piece speech from the shelter of a gazebo, figuring the day's work was done and we could get dry and get dinner. Then Reagan spotted a man in a Jimmy Carter mask.

"I thought you were in Alabama today," he said. "You know, I kind of like the contrast, though. I'm happy to be here, where you're feeling it firsthand with the economic problems that have been committed, and he's opening his campaign down in the city that gave birth to and is the parent body of the Ku Klux Klan." Now we had to get back to work. The Republican nominee had tried to link the Democratic president with the Klan, getting his facts wrong in the process. Carter had campaigned in Tuscumbia, Alabama. That is not where the Klan was founded, although one Klan organization had moved its headquarters to Tuscumbia a month before. That outfit sent about forty demonstrators to march against Carter, who said that as a southerner he was angry to see people "who practice cowardice and who counsel fear and hatred." Reagan wouldn't say any more about it that night. It turned out that he had seen a newspaper and TV report that there was a Klan office in Tuscumbia.

Instead of the feel-good show at the Statue of Liberty, the Reagan story was the flap about the Klan and the unfounded slap at Carter. The president called it a slur against him and an innuendo against the whole South. Seven southern governors joined in calling the Reagan comment callous. Reagan issued a statement saying he hadn't meant to disparage anyone and had been misinterpreted. The grand wizard of the Tuscumbia Klan office took the occasion to announce that he'd be voting for Reagan, a development that would have gained no attention at all but for the flap. All because of a news clip and some guy in a Carter mask.

For Carter, saddled with economic and hostage woes and sagging in the public opinion polls, anything that changed the subject was to the good. Outside the Ebenezer Baptist Church in Atlanta, he told us that anyone who injected "the obnoxious blight" of the Klan into the campaign was wrong. He then went inside the church and did so himself, in a political sermon denouncing "the stirrings of hate and the rebirth of code words" like "states' rights" and "the Klan" in the presidential campaign. "Racism has no place in this country," Carter said, never quite saying what he was implying—that Reagan might let it arise. In Cleveland, he accused Reagan of risking a new arms race that would heighten the threat of nuclear war. "I don't want to be misunderstood," he said. "I'm not insinuating that my opponent is for war or against peace." It only sounded that way, as it did later when Carter said he was not suggesting that Reagan was a warmonger but that the election would help decide "whether we have war or peace."

Denials meant to reinforce negative impressions of the other guy—too old, too warlike, too far right—were straight from the Richard Nixon political playbook. Reagan would be a divisive president, bad for America, Carter said. The president said that if he lost the election to Reagan Americans might be separated "black from white, Jew from Christian, North from South." It was shrill, negative, and about the only strategy Carter could use. The president couldn't claim things were going well under his administration, but he could argue that they would get much worse under Reagan. The trouble with that was the backlash. Carter looked mean, and that was becoming a problem. So his campaign managers set about changing the image. They told us that Carter would be putting more emphasis on substantive differences between the candidates on specific issues, less on his general indictments of Reagan. Maybe they'd messed up, we were told, but we had, too. One of Carter's aides told me that we reporters weren't holding Reagan to account for what he said and advocated. We were, and I didn't need a journalism lecture from a political operator, but I also understood the frustration. Reagan's misstatements were reported in full, but people didn't seem to care. His aw shucks style of fending off criticism was working. The doctrinaire conservative was playing the nice guy role, with Carter cast as the strident candidate and a meanie, too. That led the president, remarkably, to go on television and say that he didn't think he was mean, but maybe he'd overstated some points. After that the meanness issue seemed to ease, although I didn't see much difference in Carter's campaign tactics.

He had promised that he would tell the voters every time there was a prior campaign pledge he could not keep. That was a promise he couldn't possibly keep. Maybe he'd learned better. "Well, the issues are so multitudinous and so interrelated, I don't want to pursue them any further," he said one day in Portland, Oregon.

Reagan wasn't Carter's only problem. Anderson was cutting into his territory, campaigning with a liberal agenda and a Democratic running mate. The League of Women Voters was trying to arrange campaign debates, but Carter wouldn't come if Anderson did. The League had set what would become the standard test for third-candidate participation in a presidential campaign debate—15 percent support in the public opinion polls. Anderson was polling well past that level in September, so he was invited. That led to the oddest of the campaign debates, Republican Reagan versus sometime Republican Anderson minus Democrat Carter, a one-hour, televised debate in Baltimore that was a sideswipe rather than a collision. Reagan and Anderson argued their differences, but their real aim was at "the man who isn't here tonight." The League considered putting a third lectern and blue swivel chair on the stage as a reminder of Carter's refusal to come, but wisely dropped that notion rather than take sides against the president. Maybe he'd come another night, which he did. After the two-way debate the wisecrack in the pressroom was that an empty chair would have won it.

Anderson thought the debate exposure would raise his standing, make him more recognizable, and so strengthen his campaign. But that night in Baltimore turned out to be his high point. He slipped in the polls, as third candidates usually do when voters begin looking closely at whom they want to be president. It was going to be Reagan or Carter, and the president's "wasted vote" argument against Anderson started to take hold. Anderson wound up with just under 7 percent of the national vote.

With Anderson down in the opinion polls, the major party nominees finally debated one-on-one a week before the election. Reagan was the favorite and the candidate with the most to lose. He didn't. There were no landmark moments that night in Cleveland. Reagan's best line was pure actor. "There you go again," he said wearily to Carter, complaining that the president was misstating his proposals in order to criticize him. Reagan did drop in one fun-with-numbers line, a reminder of his taste for unprovable statistics. He said that if all Americans who were out of work stood in line, they would reach from New York to Los Angeles. He didn't say where he got that one. Carter walked into another round of Jimmy jokes by quoting his twelve-year-old daughter on nuclear weapons control. He said he wanted to put the issue into perspective. "I had a discussion with my daughter Amy the other day, before I came here, to ask her what the most important issue was. She said she thought nuclear weaponry and the control of nuclear arms." Cue the ridicule. Reagan said later that he used to sit around and talk nuclear policy with his kids when they were little. Carter wrote in his memoir that he had made Amy "the most famous antinuclear advocate in America."

Reagan took a moment after the debate to put it into perspective. Hollywood perspective. He was asked whether he'd been nervous at facing the president of the United States. "No, not at all," he said. "I've been on the same stage with John Wayne."

That election night was open and shut. It was Reagan, overwhelmingly, from the time the first votes were counted. Indeed, voter interviews before the polls closed told that story, and the network anchormen hinted at the outcome on the evening news. They couldn't say outright that it was Reagan because the votes weren't in yet. So they said he was faring well, or having a strong day. Carter knew it was coming, and he wasn't waiting, either. "It was obvious to everyone that I had lost, an overwhelming defeat," he wrote in his memoir. So he conceded at 9:45 election night, before the polls had closed in the West. At the time, I was trying to figure out the wording for an election story lead that would almost but not quite declare Reagan the winner, hedging because we were still counting votes. Somebody shouted across the AP bureau that Carter was about to concede. Problem solved. Carter said he'd telephoned his concession to Reagan about an hour before. No presidential candidate had conceded early since Alton B. Parker bowed to Theodore Roosevelt, at 9:00 P.M. on election night 1904.

"I promised you four years ago that I would never lie to you, so I can't stand here and say it doesn't hurt," Carter said. He wasn't the only Democrat hurting. Tip O'Neill was in a rage at the early concession he'd been unable to stop, saying it took votes from Democratic House candidates on the West Coast because when people there heard the presidential election was over, they stayed home instead of standing in line to cast ballots.

"Perhaps it was a mistake, but at the time I did not want to appear to be a bad loser," Carter wrote later, "waiting until late at night to confirm what everyone already knew."

What everyone didn't already know was that the 1980 election would prove a pivot point in American politics, leading the nation away from the legacies of the New Deal and the Great Society. Reagan said that government was the problem, not the solution. Now he and his conservatives were in charge of both. "Ronald Reagan won the White House from President Carter Tuesday night in a startling landslide that changed the face of American government," I wrote that night. It was an election that also changed the mind-set of American politics. Since the New Deal, the assumption had been that government was a growth industry. With Reagan, the premise was the opposite. In time, even Democrats were talking the language of restraint and limits—all but the old-line liberals, and they were besieged in and out of the party. Fifteen years later, a Democratic president, Bill Clinton, proclaimed, "The era of big government is over." Ronald Reagan could have said that in his political prime. Come to think of it, he did.

SEVEN

The Inevitable Reprise: Reagan Buries Mondale in 1984

Ronald Reagan was bound to win a second term in 1984 as certainly as anything can be certain in politics. His reelection was a foregone conclusion long before the ballots were cast. But the odds against the Democrats did not keep them from battering each other for the nomination to run against the president. Reagan's own campaign was not a work of political art, but it didn't have to be. He was the commanding campaign presence despite the suspicion that as president he didn't really run the show, he just starred in it. The Reagan revolution had shifted the agenda to the right as the president led the government and campaigned against it as the same time. His trademark line hadn't changed just because he was in charge—government was the problem, not the solution. Not that the president was making the government smaller; he was making it different. He expanded the defense budget and establishment, subtracted what he could from the social programs of FDR's New Deal and LBJ's Great Society, and shaped political attitudes to fit his conservative ideology. He'd joked to photographers at the end of his 1980 campaign that he'd have plenty of time to autograph the pictures they took because after he'd done away with Social Security and started a war, what else would he have to do? He'd chosen the right forum for that sarcastic comment about the image his detractors were pinning on him. The photographers didn't tell, and the remark didn't surface until long after the election.

Reagan succeeded in putting the national debate about government and politics on his terms. That was the real Reagan revolution. The assumption that new federal programs and Washington answers were the way to cope with national problems no longer applied. It had been part of the thinking even during the Republican years of Richard Nixon, who calculated that he could buy himself room to maneuver on foreign and defense matters with compromises on domestic policy. Nixon signed off on such new agencies as the Consumer Product Safety Commission and the Environmental Protection Agency. Reagan changed the attitude, although he didn't really make a dent in the federal establishment, for all his talk of cutting agencies and payrolls.

Watching it all, I thought the Reagan operation had the flavor of a sound and light show, mixed with some sleight of hand magic. Just watch the man in the spotlight and enjoy the display. Never mind the mundane details—the soaring budget deficits, the tax increases that nibbled at Reagan's big tax cut, or, worse, the casualty rate of enforcing administration foreign policy, the terrorist massacre of Marines in Beirut. The economy was up for most Americans, despite nagging unemployment. The great communicator was just that. As he said, America was back—from the fading mess of Watergate, the torment of Vietnam, and the muddled term of Democratic rule that followed Nixon's resignation and Ford's brief succession. Americans wanted to believe in themselves again, and for the vast majority, that included believing in Reagan.

At seventy-three, Reagan was the oldest man ever to run for president. So his age and his ability to handle the pressures and decisions of the office for another four years were potential campaign problems. But he had come back from an assassination attempt in which he was shot and gravely wounded by a deranged young man outside the Washington Hilton Hotel little more than two months after his inauguration in 1981. The White House told us how game he was, wisecracking to his wife that he forgot to duck and to his surgeons that he hoped they were all Republicans, and we did not know at the time how close to death the president had been. Reagan's resilience was remarkable; he was back at the White House only eleven days after the shooting. The day he was shot was the most memorable in my seven years as chief of the AP bureau in Washington. White House correspondent Mike Putzel saw it happen, and had his tape recorder running. It recorded the gunshots, pops on the tape, and then Mike's voice in the tumult that followed, telling himself what to do—get to a telephone. He did, inside the hotel, and dictated his bulletin. Grabbing a pay telephone was part of the competition to deliver the story first in that era before cell phones. Reporters' pockets jingled. When I started I always made sure I had an ample supply of dimes for pay phones. Later, of course, dimes wouldn't do; my pocket clanked with quarters.

The Democrats couldn't make age an issue in 1984 without risking a backlash, given Reagan's popularity and the fact that he didn't look as old as he was. He quipped about his age, brushing the topic away with jokes.

He said his last movie had been *Hellcats of the Navy,* and his next one would have to be *The Old Man and the Sea.* He said Andrew Jackson was in excellent shape when he left office at the age of seventy and "I know because he told me so." A faltering, halting debate performance made age a troublesome issue for Reagan late in the campaign, but only briefly. He wisecracked it off the agenda.

There was no misreading the outlook against the Democrats. Conventional wisdom before the 1984 campaign was that Reagan would win unless something disastrous happened. Something disastrous did occur, more than once. But it didn't matter. Crises that would have been the undoing of a less venerated politician flowed off Reagan as though he'd been a bystander to casualties abroad, deepening debt at home, and ethics shadows over appointees. Reagan's foes said he was a disengaged president who let his lieutenants run things in his name. One Democratic crack was that they knew he'd run for a second term because he had left a wake-up call for 1984. But the best lines the opposition could manage were no match for Reagan's winning, self-deprecating showmanship. "What's all this talk about a breakdown in White House communications?" he asked. "How come nobody told me?" Well, Reagan said, he'd fix that. "From now on, about anything that happens, no matter what time it is, wake me, even if it's in the middle of a Cabinet meeting."

Sure, there were problems as he began his 1984 campaign, but the economy was okay and while unemployment persisted as a problem, the rate was coming down. Reagan's quick answer to that issue was to point to the columns of help-wanted ads in the newspapers as evidence that there was work for people who really wanted jobs. The voters heard a man they liked and ignored the critics who talked about picky details like the fine print that showed most of the ads were for jobs that required skills beyond those of the people in the unemployment lines. There had been an economic slump at the beginning of Reagan's first term, but the arrows were pointing upward as he neared the end of it, the perfect situation for a president seeking reelection. He said his 1981 tax cuts fixed the ailing economy, and when pestered with questions about the deficits that had increased fivefold over Carter-era levels he had denounced, Reagan said that was because of the Democrats. They forced too much spending, he said, skipping past his own Pentagon spending burst. Besides, he claimed, the Democrats had slowed the Reagan recovery by approving a 25 percent tax cut instead of the 30 percent he'd campaigned on in 1980 and delaying the date it took effect. That ignored the fact that he pushed most of what he wanted past a Democratic Congress with minimal compromise.

As president and as candidate, Reagan's performance was worthy of any soundstage and the Democrats had nothing to compare. The most memorable line of the campaign for the Democratic nomination was borrowed from a hamburger ad. And the most memorable act of Reagan's challenger was to choose Geraldine Ferraro for the vice presidential nomination, making her the first woman ever to run on a major party ticket. Walter F. Mondale's gamble didn't pay off; Reagan still got a majority of the women's vote.

From the sidelines, Barry Goldwater, back in the Senate, groused about what was happening to presidential campaigns. "We're selling the presidency like we're selling a bar of soap," he complained. "You have a man to arrange your tie or a girl to make sure you don't have a shine on your forehead and make sure your hair is just right. That's no way to elect people." Besides, he said, campaigns cost too much and went on too long. They did, but there was no way to change the trend. The price of politics was going up, and for a politician with the White House on his mind it was never too early to start pursuing the goal. They'd seen the way that worked, notably for Jimmy Carter in 1976, and the trend was to longer, pricier campaigns, not abbreviated ones.

My perspective on the 1984 campaign was different because I watched much of it at a distance, with little time on the campaign road I'd traveled since 1960. My bosses at the AP promoted me to the upper realm of management. I became executive editor of the AP, stationed at headquarters in New York, off the road and off the bus for much of the campaign year. But that didn't get in the way of my candidate watching. Indeed, since I wasn't assigned to report on any one of them, I could watch all of them at once. It was part of a day's work in the new job because I was responsible for overseeing AP political coverage.

As usual, the 1984 sequence began with the assumption that Ted Kennedy could be the nominee should he choose to run, but the senator announced late in 1982 that he would not be a candidate. That opened the field and, at the same time, made former Vice President Mondale the Democrat to beat. Before the campaign year began, seven other candidates tried to do so.

Their points of entry varied. Senator Alan Cranston of California, a balding liberal with a somewhat cadaverous look, tried the Carter-tested straw polls, won the first of 1983 at his home state Democratic convention, and drew Mondale into a costly, meaningless prelude in a half dozen states. Cranston turned into a turkey after the straw counts and got out early. Senator Ernest F. Hollings of South Carolina, who shared the nickname Fritz but not much else with Mondale, made a career of campaigning in New Hampshire, where his deep drawl sounded like a foreign language. That may be why so few Yankees voted for him in the primary. His share of the primary vote worked out to fifty-one ballots for each day of campaigning, so he quit, too. George McGovern was back, with enough visibility to be assigned Secret Service protection in 1984. But the agents outnumbered his traveling campaign team so he dropped them. "I felt ridiculous and conspicuous," he said. Senator John Glenn of Ohio, the former astronaut with Robert Kennedy connections but centrist credentials, looked promising but turned out to be a bland turnoff as a presidential campaigner. "I may be dull but I'm not boring," he insisted. Actually, he was both during his futile presidential campaign. Glenn limped through the early primaries and yielded, but not before he had run up a campaign debt approaching $3 million. He took it personally, as a matter of honor, to pay back the debt in full instead of writing it off on a defunct organization as losers often did. Glenn worked at fund-raising to repay his 1984 campaign bills for years after his futile bid for the White House was a faded memory. Jesse Jackson came to the campaign as a candidate who could not be ignored, because of his influence among black voters vital to the Democrats and because he started with a triumph of personal diplomacy. Over New Year's, he went to Damascus to seek the release of a captured Navy flier, Lieutenant Robert O. Goodman, navigator on a plane shot down over Lebanon early in December. The Syrians released the black lieutenant to Jackson, who escorted him home. Even Reagan, whose administration had chafed at the freelance diplomacy, could only applaud. Jackson campaigned all spring, complaining that the Democratic rules were rigged against black voters and therefore against him, and kept sniping at Mondale after his nomination. "I'm not really aboard," Jackson said. "I'm not part of the inner circle." Defeated rivals seldom are. Atlanta Mayor Andrew Young was more quotable on the Mondale operation, saying it was being managed by "smart-ass white boys." That made for a different sort of campaign button.

Mondale's toughest tormenter was Gary Hart of Colorado, a lanky, youthful senator who came on as a new face in an old crowd. Hart wasn't all that new—he'd been in the Senate for ten years after learning the presidential campaign trade as McGovern's manager in 1972—but the image served well. Hart was a fascinating figure, especially for those of us who had traveled with the McGovern campaign and had known him as a friend on the road, at expense-account dinners, and at late-night parties. The line between reporter and political manager was always there, but with Hart, a contemporary to many of us, it blurred a bit. Not with Hart the candidate, though. The reporters who had been his pals twelve years before were harsh interrogators, with nagging questions that were a problem for him in 1984 and his undoing when he tried again in 1988.

I marveled at Hart's mastery of the expectations game, the familiar exercise of the challenger setting up the front-runner, the better to claim victory in losing. Mondale won the Iowa caucuses with 49 percent of the vote in a crowded field. Hart ran thirty-two points behind him—a landslide defeat. But Hart came in second, better than expected, he said, and the media odds-makers agreed. Hart claimed a major boost, which I thought was a stretch, but he said Iowa showed that he was Mondale's real challenger, since all the other candidates had done even worse. It worked, and suddenly Hart was on the move. His argument was that he was the candidate with new ideas, while Mondale stood for the old ways the voters had already spurned. Hart and the rest of the Democratic field hacked at Mondale as beholden to organized labor, minorities, and interest groups. Those blocs by any other name were the Democratic coalition, the party's base for fifty years. Mondale's rivals made his support among them a liability that Republicans would use in burying his ticket. Hart's "new ideas . . . new generation" theme worked beyond any expectations in New Hampshire, where he upset Mondale in the primary by a twelve-point spread. "Sometimes a cold shower is good for you," Mondale said after taking a bath in New Hampshire. There were colder showers coming, primary defeats a front-runner was not supposed to suffer, or survive. Mondale did, with dogged determination and the support of a party establishment wary of Hart. "Somebody told me this morning that this is character-building," Mondale said after Hart beat him in Maine. "I think I've got more character already than I can use."

Mondale's problem was that he was plain vanilla and Hart was the new flavor of the season. Mondale had union leaders on his side. Hart had movie and TV stars—Warren Beatty, Robert Redford, Mary Tyler Moore, Jack Nicholson, singer Jimmy Buffett, and a dozen more. Mondale had Paul Newman, the actor with his own salad dressing label. Hart's was the star-filled salad. The Hart campaign finally appointed a "celebrity coordinator" to keep track and try to make use of his star power, valuable as a fund-raising draw.

Mondale was seasoned, experienced, a solid senator from Minnesota before he became Carter's vice president. So he gained points for experience, but lost them because of his tie to an unpopular administration and the defeated 1980 ticket. Besides, he was dull, and even his best political friends said so. "He comes over kind of plastic," said Tip O'Neill. In a convoluted comparison, New York Governor Mario Cuomo likened Mondale to a flavorless cornmeal mush called polenta. And that came from politicians who were supporting him. Joan Mondale said her husband's style was part of his Scandinavian heritage. "They don't run around telling funny jokes or wearing funny hats," she said. "They're just very stable, hardworking, honest people. That's what he is. We call it Norwegian charisma." Mondale was never going to win an election on style points, and he didn't pretend otherwise. Nominated that summer, Mondale said he was taking a campaign break. "I'll sit down and read some of my old speeches because I want to get a nap as quickly as possible," he said. After his wipeout loss to Reagan, Mondale said the presidential candidates of the future would have to be better television personalities than he was. "I think, you know, I've never really warmed up to television and . . . it's never really warmed up to me," he said.

Mondale was not the candidate with whom to have a fling; Hart was. His fans saw a bit of John Kennedy in him, and Hart promoted the comparison. Kennedy, he said, "represented hope and promise, a chance for peace and progress. That's what got me into politics and that's why I'm here today." There also turned out to be just a bit of mystery about Hart. He'd changed his name from the family name, Hartpence, and he was a year older than his campaign biography said.

No big deal, he said when those oddities made the newspapers, but the disclosures set off a media frenzy, most damaging on network television when commentators began asking who this newly formidable candidate was, and political reporters started questioning what he really proposed to do as president. Mondale had been asking questions like that and now it was all over the newspapers and TV.

Mondale grilled the argument down to a fast-food hamburger ad. Debating Hart in Atlanta, Mondale told him, "You know, when I hear your ideas, I'm reminded of the ad 'Where's the beef?' " A catchy quip, particularly coming from Mondale. "Fritz, if you'd listen just a minute, I think you'd hear," Hart replied when he could make himself heard over the laughter, but that was no antidote for a three-word gibe. Mondale had a slogan, quotable and handy for TV use, and he milked it. It was no ad lib. A campaign aide claimed to have suggested the line to the candidate. Actually, Lane Kirkland, the president of the AFL-CIO, campaigning for Mondale, used the line before the candidate did. "You can apply the burger test to Hart," Kirkland said. "It's a big bun, but where's the beef?" Whatever the political authorship, Mondale had it ready when he debated Hart. It was trivial but telling, an apt trademark for a campaign that was more about maneuver and image than issues that meant something to the average American.

Jackson said Mondale was a relic and Hart was a fad. Sometimes it all sounded like a word game, but it was a numbers game, too, and Mondale had the advantage there, gaining votes for the nomination that kept him ahead in that bottom-line competition for delegates even when he was losing primaries. He got his biggest break on what should have been his worst day, when he won two states while losing six to Hart. Somehow, the TV commentators translated that into a solid showing for Mondale because Hart had been denied a sweep, a strange reading of the outcome based on inflated expectations the same commentators had created. It was a gift to Mondale, who was able to make the beating sound like a comeback even before he gained a real one in the industrial states where his labor allies were strong. He limped in— Hart won eight of the last twelve Democratic primaries—but he limped in ahead. Still, it was a near thing for Mondale, and there always was a risk that his lead would unravel.

Mondale declared that he would have a delegate majority to clinch the nomination before noon the day after the final primary in California, where Hart won. To make his claim stick, he and his people spent a frantic three hours telephoning uncommitted delegates to coax them aboard. Mondale collared the last handful and claimed victory. "It is clear I am the winner," he said. "This is a very hard count. Every one of these delegates we are claiming we know to be there." That was overstated; the Mondale people were not that certain. But they were certain that letting the clock strike noon without claiming victory on June 6 would have put all their vulnerabilities on damaging display. So Mondale declared himself the winner. He couldn't have done it without a New Jersey delegate sweep, and that probably wouldn't have happened but for Hart's own blunder in the campaign there. He joked that his wife was campaigning in California, where she got to hold cute animals, while he drew New Jersey "and I got to hold samples from a toxic waste dump." Insulting an entire state while asking its people to vote for you flunks elementary politics. The toxic waste line became the story of the week in New Jersey, and Hart sank without a delegate there. He acknowledged that Mondale had nominating numbers but said he would campaign on into overtime, trying to pry loose enough delegates to overtake him.

While Mondale was declaring Democratic victory, Reagan was showing why it would be hollow on election day. That June 6 was the fortieth anniversary of D-Day, and Reagan was in Normandy, his performance overshadowing anything a challenger could manage. In a political aside that day, Reagan said his strategy for handling the Democrats would be to "pretend they're not there." He did. The television coverage didn't go quite that far; Mondale got his mention, but he wasn't the lead. Reagan dominated the screen, from a stage near the cliffs overlooking the World War II landing zone. No TV producer could have devised a better setting, and Reagan was in his element as he looked out at an audience that included sixty-two veterans of the Army Rangers force that had attacked and captured German artillery emplacements on D-Day despite riddling casualties. "These are the boys of Pointe du Hoc," he said of the old soldiers. "These are the men who took the cliffs. These are the champions who helped free a continent. These are the heroes who helped end a war." Reagan sometimes had an off day, but not this one, and when he was on, there was no matching him.

The next act was Mondale's. Having declared himself the nominee, his strategy was to validate the claim by acting the part. He began a public shopping expedition for a vice presidential candidate to run with him. The prospects were called to his home at North Oaks, Minnesota, and although the meetings there were private, the comings and goings were anything but. The interview process was not unlike that Carter had conducted in 1976 before choosing Mondale as his running mate. But Mondale's interview list was something else. Carter had talked with prospective candidates who fit vice presidential tradition—men with records, credentials, and constituencies that might help the ticket. Mondale's interviews were with three women, two blacks, one Hispanic, and one white male senator. We'd heard hints all spring about a woman for the ticket, but that was familiar stuff. Nominees always said their tickets were open to all Americans—women, blacks, and other minorities included. That was customary and it was window dressing. The vice presidential choices that emerged had always fit vice presidential history: reliable types and usually predictable names. This one was different. The hints about a woman on the 1984 ticket became suggestions and then pressure. The National Organization for Women threatened to challenge Mondale's nominee at the convention unless he chose a she, which irked the candidate. He was tending that way but didn't need a new installment in the opposition's argument that he was too beholden to too many interest groups.

Tip O'Neill said the vice presidential nominee should be Geraldine Ferraro, a three-term congresswoman from Queens, New York. Ferraro said a woman's place was on the ticket and she'd take that place if asked. By the old rules, she wouldn't have been. She was not nationally known. While her district was solidly Democratic, she did not have a statewide constituency to bring to the ticket in New York, and there was no evidence that a woman nominee was going to improve the long odds against Mondale. Hart would have made more sense in traditional political terms. He'd won half the primaries, he had strengths to balance Mondale's campaign weaknesses, and although he had not yet folded his challenge for the nomination, he would have agreed to run for vice president in 1984. He already was looking ahead to another presidential bid in 1988, assuming Reagan's reelection in 1984, as almost everyone did. But that very assumption created a situation in which Mondale could break the mold and choose a woman for his ticket, a gamble on which he had nothing to lose.

So the cautious candidate put caution aside and chose Ferraro. "I looked for the best vice president, and I found her in Gerry Ferraro," he said. "We made history today." The latter claim was true, but there was no case to be made for the former. Ferraro would say later that she had not been chosen only because she was a woman. Not so. A backbench House member from Queens with neither a state political base nor a national reputation certainly would not have been chosen had she not been a woman. The Ferraro nomination did strike sparks for the Democrats. They were already assembling for their national convention in San Francisco, dispirited even before they got started, but you could sense a mood swing when Mondale made his move. At least something different was happening, something exciting and, just possibly, something that could change their bleak outlook against Reagan.

It got the president's attention. Reagan suggested that the Ferraro nomination was tokenism and reminded women that he'd put Sandra Day O'Connor on the Supreme Court. But Reagan's advantage was unshaken and Mondale was leading a battered party for the campaign against him. "I've paid my dues," he told black delegates the day before he was nominated, which was true but no help in the fall campaign. Lines like that made him sound like a captive of Democratic bloc politics, which was exactly the picture his opponents wanted to paint. Hart wasn't through sniping at him, saying that the nomination was "not a gold watch to be given out for faithful service" and that nostalgia was not a program. It was a final installment in the Democratic infighting

Mondale described later as a year of party bloodletting. "I hated the whole process," he said after the election. "I think it left scars that I carried with me through the rest of the campaign." Still, conventions are celebrations, and the new-look ticket gave the Democrats something extra to celebrate. It wouldn't last. While Mondale taunted the Republicans as a party of "drowsy harmony," he could only envy it. Their act was set. His was still a work in progress.

The Ferraro nomination wasn't Mondale's only campaign gamble. He also risked candor. He supposedly dug his political grave by promising to raise taxes, although that is not quite what he said in San Francisco. He said a tax increase was inevitable to deal with swelling deficits, no matter which candidate was elected, and he was right. "Whoever is inaugurated in January, the American people will pay Mr. Reagan's bills," he said. "The budget will be squeezed. Taxes will go up. And anyone who says they won't is not telling the truth . . . Let's tell the truth. Mr. Reagan will raise taxes and so will I. He won't tell you. I just did." The Republicans described that as a campaign pledge to raise taxes. I heard Mondale's words that night in San Francisco not as a campaign promise that was supposed to get votes but, rather, as a description of tax medicine Americans inevitably would have to take to deal with deficits after the election. It was an accurate forecast; that's what happened, but not until the Republicans had spent a campaign using it as an issue against Mondale.

Still, that high-risk topic was not a new one for Mondale, who had proposed a deficit-curbing tax increase early in his campaign for the nomination. He wanted one on Democratic lines, to raise tax rates on the top brackets that had benefited most from the 1981 Reagan cuts. Reagan danced around the question, saying he had no plans for a tax increase, the classic hedge for a politician who might have to do something distasteful but doesn't want to say so. He tried calling Mondale a tax-and-spend liberal. "For him, raising taxes is a first resort," Reagan said. "For me it is a last resort." That was hedged, too. Then he said taxes would be increased "over my dead body." Taxes were raised over his live body in bills he signed into law, although the overall personal tax load when he left office was marginally lower than when he began. And federal deficits were monumentally higher. When the national debt passed $1 trillion during his first term, Reagan made a big deal of it, staging a White House show in which he blamed it on the Democrats and the ways of the past. He did not hold an antidebt rally when it hit $2 trillion; that would have reminded everyone that it happened on his presidential watch.

Mondale's supposed blunder on a tax increase led at first to a fumbling Republican response. Reagan tried to say no on taxes without saying never. Vice President George Bush said maybe, a discrepancy that became troublesome. Questioned about it, Bush said he was not going to say anything further on the subject, adding, incomprehensibly, "zippedy-do-dah." Serious subject, nonsense words.

But no big problem, because while they were stumbling over taxes, Reagan's Republicans got another windfall from the Mondale camp, a controversy over Geraldine Ferraro's family finances. They'd had to pay back taxes, which she said were due to inadvertent filing mistakes. Ferraro had promised full financial disclosure, but then said her husband, John Zaccaro, a New York real estate man, wasn't going to release his own tax returns because they were separate and he wasn't the candidate. That boiled up into a flap, and even when he relented, the critical questions persisted. To settle it, Ferraro hired a hall at a Queens hotel for what turned out to be a marathon news conference. First her accountants went over the couple's finances and taxes. Then she answered questions for an hour and forty minutes, all televised. In Dallas, where the Republicans were opening their cut-and-dried convention, it was the only show on all the TV sets installed for delegates and reporters.

Republicans started speculating that the financial controversy might force Ferraro off the ticket. "Wishful thinking," she said. It was. She said she had violated no trust, that she and her husband had nothing to hide, and that their disclosures proved it. But it had been a ten-day distraction, the last thing the trailing Democrats needed, and it took the bloom off the new-look ticket. She was the first woman nominated for vice president, but she was not the first politician snared in controversy over personal finances.

It seemed that Mondale couldn't buy a break, while Reagan slid past almost every glitch.

When the president talked about the power of prayer, Tip O'Neill noted that Reagan seldom went to church, and Reagan managed to make absence sound like a virtue. Reagan said he missed attending Sunday services but "I represent too much of a threat to too many other people for me to be able to go to church" because of security concerns. Besides, the whole congregation would have to go through metal detectors. Checking the sound level before a radio address, Reagan, who had spent years trying to get rid of his quick-trigger image, spoke into a microphone that was turned on in the pressroom, where the tape recorders were running, when he thought he could be heard only in the room. What he intended as private banter became public. "My fellow Americans," he said, "I'm pleased to tell you today that I've signed legislation that will outlaw Russia forever. We begin bombing in five minutes." Just joking, he said when the gaffe was broadcast later, prompting a Kremlin protest. Embarrassing but, since it was Reagan, only a flap, not a major problem. "He screwed up," Goldwater said. "We do it all the time." When "we" means the White House, that is not usually an acceptable explanation, but Reagan was the Teflon president. Nothing stuck. Not the time he fell asleep during an address by the pope. Or the visit to Brazil where he raised a toast to "the people of Bolivia." Or the day he greeted his secretary of housing, the one black member of his Cabinet, by saying, "Hello, Mr. Mayor."

The gaffes were for nitpickers; he had his message and he stood by it. Even when he changed it. He'd once denounced deficit spending as the root of all economic travail, but by 1984 he found it no barrier to economic progress. He even disowned one of his most noted lines, denying that he had called the Soviet Union an "evil empire" when his phrase was on record and on tape. Later, reelected, Reagan changed his tune and decided he liked the line, repeating it as evidence that he hadn't gone soft on Moscow when he negotiated arms reductions with the Soviet Union during his second term. He didn't have to be consistent, he just had to be Reagan.

His campaign fare was a syrup of confidence and reassurance. It was morning in America, Reagan said, and he had a sparkling vision of even better times. "You ain't seen nothing yet," he said. You didn't see any specifics because Reagan ran on themes, not specifics. He avoided the questioning reporters who always wanted the fine-print answers. He'd walk away, or cup an ear and say he hadn't heard the question, or walk into the roar of the helicopter engines so nobody could hear anything. He wasn't going to stray off message because some reporter asked a question, and besides, the tactics protected him against questions he might not have been able to answer. Never mind the details; Reagan's staff could worry about that. Stars don't have to concern themselves with scriptwriting and stage directions.

Before he defeated Carter in 1980, Reagan had charged that a faltering foreign policy emboldened Iran to take and hold the American embassy hostages, and said he wouldn't stand by and do nothing if they were still held when he got to the White House. He lucked out—the Iranians, in a last slap at Carter, released the hostages as Reagan was inaugurated so he didn't have to say what he would have done, let alone do it. But he did say that his administration would not tolerate such acts against Americans. What happened on his watch was worse. The fifty-two hostages came home alive in 1981, although eight American servicemen had been killed in Carter's failed attempt to rescue them. The terrorist truck bombing of a Marine barracks near Beirut killed 241 American servicemen on October 23, 1983. "The United States will not be intimidated by terrorists," Reagan said, resisting Democratic calls for an end to an ill-defined peacekeeping effort in Lebanon. He changed the orders two months later, moving Marines to ships offshore. "We're not bugging out, we're just going to a little more defensible position," Reagan said defensively. In another month, that ended, too. The toll by then was 264 dead, 137 wounded.

Logically, that should have been a major issue and a damaging one against a president beginning a reelection campaign. For Carter, the hostage situation had been a constant campaign undertow. The deadly terrorism against U.S. forces in Lebanon did not register as a significant liability against Reagan, although Mondale tried to make it one.

"The president told the terrorists he was going to retaliate," he said when he debated Reagan. "He didn't. And the bottom line is the United States left in humiliation and our enemies are stronger." By then there had been another terrorist attack in Beirut, on September 20, an embassy bombing that killed nine people, two of them Americans. Reagan insisted that security had not been lax; he said safeguards were being built but hadn't quite been finished. "Anybody that's ever had their kitchen done over knows it never gets done as soon as you wish it would," he said, offering an oddly homey explanation given the deadly circumstances. Mondale said that "being president and countering terrorists is a more difficult task than fixing up your kitchen." He accused Reagan of "letting terrorists humiliate us, push us around, and kill our people." That sounded very much like what Reagan had said about Carter during the Iran hostage crisis. But Mondale couldn't make it into a telling issue. What worked for Reagan against Carter flopped for Mondale against Reagan. Two days after the Marine barracks truck bombing, Reagan ordered an invasion of Grenada, an island speck in the Caribbean Sea, saying it was to protect about 1,100 Americans there from Communists who had seized power. "We got there just in time," he told the nation. To the cynical, it looked as though he got there just in time to change the subject from losses in Lebanon to winning a mini-war.

But the administration still had the Middle East disaster to explain away. Vice President Bush said the Beirut killings were not comparable to the "humiliation" of the Iranian hostage taking when Carter was president because that involved a foreign government, not "wanton acts of terror by a shadowy group." He said of the Beirut bombings, "I don't think of those as humiliations, I think of those people as victims of horrible, international terror." When Ferraro brought up Reagan's inaction after the terrorist attacks in Lebanon, Bush tried roughly the same script—wanton terrorists in Beirut, government involvement in Iran. "Let me help you with the difference, Mrs. Ferraro, between Iran and the embassy in Lebanon," Bush began. Ferraro fumed, and when her turn came she shot back: "Let me just say, first of all, that I almost resent, Vice President Bush, your patronizing attitude that you have to teach me about foreign policy." She was not almost resentful, she was angry and it showed. The substance got lost in the spat. That was fine with Bush.

"We tried to kick a little ass last night," he told a union leader on the New Jersey docks the next day, and then realized there was a TV microphone picking up his words. "Oops, oh God, he heard me. Turn that thing off," Bush said, too late. It was on tape. Reagan instinctively denied his vice president had said it. "I don't know anything about it, but I would be inclined not to believe it," Reagan said when he was asked about the Bush remark. Bush couldn't deny it, so he defended it. "It's an old expression and I stand behind it. That's the way my kids talk. That's the way I talk," he said. "I just don't like to use it in public." More to the point, he didn't like to be caught using it in public. After that episode he minded his campaign manners. So did Barbara Bush, who had described Ferraro as "I can't say it but it rhymes with rich." She later apologized and suggested that the rhyming word was "witch," no compliment but more acceptable than "bitch."

With a campaign month to go, the age issue Reagan had been deflecting suddenly got serious for him. While he'd always made a joke of it, his strategists had been wary of the question all year. I never thought his age was the real problem; it was his disengagement, the sense that he was out of touch, the face and voice of the administration but not its hands-on executive. In 1981, U.S. warplanes shot down Libyan jets that had challenged them off the coast of Libya. That underscored toughness in administration policy, but left questions about Reagan's command of it when the White House acknowledged the president had been sleeping at the time and was not told of the episode for six hours.

Mondale kept trying to stir the disengagement question. "I'm not sure which is worse," he said, "the arrogance of Mr. Reagan's isolation or his belief that the American people would let him get away with it." Whatever the merits of the accusation, the belief was the fact. Except for Democratic partisans, people weren't concerned about Reagan's way of governing, and they liked his public, great communicator style.

The Democrats said he wasn't that good without a script, that he was a performer with prompters, using lines he knew by rote, with index card reminders always handy in case he forgot a point. A Mondale manager told me that if they could just shuffle those index cards, they'd have a chance to beat Reagan.

Mondale said Reagan had "detached himself from the details of the government." He accused Reagan of "leadership by amnesia." Reagan's retort: "I'm surprised he knew what the word meant." What it meant was that the Democrats were trying to plant the idea that Reagan was a faltering old man, not up to another term in the White House. He wasn't that old; other men in other nations had been effective world leaders well past his age. But no American president had been elected at seventy-three.

Reagan saw the problem and tried to preempt it. He chopped wood at his ranch, rode horseback, signed a magazine piece about his physical exercise routine. And he joked about it. "I've already lived about twenty-odd years longer than my life expectancy when I was born," he said. "That's a source of annoyance to a number of people." He said he didn't think age would be an issue. "Somebody tried to make it one four years ago, and it didn't work," he said, "and I've tried to start a rumor that I'm not really that old, that they mixed up the babies in the hospital." His friend and campaign chairman, Senator Paul Laxalt of Nevada, said he couldn't conceive of age becoming a problem because "he's very responsive, he's very direct, he's not absentminded." But it did become one, a month before the election.

The Democrats didn't dare to push the age question overtly because the tactic might have backfired on them. Reagan's age became an issue because his halting, confused performance in the first campaign debate with Mondale seemed to validate the subject. Reagan the communicator lapsed into bewildering numbers and befuddling sentences. He was defensive and not good at it. Reaching back for a way out, he tried his 1980 debate line to fend off Mondale's accusations: "There you go again." Mondale adroitly turned that against him, reciting what he said were broken promises of that Reagan campaign.

When the TV moderator got the debate sequence out of order and offered Reagan extra time, he fumbled even that. "I'm all confused now," he said. The moderator's mix-up gave him reason to be, but Reagan's words were an unintended self-summary of his bad night on camera.

Now the Reagan people had trouble. There's no worse moment for a presidential candidate to mess up than in one of the great debates, which command wider audiences than anything else in a campaign. A candidate has to be quick enough to avoid the traps, and in that debate with Mondale, Reagan was not. He was supposed to be the master performer. Instead, he was a lousy one for most of ninety-plus minutes on television. Now the Democrats had a risk-free way into the age issue and the Republicans were on the defensive.

Two days after the debate, the *Wall Street Journal* put it into print with a lead story asking whether the oldest president was showing his age. David Broder wrote a *Washington Post* column on the question. That made it a safe subject for the rest of the media, and the television networks blared it in unison that evening. Age was on the campaign agenda. One of the valid complaints about political reporters is that we all clamor about the same stories. That happened on Reagan and the age issue for two reasons. The first is that none of us likes being beaten to a major story or issue. When that happens, we set about catching up and trying to find out more so as to write the next chapter and get ahead of the competition. The other reason was unique to the Reagan situation. There had been Reagan age stories all season, and even in his losing campaign four years before. I wrote one in 1976 when he turned sixty-five while campaigning in New Hampshire and became eligible for Social Security benefits, which he declined. But the idea that his age was a problem and that he was slowing to a point that might be debilitating in a second term was not so much a news story as an accusation. Reporters—at least conscientious, objective reporters—do not deal in accusations. That's up to the candidates. More than once, campaigns tried to feed me damaging information about their opponents, seeking a way into print without fingerprints. I wouldn't play. An accusation cloaked in objectivity is far more effective than one lodged by a rival candidate, and good reporters don't let politicians use them that way.

But the debate and the *Journal* story had put the age issue into play. Now reporters could ask politicians about it, and we did. Laxalt acknowledged that Reagan had an off night, but blamed it on a wearing, overly intensive effort to brief him in preparation for the debate, not on "any physical or mental deficiency." Even the denial added to the problem. I wouldn't have used those quoted words in a news story until Reagan's man did. Then they were part of the dialogue.

Mondale was trying to add fuel. He said Reagan might be "out of touch with the impact of his policies . . . Maybe he doesn't understand what he has done. But we need a president who knows what is going on." His allies worked the issue, too, including, remarkably, eighty-four-year-old Representative Claude Pepper of Florida, the political patron of all elderly causes. Pepper said Reagan was showing signs of old age. He said Reagan's lapses in the debate "might well be attributed to his increasing years." I guess it took one to know one.

The White House chose the week after the TV debate to release a doctor's report saying the president's health was fine. Coincidence, they claimed; the release had been planned all along. "I wasn't tired" in the Mondale debate, Reagan said. "And in regard to the age issue and everything, if I had on as much makeup as he did, I'd look younger, too." Reagan said he had never worn makeup, "even when I was in pictures," but we found makeup artists who recalled otherwise. There also was the persistent rumor that he dyed his hair to keep the gray out, which the Reagan people always denied. The cynical response around Washington was that he might just be prematurely orange.

Let Reagan be Reagan his followers said, complaining that he had been crammed with too many facts and figures to be himself in the debate. "I was overtrained," the president agreed. Reagan's team wouldn't let that happen again. He'd be rested and ready for the final debate, two weeks after the first.

Mondale went in on the offensive, saying Reagan was out of touch. He questioned whether Reagan was "in charge of the facts" and exercising real authority over his own administration. Reagan fended him off until the debate got to the Question. "You are already the oldest president in history, and some of your staff say you tired after your most recent encounter with Mr. Mondale," said Henry Trewhitt of the *Baltimore Sun*. "President Kennedy had to go for days on end with very little sleep during the Cuban missile crisis. Is there any doubt in your mind that you would be able to function in such circumstances?"

"Not at all, Mr. Trewhitt," Reagan said. Then, with one line, he shelved the issue. "I want you to know that also I will not make age an issue of this campaign," the president said. "I am not going to exploit for political purposes my opponent's youth and inexperience."

That drew laughter from the audience and a smile from Mondale, who said long afterward that it was a smile through tears because at that moment he knew the election was hopeless.

Not that Reagan was a champion debater that night, either. His bumbling summation was as addled as anything he'd said in the first debate. He got his time frame confused and said voters had to decide whether they wanted to "return to the policies of weakness of the past four years," which obviously was not what he meant to say about his own first term. Then he rambled through an account of writing a letter to be put into a time capsule, which made no sense literally or politically. I wrote that night that Reagan had not been at his televised best but probably had been good enough to avoid further debate damage and hold his lead. I underestimated the power of Reagan's one best line, the comeback on the too-old question. With it, the president deflected and deflated the age issue. That helped him get past the more significant question of whether he was a commander in chief who had ceded real command to his committees, consultants, and advisers. There certainly were grounds for wondering about that, but it made no difference. "I know it will come as a surprise to Mr. Mondale, but I am in charge," the president said, and voters took his word for it. Reagan was Reagan again, and that was enough. Fifteen days later Mondale was buried in a 59 percent Reagan landslide. He won only in Minnesota and the District of Columbia, the worst electoral vote drubbing in history. "My chance of winning disappeared at the end of the second debate," he said. "The president sufficiently reassured Americans."

Reagan won a mandate without a blueprint in his last, best landslide. So he had ample room to maneuver in his second term. The hawk didn't go dovish, but Reagan negotiated for arms reductions with Moscow and boasted of "a satisfying new closeness" in relations. Still claiming to be the champion of tax cutters, he signed thirteen bills that raised taxes while insisting that he had opposed them all. Administration operatives traded arms for hostages in the Middle East and misspent the money the weapons brought. Reagan denied it, then had to admit it—but said even then that his heart and his intentions told him that what he was confessing wasn't so.

When Reagan left office in 1989, he had the highest job approval ratings an outgoing president ever held, 68 percent. He was the first president in sixty years to turn the job over to an elected successor of his own party. His genius was not in the details but in avoiding them. In the sad retirement that took him from the stage as a victim of Alzheimer's disease, the biggest federal office building in Washington was named for the president who had demanded smaller government. That was only the beginning of a naming frenzy led by conservative activists to get highways and government installations named for Reagan in every state. After the Republicans took control of Congress, they voted to change Washington National Airport to Ronald Reagan Washington National Airport. I thought George should have had his first name in there, too, but the nostalgia was for the fortieth president, not the first.

In an uncertain world, Reagan stood for certainty, I wrote as he left office. He was unwavering, absolute in his convictions, never more so than when he was changing them. His style not only succeeded, it triumphed.

"They call it the Reagan revolution and I'll accept that," Reagan said in farewell. "But for me, it always seemed more like the great rediscovery, a rediscovery of our values and our common sense." Whether by revolution or rediscovery, Reagan had rewritten the agenda.

EIGHT

Flag-Waving, Lip-Reading, and Liberal-Baiting in the Campaign of 1988

W hen monkey business toppled the leading Democratic candidate, the presidential campaign of 1988 got down to really
vital matters—such as flag-waving, prison furloughs, and the questions of whether Vice President George Bush was a wimp and Democrat Michael Dukakis was an emotionless ice man. It was a campaign
that enthroned irrelevance. In snide shorthand, the field of candidates
for the Democratic nomination was called the seven dwarfs; the
Republicans had a six-pack. The candidates traded trivia and sloga-
neering, tone-deaf to the real problems facing Americans and the next
president. Bush ran as the heir to Ronald Reagan and his promise in
chief was the "read my lips" vow of no new taxes, which he broke as
president. Dukakis, the all-business governor of Massachusetts, said
the question was competence, not philosophy, bristling when the
Republicans called him a liberal but eventually, curiously, changing his
tune to say that he was one and proud of it.

While the 1988 campaign was not enlightening, neither was it elevating. It was the campaign that took adultery out of the bedroom
and put it into presidential politics as a question for candidates. After
the aborted campaign of Gary Hart, intimate, personal topics were in
bounds, part of the process. Gossip always had been part of politics,

but in whispers. Now the volume was turned up and almost any rumor was treated as fair campaign game, grounds for questioning of the candidate, which, obviously, put such stuff on the public record.

The year of nasty politicking showed the power of accentuating the negative, which was at the center of the Bush strategy. Going negative was nothing new, and I never saw a candidate who didn't do it while denying it. The cover always was, and is, the same: Denouncing the other guy is comparative, not negative. Actually, it is both, because no candidate is saintly enough to run entirely by promoting his ideas, programs, and leadership style without tearing down those of the other side. The Bush campaign took that reality to a new level with a concentrated attack plan that succeeded and kept Dukakis defending himself much of the season. The Bush offensive wouldn't have been that effective against a more adept Democratic candidate, but Dukakis had not found his footing nationally. As Republican attacks escalated, Bush worried that the tactics might backfire. So one night on the floodlit lawn of Bob Hope's Hollywood estate, Bush promised some fine-tuning. "We're not going to be talking on the negative side anymore," he told Republican donors there. "It's going to be a kinder and gentler finish to this campaign." Sure it was. Within a day, Bush described Dukakis as a sexist who would torpedo American prosperity and bring the nation to gloom and malaise.

Before it was done, Richard Nixon had called the campaign fare trivial, superficial, and inane, and Barry Goldwater had sent public word to Bush that he ought to start talking about real issues instead of fake ones. The vice presidential nominees traded insults, Republican Dan Quayle saying the Democrats were dealing in sludge, Lloyd Bentsen complaining of GOP mud wrestling. Dukakis said Republican tactics smacked of racism. Jesse Jackson complained that all the nominees were doing was exchanging one-liners, criticism that came from an expert since Jackson spouted them himself, sometimes in rhyme.

Vice President Bush began with the advantage in his second campaign for the Republican presidential nomination. No modern vice president who sought his party's nomination for the White House has been denied it, with the exception of Alben Barkley, who was seventy-four when he tried, briefly, in 1952. In nine of the thirteen presidential campaigns between the end of World War II and the end of the century, one ticket or the other has been headed by a vice president or a former one. Former ones did better. No incumbent vice president was elected president between 1836, when Martin Van Buren won the White House, and 1988, when Bush finally did. Despite his advantages, Bush's route to the Republican ticket was an obstacle course. He had to deal first with his own image—the dutiful vice president scorned by his opponents as "the résumé candidate" because he hadn't won an election on his own since 1968, the second of his two terms in Congress from Houston. He left the House for an unsuccessful campaign for the Senate in 1970. He had foreign policy experience as U.N. ambassador, envoy to China, and, briefly, CIA director. He melded his moderate views with Reagan conservatism when he joined the ticket in 1980, which led cartoonist Garry Trudeau to depict him in "Doonesbury" as a candidate who had put his manhood in blind trust. Bush said it bothered him at first, but then he decided not to be uptight because Americans didn't believe the comics about him. " 'Doonesbury,' my God," Bush said. "He speaks for a bunch of Brie-tasting, Chardonnay-sipping elitists." Besides, he didn't "understand 'Doonesbury,' even when it's about me."

Bush's tendency to mangle his wording didn't help. "I have opinions of my own, strong opinions," he said in 1987. "But I don't always agree with them." He wasn't joking, just misspeaking. We called it Bushspeak, apparently a family trait, since his son later delivered convoluted sentences, too. On the day he declared himself a candidate for president, October 12, 1987, *Newsweek* hit the stands with a cover story on the vice president and his prospects, headlined "Fighting the Wimp Factor." The story included a public opinion poll in which more than half the people said the wimp image would be a serious problem for candidate Bush. The wimp talk was a cheap shot, Bush said, from nitwits who didn't know what it was to fly World War II combat missions in the Pacific—he flew fifty-eight—or to be shot down at age twenty. What's more, he said, "I like pork rinds, but that doesn't fit the mold."

The campaign for the Republican nomination began two years in advance, forcing Bush into political action far earlier than the front-runner wanted to start. Michigan Republicans had set up a bizarre system of caucuses to award their 1988 nominating votes, with the first installment of the competition in 1986. Pat Robertson, the television preacher who said God had called him to run for president, campaigned intensively there, forcing Bush into a costly, premature contest. The vice president eventually won, but he paid a toll in diverted resources and political energy. Senate Republican Leader Bob Dole was concentrating on Iowa, and Robertson was competing there, too, with a built-in constituency of conservative Christians, a bloc strong enough to prove potent in the caucuses. With the farm economy sagging, the Reagan connection was little help to Bush in Iowa.

The vice president's start there was not promising. When Robertson won an early straw poll, Bush said he would have done better but his supporters were busy: "A lot of people that support me, they were off at the air show, they were off at their daughter's coming-out party, or they were off teeing up on the golf course for that all-important last round." There are more plowing contests than debutante balls in Iowa, but Bush tended to say odd things like that. When a TV interviewer questioned whether he was tough enough to deal with the Soviet Union, Bush said he was and could prove it: "You've seen me striding down the sixteenth fairway with blood in my eye." That certainly would cow the Kremlin. And such lines were no help as the candidate tried to shed the image of an aging preppy. He said and did things that made it stick. Traveling with the Bush campaign that fall, I bumped into the vice president at his Detroit hotel one morning, and he was miffed. He'd just been in the sauna, and a reporter had cornered him there and tried to interview him. Bush wanted to know whether I thought that was fair. I said I thought it was difficult because it would be hard to take notes in a sauna. "Well," he said, "you missed your chance to see me naked." I didn't think that was part of the job description, so I just smiled.

In the first test of the campaign for the Republican nomination, Dole won the Iowa caucuses, a defeat the Bush people tried to explain away as a regional thing, midwesterners voting for a candidate from the neighborhood. That might cover Kansan Dole, but what they couldn't alibi was the far more damaging fact that Bush lost to Pat Robertson, too, and ran a weak third in Iowa. Those were the caucuses in which Bush had upset Reagan in 1980, and four years later he had the advantages of national office. But there wasn't any "Big Mo" for Bush the second time around.

That wasn't all. Bush was dogged by the Iran-Contra scandal in which the Reagan administration traded arms to Teheran in 1985 and 1986 in exchange for the release of U.S. hostages in the Middle East. A special prosecutor was on the case by campaign time, a political peril for Bush, who insisted that he hadn't known of the deal that breached American policy. He said he had been out of the loop and nobody proved otherwise, despite evidence that he had been present at meetings at which the illicit deal was discussed. He denied everything and claimed that he had answered every scandal question except one: He would not say what he had told Reagan about Iran-Contra while it was happening. "I'm not a kiss and teller," he Bush-spoke. Bush said if he had known about it, he would have opposed it. He never explained how he could have been at meetings where it was discussed without knowing anything about it.

He'd argued the case on network television before the Iowa caucuses, and while it wasn't enough to salvage him there, the episode turned to his advantage on both Iran-Contra and the wimp problem. Bush agreed to an interview with Dan Rather on CBS, for what he thought was to be a political profile. He insisted that the interview be live so that his answers could not be edited before they were broadcast. The interview ran on for over nine minutes, an extraordinary segment on a tightly timed network news program, and Rather's questions dealt entirely with Iran-Contra, which angered Bush. "You've impugned my integrity," he told the anchorman. It turned into an argument, both men speaking at once, making it impossible to understand either. Bush said it wasn't fair to judge his whole career "by a rehash" of Iran-Contra accusations that had been investigated and disproved. He made it personal, asked Rather how he would like being judged by the seven minutes of blank airtime when he stormed off the CBS set in 1987 because a tennis match had cut into his nightly news time. Rather said the presidency was more important than a TV flap, but in a debate with a television anchorman, Bush couldn't lose. People like beating on the media and Bush was doing it for them. Off-camera in his Capitol office—Rather was in New York—Bush vented his rage into a microphone still open to monitoring reporters. "The bastard didn't lay a glove on me," he snapped. He hadn't looked like a wimp and he certainly didn't sound like one. His son George W. took up the family cheerleading. "It's reinforced the image of George Bush, that he's a strong, stern man when his integrity had been questioned," the younger Bush said. "I know, I've been on the wrong side of his lectures before."

But the embarrassment of Bush's sorry showing in Iowa sent him limping into the New Hampshire primary with his campaign tottering. In the public opinion polls there, Dole overtook Bush and edged ahead of him. Another defeat and the front-runner could be a goner, so Bush went on the attack. Robertson's early showings had embarrassed the vice president, but Robertson wasn't going to be the Republican nominee, notwithstanding the summons he claimed to have received from God. Dole was the real rival, and Bush accused him of tolerating tax increases, anathema in a state with no sales or income taxes. The Bush campaign broadcast a TV commercial that showed Dole with two faces. "Taxes, he can't say no," the ominous ad voice said. "Bob Dole straddles, and he just won't promise not to raise taxes. And you know what that means."

In a campaign debate, Pete du Pont, the former Delaware governor running but going nowhere, pulled out the New Hampshire pledge, a fixture gimmick in which candidates signed a promise not to raise taxes. "Sign it," du Pont demanded of Dole. "I'd have to read it first," the senator replied. "Maybe George should sign it." Those debate theatrics aside, Bush's campaign strategy was built on repeated promises that he would not permit tax increases. Bush easily beat Dole in the New Hampshire primary, and Robertson wasn't even close. So the vice president was back on track. After the outcome was reported,

Tom Brokaw of NBC got Bush and Dole on television, separately but simultaneously. He asked whether the vice president had any message for Dole. "No, just wish him well and meet in the South," Bush said mildly. Brokaw asked Dole whether he had a message. "Stop lying about my record," Dole snapped, glowering darkly. He looked like some political Dracula. The problem was bad lighting as well as a bad mood, and the grim visage stuck. In fact, Bush had twisted Dole's record against him, but it was the image that counted—nice Bush, mean Dole.

Dole had called Bush all résumé and retinue, saying the vice president could not point to one thing he had accomplished during his eight years with Reagan. Vice presidents don't get to make decisions, so that is an easy shot for a candidate running against one. But Dole withheld a particularly harsh campaign TV ad that dramatized his point, wary of attack tactics that would remind voters of his reputation as a political hatchet man. The ad showed a man walking through the snow without leaving any footprints, while the announcer recited Bush's résumé and the achievements the vice president claimed. The Dole campaign didn't broadcast it in New Hampshire, where the snow commercial made sense. They shelved it because they were worried it might be too tough and could backfire. "After a lifetime of walking in the shoes of giants, isn't it interesting that George Bush has never left a single footprint behind?" the announcer's voice intoned. The Dole campaign finally used the footprints ad in Florida, where people go to stay away from snow and where it did no good anyhow. Florida was one of the sixteen states Bush carried on March 8, dubbed "Super Tuesday" for all the primaries on a single day. With that, Bush was all the way back, his nomination clinched, his rivals dropping out.

But not Pat Robertson, who conceded the nomination to Bush but wouldn't quit the campaign. "This is an enterprise the Lord sent me on a year or so ago, running for president," he told about three thousand people at the Happy Church in Denver. Figuring out that political theology defied my powers of analysis, and I wasn't alone. When the National Association of Evangelicals polled delegates to its convention, Robertson ran fourth among Republicans. Dole, who claimed no divine mandate, withdrew at the end of March, went to the White House, and told Reagan, "I'm reporting back for duty" as Senate leader. Quitting the campaign, Dole said: "I have been beaten before and no doubt will be again. But I never have been defeated and never will be." That sounded good, even though the dictionary says the two words are synonyms.

So the Republican nomination belonged to Bush, five months in advance. His task became one of commanding political attention to keep his name in the newspapers and on TV until the Republican convention, while the Democrats were still competing in primary campaigns, which put them in the news automatically. That's always a challenge for a candidate who clinches the nomination early in the season, but it beats the alternative of scrambling in competition all the way to the convention.

For Dukakis, that alternative was the reality, a springtime of contention with Jesse Jackson after the rest of the field had surrendered. Gary Hart, who had made a national name in defeat in the 1984 Democratic campaign, began his bid for the 1988 nomination as the Democratic favorite. But he had to cope from the start with what is euphemistically called the character issue. Translated from political journalese, that meant that he had a reputation as a ladies' man with a wife back home. He'd socialized with reporters in 1972 when he was managing McGovern's campaign, and they remembered the bar talk from those days. He'd twice been separated from his wife, Lee, although they were back together when he ran. Hart denied all rumors but they persisted as he declared his candidacy in the spring of 1987. He told interviewers he had nothing to hide. Reporter E. J. Dionne Jr. wrote a profile for the *New York Times Magazine*, and Hart told him: "Follow me around, I don't care. I'm serious. If anybody wants to put a tail on me, go ahead. They'd be very bored."

They did, and they weren't. The *Miami Herald* had been tipped that the rumors were true and that Hart had invited a Miami woman to his town house on Capitol Hill. *Herald* reporters staked out the place on May Day 1987. They spotted Hart going in with a blonde who spent the night. The *Herald* story was published on May 3, the same day the Dionne piece appeared in the *Times*. In political mythology, Hart was followed after he'd challenged reporters to tail him. In fact, the stakeout came first. When *Herald* reporters confronted Hart outside his home, he said no one was staying at his house, that he was not involved in any relationship, and that he was being set up.

The *Herald* story said Hart, "who has dismissed allegations of womanizing, spent Friday night and most of Saturday in his Capitol Hill townhouse with a young woman who flew from Miami and met him. Hart denied any impropriety." Hart tried to tough it out with denials, saying that the story was misleading and false and that his mistake was to put himself in circumstances that could be misconstrued. Beyond that, he said, "I have nothing to hide," and went back to the campaign. At a news conference in Hanover, New Hampshire, reporter Paul Taylor of the *Washington Post* asked Hart the question that changed the boundary of campaign scrutiny. "Have you ever committed adultery?" he asked. "I do not think that's a fair question," the candidate replied, and they fenced over wording. Taylor asked the question again, and Hart said he was not going "into a theological definition of what constitutes adultery." I thought that made him the champion of political haggling about the definition of a simple word until Bill Clinton took over by dodging a question by saying it depended on what the meaning of "is" is. The blunt, direct question of adultery hadn't been put to candidates before 1988. With it, for political good or ill, the most intimate, personal matters about a candidate were opened to attempted inspection.

The other woman was Donna Rice, a Miami model, and it would later be disclosed that she and Hart had cruised overnight from Miami to Bimini with another couple. On June 2, the supermarket tabloid *National Enquirer* published a photograph of Rice sitting in Hart's lap. He was wearing a T-shirt emblazoned "Monkey Business Crew," for the name of the yacht. But by then, Hart had conceded that "under present circumstances, this campaign cannot go on." He was still defiantly denouncing "reporters in bushes" and their "false and inaccurate stories," saying they made a mockery of the system. But he had been confronted with accounts of another affair the winter before. The

Washington Post had the outlines of the story and photographs of him leaving that woman's home. The story was never printed. Hart got out first.

"I am what I am," Hart said in dropping his campaign. "I don't want to be the issue." But the candidate is, inevitably and properly, an issue. No one can run for president without facing and withstanding the glare of unrelenting scrutiny. The question, and no one has or will find a pat answer, is how intrusive that scrutiny should be regarding the personal lives of candidates. My own answer as a reporter was that the personal attributes of candidates are issues and appropriate ones. The voters are not choosing among position papers or abstractions. The choice is among real people with personal as well as political records. Candidates can and do change positions on policies, but they can't change themselves. I think voters are entitled to know who they are as well as what they propose to do in office. How personal that gets depends on the behavior of the candidate. And also, realistically, on how discreet a candidate is about personal behavior. By latter-day accounts, JFK's personal affairs involved more than one woman, but he kept his private dalliances quiet. When Hart got into trouble in 1988, a seasoned adviser to Democratic presidents said it was because he was impatient and wouldn't wait until he got to the White House, where he could carry on behind iron gates and armed guards. Rumors of Hart's involvements with women had persisted for fifteen years, and he had heatedly denied them in declaring his candidacy for the 1988 nomination. Within three weeks he had validated them, which seemed to me as arrogant as it was indiscreet.

Eight months after he dropped his campaign, Hart suddenly reappeared, entering the New Hampshire primary. "The public does not have a right to know about everybody's personal life," he said. But a candidate for president is not everybody. Then, in an interview with the *Des Moines Register*, Hart said that if he was elected, he would not be the first adulterer in the White House. "I may be the first one to have publicly confessed to that sin, but I won't be the first one." He had, at least, figured out the meaning of the word. But by then, he was a hopeless political case, a joking matter on late-night TV. "He said that if he was elected he would not be the first adulterer in the White House, but he would be the best," Johnny Carson quipped. When President Reagan had his annual physical and was pronounced fit, David Letterman said, "Reagan says he has the body of a twenty-year-old, which, if I remember correctly, is very much like the Gary Hart campaign slogan."

Hart quit for good after a hapless showing in the first primary. But the imprint of what happened to him lasted. In the fall of 1987, there were rumors about George Bush and another woman. Adultery? Son George W. dealt with the matter: "The answer to the big A question is N-O." The topic made a comeback two weeks before the presidential election when the *Wall Street Journal* blamed a stock market decline on October 20 on rumors that the *Washington Post* was about to publish a damaging story about Bush, which didn't happen. That frustrated the Dukakis people. Donna Brazile, a field director at his campaign headquarters, stoked the gossip the next day. She said she hadn't been on Wall Street but understood "they got a little concerned that George was going to the White House with somebody other than Barbara. I think George Bush owes it to the American people to fess up." Dukakis apologized to Bush, and Brazile resigned from his campaign. Her skills kept her at work in Democratic politics, and in 2000, she was Al Gore's campaign manager.

As for the impact of Bush's bedroom behavior on the stock market, I imagined a telephone call to a broker. "Sell," the customer cries. "George Bush has been fooling around." The story evaporated, Bush was elected president, and the day after he won, the market went down again.

Dukakis began the 1988 campaign as an unlikely nominee but he methodically climbed past the field, until the persistent Jackson was the only rival left. The voting began in Iowa farm country, where the governor of Massachusetts was an alien and quickly proved it by suggesting that farmers suffering from sagging prices should diversify their crops from corn and soybeans to fruit, flowers, and Belgian endive. Most of us weren't sure exactly what Belgian endive was—I had to look it up. It is a lettucelike plant with narrow curled leaves, used in salads. Obviously not a crop option for a grain farmer in the Midwest. An anti-Dukakis ad broadcast by Missouri Representative Richard A. Gephardt ended with the announcer asking incredulously: "Belgian endive?" Gephardt won the Iowa caucuses; Dukakis ran third. Then the competition moved east, where Dukakis was in home territory and swamped Gephardt in the New Hampshire primary. Running in the state next door was an advantage, but not an unmixed one. Southern New Hampshire was becoming a commuter tax haven for people fleeing the high rates in Massachusetts, and many of them blamed Dukakis. Bush tried to capitalize on that in the fall campaign, with his strange syntax: "You know the governor of Massachusetts— I don't know why they call it Taxachusetts. I didn't name it Tax- achusetts. The people in Taxachusetts named it Taxachusetts." Bushspeak again; he could step on any line they fed him.

Jackson entered the New Hampshire primary to hold his place in the constant series of Democratic candidate debates, but it wasn't his kind of state and he ran a limited campaign. I heard his personal view of New Hampshire in an odd and unintended way. That January, the *News-Gazette* of Champaign, Illinois, reported that Jackson had been forced to drop out of the University of Illinois because of pla- giarism. He said his record was clean, and that the university would vouch for it. The AP picked up the *News-Gazette* story and it moved on our wires. I was executive editor and I got a call one evening from Frank Watkins, Jackson's aide and spokesman, saying that the rev- erend wanted to talk with me. I said fine, put him on, but Watkins said he wouldn't be available for a couple of hours. So I gave him my home telephone number in Brooklyn. Watkins called me there that night, and Jackson clicked onto the line. He wanted to complain about the plagiarism story, which he wanted eliminated. It had gone out on the AP wire the day before, so that would have been impossi- ble even had I been willing, which I wasn't. I told Jackson we'd carry any denial or comment he wanted to make, but he wasn't interested in that. He knew that anything he said in rebuttal would just keep the story going. So we agreed to disagree and said good night. I hung up and had to make another call a few minutes later. Watkins and

Jackson were still on my line. I cleared my throat politely to let them know I was back, but my end of the connection had been partially cut—I could hear but I couldn't be heard. I hung up the phone and waited a while, but when I picked it up again they were still talking. Well, I figured, it's my telephone and they won't get off it. So I listened. Jackson, it turned out, was in New Hampshire, his aide in Chicago. Watkins asked him how the primary campaign was going. Great, Jackson said, telling him he'd just come back from two rallies that drew packed houses. "But I'll tell you one thing," he said. "It is motherfucking cold in New Hampshire."

Not for Dukakis. New Hampshire got him going, and he didn't stop. Three weeks after that first primary the Democrats voted on Super Tuesday, a mega-election day designed by southerners to give them more clout in choosing the nominee. Fourteen southern and border states were among the twenty voting that day. The political designers figured that their regional vote would favor a candidate more in tune with their relatively conservative views than Mondale had been in 1984. It backfired. Dukakis won eight states, although only three in the South. Senator Al Gore Jr. of Tennessee won six, although he couldn't capitalize on it and dropped from contention in the rest of his primaries. The chief beneficiary was Jackson, who carried five Deep South states on the strength of massive black turnouts, his best day as a candidate. A black activist from Chicago was not the beneficiary the architects of Super Tuesday had intended. Gephardt was finished, able to win only at home in Missouri. That left three candidates.

Gore had nagged the other Democrats on issues like defense, saying he was for strength and they were not. Gore also was the candidate who first raised the issue of prison furloughs in Massachusetts and the case of Willie Horton Jr., which damaged Dukakis all year. Horton was a convicted murderer who'd slashed a Maryland man and raped his fiancée while on furlough from a life sentence in a Massachusetts prison. It became a fixture in Bush's attack strategy; proof, he said, that Dukakis was soft on criminals.

Gore's last stand was in New York, where he got the backing of Mayor Ed Koch, who declared war on Jackson and admitted after the primary that his tactics were a mistake. While Koch ranted, Gore looked like the guy assigned to hold his coat. Where the candidate went the mayor went, claiming the headlines with his invective, not against the leading Dukakis but against Jackson, who, Koch said, had slurred Jews. Koch called Jackson a liar for at first denying he'd called Jews "Hymies" and New York City "Hymietown" in 1984 in a conversation with black reporters. Jackson later acknowledged he'd said it and was sorry. The mayor wasn't forgiving him for that or for what he deemed other slights. "Jews would be crazy to vote for Jackson," Koch said. It sounded like a personal vendetta, not an attempt to help Gore. And Koch's candidate was the big loser in all of this. Gore managed only 10 percent of the vote, and his campaign was over. "I was doing great until I turned forty," he said when he quit. He also said that he wouldn't be interested in the vice presidential nomination. "It is a political dead end," Gore said of the role he would welcome in 1992.

Dukakis came away the easy winner but uneasy leader because he still had to cope with Jackson, who wasn't going quietly. Jackson couldn't win, but he couldn't be ignored. He said he deserved consideration for the vice presidential nomination, and the Congressional Black Caucus said he should get it. There was no way the Democrats were going to risk putting a black vice presidential nominee on the ticket, but it would have been good political sense—and manners—to let Jackson down easy. The Dukakis camp botched that; when the governor chose Senator Lloyd Bentsen of Texas to be his running mate, nobody in the campaign told Jackson in advance, which made him angry. "It takes two wings to fly and so far our wing is not connected," he said. Jackson wanted a piece of the Democratic platform written his way. He wanted party rules changed so that black primary voters would get more influence, and, as always, he wanted attention. Dukakis had the nomination locked, but the Jackson show was not closing yet. Jackson staged a three-day "Rainbow Express" bus trip from Chicago to the convention in Atlanta. He said former President Carter should serve as mediator between him and Dukakis, who wasn't interested in that showboating proposition. But in defeat,

Jackson remained politically powerful for his influence among the black voters Dukakis needed in the election.

So Dukakis had the same problem Mondale had faced four years before; he needed to enlist Jackson without pandering to him and caving in to his demands. Mondale had suffered for the appearance that he'd catered to the special interest named Jesse. Jackson played it all out, got some of what he wanted from the party, and came around with his endorsement. But I wrote at the time that Jackson's political blessings were not unmixed. He would have been a dangerous dissenter but he also was a difficult ally, never quite satisfied with his role and seldom reluctant to say so out loud. He said he was allied with Dukakis to beat the Republicans, but that he disagreed with the nominee on some important issues and was going to make sure that his ideas were represented in the campaign. Before the Democrats broke convention camp, the Republicans were saying that Jackson had been installed as a campaign boss and that his role proved Dukakis was just another old-style liberal, not the competent centrist he claimed to be.

At least there were some laugh lines in Atlanta, although not from Dukakis, who wasn't much for quips. It started a battle of insults in which the Democrats got the early lead. Their orators called Bush a toothache of a man, said he'd been born on third base and thought he was there because he'd hit a triple. They said he'd left no landmarks for all his résumé entries. "Where was George?" they chanted at the convention hall. "Poor George, he can't help it," said Ann Richards, then the Texas state treasurer. "He was born with a silver foot in his mouth." That line really bugged Bush; he'd cite it when people accused him of getting negative and say they started it. The Bush family got even. Richards went on to become governor of Texas and was denied a second term when George W. Bush beat her in 1994.

When the Republicans held their convention in New Orleans, they said they were going to skip the epithets in favor of substance, which probably was a good idea because they had no knack for pithy put-downs. The quotable political insult is a one-liner and Republicans tend to take longer. Bob Dole delivered quickies, but his attempts seemed strained, as when he called Dukakis a liberal with

"Dukak-eyed ideas about the way the world works." Former Secretary of State Alexander Haig, who got nowhere in his own campaign for the nomination, produced a more typically Republican slap, saying the Democratic ticket was like a bat, flying erratically and "hanging upside down for extended periods in dark, damp caves up to its navel in guano." Too long, too complicated, and too untidy to rank as an effective political insult. The Bush people had wanted him to skip that line or tone it down, but he wouldn't. Haig also called Dukakis "a diminutive clerk from Massachusetts," and the Bush campaign said that was inappropriate. It wasn't funny, either. Jerry Ford tried name-calling, but he never had been any good at it. He described Ted Kennedy as "that creature" and "some nonentity." Take that, Ted. What I found funny was the Republicans' inability to come up with quotable insults or to agree on how nasty to get. Dole did deliver one good convention wisecrack, but not about the Democrats. He said he'd gone to see Indiana Senator Dan Quayle, the youthful, surprise vice presidential nominee and found him shaving "for the first time."

New put-downs were not what Dan Quayle needed. From the moment Bush picked him for the ticket, Quayle got plenty of them. His name had turned up on the lists of prospective nominees before the convention, but that didn't mean much. Every potential running mate gets mentioned in advance; it is a way presidential candidates can flatter politicians who might be picked for the ticket without having to actually pick them. There's always a list and it isn't hard to get a name on it. In 1992, Bill Clinton was shopping nominee names, and my friend Bill Richardson, then in the House, wondered why he wasn't getting mentioned. Since he was interested, and a prominent Hispanic among Democrats, I figured he bore mention so I put his name in a column. Within days, Richardson was on the *New York Times* list of possible candidates. He thought that proved my vast influence, which didn't exist, but I didn't deny it. Being mentioned is a self-fulfilling prophecy.

So Quayle had been on the speculation lists, but that did not make it less startling when Bush actually chose him. It looked to me as though Quayle was startled himself. Bush told him by telephone but

Quayle still looked giddy about it when he went to the New Orleans docks for the announcement. Bush had made his grand entrance into the convention city by riverboat. Quayle put his arm on Bush's shoulder and looked as though he wanted to hug the man. At forty-one, the second-term senator from Indiana seemed overwhelmed by his sudden promotion to the national stage. The Bush people hadn't prepared him for the role or the moment, nor had they bothered to do much checking into his background. I thought Quayle was in over his head. He told me later that he had been put in the line of fire without so much as a preparatory briefing from the Bush high command.

Bush praised him as "a man of the future," but Quayle began the campaign bogged in questions about his past, particularly about the way he'd gained a slot in the Indiana National Guard in 1969, avoiding the Vietnam draft. Was it the influence of his powerful family, owners of the *Indianapolis Star* and *News*? Quayle said there might have been phone calls on his behalf, but no improper influence. Still, a National Guard general who had helped him enlist was an editor at the *News*, a business-family connection that didn't help his defense. Then there was another problem—the Paula Parkinson outing. When Quayle went on a 1980 Florida golf trip with two other House Republicans, one of them brought his lady friend, Paula Parkinson, a voluptuous sometime lobbyist. She was at the center of a sex-and-influence scandal in 1981 that prompted a House investigation but did not lead to any charges of wrongdoing. When Quayle was asked about the outing, he said, "That has been covered and there is nothing to it." In one day as Bush's running mate, he'd had his first two controversies. Nothing came of either, but for the Bush ticket, just then pulling even in the public opinion polls, any distraction was one too many. Parkinson later claimed to *Playboy* that Quayle had come on to her at the Florida outing. He called that an outrageous lie, but the most compelling rebuttal came from Quayle's wife, Marilyn, who said it didn't worry her because she knew her husband and he'd choose golf over another woman any time. I usually was skeptical about things politicians said in self-defense, but I didn't doubt that one. Quayle was a talented, dedicated golfer, not to be distracted from his time on the course by some woman named Parkinson. I played with him—and lost to him—often enough to know that.

While Bush said he had chosen Quayle to represent a new generation and to show that he was looking to the future, I always thought the selection was a sort of declaration of independence. Bush's surprise choice, I believed, was intended to prove he was his own man, not beholden to the opinions of party leaders bequeathed by the Reagan era or, for that matter, his own campaign advisers. Quayle wouldn't have been their pick, and Bush knew that. So it was a way to show that he was in command now. A wimp would have looked for a consensus running mate. As for Quayle, his vice presidential debut tagged him with a reputation as a bungler, and he never got rid of it. His sometimes-mangled sentences and spellings as vice president only made it worse. He was smarter than the image he never overcame. He'd been an increasingly effective conservative senator, but he was a stumbling national candidate.

When the new ticket headed off to campaign, Quayle's first stop was his hometown, Huntington, Indiana, and the National Guard mess got worse. He gave a speech on the courthouse steps and then answered questions from reporters, all over the speaker system. It was the unruliest of news conferences, with the crowd jeering the press and chanting Quayle's name to cheer his answers. "I got in fairly," he said. But he also said that a call from the friendly general probably helped, and then described what he'd done in terms that were not at all vice presidential. He claimed that what he'd done was what any normal person would do at that age, twenty-two. "You call home to mother and father and say, 'I'd like to get in the National Guard.'" That bizarre description of normal behavior for a man in his twenties only fueled more questions, presuming, as it did, that Mother and Dad could do something about it. The news conference questions were shouted and shrill. One woman reporter got so argumentative in what passed for questioning, suggesting that Quayle had ducked duty while other young men were dying, that her newspaper pulled her off the campaign.

The Quayle problem was of Bush's making. He'd had more than five months as the certain nominee to make a careful, thorough search of the field for a running mate, and make sure his man was prepared. He didn't do it that way. Quayle came unschooled to the national stage to face an onslaught like nothing he'd seen in his two campaigns for the House and two for the Senate. He was supposed to be the fresh face to counter the sixty-seven-year-old Bentsen, who had his own political scars, notably his admitted blunder in setting up a high-priced breakfast club at which lobbyists paid to dine with him when he was chairman of the Senate Finance Committee. When that became public he called off the breakfasts, gave back the money, and apologized. The pricey breakfast club was history by the time Dukakis put him on the Democratic ticket. In contrast, Quayle's troubles began after he was chosen. Following a weekend of ineffectual, defensive campaigning, he was called back to Washington for basic training on national politicking. "This hit him out of a clear blue sky," Bush explained. It did, and it was Bush's fault. Belatedly, the Bush campaign assigned aides to look after Quayle, "baby-sitting the vice presidential nominee," one of them said, an inside slap that infuriated the senator.

The Quayle keepers were on the job before his vice presidential debate with Bentsen, and they'd told him what not to say. He said it anyway. Smarting from all the put-downs, Quayle had taken to mentioning that his congressional experience matched John F. Kennedy's, which it almost did, but his coaches didn't want him saying that in the debate. It was too risky, a batting practice pitch Bentsen could swat. Facing debate questions about experience and qualifications for the vice presidency, Quayle either forgot or defied his handlers' instructions. "It's not just age, it's accomplishments, it's experience . . . I have as much experience in the Congress as Jack Kennedy did when he sought the presidency." Actually, he was two years short of JFK, but that didn't matter. The comeback did. "Senator," Bentsen said with a theatrical glare, "I served with Jack Kennedy. I knew Jack Kennedy. Jack Kennedy was a friend of mine. Senator, you are no Jack Kennedy." On TV, Quayle looked as though he'd been hit, which he had. All he could manage as a comeback was to tell Bentsen "that was really uncalled for," to which his rival replied that Quayle was the one who had made the comparison. The line stuck to Quayle. Democrats taunted him with it for the rest of that campaign, and it became part of his boilerplate biography. It led to a barrage of ridicule from Democrats who said Quayle had claimed to be an incipient JFK. He never did that, but to invoke the name of the assassinated president is to enter a political realm in which the details don't count, only the images and memories.

While the Kennedy exchange was the only memorable one of the 1988 vice presidential debate, I thought the most telling moment came when Quayle botched an obvious question: What would he do should he succeed to the presidency? That insurance role is the only really important one a vice president has, but Quayle hadn't even considered it. So he winged a halting answer: "First, I'd say a prayer for myself and for the country I'm about to lead, and then I would assemble his people and talk." He meant the president's people. Pressed, he said he wouldn't get into hypotheticals but that he was capable and qualified to take over as president if need be. It wasn't until the next day that he figured out the right answer and said that he would continue Bush's policies and programs. "I hadn't thought about that question before," he said lamely. The first answer stuck. Quayle's growing corps of detractors said that if he became president, every American would need to say a prayer for the country.

Quayle's travails continued. The Holocaust, he said, "was an obscene period in our nation's history." Reminded that it was not our nation that did it, Quayle clarified: "We all lived in this century—I didn't live in this century—in this century's history." In a defense policy speech he sort of quoted the Indiana University basketball coach. "Bobby Knight told me this: 'There is nothing that a good defense cannot beat a better offense.' In other words, a good offense wins." He may have known what he meant, but nobody else did. Sometimes Quayle ignored the texts he was handed and made it up as he went along.

So did Bush, and when he strayed from his set-piece campaign speech, his utterances could be odd. "I hope I stand for antibigotry, anti-Semitism, antiracism," he advised one crowd. "That is what drives me." He didn't mean anti-Semitism, of course, but by the time he said so, the rally was over. Dukakis was too weak to stand up for America, Bush contended, promising, "I will never apologize for the United States—I don't care what the facts are." He moved the date that will live in infamy by telling an American Legion convention on September 7: "I wonder how many Americans remember—today is Pearl Harbor Day. Forty-seven years ago to this very day we were hit and hit hard at Pearl Harbor." That would have been December 7, 1941, and Bush corrected himself.

When Dukakis needled him about that lapse Bush countered, "It must be nice to be an ice man and never make a mistake." Bush's mistakes sometimes were classics. In Twin Falls, Idaho, he bragged about his close ties to Reagan. "For seven and a half years I've worked alongside him and I'm proud to be his partner. We've had triumphs, we've made mistakes, we've had sex—" When he could be heard over the laughter, Bush corrected himself. "Setbacks. We've had setbacks."

But such babbling sentences didn't do any lasting damage. And the misadventures of Dan Quayle proved one point: People vote for president, not vice president. There was no evidence Quayle cost votes in the 1988 election. Nor did he add any, except perhaps back home in Indiana, where the Republican ticket was a lock with or without him. The election was Bush or Dukakis; at the polls, running mates were afterthoughts, if that.

Lagging early, Bush came on tough against Dukakis. He shook off the wimp factor and ducked the Iran-Contra mess, getting a break when a trial in that scandal was postponed from the fall of 1988, in the middle of the campaign, until 1989, well after the election. The new Bush was on the attack, a bare-knuckles kind of a candidate. "I will not be deterred by the age-old ploy of calling it negative campaigning," he said, and he certainly kept that pledge. Bush spent his campaign time arguing that Dukakis had been a lousy governor and would be a worse president, reciting his own credentials and delivering only one central promise, which wasn't about what he would do but about what he wouldn't. "Congress will push me to raise taxes, and I'll say no," he said. "And they'll push again and I'll say to them: Read my lips. No new taxes." With minor variations that was part of every speech. It was so familiar that his supporters started reciting it with him at campaign rallies. It was so indelible a trademark that when he reneged and made a tax increase deal with Congress as president, the scars were part of his political undoing. But in the heady rhetoric of the 1988 Bush campaign, "Read my lips" sounded Reaganesque. Nothing preppy about that and besides, it tied the vice president to the old president's favorite issue. He'd be strong against taxes, firm on defense, and stern against crime. He argued that Dukakis was none of the above.

Bush pointed to the Willie Horton case as his evidence on crimefighting. "What did the Democratic governor of Massachusetts think he was doing when he let convicted first-degree murderers out on weekend passes?" Bush demanded. That was his handle on the soft-on-crime accusation Republicans always used against Democrats. The Bush offensive featured a television commercial showing inmates walking through a revolving door. A more racially charged ad showing a menacing black man—Horton was black—was broadcast by an independent Republican organization, and while the Bush campaign disclaimed sponsorship, the commercial worked to his advantage. And it put race into the campaign, although the Bush people tried to keep their fingerprints off that aspect of the issue. The Republicans found Horton's stabbing victim, Cliff Barnes, and enlisted him. The most effective attack issues are the simplest, the ones that lend themselves to political shorthand. That was Willie Horton. Obviously, Dukakis didn't let the man out, but he was the governor in 1987 when Horton got his furlough, his tenth furlough as a Massachusetts convict, and found new victims.

The Horton case didn't tell a voter anything about who'd be the better president. Nor did it draw any lasting attention to prison furloughs in which convicts, even lifers, were getting time off from their sentences. Forty-five states and the federal prison system had some form of furlough programs in 1988 and at least sixteen granted them to prisoners convicted of murder.

Then there was the flag issue, more specifically, the Pledge of Allegiance to it. Bush waved the flag and said Dukakis didn't want kids required to recite the pledge in school. Dukakis waved it and said he did, too, but that compelling the pledge in the classroom was constitutionally dubious. He had vetoed a bill that would have required teachers to lead pupils in the Pledge of Allegiance every school day. Dukakis said he had to veto the bill because the state supreme court had ruled it unconstitutional. A wiser politician would have signed it and let the courts knock the statute down if they chose, but Dukakis didn't operate that way.

To counter the problem, Dukakis began his fall campaign at a rally that looked like a Flag Day celebration, a giant one behind him, scores waving on and near the platform, miniature flags passed out in the crowd. Bush certainly wasn't being outflagged; he even went campaigning at a flag factory in Bloomfield, New Jersey. I was traveling with Dukakis that day, and he was dealing with a serious issue, health care insurance for Americans who lacked coverage. He said Bush ought to come out from behind the flag and say what he was going to do about health care. It was a frustrating campaign day for the Democrats. Health insurance briefings do not make good television footage. Flag factories do. The Bush show got the television coverage that night, the Dukakis proposal a brief mention.

Even on an issue as simple as the flag, Bush could flub a line. "I think it is good to have children sign the pledge—er—say the pledge," he told one audience, as he claimed that Dukakis must not think so. When they debated, Bush said he was not questioning Dukakis's patriotism with the Pledge of Allegiance offensive, to which the governor heatedly replied that he certainly was.

Both sides took to handing out small, plastic flags at campaign rallies; on some, the fine print labels said the U.S. flags were made in Taiwan. The 1988 flag campaign did leave one lasting imprint: Republicans got the House of Representatives to open each day's session with the Pledge of Allegiance to the flag, which had not occurred to anyone there before.

Dukakis was trying to conduct what amounted to a classic Democratic campaign, promising better jobs at better wages, accusing Republicans of catering to the rich, saying he'd reform the military to better arm America's soldiers instead of pouring money into things like Reagan's Star Wars missile defense system. Bush said Dukakis had a "Disneyland defense" plan. And Dukakis made it look that way by climbing into a tank at a defense plant in Michigan for a ten-minute ride around a test track with his helmeted head sticking out of the turret. The helmet had his name on it, and he looked like Snoopy out for a ride, which is to say silly, in person and in the photograph that made newspaper front pages. Somebody should have reminded him of John Kennedy's unbreakable rule against putting on funny hats, Indian feathers, or other headgear handed him as he campaigned. The head in the helmet did not look like the head of a president.

Bush didn't let it go with flag waving and crime talk. He took a ferry tour of Boston Harbor and blamed Dukakis for the sewage-polluted water. Bush called himself "a Teddy Roosevelt Republican," all for conservation, although he'd served an administration with a dismal record on environmental enforcement. "In terms of the environment, I will be a good president because I know in what kind of decade to leave the kids, not what we're in right today," Bush claimed, in another of his coded sentences. For good measure, he accused Dukakis of trying to sneak sewage out of state. He said that the Dukakis administration applied in 1985 for a permit "to dump Massachusetts sewage sludge off the coast of New Jersey." Way off, a check of the record showed. Massachusetts sought permission to dump sludge at a site 106 miles offshore, where New York and New Jersey already had dumping permits.

Then, too, there was the L word. Liberal. Dukakis had shunned the label, styling himself a centrist and promising competent management that he said was more important than ideology. The Reagan years had shifted political attitudes to the right, and the 1984 landslide against Mondale had shown the fate of an old-fashioned liberal campaigning against the trend. Dukakis would have done better to accept the label and define it his own way. Instead he avoided the word, complaining that Bush and Reagan kept calling him liberal, liberal, liberal. Well, Bush said, Dukakis had claimed to be one before he ran for president. And not just a liberal. "He said, 'I am a card-carrying member of the

American Civil Liberties Union,' " said Bush. So the ACLU was added to the lengthening list of irrelevant campaign topics. Dukakis didn't burn his ACLU card, although it might have been a useful comeback to Bush. He simply said that membership did not mean he agreed with all the positions of the organization, which often championed unpopular causes and cases in defense of what it considered to be civil liberties. "The liberal governor of Massachusetts" Bush called Dukakis, the ACLU guy. Again, he had slogan-sized phrases, and never mind the details. Dukakis could try to deal with those.

Finally, nine days before the election, Dukakis came around to the self-description he should have applied all along. "Yes, I am a liberal, in the tradition of Franklin Roosevelt and Harry Truman and John Kennedy." Good line, too late. "Miracle of miracles," Bush taunted. "The big L word." By then, Bush had succeeded in defining "liberal" as meaning someone lax on crime, soft on national defense, and prone to spending money and raising taxes. Accepting the term, Dukakis rejected the definition. He said that to be a liberal was to work for the average American, to help people in need of help, and to pay the government's bills at the same time. But Bush's take on the term was the one that stuck. And when Dukakis was prodded to say whether his list of liberals also included Walter Mondale and George McGovern, he ducked, saying, "I'm not going to go through a litany of people."

Dukakis should have seen the big L problem coming. A campaign with a clear game plan would have defined its candidate's philosophy up front instead of defending it too late. Bush had told the Democrats he would come at them on ideology, back when Dukakis argued that was not what the election would be about. Dukakis said the question should be competence, but he was kidding himself. "Competence is a narrow ideal," Bush countered. "Competence makes the trains run on time but doesn't know where they're going. Competence is the creed of the technocrat." Presidential elections are not all about competence, they are about personalities and, as Bush said going in, shared beliefs and values, and the proposals that flow from them. Besides, Bush was a pro at ideology adjustment. When he ran for the Senate and lost in 1970, it was as a relatively liberal Republican, outflanked on the right on some issues by the Democrat who beat him, Lloyd Bentsen. In his campaign for the 1980 Republican nomination, he was cast as the moderate candidate against the conservative who won. When Reagan then chose him for vice president, it drew protests from some conservatives who thought he was a closet GOP liberal. I wrote at the time that Bush was no flaming liberal although he might be a smoldering moderate. Either way, he knew whom to salute, and for eight years that was Reagan, to the point that critics called him a lapdog with no firm beliefs of his own. You could make that case, but Bush wouldn't help you. By 1988 he was a Reagan conservative, with no apologies or explanations for the turns that got him there.

Under Bush attack, Dukakis banked on the presidential campaign debates as a way to get even. That wasn't happening, even before he suffered the most memorable cheap shot question in the annals of the great debates. It was the first question asked in their second debate, in Los Angeles, by moderator Bernard Shaw of CNN. His tone was bland, his question savage. "Governor, if Kitty Dukakis were raped and murdered would you favor an irrevocable death penalty for the killer?" Shaw asked. He said afterward that he had asked it in order to get an answer that wouldn't be the usual campaign boilerplate. It looked to me like a question asked for shock value and TV showmanship. The way to force a candidate's hand in a debate is to check the record and confront him with facts, not to invent a shocking, hypothetical question.

I waited for Dukakis to tell Shaw that the question was offensively out of line. He didn't. Instead, he accepted the question and answered like the technocrat Bush said he was. "No, I don't, Bernard," Dukakis replied. "And I think you know I've opposed the death penalty during all my life. I don't see any evidence that it is a deterrent, and I think there are better and more effective ways to deal with violent crime." No emotion, no comment on the extraordinary nature of the question. The ice man at work.

It wasn't for lack of debate practice. He'd been involved in more than two dozen debates during the campaign for the Democratic nomination and for the White House. Years later, when I called Professor

Dukakis, the retired politician, and interviewed him for a column I was writing on presidential debates, he laughingly cautioned me not to consider him an expert on the subject. He said that if he'd been any good at it, he might be talking to me in a different role.

Bush won the election with 54 percent of the vote and forty states in his column. The president-elect then went on a fishing vacation off Florida. Not Dukakis. He conceded the White House and in ten hours, early the next morning, the governor was back at his desk at the statehouse in Boston. It was a weekday so it was a workday.

I interviewed Vice President Bush just before he was inaugurated to succeed Reagan. "There's going to be change, but hopefully, a building on what's happened," he said, no sharp turns from the Reagan years. Bush told me the tie to Reagan was on his mind when he presided over the "antiquated drill" in which Congress formally registered the electoral college vote that made him president, and the time was at hand for him to put his own imprint on the office. "Style, message, people, be yourself," he said. Never mind the gossip that it was going to be Reagan III. "I'm the one calling the shots. I'm the one who's going to set the agenda." The agenda might read much like Reagan's, but the Bush trademark would be on it.

"Automatically, that happens," Bush said. "That happens at the time when I put my hand on that Bible and hold my right hand in the air and say that oath. It happens." So it did, but within weeks, Bush found it necessary to deny that his new administration was drifting without clear purpose, that it was in disarray, that his government was suffering malaise, the political affliction diagnosed in Carter's presidency. Reagan had come to power with a clear mission: Rein in government and cut taxes. Bush had no such turning point agenda for change. "That's not what I am about," he said. "People understood that when they were voting. They weren't looking for a radical shift." But they got one: Bush's reversal of his own "read my lips" vow against new taxes. As his political fortunes sagged near the end of his single term, he said that was his worst mistake. It put him, in the epitome of Bushspeak, in "deep doo-doo."

NINE

The Comeback Kid
Overcomes the President
in 1992

The liabilities Bill Clinton carried into his presidential campaign
were enough to sink another candidate, but he wasn't just
another candidate. Clinton was a master campaigner and a very lucky
one. He was glib, too, crafty and smooth enough to talk his way out
of almost anything. Clinton had a woman problem beyond the kind of
fling that drove Gary Hart out of presidential politics. His draft-
ducking agility made Dan Quayle look like a willing warrior, if a
weekend one. He rose from the Democratic field to become the
preprimary leader, then plunged more sharply than any early front-
runner since the early slump that sent the favored Ed Muskie to early
defeat two decades before.

It read like the résumé of a loser, a compilation of woes that had
damaged or undone a succession of campaigners. But for all of it,
Clinton ran off with the 1992 Democratic presidential nomination
faster than any contested candidate ever had. The guy was that good.
He was smart, adroit, a political actor to rival Reagan, with a sack of
tricks Nixon would have admired.

Then, too, he was running in a weak Democratic field, the star in
a cast of mediocre candidates. The rivals who would have been most
formidable all declined to run, stepping aside before the campaign

year began, when President George Bush was riding record-high readings in the public opinion polls. Bush was the president who won a war in the Persian Gulf, the president during whose term the Cold War ended in victory, the Berlin Wall was toppled, and the Soviet Union unraveled. But recession at home trumped victory abroad, especially for a president who had no discernible program for dealing with the economic slump. He'd reneged on his "no new taxes" pledge of 1988. His reelection campaign was tardy and remarkably disorderly for a candidate with the advantages of the White House at his command. Besides, Bush was a lousy candidate. Watching him, I sometimes wondered how much he really wanted a second term.

The campaign of 1992 was my first as a full-time columnist for the AP, with a new set of deadlines—three columns a week. But I wasn't ready to part with the old ones, the spot news deadlines I'd been handling all my career, and I wasn't comfortable being "just" a three-a-week columnist, although colleagues said that was more than full-time work. When I went on the road with the candidates, I wanted to write the news, the major developments of the campaign day, too. It was satisfying work and it kept me in the flow of events, invaluable for the analytical columns I wrote. I covered the news, and then I tried to explain it, fill in the background blanks and put things into context. My columns offered analysis, not opinions. I never had any use for the pontificators who wrote what they thought and told readers to think likewise, although that became a growth industry as cable television put the loudest mouths on the air. I thought it most useful to make my case with facts and history and let the reader decide whether my conclusions made sense. The role added pressure but also extra satisfaction.

The 1992 election was a three-way choice, Clinton versus Bush versus Ross Perot, the crankiest of candidates. He ran; he quit; he ran again; he griped about one-liners while spouting them. Perot obviously detested Bush, although he claimed his campaign was nothing personal. Perot's popularity testified to the voters' disenchantment with the president and with politics in general. Perot had no real program, falling back on the time-tattered claim that he could save the government billions by cutting out waste, fraud, and abuse. Elect him and he'd tell us where and how much.

It was the campaign of the TV talk shows. Watch Larry King on CNN long enough, and you'd see everybody who was running. That's where Perot declared that he might run, where he went for airtime after dropping out, and where he appeared after renewing his candidacy, reentering with the antic explanation that he'd quit only because Bush's Republicans were plotting to sabotage his daughter's wedding. Perot's was the strangest performance I ever saw in national politics. The guy was a nagging oddball, but that's what his supporters seemed to want. Talking with them at Perot campaign outposts that fall, I found his volunteers zealously committed to their man, a mood that was not matched by supporters of the major party candidates. Rank-and-file workers for Bush or Clinton were dutiful. The Perot crowd was devoted.

A succession of potential Democratic challengers to Bush stepped aside before the campaign began, narrowing the field to the untested and the unlikely. Ted Kennedy, who wasn't running, said in 1991 that the party was essentially conceding Bush a second term. It did look that way. Clinton did not seem a formidable figure. At first, he was the Republicans' favorite choice for challenger, given the character questions and the personal baggage he carried into the campaign. But he checked the bags skillfully and got past the problems. He'd been governor of Arkansas for a decade but had no national profile. His debut on the national stage was laughable—a thirty-two-minute run-on introduction of Michael Dukakis at the 1988 convention during which, he ruefully acknowledged later, the only applause line was "in conclusion." However, he was an emerging leader of the centrist Democrats who saw the old liberal ways as a political dead end and knew that to win, the party would have to adapt to the landscape shaped by the Reagan revolution. The dwindling Democratic field handed Clinton his first break because it left him running against three little-known senators, a flaky former governor, and a solid but electorally improbable one-term senator from Massachusetts who had dropped out of politics for five years for treatments to fight off cancer.

Senator Al Gore, the failed candidate of 1988, was a prime prospect for 1992 until a personal trauma led him to say he wouldn't run. Gore took his son, Albert III, to the Orioles game in Baltimore on opening day in 1989. As they left the stadium, the boy pulled his hand out of his father's and ran into the street, where he was hit by a car and gravely injured. He recovered, but Gore said later that the accident changed the way he looked at his life and politics and led him to decide against running in 1992 because his family needed him at home. I always thought that if he had run, Clinton might have remained a footnote. Not that Gore would have won the nomination, but with the senator from Tennessee on the primary ballots of the South, the governor from Arkansas would not have had an easy ride through the Super Tuesday primaries that made him the dominant Democrat.

When Clinton's personal excesses overtook him in the Monica Lewinsky affair, nobody could claim there had not been storm warnings long in advance. His flaws and his deceptions were on display in 1992, but the voters chose him anyhow. He was the slick standard-bearer for change over the Republican president who couldn't seem to convince people that he really cared about their problems. When Bush's handlers tried to fix that problem at the start of the campaign, they gave him a reminder on an index card, an explanation of how concerned he was about the economic plight of too many working Americans and how he meant to do something about it. Instead of a dissertation, the audience got the cue card. Bush glanced at it and read it aloud. "Message: I care," he declaimed. No details as to what he'd do about the economy; Bush promised those later. When they came, they amounted to a warmed-over pudding of what the administration already had offered, with a gimmick or two to touch up the product.

Clinton was the new guy from the baby boom generation. He'd been reelected governor of Arkansas in 1990, fending off Republican claims that he only wanted to keep the job as a stepping-stone for a presidential campaign by promising that he would serve all four years of the term. He hadn't finished one year when he declared his candidacy for the Democratic presidential nomination. He dodged the promise by asking his audiences in Arkansas whether they thought he should run for president and, wonder of wonders, read the applause and decided they wanted him to go for it. He said his campaign wouldn't offer a choice of liberal against conservative. "It's both and it's different," he said.

Clinton had been drawing notice as a promising Democrat since he got to the statehouse in 1978 and began claiming leadership among the party's centrists in the 1980s, although he lost his reelection bid in 1980, regaining the governorship in 1982. By the time he ran for president, they said he was the only politician around who had been proclaimed a prodigy in three different decades: the '70s as a promising newcomer, the '80s as a governor with national potential, and the '90s as candidate and president. The liberal label that had haunted Dukakis wasn't going to be stuck on Clinton. He said the 1992 campaign had to be about curing the economic woes left by the recession of 1991, the slump that undid Bush's towering support after the Persian Gulf war and left him fumbling for answers.

The 1992 campaign and election proved again the oldest political lesson: Bread-and-butter issues trump everything else when economic times are hard. That was a ready-made theme for a Democratic challenger, and with the Democratic heavyweights out of the way, it was waiting for Clinton. "The economy, stupid," read the sign on the wall in his Little Rock campaign headquarters, the reminder to stay on the central message. Bush handled it as though he thought it was just the stupid economy, getting in the way of the great international undertakings he wanted to pursue. He said he preferred foreign affairs, on which he could act by himself, to domestic ones, which required him to work with that pesky Democratic Congress.

In the fall of 1991, Clinton delivered three issues speeches at Georgetown University to show he had a grasp of national and international issues, and that he was a major-league candidate, not just a governor from a minor-league state. He claimed the political center, a departure among Democrats. Clinton went before the councils of the more liberal Democratic establishment seeking to erase their reservations about his centrist stance, saying he wanted to "push this party into the future, not pull it to the right or left." He drew good reviews from politicians and in the news media, and before the election year began, they anointed him the front-runner, with both the risks and the advantages of being the man to beat. He was rated the leader going into the New Hampshire primary campaign—until January 16, when the *Star*, the supermarket tabloid, reported that a woman named Gennifer Flowers, a sometime nightclub singer who'd gotten a minor state job in Arkansas with the help of the governor, had been Clinton's mistress. The accusation had been made before, during Clinton's 1990 campaign, but he had an easy comeback because it was raised by a state employee who had been fired for misconduct. The man filed a lawsuit claiming Clinton had spent state money on dalliances with Flowers and four other women. Reporters checked it out, found no proof, Flowers denied it, and the story didn't make print. That's the reason most political sex stories were spiked before they were printed. One of two participants in an affair had to go public to make rumor into publishable fact, although the bar was lowering, first with the tabloids and then with Internet gossip that didn't meet the traditional tests of responsible journalism. With Clinton running for president, the *Star* published its version and made Gennifer Flowers a sudden campaign sensation. Clinton certainly knew her—in every sense of the word, it turned out. I thought he'd asked for trouble when he got cozy with a woman who spelled Jennifer with a G.

The episode was a seamy landmark in the way political campaigns are reported. Before Flowers, we who styled ourselves the "mainstream press" did not deign to pursue, let alone pick up, the findings of the bottom-feeding supermarket sheets that thrived on sex, scandal, and occasionally space aliens. But not after the Clinton-Flowers episode. The *New York Post* and the *Daily News* went with the story and it spread into print elsewhere. Clinton said the accusation had been thoroughly investigated before and found false. Not thoroughly enough. It was true, as Clinton finally had to admit in 1999. In 1992, he called the allegations "totally bogus." The establishment newspapers still weren't buying the story, although they began backing in with accounts of the way the New York tabloids were handling it, which put the accusations in print on their pages. Then the moderator of a televised Democratic debate raised the question of women trouble, and while Clinton called it all "a pack of lies," the story got a new cycle, revived in the next day's newspapers and TV shows. The *Star* delivered a follow-up punch: Flowers told all about it in a first-person account of what she said was a twelve-year affair, and supplied tape recordings of telephone conversations with Clinton as recent as the fall of 1991. Clinton denied the affair again, but he couldn't deny the tapes, so he said he'd talked to Flowers on the phone because she was being harassed and frightened by people trying to get her to change her story. He said he'd called her only after checking with his wife, Hillary, first, every time. He also said Flowers obviously had been paid to tell her story to the *Star*, which was true, business as usual for the supermarket tabloids, which pay for scandal stories. By now, with Clinton talking about the whole business, the mainstream press had a way into the story. Denials keep a story going because we recount the accusation in reporting what a politician is denying. An accusation a good reporter would not repeat in print becomes fair game when the candidate talks about it in denying it.

The effect of all this can be to reduce political journalism to the lowest common denominator—to report things because another outlet has reported them, to go with the story because somebody else did. It is an old dilemma, and it worsened as the number of outlets multiplied, from the supermarket scandal sheets to the talk shows to the cable TV cacophony to the Internet with its unlimited rumor-exploding capacity. Clinton was the one lying in 1992, although we didn't know it until long after, when he confessed in a deal with a special prosecutor that his sworn denial of the Flowers affair was not true. As was his habit, he tried a tricky way out. He said it was only a one-night stand and that what he'd denied under oath was a long affair, twelve years by her account.

Trapped in the Flowers mess, the Clintons made their remarkable appearance on CBS's *60 Minutes* on Super Bowl Sunday to talk about their marriage. The candidate admitted that he had been guilty of wrongdoing and causing pain. He wouldn't be more specific, but he said that the people watching would "know what we're saying, they'll get it." In Clinton code, that meant he'd had his affairs and people would figure it out without his saying so directly. Beyond what he'd said, Hillary put in, what happened in the privacy of their lives together was just that, private. But there was one more installment. The next day, the *Star* produced Flowers at a New York news conference and played edited excerpts from the telephone tapes, her voice and Clinton's. Nothing in the tapes played that day proved an affair, but Clinton's advice to Flowers certainly proved an embarrassment. CNN televised the show as Flowers, in a bright red outfit, said she had been Clinton's lover and had lied to protect him. The performance featured twelve minutes of edited tapes, including one in which a man whose voice matched Clinton's described New York Governor Mario Cuomo as a "mean son of a bitch" and agreed that he acted like a man with Mafia connections. There was no date on the conversation but it would have been before Cuomo stopped hinting he might run for the nomination himself and announced that he would not. That sequence put Clinton in an odd position. He wouldn't acknowledge that the tapes were valid, but he said he was trying to telephone Cuomo to apologize. Cuomo sniffed that Clinton should save the telephone toll.

Perhaps the most telling line on the tape—given what Clinton did and said after he was president—was this advice to Flowers: "If they ever hit you with it, just say no and go on. There's nothing they can do . . . If everybody is on record denying it, no problem." That would be his strategy and almost his downfall in the Monica Lewinsky sex scandal in 1998. Dishonest denials got him impeached by the House; political survival tactics got him acquitted by the Senate to finish his second term.

In New Hampshire, Clinton said it was up to the voters to determine whether his almost-admitted straying from Hillary would disqualify him from the presidency. "We're putting this in your hands. You get to decide." The questions wouldn't go away, though. In a Democratic debate, all the candidates were asked to speak on the issue of character. They began politely, bypassing Flowers. Not Jerry

Brown, the former California governor who played the wild card in the campaign. He said the others weren't being realistic. "I mean, what's the biggest character issue out there right now? The stories on Bill Clinton, isn't it? And whether or not there's an issue there . . . that's what everybody's thinking about, they're looking at that . . . whether it's legitimate or not."

Clinton played the long-suffering victim. "I think I've said all I need to say about that and I think the American people have got more of me and my wife together than they ever thought they'd get in the primary process."

The Flowers episode stalled Clinton in New Hampshire. The lead he'd been opening in the polls sagged and his leading primary rival, former Senator Paul Tsongas of Massachusetts, gained on him. Tsongas was an engaging, open man who only looked dour. He was from Lowell, Massachusetts, a short commute down the interstate from New Hampshire. He'd served only one term in the Senate, dropping out of politics in 1984 after he was diagnosed with cancer. Now he was back in action, saying he'd beaten the disease and had the right answers to the economic slump. His campaign manifesto was *A Call to Economic Arms,* an eighty-six-page pamphlet that broke with Democratic orthodoxy to advocate spending cuts and business tax incentives. The booklet was bound in gray, a shade that fit the content. Watching Tsongas autograph copies after his rallies, I suspected that he was signing a lot more of them than people were reading. Tsongas was against the middle-class tax cut Clinton was promising. The liberals said he was a closet Republican. But his bigger problem was the need to convince people that he would have a chance of winning in a national election in the fall. He joked he had the burden of being another Greek from Massachusetts, four years after Michael Dukakis's defeat. A heavier burden was not openly addressed. It was his health, and while he said he was fine and past the cancer, you could hear people murmuring about it in the campaign crowds. (Tsongas died of pneumonia in January 1997, at the age of fifty-five.)

Despite the Flowers furor, Clinton held his edge in the primary polls in New Hampshire and actually widened his lead over the

Democratic field in national surveys. But there was another storm coming, this time over the Vietnam-era draft and the way he'd ducked around it. This one didn't start in some tabloid. The *Wall Street Journal* broke the story, reporting that a former recruiter said Clinton had manipulated an ROTC deferment to avoid being drafted. The secretary of the draft board back home said Clinton had been given special treatment because he'd asked to stay at Oxford University and they liked having a hometown boy over there in England as a Rhodes scholar. Clinton had dropped the ROTC deferment in 1969, asked to be put into the draft lottery. Questioned about it in New Hampshire, Clinton said he'd opted for the lottery instead of keeping his ROTC deferment "because I didn't think it was right" when friends from Arkansas were dying in Vietnam. The Clinton organization said it was old stuff, nothing wrong, all plowed over before in his Arkansas campaigns. But it also was sensitive stuff, and with the Flowers uproar subsiding, the draft questions took over. "All I've been asked about by the press is a woman I didn't sleep with and a draft I didn't dodge," Clinton complained. But it all depends on what dodge is. He avoided the draft legally, but he certainly had played games with the system in order to do so. It looked questionable, not a topic a politician would want raised as he went to the voters in the first presidential primary. When Dan Quayle was battered in 1988 over the appearance that he'd used family influence to get into the Indiana National Guard and out of the draft, he had said he would have done things differently if he'd known he would be running for vice president twenty years later. Clinton wasn't so candid.

What the Flowers case hadn't done, the added drag of the draft questions did. Clinton sank in the New Hampshire polls and Tsongas took over the lead with the primary little more than a week away. The Great Denier was still at work. "The key issue is that I made myself available for the draft," Clinton said, but there was more to it. Clinton put his name into the draft lottery late in 1969 and drew a predictably high number—quotas were down and the odds were against being called. He then wrote a letter to the director of the ROTC program at the University of Arkansas to thank him "for saving me from the draft" and to explain what he'd done. Clinton wrote that the draft was interlocked with his opposition to the Vietnam War.

"I decided to accept the draft in spite of my beliefs for one reason: To maintain my political viability within the system," Clinton wrote. That 1969 explanation didn't fit the claim of the 1992 presidential candidate, who said he had been driven by conscience. The deceptions were accumulating, and I thought they were enough be his campaign undoing. I thought wrong. "I don't think it's undermined my electability," Clinton said in a paid TV appearance with a panel of New Hampshire voters. "If you say I'm electable on Tuesday, by definition, I'm electable." Enough of them said he was to keep him going, into primaries in which the sex and draft issues wouldn't be so fresh and so damaging. Weeks later, Clinton did have one last draft item to admit, when it developed that he had received an induction notice in April 1969, before he signed up for the ROTC program that got him deferred. He said it hadn't "occurred to me that this was relevant to the story," so he didn't mention it during the earlier controversy. He'd gotten permission from the draft board to finish his term at Oxford, and then temporarily joined the ROTC. No big deal, he claimed, and it had just slipped his mind. I didn't believe him. No man who ever has received a draft induction notice brushes it off as irrelevant. It gets your attention. I remember mine, nearly fifty years after I got it. I'd already joined the Vermont Air National Guard when it came, so I was off the hook. There was no war on at the time but I didn't want to spend two years in the Army instead of at work on my career as an AP reporter, so I opted for a brief tour of active duty and then weekend service. I even got a commission for which I was totally unqualified. That happened because the commanding officer of my unit was at the statehouse one day and saw me in a friendly chat with the governor. He figured if I knew the governor that well, I ought to be an officer, so they made me a second lieutenant. Later, after I'd transferred back to Boston, I drew duty one rainy night at a base in the city and was walking to my post when a general shouted at me. "Lieutenant," he said commandingly. "Stop." I stopped and thought, "Damn, I forgot to salute again." So I walked his way and saluted.

"No problem," the general said. "It's just that I haven't seen a second lieutenant since World War Two."

So I understood a bit about dealing with—and around—the draft. I thought Clinton inflated the topic with his deceit about it. Candor would have cured the problem, or at least minimized it, but candor was not Clinton's way.

In the 1969 draft letter, Clinton also wrote that he hated and despised the Vietnam War and demonstrated against it not only in the United States but as a protest organizer at Oxford. I never covered the war, but I did cover the mass protest rallies against it in Washington. In one, guards made the Nixon White House into a barricaded haven, surrounded by city buses parked bumper to bumper. As a reporter, I kept my views out of my copy, but I thought the war was a disaster from the beginning, a wrong-minded policy that killed young Americans who deserved better from their government. It poisoned American politics. The excesses and deceptions that went with it twisted the 1968 campaign, planted the seeds of Watergate—which began with covert, illicit attempts to plug leaks about the war—and led to the cynicism and mistrust of government that persists, long after the U.S. withdrawal from Saigon. I finally saw Vietnam in 2000, covering Clinton when he became the first American president to go there after the victory of the North Vietnamese Communists in 1975. We got to Hanoi late at night, and when my story was done, I walked down the quiet street from the hotel and just stood for a while, marveling at the delusions that had led American policy makers to decide that what happened in this small corner of Southeast Asia was so great a threat to the United States as to warrant more than a decade of war.

In 1992, the history of the war wasn't at issue. The personal history of candidate Clinton was. He tried to stay on his economic message, but we'd heard all that and we kept questioning, and writing, about his alleged affair and his draft avoidance. They added up to the character issue and it was costing him support. By primary time, the New Hampshire polls favored Tsongas. Clinton, the early front-runner, was braced to be beaten his first time out, and he was. Tsongas won easily with 33 percent of the vote. Clinton got 25 percent.

History's lesson was that an early front-runner couldn't afford that. Muskie had won the 1972 New Hampshire primary by nine percentage points, the victory that began his undoing because it failed expectations. But the old rules didn't apply to Clinton. He was a survivor, as skilled and agile a candidate as I ever covered, and his campaign hatched a plan. Clinton would ignore the defeat and claim that he had actually won by doing as well as he had, no matter what the numbers said. Clinton ran second, with the rest of the Democratic field far behind and discredited as contenders. The returns were still being counted when Clinton held what amounted to a victory rally. "New Hampshire tonight has made Bill Clinton the comeback kid," he told his cheering supporters. Tsongas had won, but Clinton made it sound as though he had, and grabbed the TV attention before the real victor got to celebrate. Only a candidate as sly and skilled as Clinton could make that setback into a send-off. I wrote about what really had happened, but there was no avoiding the fact that Clinton was the quotable Democrat. He had another advantage that night: Bush won the Republican primary, but upstart conservative Pat Buchanan drew a hefty vote against the president, and that became the major story of the New Hampshire primary. The political troubles of the president trumped the maneuvering of his would-be Democratic challengers, and that emphasis helped Clinton. His defeat was the second paragraph; the lead was the Republican outcome, Bush's victory over an unexpectedly strong Buchanan challenge. Clinton pretended he'd won. Bush sounded almost as though he'd lost.

Within six weeks, Clinton had validated the claim with victories in the South and the Midwest that effectively clinched his nomination on March 17. Even Clinton was surprised. "Son of a bitch," he said in a telephone chat with an AP colleague. "It's only the middle of March." Tsongas withdrew, saying he wasn't going to be the man who split the Democrats: "I did not survive my ordeal to be the agent of George Bush's reelection." That left Jerry Brown as Clinton's sole rival, but he was a protest candidate, not a real threat. He kept going, and not quietly. He said the nomination of Clinton would ruin the Democratic Party, that "I am not the spoiler, Slick Willie is the spoiler." He said Clinton was unelectable, "the prince of sleaze." In New Hampshire, Tsongas had called Clinton "pander bear," claiming that Clinton wanted to please everybody at once, and had sometimes waved a teddy bear as a visual aid. The character questions had not gone away, but they had come early in the game and Clinton won in the primaries despite them. What I'd once thought would cripple him strengthened him instead. The early disclosures and rebuttals did not immunize him on the women and draft questions, which would come up again in the fall, but they did take the edge off the stories. Had either or both broken in the middle of the general election campaign, the spotlight would have been far more glaring, the damage far more telling. Instead the Republicans were left trying to revive what essentially was old news.

For Clinton, evasiveness seemed to be a habit. He was deceptive even when there was no point to it. On his youthful experiment with marijuana, for example. That was not a new question; other presidential candidates had answered it honestly and said yes, they'd tried the stuff years before. Gore was among them, saying he'd sampled it when he was in the Army in Vietnam. So it was no surprise that Clinton was asked about drugs. "I have never broken the laws of my country," he answered. He did not mention anybody else's country because we didn't think to frame the question that way. We should have known better; Clinton found the loophole and took it. Finally, a New York TV reporter had the sense to restate the question to include state laws or laws outside the United States. "I've never broken any state laws," Clinton repeated. "And when I was in England I experimented with marijuana a time or two. And I didn't like it and I didn't inhale." Why the obviously evasive answer until then? "No one had ever asked me that direct question before," he said. Nobody ever asked him whether he'd inhaled; he volunteered that odd information because he instinctively looked for cover by talking his way around potential problems. All that one did was draw ridicule. Clinton said later it was just that he didn't know how to inhale. "I took it, and I tried to smoke it like a cigarette," he said on a TV talk show. "I did my best. I wasn't trying to get a good conduct medal."

Richard Nixon's performances wrote the text on political image problems and sly evasions to get around them. I thought Clinton was struggling with the sequel. "Tricky Dick, meet Slick Willie," I wrote that spring. Clinton was trying to dispel character questions he said were the creation of strangers repeating the worst about him. When a TV questioner told Clinton that changing positions might account for the "Slick Willie" label, the candidate said the question was wrong, that he had been consistent. "And you see, one of the reasons that you get a Slick Willie attack is if someone like you mischaracterizes my position." Clinton said voters were being fed "bad stuff" about him, that he was being made a punching bag.

Nixonesque problem, Clintonesque answer. But there was more than a political divide between the two politicians. Nixon was awkward and often aloof, a man with few friends. Clinton was the opposite. You couldn't help but like him. He'd drape an arm over your shoulder and treat you like a pal, whether you were or not. Later, when Clinton was president, I took my boss to the White House to see him. While we were talking, Clinton's dog Buddy started licking the boss's well-shined shoes. Without missing a word of the conversation, Clinton grabbed a Kleenex from a box and crouched down to wipe them clean. It looked as though he were giving AP President Lou Boccardi a shoeshine.

Clinton could explain away anything, or try to. The character doubts were just "a case of buyers' remorse" about a nominee who had sold himself to the Democrats so quickly. "I'm the most investigated, examined, gone-over person running for president."

Overall he won primaries in twenty-nine states, but even so, his favorability and trust ratings in the public opinion polls were lousy. He blamed the process he'd just come through, saying that the primary campaign "kind of clouds and muddles your image with people." That struck me as strange because unless campaigns tell the people who the candidates are and what they propose to do in office, there is no point in the exercise. Clinton said otherwise. "The American people are so disgusted with both political parties—and I don't blame them—that anybody who's gone through this primary process winds up weaker coming out than they went in because you become like a politician," Clinton said. Odd; I'd thought he was a politician all along and a very good one.

Clinton also came through the primaries with an advantage no candidate had gained since Jimmy Carter's winning campaign in 1976: He did not have to guard his left flank by catering to interest groups there. That had been a primary campaign necessity and a general election liability for Democrats since their reformers took the nominating clout away from party leaders and delivered it to the primary election voters. Nixon's Republican tenet was that a candidate had to move far enough right to win the nomination and far enough center to win the election. In the Democratic mirror image, candidates usually had to move left to win nomination and then try to get back toward the middle, which was sometimes a struggle, as it had been for Dukakis and for Mondale before him. Both Democratic losers were saddled with the impression that they were beholden to liberal and labor interest blocs. Dukakis had tried to shun left-right philosophy but was stuck with it anyhow, with a capital L. Nobody was going to pin that on Clinton. When Bush said Clinton's middle-road, moderate stance was only camouflage for a liberal Democrat, the candidate from Arkansas said that was an old dog that wouldn't hunt again. "People try to put on yesterday's broken record that sticks in the same old place in the song: tax and spend, tax and spend . . . liberal, liberal, liberal," he mocked, saying that it wouldn't work this time. Take the Republican effort to win points on crime control and capital punishment. Clinton said Bush could only talk about law enforcement, whereas "I'm the only one who's carried it out," by signing off on four executions as governor of Arkansas.

Besides, Clinton didn't have to defend his left flank because there were no rival candidates there. New York's Cuomo, the heavyweight contender waiting in the locker room, never came out. The opinion polls rated him a powerful candidate, the traditional liberal versus the centrist Clinton. An airplane was idling on the Albany runway, waiting to take Cuomo to Concord to file entry papers in the New Hampshire primary, when he said no. The cliché was to call him the

Hamlet of the Hudson. I always considered him a realist, a man who knew that he would have been an awful candidate for president. He did not suffer foolish questions, let alone fools, lightly. He'd said in 1988 that Dukakis had a problem in campaign debates because he was too intelligent for the format. "A lot of people find it difficult to take these complex subjects and distort them into a twenty-second sound bite," Cuomo said. He certainly did. He also had political rabbit ears, like the ballplayer (he'd been one, with big league prospects in his time) who hears every jeering fan. He was given to telephoning reporters and columnists who wrote things about him he didn't agree with or just didn't like, to complain and debate the matter. No presidential candidate could operate that way.

In December 1991, on deadline day for filing in the New Hampshire primary, Cuomo went to the brink of entering. If that waiting plane couldn't get to Concord in time, duplicate papers already were in the hands of his supporters in Concord. Only then did Cuomo announce that he would not run. He said he had hoped to, but he had to stay in Albany to deal with a state budget crisis. Nor would he leave open the possibility that he might enter later. He said he was out, period, although he seemed to flirt with running now and then. He neither promoted nor discouraged a New Hampshire write-in effort, calling it flattering. It flopped. Cuomo still ventured unsolicited advice to Clinton. On taxes, for example. He said Clinton should tell people, "Look, I'm Bill Clinton. I am going to solve your problem but I'm going to have to raise some taxes. I know Mondale said that and lost." Somehow Clinton never got around to saying such things, although he did get some taxes raised as president. As candidate, he promised a middle-class tax cut, but that idea was gone before he was inaugurated.

After entering three Democratic campaigns, Jesse Jackson did not run in 1992, which eliminated another pressure point on the left. Jackson sought and got concessions from the prior Democratic nominees before endorsing them, deals so publicly done as to cement the impression that they had bowed to his demands in order to get black votes. That fit the Republican argument that the Democratic candidates were captives of liberal interest blocs. Clinton knew that trap, and he meant to avoid it. He appeared determined to snub Jackson to underscore his own independence of the old liberal coalition. During the primaries Clinton was told, incorrectly, that Jackson had endorsed a rival in South Carolina and blurted into an unexpectedly open radio microphone that it was "dirty double-crossing back-stabbing." It was accidentally broadcast, and he apologized to Jackson, but I always suspected that Clinton didn't regret it all that much. There was no doubt about his intent when he spoke to Jackson's Rainbow Coalition and criticized the organization for giving a black rapper called Sister Souljah a place on the program after she'd said that in view of the Los Angeles race riots, blacks should consider killing white people instead of each other. Clinton said that reflected "a kind of hatred" at odds with what he understood to be the aims of the organization. Jackson was furious at the slap from his own platform, complaining that Clinton owed him advance notice of what he was going to say. Clinton countered acidly that he had no reason to because Jackson was "not in the habit of clearing his public remarks with me."

"If you want to be president, you've got a responsibility in a consistent way, even when it's unpopular, to stand up for what you think is right," Clinton said. The calculation was evident: He needed black votes for the Democratic ticket, but he needed independence more. Clinton already had told Jackson that he would not be considered for the 1992 vice presidential nomination, which never had been a real possibility in earlier campaigns but had not been so clearly ruled out so soon by the nominees. Jerry Brown said that if he was nominated, he would ask Jackson to be his running mate, and Jackson said he would be honored to accept. It was all fiction, since Brown wasn't going anywhere. "If Jerry Brown is the answer, it must be a damned peculiar question," Senator Lloyd Bentsen had observed.

While Clinton was declaring his independence of the Democratic left, and even of the Democratic Congress, Bush was struggling with a problem on the Republican right. He never overcame it. The problem had a name: Patrick J. Buchanan. Conservatives were angry before Buchanan entered the campaign, declaring his challenge to Bush only ten weeks before the New Hampshire primary. The Republican right had been miffed since Bush's "read my lips" bravado against new taxes had vanished in surrender to Democratic demands in budget bargaining. Bush agreed to "tax revenue increases" in June 1990, enraging antitax conservatives. But their anger was submerged by conflict abroad, first the buildup in the Persian Gulf against Iraq's invasion of Kuwait and then, in 1991, the Gulf war itself. Bush's popularity soared to record approval in the public opinion surveys, but the economy slumped and his polls soured. He was still paying that toll as he geared up for his reelection campaign. His initial campaign plan did not make provision for the primary elections; the president didn't know that would be necessary, but Bush was forced to defend his right to run again. Protest votes against presidents are nothing new, and usually are inconsequential. Nixon was at the peak of his political power when he ran in 1972, and two GOP congressmen who ran against him in the New Hampshire primary came away with 32 percent of the vote anyhow. Bush was in a political slump in 1992, reflecting the economic one for which he seemed to have no answers. Enter Buchanan, and the president who intended to concentrate on the national campaign could not because he first had to defend himself in the primaries. Buchanan began with an influential ally in the reliably rightist *Manchester Union Leader*, which always had been down on Bush. He had the issue of the economic situation, more severe in New Hampshire than elsewhere with lost computer industry jobs and plunging real estate values. And he had his ardent conservative message. "We put America first," he declared, accusing Bush of a seedy, backroom deal on taxes and of surrendering to the Democrats in signing a civil rights measure conservatives called a job quota bill. His face was familiar; voters had seen him on TV and heard him argue the conservative line. Still, he was just a right-wing commentator, and George Bush was president. For Bush to pay him too much heed would risk elevating Buchanan's political status by giving him a rebuttal platform. To ignore him would risk letting him elevate it himself by showing strength in the primary.

Buchanan knew all that and he knew the territory. I first met him in 1968 in a cocktail lounge in North Conway, New Hampshire, when he was a media aide and speechwriter for Richard Nixon. He was an engaging guy, quick with a wisecrack and a laugh, most heartily at his own jokes. To Pat, right was right and everything else was wrong. He had worked for Nixon in the White House—it was disclosed years later that he'd had a hand in some 1972 dirty political tricks—and later for Reagan. Between those White House stints and since them, he had become the voice of the Republican right on CNN. He found a vein and a nerve in unhappy New Hampshire voters, not only textbook conservatives but also working-class men and women who saw jobs and salaries eroding in the slumped state economy. Bush couldn't ignore Buchanan, so he spent the first day of his reelection campaign there, six stops beginning with a confession that had been long in coming:

"I know times are tough. This state has gone through hell, extraordinarily difficult times. And yes, people are hurting, and I am determined to do something to turn it around . . . I've known the economy is in free fall. I hope I've known it. Maybe I haven't conveyed it as well as I should." It struck me that he hadn't conveyed it at all. Instead he had taken to reciting the forecasts of economists who said times were getting better, or would soon, which was of no help or interest to people who weren't drawing a paycheck.

Bush declared that his answers would not be the Democratic medicine of a Congress "that's still back in the dark ages of government intervention, liberal spending, and more taxes." Enough of that, he said, and lapsed into Bushspeak. "I am getting sick and tired of every single night hearing one of these carping little liberal Democrats jumping all over my you know what," and that was just the warm-up. Bush said he'd intended to stay calm. "But I'll tell you something, I'm a little sick and tired of being the punching bag for a lot of lightweights around this country yelling at me day and night." At his next stop, he described his health as fine despite the illness that hit him in Tokyo and caused him to vomit in the lap of the Japanese prime minister. "Jeez, you get the flu and they make it into a federal case." And later, he declaimed: "Don't cry for me, Argentina." Which made no sense at all. Times were hard, Bush acknowledged, but they would get better.

Always had. "If you want to see a rainbow you've got to stand a lit-tle rain," he said, borrowing a lyric from the Nitty Gritty Dirt Band. Except that Bush called it "the Nitty Ditty Gritty Bitty Great Band." He drew good crowds, though, and the nonsense lines didn't bother them. I never saw political vaudeville to compare to Bush's six-speech outing that day, before or since.

Bush was an easy target and he made his own problems, but he also took some cheap shots from the media. One notable example was a *New York Times* story that fed the old preppy image by reporting that Bush had been amazed to see the way a supermarket checkout line works. It was raw material for cartoonists, for comedians, and for media commentators who reflected scornfully on Bush's life in splen-did isolation. It is a fact that presidents are isolated; they don't run out to the supermarket. But when Bush toured an exhibit at a grocers' convention in Orlando, Florida, he was shown a newfangled scanner that got the price right with the label ripped to pieces. He said he was amazed at the technology. Told that way it wasn't much of a story. Indeed, the reporters who actually accompanied Bush on the tour didn't give it more than a mention in their own stories. The *Times* reporter was not among them. His piece was written from a pool report, notes distributed to the White House press corps by a small group of reporters designated to represent the rest when the whole crowd won't fit.

White House reporters take pool turns by rotation. That is a seldom-mentioned secret of the coverage—most reporters don't get close to the president but wait in the pressroom for the pool reports. It is unavoidable given the planeloads of print and broadcast news-people who travel when the president does, and it is sometimes abused by the White House to restrict coverage even when there's room for everybody to watch. I always thought it was pointless to fly thousands of miles to sit in a media center and write stories based on speeches piped into the pressroom and on details put together by the pool and handed out to everybody. But that's the routine. Set up your laptop and you can cover everything without ever leaving the press center. It wasn't a problem for me and my AP colleagues because the Associated

Press always has a spot in the pool as the wire service that delivers coverage to every significant American newspaper and broadcaster and to thousands more internationally. AP people are there to see and hear what we report, and if it isn't always perfect, it is firsthand. It's also straight, not bent to make a point the way that supermarket scanner story was.

The facts never caught up with the notion planted in that 1992 *Times* story that Bush was so out of touch with the real world that he was totally alien to supermarket checkouts. The Democrats needled him about it all campaign, and the impression stuck afterward as part of the Bush legend.

Buchanan kept sniping at "the hollow army of King George" in New Hampshire, saying that in the primary, his conservative brigades would cut through it like a knife through butter. His rebellion forced Bush to play defense. Bush still seemed tone-deaf to the economic travail he'd walked into. One of his lines was that what happened to New Hampshire happened to him because when a hurricane hit the coast there it hit his home in Kennebunkport, Maine, next. True enough, but not a useful example when he was talking about a rambling family vacation home and the New Hampshire voters were worried about keeping jobs or finding work to pay their mortgages.

When the primary votes were cast, Bush and his people made a bad situation worse by reacting to what they thought was a stronger Buchanan uprising than the challenger actually delivered. The day was marked by premature exit polls—network projections based on interviews with people after they'd voted, compiled before the real results were counted but supposedly confidential until the election was over. The confidentiality is fiction. Reporters know what the exit polls are showing, and that means politicians know. You swapped information. You gave a candidate a heads-up on the trend, and you got an election night telephone interview in return. In 1992, the New Hampshire exit polls began leaking to the White House in midafternoon, and they were not promising for Bush. The partial poll results also were wrong, which should not have been a big deal because the full survey and then the actual returns were what counted. But the White House picked up word that the first exit polls showed Buchanan running even with the president and possibly even winning the primary. The projections shaped first impressions of the New Hampshire primary, including Bush's own, making Buchanan a bigger threat than he was. With only partial returns counted that night, Bush issued a victory statement that sounded like a concession: "This election was far closer than many had predicted. I think the opponents on both sides reaped the harvest of discontent with the pace of New Hampshire's economy. I understand the message of dissatisfaction."

For Buchanan it was an uprising to celebrate. He thought he'd gotten at least 40 percent of the vote, and in acting as though he had, the White House magnified his showing. It turned out to be 37 percent. Bush got 53 percent of the Republican vote in New Hampshire, a sorry showing for an incumbent president and one he made worse with his own reaction. He wouldn't fare that badly against Buchanan in the later primaries, but the game had changed. Buchanan could not deny Bush renomination, but now he was more than an upstart right-wing commentator. He was the vehicle for a protest vote that harried Bush into catering to the Republican right when common political sense was to seize the center, especially once Clinton was installed as the opposition. But Bush couldn't seem to get over the scare he got in New Hampshire. Buchanan made the Georgia presidential primary his next, and really his last, major stand. Bush trounced him, 64 percent to 36 percent. "I hear your concerns and understand your frustration with Washington," Bush said in the oddest of victory statements. As for Buchanan, he said that night that Bush ought to withdraw. "I'm the only guy in this race who has a snowball's chance," the loser blustered.

Bush may have been getting the message, but he wasn't doing anything about it. He was stuck between voter discontent over the economic situation on one side and, on the other, the rebellious conservatives who thought job programs and economic bailouts were for Democrats. So he stayed put and ventured no new answers on the economy.

If the voters were frustrated, Ross Perot knew whom to call: Ross Perot. He was just a temperamental tycoon, in one of Quayle's better lines, but there was a vein of voter anger and discontent with the major parties and the whole campaign just waiting to be tapped. So the short, wiry billionaire with the grating voice edged toward his third-man campaign. There had been a draft Perot movement for months and he'd been saying no. Just after the New Hampshire primary, he turned up on Larry King's CNN show and said maybe. He would run if his volunteers got the petition signatures to put his name on the ballot in all fifty states. But he'd be different, he claimed, calling Washington a place of "sound bites, shell games, handlers, and media stunt men who posture, create images, and talk." After scorning those political hired hands and tactics, he used them all himself. He was the king of the sound bites, and he usually bit Bush with lines like "We are now in deep voodoo, I'll tell you that. We got into trickle-down economics and it didn't trickle."

"I don't want the job," Perot drawled. "That makes me weird, right? Because everybody else out there would kill his mother to get the job." Feigning disinterest was good politics in a time of voter resentment against Washington and politicians in general. It also was disingenuous, because no candidate who really meant that would have been campaigning for the White House. Perot postured that he'd run only out of a sense of duty "to my volunteers," as though he wasn't the one egging them on. He had no program and no patience with reporters when we tried to find out what he proposed to do as president. "If I ever get stuck up there, give me thirty days, and I will have access to the numbers and I can tell you," he snapped. Until then, leave him alone. Perot was a political sniper given to outrage when anybody shot back. He claimed to be the outsider, different from all those other guys. He wasn't, and Nixon-era papers in the National Archives proved it. In 1969, according to White House memos, he offered Nixon $50 million to finance a public relations campaign that was supposed to include outright purchase of a newspaper and television outlet. He pledged another $10 million to create a pro-Nixon think tank. Nixon accepted both offers, the memos reported, but Perot never delivered on either. In 1992, Perot contended it was all "fantasyland stuff" invented by Nixon aides. Other documents showed that Perot sought and got White House help on tax and business matters. When reporter John Solomon of the AP disclosed those facts, Perot said the Bush White House put him up to it, which wasn't so. Solomon got the story by pursuing clues he had picked up in interviews with Perot himself. When a reporter asked Perot at an editors' convention about his earlier idea of house-to-house drug searches, he denied advocating it (he had) and then got personal, calling the reporter a woman given to flights of fancy who couldn't hold a job. To disclosures that he had private investigators look into the lives of people with whom he had differences, Bush among them, Perot denied all and said the system was out to get him. That always was the answer—deny everything and change the subject.

No matter. Disenchanted voters heard what they wanted to hear, and public opinion polls showed him running strong against Bush and Clinton, even leading in some surveys. He said the volunteers were "the owners" of his operation, although I thought that any of them who tried to act like proprietors would be gone in minutes. Perot was his own show, even after he hired two veteran political advisers—a Democrat and a Republican—and a campaign spokesman, all in the traditional mold he supposedly was shunning. Perot never announced that he was a candidate for president, he just became one. He worked the TV talk shows as no candidate ever had. Bush and Clinton didn't know how to handle him. This wasn't a regional challenge like that of George Wallace in 1968. When John B. Anderson had run as a third candidate in 1980, it was as a dissenting liberal Republican. Perot came with no identifiable cause, no evident philosophy, and no clear programs. I thought he was as paranoid as the White House said he was, and as phony as any politician I'd seen. Phonier, perhaps, because he pretended not to be a politician at all. Then, hours before the Democratic National Convention nominated Clinton, Perot announced in Dallas that he wasn't going to run after all. He said the Democratic Party "has revitalized itself," which led him to conclude that he couldn't win the election but might force a deadlock that would have to be settled by the House of Representatives, and therefore would be disruptive to the country. Perot said he'd answer questions about what he was doing, but immediately took offense at the tone of them and walked out of his own news conference.

I watched in our convention newsroom at Madison Square Garden, no less surprised than anybody else at the campaign upheaval, but not at Perot's erratic performance. I'd always doubted he could take the questions and criticism a candidate gets, or at least that he would accept them. Billionaire businessmen can have it their own way. So he got out, although he didn't shut up. "I could have been an effective president if we didn't have this partisan stress," Perot said. "I didn't realize how vicious it was, how petty it was."

Presidential campaigns can indeed be petty, nasty, off the point, demeaning, too long, too expensive. Despite all those flaws and more, nobody has devised a better way to test and choose among people who want to be president. One reason is that campaigns force accountability for past performance and for new ideas. Perot flunked on both counts. He wanted to be crowned president or, better still, to crown himself. So he got out, leaving a constituency without a candidate, which led both Bush and Clinton to remember just how much they'd admired him all along. They couldn't wait to call him up and tell him so, each trying to woo Perot supporters to his side. Perot said he wasn't endorsing either man, and he kept his ballot petition volunteers going. The guy was craftier than we credited. He still had a hand to play.

In mid-September his movement met his original condition for candidacy by qualifying him for the ballots of all fifty states. The major party nominees sent delegations, hats in hands, to audition for his support, missions I thought both crass and humiliating. Perot pretended that he was going to settle his 1992 campaign course only after talking it over with his supporters. "My volunteers decide," he claimed, having already decided himself, since he said that quitting was a mistake. So he surveyed his troops, which was a farce because their advice was obvious: Run. On October 1, he was back. He said he would not be answering any more questions he did not think relevant, and when he didn't like what he was being asked, he ended the news conference he had called on his reentry by stalking out of the room. While he'd claimed in quitting that he was concerned about disrupting the election, his explanation now was that the Bush campaign had been planning to sabotage his daughter's wedding in August. He claimed to have multiple sources for that strange alarm, but they all seemed to stem from a private eye as wacky as the explanation. I thought it was a laughable performance, but Perot had his following, and he was back in the game he supposedly disdained, making his own rules. Pandering to the Perot vote, both Clinton and Bush had offered him a third seat in the fall campaign debates, so Perot came back with his ticket punched for television. He'd get equal billing with the major party nominees, although the polls he once had led in his days as a novelty item now showed him third and more people had negative than positive opinions of him. So it was a threesome. "The more the merrier," said Clinton. And the odder, with Perot sniping at will while both Clinton and Bush granted him a kind of campaign immunity, wary of taking him on lest they offend his supporters who might still be sensible enough to switch to one of the nominees with a chance of winning. "We haven't said the first unkind word about Ross Perot," said Al Gore, the Democratic vice presidential nominee.

Before the Democratic National Convention in New York, I was having dinner with John King, a skilled, relentless political reporter then with the AP, when he got the scoop on the Gore selection. King had arranged with a Clinton insider to call him with word of the vice presidential choice before it was announced. But the Clinton camp clamped down to prevent leaks, and the guy couldn't say the name for risk of being overheard. Instead, he called King's pager and left a cryptic message—the number 4673. Not a number you could call back, which puzzled John, who hurried off to work the telephone. When he looked at a telephone keypad he got the message. Translate the four numbers into the matching letters on the phone, and it reads G-O-R-E. With that to go on and a couple of calls to confirm it, John filed a bulletin story that beat the competition, as was his usual standard.

Clinton scrapped the traditional rules of ticket-making when he chose Gore for vice president. They both were centrist Democrats, from adjacent states, same generation, similar politics. The idea of balancing regions and party wings in selecting running mates didn't apply to their ticket.

Bush and Quayle had been renominated at a Republican convention that added to their campaign liabilities with a shrill turn to the right. Buchanan hadn't quit his challenge, although he had long since conceded that he didn't stand a chance. He'd agreed to endorse Bush, but he wanted a prime-time convention slot when he did it. The Bush camp agreed, and Buchanan appeared on opening night with a theocratic diatribe against the Democrats: "There is a religious war going on in this country for the soul of America. It is a cultural war . . . for the soul of America." His speech set a tone for the convention that catered to the conservatives while stirring a backlash, not only from the left and the interest groups Buchanan denounced, but also from moderate Americans who didn't care for religious ranting about political choices.

Bush kept tuning his message, trying to find one that registered with voters. He changed campaign management. Just watch, he would say, now I'm really going to get tough. He'd been saying that periodically all year. "I'm starting to dish it out," he announced six weeks before the election. It struck me that the dish was skimpy and stale. He repackaged his economic proposals and his campaign issued them in a blue-covered pamphlet, stale wine in a new bottle. His wheels always seemed to be spinning.

Dan Quayle was back. There had been rumblings from his Republican detractors about dumping him in 1992, but Bush decreed long in advance that Quayle would absolutely be on the ticket. He'd produced a dossier of gaffes as vice president. I thought he peaked with his contorted attempt to recite the slogan of the United Negro College Fund. "What a waste it is to lose one's mind or not to have a mind, is being very wasteful. How true that is." Yes, a mind is indeed a terrible thing to waste. His most convoluted sentences notwithstanding, Quayle was no dummy. To borrow the line used against him in that 1988 debate: I knew Dan Quayle, Dan Quayle was a friend of mind. I thought he was a competent man and a competent senator who would have been better off had he stayed in the Senate. He was better than his reputation and his worst lines, but in over his head as vice president. He thought all the gibes and put-downs were unfair. When he tried to run for president himself in 2000—his campaign quickly sank from sight—he told me, "They can't do that stuff to me again." I said he was kidding himself, and he was. Any slip was a blow to a man who was strangely prone to them. One of his aides once told me, jokingly, that he thought maybe Quayle was dyslexic because he was smarter than he seemed able to express. One personal Quayle memory: I was on the practice range at the Burning Tree Club one Sunday afternoon, hitting golf balls when his motorcade pulled in, and the vice president came over to ask whether I wanted to play. I did, and we set out in a golf cart, betting a few dollars on a game in which I got, and badly needed, handicap strokes against him. Quayle was a fine golfer. He was keeping the scorecard and a few holes in, I looked at it to see how the bet stood. He'd put our names on the card as "Walter" and "VP."

In 1992, Quayle filled the campaign role customary for the VP: He was the attack man. He took on the trust and character offensive against Clinton. He told people that they would be wasting votes by casting them for Perot. He also chafed at the way the campaign was being run. Over dinner on Air Force Two shortly before the election, he bristled that it was the lousiest campaign operation he'd ever seen.

Clinton was rolling. He hammered Bush on the economy, and the president had no comeback except to say things were going to get better. Clinton and Gore broke another tradition, campaigning together for almost three weeks when the theory always had been that running mates worked separately to cover more territory and broaden the reach of the ticket. They did a lot of their tandem campaigning on eight bus tours in nineteen states. You could get really tired on those bus rides. They always ran late, sometimes hours late, because of extra stops and extra long speeches. The candidates spent all day riding together and then had late-night bull sessions that sometimes ran long past midnight while the rest of the entourage waited, scores of aides, Secret Service agents, and reporters, weary but stuck until the candidates decided it was time for bed. Their campaign theme song was Fleetwood Mac's hit "Don't Stop Thinking About Tomorrow," sometimes played at a volume that prevented you from thinking about anything at all. In Hannibal, Missouri, the music that brought them on and off the platform was so loud that my laptop computer malfunctioned as I tried to write and file a story from the press table behind the stage.

There were three presidential campaign debates, plus one among the nominees for vice president. Bush took the hits; Clinton and Perot delivered them. By debate season, Clinton had a lead to protect, and did. I think Perot would have been relegated to the minor share of the vote third candidates usually get had he not been put on equal footing with the major nominees in the campaign debates. He nagged at the others but said little of substance. The line I remember best was an unintended self-portrait. "I'm all ears," Perot said, and had to wait for the laughter to subside before he went on. Bush's worst night was in Richmond, Virginia, an audience participation debate in a format he had tried unsuccessfully to avoid. Clinton thrived as an up-close campaigner, strolling the stage, walking to the edge of the audience like a talk show performer. Bush was uncomfortable and awkward. The telling questions could have come from Clinton's speechwriters, or perhaps Perot's. One was a challenge to the candidates to stop negative campaigning, clearly targeting Bush, who fumbled it by hedging. "I think it depends how you define it," he said, arguing that Clinton started it and he was only responding to attacks. "I'm not going to sit there and be a punching bag." But he was one, again. "I'm just as sick as you are of having to wake up and figure out how to defend myself every day," Clinton answered piously, as though attack tactics were not part of his arsenal. "I'll take the pledge because I know the American people want to talk about issues and not tabloid journalism." Perot pledged purity, too. Bush was stuck as the odd man in the threesome.

He took another hit when he got a question that made no sense and tried to answer it sensibly. The question was how the national debt had personally affected each of the three candidates. It hadn't; the national debt doesn't do that. What the woman really wanted to know was how the economic slump had affected them, but that is not what she asked, and Bush talked about the national debt, saying it affected interest rates, and then lapsed into double-talk about his grandchildren having to pay for it. "I'm not sure I get it," he went on. "Help me with the question and I'll try to answer it." The Democrats taunted Bush for the rest of the campaign as the president who didn't get it. Bush also gave them a visual aid that night in Richmond. The camera caught him glancing at his watch while Clinton was talking. It looked as though he just wanted to be out of there, which he probably did. That was the image that played in the TV spots.

In the vice presidential debate, Quayle and Gore pitched their tickets with tough lines, wisecracks, and no blunders. Perot's running mate was the more interesting figure. "Who am I? Why am I here?" asked retired Admiral James B. Stockdale, trying to answer his own questions and never managing to do so. He was literally the man in the middle, at the lectern between Quayle and Gore, admitting that he felt like an onlooker at a Ping-Pong game. He fumbled with his pen, missed hearing one question, saying his hearing aid had been off, presented himself as an amateur and proved it. There was a naïve charm about his performance in contrast to the practiced politicians on either side of him.

There was one last bit of Republican sleaze to come. It was delivered by a lame duck congressman from Michigan, Guy Vander Jagt, who had lost in a primary but was still chairman of the House GOP campaign committee. At a news conference the night before the election, Vander Jagt charged that Clinton was having an affair with a wire service reporter covering his campaign. It was a slanderous lie. The Republicans repeated it in a press release and sent that by fax to newspaper offices that night. No name, but there was only one woman covering Clinton's campaign for a wire service, a talented, dedicated reporter for the Associated Press. I seldom lost my temper about politics, but I was damned mad that night. The Republicans disgraced themselves with that performance. They acted like the losers they were going to be the next day.

Clinton won with 43 percent of the vote, to 38 percent for Bush. Riding the wave of voter disenchantment and inflated by the debates,

Perot got 19 percent, the strongest popular vote showing by a third-party entry in sixty-eight years. My guess is that Clinton would have won a two-man election because the Perot voters obviously wanted a change in the White House and might have stayed home from the polls had he not been on the ballot, but probably would not have gone to Bush. That said, no one can be certain what would have happened without Perot. What happened with him was that Clinton's call for economic change overrode persisting doubts about character and trust. Well-founded doubts, as we would learn in the White House sex scandal that scarred his second term. It wasn't as though people hadn't been on notice. They weren't saying they'd trust Clinton with their daughters. They did trust him to deliver economic revival, and no candidate ever lost an election by promising to see to everyday, bread-and-butter issues.

TEN

Bob Dole's Turn and Clinton's Return in 1996

When a president is running for reelection, his standard keynote message is to point with pride at what he has done the first term and promise even better results in a second. Presidents who can't make claims to fit that formula usually have trouble winning another four years. Bill Clinton didn't have much to boast about in 1995 after the voters repudiated his Democrats and Republicans won Congress. He got over it and won, boosted by an adroit early campaign, an inept Republican challenge, and an economic revival. But going in, he sounded defensive and sometimes dispirited. He said he knew that Americans were insecure, worried about the uncertain economy and distrustful of political leaders, including the president. "I'm trying to get people to get out of their funk about it," Clinton said in September 1995. I thought I heard an echo of Jimmy Carter in 1979. Malaise by any other name is not a promising diagnosis for a president to deliver when he is asking voters to reelect him. In his own slump after the trouncing of the Democrats in the 1994 congressional elections—a beating many of them blamed on the president—Clinton was reduced to arguing that he was still relevant to what was happening in Washington, even with the new Republican Congress at center stage. A president who has to deny that he is irrelevant is a politician in trouble.

"They used to call me the comeback kid," Clinton said as his approval ratings sank. Actually, "they" didn't. He called himself that. Now the title was "president," and Clinton needed a real comeback, not just a campaign gimmick. He got it, with the unwitting, sometimes witless help of those same Republicans. They were running Congress for the first time in forty years, and they didn't remember how to be in charge. Zealous conservatives commanded the House, and they overplayed their hand, which played into Clinton's. So by the time the 1996 campaign began, the oversold Republican revolution was slumping and Clinton was resurgent. Maybe he was a bit sleazy, but he came across as a leader who cared about people and their needs, an image drawn more sharply as the GOP House tried to slash away at social programs. When the government ran out of money and shut down some operations in a budget deadlock, the Republicans figured Clinton would get the blame, but they did.

Clinton's presidential beginning had been shaky, with lurches to the left, mishandled choices for the Cabinet and top administration jobs, and then, worst of the lot, his failed attempt to decree an overhaul of the nation's health care system.

The moderate, middle-road course Clinton had advertised in 1992 seemed to have veered from his map and the Democrats suffered for it in the 1994 elections. But Clinton was adaptable. He said the message was that people still thought the government was more often the problem than the solution. That was, of course, a Ronald Reagan line, and if the voters wanted to hear it from a Democrat, Clinton would oblige them. Before the 1996 election, the conservative good news–bad news joke was that the next president would be a Republican—and that his name would be Clinton.

The other name was Bob Dole, finally nominated on his third attempt, after a Republican contest that was brief but scarring. It was as though Dole had been awarded a gold watch for long, faithful service to the party, which he certainly had delivered for more than thirty years, eleven of them as the longest-serving Senate Republican leader. By the time Dole clinched his nomination, Clinton was back in full stride, flush with campaign funds—some of them tainted, his liberal dalliances, if not his sexual ones, behind him.

The field included some of the usual suspects, among them Pat Buchanan on the Republican right and Ross Perot, back as a candidate with his hypocritical, grating claims that he didn't want to be president but had to run for the job in answer to a call to duty, which only he heard. There was a boom for Colin Powell, who did nothing to disown it until his 1995 book publicity tour was over, and *My American Journey* was a raging best-seller. Steve Forbes showed up with his publishing fortune and his flat tax notion, climbing the charts in what turned out to be a fad that faded, out of pocket $36 million when reality hit and he quit. Lamar Alexander, former Tennessee governor, former Cabinet member, roamed the early primary trail in his plaid shirt, as though that would make him the political outsider he pretended to be. I thought Alexander probably would have been the strongest nominee against Clinton, without the lumberjack getup. But he couldn't get past the early primaries, and when he tried again four years later, he didn't even make it that far.

It was a campaign that set new highs for spending and a new low in the conduct of hired gun campaigners when Dick Morris, who advertised himself as the genius behind the president's remodeling, landed in a sex scandal. Morris lent spice to the dull Democratic National Convention when he was forced out of the campaign over his conduct with a pricey prostitute, who sometimes listened in on a telephone extension while he counseled Clinton.

"Pricey" was the word for the campaign, too. Clinton's comeback plan required big spending early in the season, and Democratic fund-raisers went after it with tactics that were borderline at best, illegal at worst. Republicans said Clinton turned the Lincoln Bedroom into a money-raising motel, offering overnight stays for high-roller Democratic donors. The Republicans had their own money hunt. Texas Senator Phil Gramm, whose view that he should be president was not widely shared, said that to be competitive, a candidate for the nomination would have to have at least $20 million in hand on January 1, 1996. Gramm raised that and more, but not even his $26 million bankroll was enough to buy him a way into real contention, and he quit before the first primary.

The reform lobby Common Cause reported that between them, the two national parties raised $231 million in unrestricted contributions for the 1996 campaign, "soft money" in Washington jargon. That was more than triple the take for the 1992 elections.

Dole was the leading Republican candidate from the start, "tempered by adversity, seasoned by experience," he said. He'd be getting more of both. Bob Dole was one tough politician. His right arm was shattered in World War II combat that almost killed him, and he never recovered full use of it, a particularly difficult disability for a politician because constituents and voters always want to shake hands with the senator. He usually carried a pen in his right hand, shook hands with his left. When you got to know him, you'd extend your left hand, too. The hatchet man of the 1976 vice presidential campaign had mellowed, but the new, older Dole still had to be careful not to revive the dark-side image. "I went for the jugular," Dole said of his caustic campaign history. "My own." In the 1976 campaign, Dole sent an aide to a hardware store in Jackson, Mississippi, to buy him a hatchet. The guy had to go through a security obstacle course to get it to the candidate, but did, in time for the evening's rally. "I pulled it out of the sack," Dole remembered. "I said, I'm supposed to be the hatchet guy. Here's my hatchet."

"I," incidentally, was a pronoun he seldom used as he campaigned in 1996. He referred to himself in the third person, as in "Bob Dole is a man you can trust," or "Bob Dole's policy would be to cut taxes." It was an odd affectation, apparently cured by defeat because he went back to the first person singular after the 1996 election.

While Clinton needed a political revival, he had one advantage no second-term Democrat had enjoyed since Franklin D. Roosevelt: He was unopposed for renomination. Dole began with a lead to defend in a widening Republican field that would reach ten before his rivals faltered. Even so, I always got the sense that I was on a nostalgia trip when I traveled with the Dole campaign, that it was one last tour for the veteran, and that it would end in retirement, not the White House. It was Dole's turn at last. The establishment was with him. When his people tried to get an early endorsement from the governor of New Hampshire, Steve Merrill jokingly wondered why, when "they've already got everybody but U. S. Grant."

Dole got started a full ten months before the New Hampshire primary with a kickoff rally at the colonial town hall in Exeter, entertainment provided by a skydiver and daytime fireworks. The show was on. Every fourth winter, the New Hampshire primary campaign draws droves of reporters and TV cameras, some crews from as far off as Sweden and Japan, to interrupt the customary peace of historic streets and town squares. Yankees welcome the business. Hotel rates go up, and the restaurant menus are at summer tourist prices, not winter bargain rates.

Dole was a skilled and seasoned legislator who knew the realities of budgets and taxes and, responsibly I thought, always had resisted the political allure of promising never to raise taxes. But he had suffered on the tax issue in his first two presidential campaigns, and he wasn't going to risk votes on it again, so he took the position he'd considered irresponsible and said flatly that taxes would not be raised. He signed the Pledge, the gimmicky promise the antitax lobby regularly pushed on Republican candidates, promising that he would tolerate no increases. It was playacting, a commitment that could not be kept forever, as Dole knew, and as George Bush had discovered in reneging on his antitax vow of the 1992 campaign. But Dole took it anyhow as insurance against tax hits, cover he needed with his critics trotting out an old Newt Gingrich quote. In his days as a backbench rebel, the speaker of the House had called Dole "tax collector for the welfare state."

Dole wasn't the only Republican doing advance work in New Hampshire that spring. I turned on the radio in my rental car, and there was Pat Buchanan on a call-in show, disputing a questioner who said he had fascist tendencies. Buchanan said it wasn't so. He said Italian dictator Benito Mussolini was the prototype fascist, wore uniforms, and invaded Ethiopia. Buchanan said he wore suits, not uniforms, and put America first. At least it was a unique commitment: I never heard another candidate promise not to invade Ethiopia.

"If I get elected at my age, you know, I'm not going anywhere, I'm just going to serve my country," observed Dole, who was seventy-three. His sentences tended to drift. "Whatever," he sometimes concluded. He was given to talking in the jargon of the Senate cloakroom, an alien language to puzzled voters. He never got over that problem. "I'm going to say this slowly because it will make your eyes glaze over," Dole prefaced a campaign talk on his economic proposals, once he had some, after wasting months casting for a theme. "We're starting to get some ideas out there," Dole observed, the implication being that his campaign hadn't started with any. His Republican rivals were no better at what George Bush had called "the vision thing." They were, as right flank Representative Bob Dornan of California said during his brief, fringe candidacy, "charismatically challenged." Steve Forbes did have one specific new proposal, although only one. He wanted to replace the federal income tax with a flat tax, which caught on as a topic, a sort of flavor of the month, especially after he began pumping money into television ads for the proposal. Then it ebbed, and so did the Forbes campaign. When the Republican candidates debated in the fall of 1995, they came on as ten men in dark business suits, talking about change but looking like a board of directors bent on business as usual. They'd been maneuvering and arguing with each other for months, long enough to be repeating themselves to the point of boredom, especially among the reporters who heard it every day. We do tend to have short attention spans.

That was the setting for the Colin Powell phenomenon. The retired black general who hadn't even declared his party preference became a media star, cover man in the newsmagazines, soaring in the polls—all of which diverted attention and effectively stalled the Republican campaign until he quashed the speculation that he would run. I went to see Barry Goldwater, then eighty-six, in Phoenix that spring. Goldwater had dutifully endorsed Dole, but he wasn't enthusiastic about it. He said he preferred Powell. "If Powell decides to run, he'll get elected president," Goldwater said. "If he runs as a Democrat, I might turn into a Democrat." Powell didn't buy into the rumors, but he knew the game, and he played it to advantage—a gesture here, a companionable telephone call there, and the media stars kept his stock rising. His twenty-three-city book promotion tour took on the flavor of a political swing. In November 1995, he declared himself to be a Republican and said that he would not run. "I understand that they are looking for new ideas and fresh faces in American politics, and I certainly was one," Powell said.

I never thought the Powell boom was more than a bubble. It was politically incorrect to say so, but a black candidate had no chance of winning the election. The race factor didn't come into play because the candidacy was theoretical. Put a black candidate into real contention for the White House and racial politics would have risen again. Nor could Powell have been nominated by the Republican Party. Conservatives dominate the GOP establishment, and they wouldn't accept rational compromise on social issues, let alone a nominee who supported affirmative action and a woman's right to choose an abortion. One of Powell's exit lines seemed to me to cover both barriers. He said that when he talked about his views on social issues "instead of being burned at the cross immediately," he found some Republicans actually willing to listen.

With Powell out, the lineup was set. Dole was still at the head of it, a particularly advantageous position given the latest round of Democratic tinkering with the rules, which accelerated the primary election schedule again. Political junkies called the result "front-loading," and in 1996 that meant thirty-two states would be voting in the first six weeks of competition, a pace that favored the favorite, even a shaky one. And Dole certainly was that. Forbes was gaining headway with his TV barrage of flat tax ads. "If you take away the tax code, you take away the power of the Washington politicians," Forbes advertised. A companion ad said Dole was just one of those old-fashioned politicians, that he was against change and had been voting for tax increases for years. Forbes, of course, hadn't voted for or against anything because he'd never held office. Now he was the new-look cover boy of the Republican field. Before he was finished, which was soon, Forbes had spent millions of his own dollars, most of the money on TV ads that scarred Dole all season. "Millions of dollars of negative advertising," Dole complained. "It's terrible. I might not even vote for myself." The real problem was that the Forbes offensive forced Dole to spend more of his legally limited campaign funds in the winter than he could afford, leaving him strapped in the spring, when he had the nomination locked up but little money to put into a national campaign against Clinton. Forbes's speeches were monotone, his campaign mono-issue, his attempts at humor as flat as the tax idea. But his scrap-the-tax-code notion took hold, and soon all the Republican candidates were talking about flat, or at least flatter, taxes. Dole promised "an entirely new tax system," although he'd been around the old one long enough to know that it is resistant, if not impervious, to an overhaul. In 1976, Carter had called the tax code a disgrace and promised to scrap it for a simpler one, but he left the system more complex than he'd found it. Taxes were always campaign fodder, and the simplicity theme put a twist on it, so Forbes hit a political nerve twenty years after Carter with his promise to make it so simple that a return would fit on a postcard.

But it was the belligerent Buchanan who closed in on Dole when the voting began in Iowa. Dole led the field but didn't dominate it—26 percent to Buchanan's 23, a margin of only three thousand or so votes. Alexander ran third and claimed satisfaction. The playing field moved to New Hampshire, but the game didn't change. It was everybody against Dole, with Buchanan urging his forces on the right to "lock and load" and fire at the establishment. Alexander told anyone who would listen that the front-runner was a voice from the past, out of ideas and out of his time. Dole's performance was not inspiring. "I didn't realize that jobs and trade and what makes America work would become a big issue," he confessed after touring a New Hampshire factory just before the primary. That was as silly as it sounded, and Dole knew better, but he was stuck with what he'd blurted. Dole couldn't break his unhappy habit of using congressional jargon about amendments to amendments and the like, baffling code to most people, instead of talking in terms voters could understand. What made sense at the Capitol made none in a New Hampshire town hall.

Dole got what seemed like a boost when Gramm conceded that he couldn't win, quit before the primary, and endorsed the Senate leader. It was a so-what plug because Gramm had scant support and no way to transfer it to Dole anyhow. And it backfired because it took a conservative figure out of the running, which I thought could only help Buchanan, who stood to inherit any stray votes on the right.

He did, and he won the primary, with a 1 percent margin that shook the Republican hierarchy. "All the peasants are coming over the hill with pitchforks," Buchanan crowed. He said he had the knights and barons of the Republican Party on the run. They didn't run far; they ran to Dole, fearful that a Buchanan rebellion would wreck the whole ticket in the fall. Buchanan beat Dole by only 2,274 votes, not even a droplet in a national election bucket but enough to hobble the leader and shake the party. A holy war like the one he'd tried to declare at the 1992 convention was only going to help the Democrats. In party councils and in the political media, Buchanan was not treated as an upset giant killer but as a threatening loose cannon of a candidate. That led to another reverse spin. I later concluded that losing New Hampshire helped Dole clinch the nomination quickly. He wasn't inspiring, he was the same old face, but he was safe, not menacing.

Appropriately enough, a dense winter fog shrouded Concord the morning after that New Hampshire primary. Dole was a shaky frontrunner at best and the Republican situation was as murky as the weather. But Dole still had the strongest national organization and the healthiest campaign treasury for the rush of primary elections just ahead. Besides, losing to Buchanan was not as damaging to Dole as if he had been defeated by a credible candidate for the nomination. Buchanan was not going to be on the ticket; Republicans might turn to the right but not that far. He'd had his best night in New Hampshire in 1996, just as he had four years earlier in his losing challenge to Bush. "It's the mainstream versus the extreme," Dole said. But Buchanan wasn't his only problem. Forbes was still at it despite a sorry showing in New Hampshire. He won a primary in Delaware, where nobody else campaigned, and he bought one in Arizona, where nobody else spent the kind of money he did—$4 million on a TV ad onslaught. Forbes said he was writing the obituary of conventional political punditry. Actually, he was buying his own campaign obit. He faded and Dole soon clinched the nomination.

Strangely, a day after Dole swept eight presidential primaries and all but certified his ticket, Jack Kemp, the former congressman and Cabinet member, declared that he was for Forbes. Kemp acknowledged that he was somewhat late in backing his flat tax pal. He was very late. Eight days and one more beating after Kemp had boarded his sinking political ship, Forbes quit the campaign and said he'd support Dole. And five months after that, Dole made Kemp his vice presidential running mate.

Kemp had a long history as a tax cut champion. As a representative from New York, he had joined Senator William V. Roth of Delaware in sponsoring the tax bill that was the prototype for Ronald Reagan's tax cut in 1981. Kemp had been a pro football quarterback in San Diego and Buffalo, and he was almost as athletic in promoting his bill. Kemp was the showman, Roth the toupeed elder of the two sponsors. I interviewed them together in a cubbyhole Capitol office back in the Reagan era. Kemp waved his arms as he argued his case. At one point, his gesture just missed the senator, who lurched back so hard his toupee went awry. Dole didn't buy Kemp's economic and tax theories, and their differences in those years got down to personal insults. Kemp said Dole was devoid of vision. Dole sniped back that Kemp was a pretty boy who wanted "a business deduction for hair spray." Those tiffs were forgotten when Dole swallowed hard and asked Kemp to run with him that summer.

When Dole nailed down his nomination, the realistic rivals got out of the way. Buchanan was a different story. He'd concede the nomination was Dole's, but he wouldn't concede the campaign. He wanted clout and a platform at the Republican National Convention. So he kept running, although he shelved his active campaign for a while. "Bring the pitchforks, we're going all the way to San Diego," he told his supporters after losing twenty-five primaries in a row. He did nothing to dispel the scary image. At one point he peered out from under a broad-brimmed black hat, brandishing a shotgun over his head. Denouncing the North American Free Trade Agreement, he told people not to eat Mexican avocados because they had bugs. By then he sounded buggy himself. Bush had tried to placate the right with concessions to Buchanan in 1992. All that got him was trouble, and Dole wouldn't do it. Buchanan said it would be a calculated insult if he was denied a prime-time speaking role at the San Diego convention. He was, and couldn't do anything about it. Buchanan's campaign finally ended with more whimper than bang in August, the day before the convention roll call that ratified Dole's nomination. Buchanan issued a one-page statement endorsing Dole, with a hollow claim of triumph and vindication because the Republicans had adopted a conservative platform. They always did, and it would have happened with him or without him; if anything, his weekly primary defeats had shown signs of weakness on the right, not strength. He could fight Republican resistance and fire back at ridicule, but there was no defense against irrelevance. "He's a commentator, not a candidate," Dole had said while Buchanan was a holdout campaign challenger. Soon, Buchanan was back on the air, a commentator again—until the next presidential campaign.

His nomination secure by mid-March, Dole was a winner with a money problem. He'd had to spend most of the $37 million the law allowed for a primary candidate who got federal campaign subsidies. That led him to a silly suggestion. Clinton had no opposition for renomination so Dole said the president wasn't morally entitled to the $12 million in federal funds he had received. "He ought to give the money back," said Dole, as improbable a demand as I ever heard a candidate make. Clinton had more than $20 million to spend that spring and early summer before he hit the ceiling. By mid-April, Dole was bumping against the limit. Clinton's bankroll went into television advertising, beginning his national campaign long before Dole could afford to start his. At the same time, Clinton was out raising more money, with tactics and sources that skirted and sometimes crossed the line of legality. By the time Clinton and the Democrats got into trouble over fund-raising conduct, they had spent the money to take command of the campaign, no matter that some of it had to be given back to illicit donors after the election.

Still, Dole had a card to play. This was going to be the campaign of Pennsylvania Avenue, the Republican leader of the Senate against the Democrat in the White House. A test of men in charge not only of rival parties, but of branches of government. That never had happened before. So the Senate would be Dole's stage, his campaign would be centered there instead of on the road, which made sense with the travel budget about spent. "I'm going to be a full-time senator," Dole said. And not just the senator from Kansas; he was going back to his job as the majority leader. "It's just something I do fairly well." In fact, he did it very well, as minority and then as majority leader. He knew how to make the wheels turn, when to lubricate them with compromise, how to get things done in the Senate. When a Democratic senator said he should quit as GOP leader in order to be a presidential nominee, Dole said if he was supposed to do that, Clinton should quit the presidency to run for it again. But the strategy of campaigning from the Senate was a flop. Within two months of announcing it, Dole resigned not only his leadership but his Senate seat, too, in an attempt to jump-start his stalled challenge to Clinton.

With the presidential campaign on, the Senate, balky and cantankerous at best, was at its worst, stalled and snarled. The Senate job that was supposed to be a springboard for Dole was turning into an anchor. Congress was gridlocked, and Clinton was making it a telling issue against Dole. Besides, while the Senate is a farm system for presidential candidates, senators seldom win. Only three men have won the White House while serving in the Senate, only two, Warren G. Harding and John F. Kennedy, in the twentieth century. Slumping while Clinton gained in the public opinion polls, Dole offered up his dramatic sacrifice, forsaking the Senate after thirty-five years in Congress. On May 15, he announced he would quit within the month. He sobbed when he told his Senate staff, showing the private Dole the voters never saw, the human side of the tough guy. His voice choked as he announced he was resigning, but he kept his composure.

"I will seek the presidency with nothing to fall back on but the judgment of the people, and nowhere to go but the White House or home." Not that home meant he was going back to Kansas. Home was a fancy apartment at the Watergate. And the fallback would turn out to be a marquee role with a Washington lobbying law firm, a rainmaker, as figures like Dole were called in the Beltway world.

Dole's campaign motto claimed that he was a doer, not a talker. That wouldn't fit after he resigned from the Senate, and he had a lot of fast talking to do to reinvent himself. He'd already acknowledged that he could not match Clinton as a performer, conceding that the president was "a good speaker, a better speaker than I am." And ex-senator Dole had the challenge he'd always faced: defining goals and programs that would convince Americans they should unseat a president even though things were going fairly well. Dole had answered like the legislator he was, dealing with campaign issues by talking about bills and amendments, proposals that could not be enacted but might serve as political sales points. Stalls, filibusters, and Democratic parliamentary ploys blocked that path and made the Republican Congress look hapless, a target the Clinton campaign couldn't miss. Dole's allies said the Senate had become his prison. He was out, but only on probation.

While Dole was trying to transform himself, Clinton already had, adopting an old-fashioned strategy with a newfangled name: triangulation. It was a fancy label coined by Dick Morris, the self-advertising campaign consultant. In Franklin Roosevelt's time, a passion for anonymity was a job qualification for presidential advisers. Morris had a passion for promoting himself as the brains behind the Clinton revival. Triangulation meant blaming the Republicans on the right when things went wrong, scorning the Democrats on the left, and planting Clinton back in the middle. That was the solid ground on which Clinton had won the White House in the first place, before straying off into such issues as gays in the military and his futile attempt to overhaul the health care system all at once. He said in 1995 that he had been too obsessed with trying to do too many things at the same time. Forget that. Clinton declared an end to big government in his election-year State of the Union address. The Republicans complained that the Democratic president was trying to sound like Reagan. He was, of course, but there was no political patent on rhetoric. Speaker of the House Newt Gingrich said Clinton wanted to talk in the center, govern on the left, and hope nobody noticed the difference. The Republicans had figured out the Clinton strategy. But they never figured out how to counter it.

Indeed, Gingrich and company blundered into helping Clinton make the game plan work when the Republicans balked at budget compromises in late 1995 and early 1996, leading to selective shutdowns of federal agencies for lack of appropriations. The Republicans believed the president would suffer politically for the stalemate. Wrong. They did. And the episode, illustrated on Democratic terms with the temporary closing of sites like the Washington Monument, propelled the Clinton comeback. In the Republicans' heady First Hundred Days in command of Congress, Clinton was the afterthought in the White House. "The president is relevant here, especially an activist president," Clinton said. It was a forlorn claim; no other president had to argue that he really was a big shot in the Washington scheme of things.

But Morris was already at work on a campaign revival that began with a barrage of television advertising in 1995. They were ads for Clinton but they were disguised as more general Democratic commercials. That way the party could pay for $32 million worth without counting the spending against Clinton's account or disclosing the sources of the money. The spending was supposed to be independent of the candidate and his operation. But the candidate was the president, and the independence was a fiction. It was the start of the anything-goes fund-raising that became one of the chronic scandals marring Clinton's second term. The fund-raising abuses surfaced before the election but never caught on as an issue against Clinton. Never mind the potential consequences after the election; the big money, big TV strategy was working in the world of political operators like Morris and that's all that mattered.

The day before Clinton's renomination at the Democratic National Convention in Chicago, Morris held forth for a select group of political columnists and commentators. I was supposed to be there, but I'd been knocked out of action by an intestinal infection. That Sunday, the day before the convention began, I wrote a piece recalling the tumult of the last time the Democrats met there, in 1968. It was a reminder of my seniority—there were not many of us covering the 1996 convention who had been there twenty-eight years before. I got a more painful reminder as I finished my story, a sharp pain in the stomach. I figured it would go away, but it got worse, to the point that I had to be taken to the emergency room. I spent the convention at Northwestern University Hospital with an IV pumping antibiotics into my arm to treat diverticulitis, drowsily watching the proceedings on television, out of convention action for the first time since 1964. There always is an air of excitement at a national convention hall, even when all the decisions have been made in advance and the proceedings are only a show. I found nothing exciting in what I saw on TV from my hospital bed. I don't know whether it was the doses of medicine or a dose of reality.

At that lunch with the columnists, Morris boasted of the way he'd put the whole campaign together and theatrically excused himself to make a private telephone call, leaving the impression that he'd had to tell Clinton what to do next. What Morris had to do next was resign the following day, when accounts of his kinky sex with a Washington prostitute made the newspapers. Clinton said Morris was "my friend and a superb political strategist," and privately kept in touch with him later in the campaign. And Morris was the man Clinton called in 1998 when he was trying to decide how to deal with the Monica Lewinsky scandal. They hatched a quick poll on the impact of confession versus denial, and Clinton then decided to dishonestly deny everything. In 1996, the Morris episode was a flap but not an issue. "It says something about who you surround yourself with, doesn't it?" Dole asked archly. It said more about the way consultants with loyalties for sale had perverted campaign politics. Morris had worked for Republicans before he went back to Clinton's campaign payroll in 1995. One of his clients was Senator Trent Lott of Mississippi, the man who succeeded Dole as Senate leader. Morris had been calling Lott in 1996, sometimes with inside campaign information, even after the White House reprimanded him for leaking polls on voter attitudes about a budget dispute in Congress.

After Morris quit he signed a big money deal for a tell-all book, which came out under the title *Behind the Oval Office*. Essentially, Morris wrote that he was. Clinton responded sarcastically that he'd had something to do with his own reelection. Within months of his forced exit from the 1996 Clinton campaign, Morris was back on the TV talk show circuit, and political writers were calling him for talking-head comments on the election and the second Clinton term. He later became a columnist for the *New York Post*, the newspaper he had accused of yellow journalism for publishing the prostitute story that drove him out of the Clinton campaign in the first place. Notoriety was its own reward.

In the 1996 campaign, my role was as an observer and analyst for my AP columns, with less hands-on news reporting than before. I still took a turn at my old spot-newswriting specialty now and then, but a new generation of AP reporters was taking over, and I didn't want to be in the way. It was a season of nostalgia but also of satisfaction because my successors were people I had tried to guide and help on the way. My columns were appearing in hundreds of AP newspapers— they went to more than 1,500 newspapers three times a week. Editors told me they liked what I was writing and wanted more, which I appreciated. But I kept in mind the advantage I enjoyed over my syndicated rivals in column writing: Their columns had to be sold while mine were part of the basic AP service to newspapers, no extra charge.

Dole struggled all that spring and into the summer for lack of money. He had $62 million in federal campaign funds coming when he was actually nominated by the Republican National Convention in mid-August, but until then he had to scrimp. He tried to make ethics an issue, but survey after survey showed that while people rated Dole higher for honesty and integrity, Clinton was their preference for president. The Republicans said Clinton was hijacking their issues. He was. He was frustrating them because he was so good at it. Welfare reform was a campaign-year topic in Congress. As a candidate in

1992, Clinton had promised to "end welfare as we know it," but he shelved the idea, taking on health care and leaving welfare for later. My guess was that if he had kept the welfare commitment instead of overreaching on health care, he and the Democrats would not have taken such a beating in the 1994 elections. After the Republicans won Congress, they pushed through tough welfare terms, but Clinton vetoed their bills twice. Then he bent, compromised, and signed a GOP-drawn welfare bill despite liberal Democratic protests, accepting provisions he said went too far in restricting benefits. Swallowing that Republican medicine, he made it sound as though he had written the prescription himself, erasing an issue Dole had tried to claim as his. Clinton said, disingenuously, that he'd never worried about the political impact of the welfare debate. Then again, Dole had claimed that his resignation from the Senate had nothing to do with the polls that showed him lagging behind Clinton. That was about as credible.

With the lead in hand, Clinton waged a low-risk campaign without major proposals for change, only minor ones. He had plans to deal with deadbeat fathers, with wife beaters, and to take unspecified steps against overseas sweatshop labor on imported goods. He favored school uniforms so that inner city kids wouldn't fight about clothes. There'd be a toll-free number for victims of domestic violence. He wanted a second emergency line in case 911 was busy. He supported local curfews for teenagers. He favored cautious tax reductions for the middle class, balanced by spending cuts. He wanted literacy tutors, family leave laws, and school computers. Clinton's mini-agenda kept him safely in the center, away from the costly social programs of the liberal Democrats. Listening to some of them I thought he sounded like a candidate for county council, not president. But his tactics succeeded.

I never did figure out what Dole's strategy was. I don't think he did, either. He thought the character issue would boost him against Clinton, saying that "the drip, drip, drip" of ethics accusations would erode the president's standing. But until the latter days of the campaign, he shied from a direct challenge on Clinton's ethics, wary that to do so might revive his old image as a political knife fighter. Dole stepped on his own lines. He'd once said that he was running for president because every country ought to have one, and now he seemed to have no better explanation, no blueprint for a new government. He sounded defensive, not a good omen for a challenger. "I'm not some extremist out here," he said in one of his debates with Clinton. "I care about people."

It was midsummer before he settled on a centerpiece issue: He'd cut taxes by 15 percent. He'd always been skeptical of the Reaganomics idea that tax cuts would pay growth dividends and bring in more money at lowered rates, but now he not only signed on, he signed up the political guardian of that theory, Kemp, to run with him. It wasn't an easy match between two men who had been scorning each other's ideas for years. Dole went shopping for a vice presidential nominee who might shake up the sluggish Republican campaign but couldn't find one among the two dozen more companionable names on his prospect list. None of them seemed likely to be much help. "What about the quarterback?" Dole finally asked his advisers, who hadn't thought he would turn to Kemp. The two men had feuded across the Capitol when Kemp was in the House and as rival candidates for the 1988 nomination. But Dole didn't need a pal on his ticket, he needed a push. Maybe the energetic, photogenic Kemp could provide one. At least the selection was unexpected, which was not the case with anything else that happened at the Republican convention in San Diego. That was the convention at which ABC's Ted Koppel announced that he was packing up his *Nightline* show and getting out of town because there wasn't any news. "Nothing surprising has happened," he explained to his TV audience. "Nothing surprising is anticipated." I thought that was showboating because we all knew going in that nothing surprising would happen at the convention. Koppel certainly knew that when he got on the plane to San Diego. He could have saved the airfare, but if he hadn't come at all he couldn't have made himself a news story, if a brief one, by leaving in midconvention.

It was a three-convention summer: Republicans, Democrats, and Ross Perot's Reform Party. Perot was on the TV interview circuit early, on the road in the spring, pretending he was not a candidate—although he said he would run should he be drafted by the Reform Party. "This is not about me," he claimed. But the Reform Party was Perot's creation. His share of the 1992 vote entitled its nominee to more than $29 million in federal campaign funds. I couldn't imagine that anyone believed Perot had built a party to be a vehicle for an ego trip by any candidate but himself. He kept saying he really didn't want to run for president again, and Dick Lamm, who had been governor of Colorado as a Democrat, announced that he would seek the Reform nomination. Suddenly, but not surprisingly, Perot then decided that he'd have to run after all because "the American people want me to do this." There were dissenters in the Reform Party, but the "contest" for the nomination, with voting by mail and computer, was a sham. Perot, of course, was nominated. He never came close to the standing he'd gained in the 1992 campaign, and he couldn't get into the 1996 campaign debates, although he sued trying. The candidate who once had complained that he was sick and tired of having people ask him to spell out his positions had a worse political headache now: Nobody much cared.

Dole fretted about the Perot vote and made the mistake of asking him to endorse the Republican ticket late in the campaign. The appeal was supposed to be secret, but it leaked instantly, making Dole seem desperate, which he was. Perot said the plea was weird and inconsequential. Still, if he wouldn't endorse Dole he would denounce Clinton, saying the president was so ethically flawed that he might be forced out of office in a second term. "How could you even consider voting for a candidate that has huge moral, ethical, and criminal problems facing him?" Perot asked.

There was a sexual harassment suit pending, four special prosecutors were investigating Clinton and Cabinet officers, and prosecutor Kenneth Starr's investigations of the Clintons' role as investors in a failed Arkansas land deal had been broadened to cover a purge of the White House travel office and the improper handling of confidential FBI files on Republican figures. Dole tried to stir the ethics issue by indirection, saying he was a man to be trusted without saying flatly that Clinton was not. He got more explicit late in the campaign, accusing Clinton of betraying the public trust, but he still couldn't ignite the character question. Clinton piously said people wanted a campaign of issues and ideas, not insults.

Traveling with the Dole campaign, I saw the frustration of his balancing-act attempt to cut down the president without a backlash. What Dole might gain by getting tough he could lose by looking nasty. "Where's the outrage?" Dole kept asking. It never surfaced. The outlines of Democratic financial misconduct were on the record long before the election. The Democrats were raking in illicit foreign money; the party was forced to return about $3 million after the election. There were the White House sleepovers for fat-cat donors. There was TV tape of Vice President Gore's bizarre performance at a fundraising session at a Buddhist temple near Los Angeles in April 1996. Gore said he thought it was a "community outreach" event and hadn't realized that the reach was for campaign contributions. I thought that all those nuns in saffron robes should have been a tip-off that it wasn't a good setting for politicking, but Gore had smiled, steepled his hands, and stayed, to his regret. The illegal and borderline 1996 fund-raising didn't do Clinton significant political harm because he was reelected before the official investigations began but haunted Gore as he readied his campaign to succeed the president in 2000.

Dole could have challenged Clinton directly on ethics and character when they met in the first of their two campaign debates. Dole was asked an ethics question that amounted to an invitation to attack, but he didn't, perhaps wisely because his harshest words drew the most negative reactions in a postdebate opinion survey conducted by the Republicans. That's the trouble with the character questions: They make voters uncomfortable. "Some people think I'm not tough enough, but I'm working on it," Dole told us after the debate. Kemp took his turn next, and the opening question in his debate with Gore was down the middle of the plate: Should ethics be an issue against Clinton? Kemp didn't swing at it. "In my opinion it is beneath Bob Dole to go after anyone personally," Kemp replied, saying his ticket was for campaign civility. Gore thanked him for saying so. Kemp certainly had earned Democratic thanks by shelving a difficult topic.

Gore, incidentally, had become something of a campaign humorist, at his own expense, as he traveled for the Democratic ticket. The jokes were about his own reputation as a stiff. "Al Gore is so boring his Secret Service code name is Al Gore," he would say, a sure laugh line. Or, "If you use a strobe light, it looks like Al Gore is moving." Or, "I'd like to do the Al Gore version of the Macarena." He would stand motionless for a moment. "Want to see me do it again?" It was a funny routine, and I'd played a role in it. Jokes about Gore's dull stiffness once were put-downs. The laughter was at the vice president, not with him. In 1994, I became president of a Washington institution called the Gridiron Club, which satirizes politicians and hears them joke about themselves at an annual white-tie dinner. I asked Gore to join the humor with a funny speech. It was casting against type and it interested his image-makers. Gore had himself wheeled in, board stiff, on a handcart. I had to sign for the delivery before he took the microphone. It was his debut as a self-deprecating humorist, and he was hilarious.

By the time of the second presidential debate, Dole was out of options. He had to come on strong or forget it. So he went on the attack, sharp and persistent in challenging Clinton on trust and integrity. Even when the question was why Americans couldn't be more united, Dole's answer was stridently on his message: "There's no doubt about it that many American people have lost their faith in government. They see scandals on an almost daily basis. They see ethical problems in the White House today." Clinton had his script, too, and it did not include a response to Dole's accusations. He'd rehearsed the role of the patient, tolerant target. He said he could have answered Dole tit for tat but would not because he wanted to talk about America's future and because attacks did not solve problems. He'd watched Bush stumble in the 1992 debates by refusing to promise not to go on the attack. Sometimes the most effective defense against a rival's offensive was no defense at all.

Besides, that way his postdebate cheerleaders could tell us how Clinton had conducted himself with presidential gravity while Dole was just a complaining candidate. They were both candidates, of course, and candidates do whatever they think will get the most votes. The Republican rooting section said Clinton's refusal to answer Dole's accusations was the next thing to a confession that he'd done all those awful things. He hadn't, only most of them. But neither reporters nor voters would find out about that until he spent his second term under investigation, eventually under impeachment, and was ultimately spared dismissal from the White House when the Senate voted to acquit him on two counts early in 1999.

Presidential campaign debates beget self-serving partisan appraisals of the candidates as soon as they go off the air. In one of the odd rituals of modern campaigning, each side sends its supporters to what politicians and reporters all call Spin Alley, at the front of the cavernous press centers set up for debate coverage. Rival politicians had been trying to convince us to see debates their way in every campaign since debating was revived in 1976. The game of trying to spin the story their way became more intensive, more organized, and, I thought, sillier each campaign season. Only a handful of reporters get into the actual debate theater to see what happens off camera. The hundreds of others work in nearby ballrooms or conference halls, watching the proceedings on television like the rest of the country. That's where the political impact lies anyhow, in what the nation sees and hears. Trying to color what is written and said about the debate while it is happening, the rival campaigns assign teams of operatives to crank out news releases point by point, arguing that the other guy lied about his record or his program, and send young volunteers running among the press tables, piling up the paper. If you want to concentrate on what is happening between the candidates, you have to pitch the handouts or your laptop keyboard will vanish in all the paper, so it piles up around you. The useful paper is the debate text, delivered in sections that have to be grabbed quickly to make sure those pages don't get buried in all the other stuff.

Actually, the claims and counterclaims begin before the debating does, when the candidates' partisans show up in the pressroom to boast how well their man is going to do—meaningless bluster, but they get some TV time because the cable types have to put something on their nonstop news. For print, it is uselessly outdated the moment the debate begins.

As part of the bizarre rites of debate spinning, Cabinet members, congressional figures, governors, political operators, spokesmen, apologists, managers, you name it, crowd into the press center to try to tell us what to think about the debate we all just observed. I always figured that if I didn't know better than they did, I shouldn't be writing about it. At the 1996 debates in Hartford and San Diego, the Republicans boasted about how well Dole had performed, the Democrats solemnly pronounced Clinton the clear winner, and only the gullible paid any attention. "We're burbling banalities," admitted Mike McCurry, then Clinton's press secretary, as he extolled his boss. To make clear who was babbling, campaign gofers carried placards with the name—or title—of the spinner. I thought it was demeaning to Cabinet members to parade in the pressroom under signs announcing who they were, but that became the custom. It reminded me of a wisecrack delivered by Jack Germond, who said after a senator had delivered his vacuous thoughts to reporters at a Capitol news conference that it amounted to casting imitation pearls before real swine.

In the end, the 1996 election fit the form charts. Clinton won with 49 percent of the vote to Dole's 41 percent. Perot got 8 percent, not bad for a third candidate but not half what he'd polled four years earlier. It was enough to entitle the Reform Party nominee to government campaign funds in 2000, which would prove the rule of unintended consequences when Pat Buchanan claimed it. In polling place surveys, most voters said they were more interested in policies than in character, and the people who felt that way voted overwhelmingly for Clinton. A majority said they did not think Clinton was honest.

Long afterward, in the final months of Clinton's term, I sat down with Dole amid the trophies, photographs, and mementos of his long political life as he reflected on it. He recalled the morning after the 1996 election when he got a call from a Democrat, a fellow in the select company of defeated presidential nominees. "Don't despair, it's just going to be different," former Senator George McGovern told former Senator Dole.

"I ran for president," Dole told me that day. "I did the best I could. We didn't win. So get on with your life. Politics isn't everything. I think as long as you behave yourself and just become sort of a senior something—" The thought drifted away.

Politics was everything for Clinton, I thought. After an interview on Air Force One late in 2000, with the disputed presidential outcome still unsettled, Clinton went into an hour-long soliloquy about House seats and states the Democrats had lost, and where he thought he might have tipped the outcome had he been asked to play a major role in the campaign. The two of us who had interviewed him and the aide who sat in could only listen; Clinton did all the talking. It was as though he were alone, reflecting.

He'd struggled to get past the stain of impeachment, even suggesting that it might become a positive part of his legacy: "I think when historians get a little space they will say, 'I don't know how those people stood up to that but, boy, I'm glad they did because it preserved the Constitution.' So I think history will view this much differently." But probably not unless Clinton is writing it, or rewriting it. Certainly Clinton was concerned about his legacy and bent on polishing it, in and after office. But it seemed to me he had another, simpler, concern. He just didn't want to be out of the game. He was a masterful politician, sentenced to early retirement at fifty-four, the youngest ex-president since Theodore Roosevelt.

Dole, two decades Clinton's senior, was more philosophical. "Losing," he told me, "means that at least you were in the race."

ELEVEN

Overtime: The 2000 Election

Before the pollsters, the computers, and the projection wizards came to power, election nights in close contests were suspense stories, stretching through hours of uncertainty as the votes were counted. In all but the landslides, writing about elections was telling a story as it happened, unfolding toward an often unknown ending. You could read the clues and anticipate the winner, but you couldn't be sure. Come the millennium, all that suspense and excitement was history, we thought. In the last campaign of my career as a political reporter, I harbored a nostalgic wish that there might an election to defy the system—the art, science, or whatever it was—of projecting the outcomes before a vote had been counted. But by 2000, we thought the process of voter polling and computerized projections had to be infallible, or close to it.

The experts were always right, or almost always. They'd blown a New Hampshire Senate election call in 1998, declaring the wrong winner, but that was just a glitch, the projections people said, and they'd made the system failproof for 2000. Sure they had. I got my suspense that election night and five weeks beyond it as George W. Bush and Al Gore struggled for the presidency in a deadlock over Florida, where the margin was too close to call with certainty even after the state's electoral votes and so the presidency were awarded to Bush.

Neither Bush nor Gore nor anybody else will ever know who really got more votes in Florida. At 0.00009 of 1 percent of the vote, the margin by which Bush was certified the winner and ultimately the forty-third president, there could be no absolute proof of the outcome. Despite the never-again promises of Congress and the states to create a more perfect process for casting and counting votes, no voting system could guarantee the accuracy of a count as close as Florida's in 2000. Perhaps in a laboratory scientists could engineer one, but not in the schoolhouses, town halls, and myriad other precinct settings of a diverse American election. (The organization that conducted voter exit interviews and projected outcomes for the media, Voter News Service, a consortium of the TV networks and the AP, not only failed in Florida in 2000, but a two-year effort to fix the system failed as well. Before the polls closed in the election of 2002, VNS said it could not deliver reliable data and gave up for the night. After those failures, VNS was disbanded in January 2003.)

Presidential elections usually are settled by clear margins, two or three percentage points even when they are close. When the vote count is even closer, as between Kennedy and Nixon in 1960, the electoral college system tends to magnify the winner's margin. In 1996, Clinton was reelected with less than half the popular vote but a 70 percent count in electoral votes. But in 2000 the old generalities didn't apply; the projections were not reliable, and the TV commentators had to swallow their announcements that Bush had won, made and retracted in the early morning hours after election day. The election of November 7 was settled for Bush on December 12, after the Supreme Court ended the Florida recounts. Bush lost the national popular vote but won the White House with an electoral college majority plus one.

It was the election that ran overtime. My career did, too. I was sixty-five years old that January 11, retirement age. It was not mandatory for me to retire as a reporter, but as an AP vice president, I served one-year terms and thought I was in my last in 1999. After nearly forty-five years, it was time to go. Then Lou Boccardi, the AP president, asked me to stay through the 2000 election and cover one last presidential campaign. I was flattered and delighted.

The first campaign of the twenty-first century began taking shape two years before the millennium, with Vice President Gore and Texas

Governor Bush installed long in advance as the consensus front-runners for the presidential nominations. For both men, politics was the family business. I'd reported on their fathers, the first Tennessee Senator Gore and the first President Bush. The vice president and the governor had the name recognition, the poll ratings, and, therefore, the campaign cash to become the favored candidates of their rival party establishments. That standing propped them up when they slipped, enabling them to withstand the challengers who stalled each of them early in the 2000 primary election season.

I first encountered George W. Bush in 1988 as he traveled the presidential campaign path with his father. "I was a loyalty enforcer and a listening ear," he said later. "I earned and deserved a reputation for being feisty and tough, sometimes too tough." The younger Bush was a brusque-to-bristling insider who usually kept reporters at a defensive distance. As the political saying goes, he wouldn't tell you if your pants were on fire. He was an unofficial adviser in the Bush White House, the guy who got the tough assignments, including the task of telling Chief of Staff John Sununu that he had to go in 1991. George W. was aboard the 1992 reelection campaign, too, and no friendlier, especially as the odds worsened for his father against Clinton. The uptight style and the hard edges yielded to the more relaxed, cordial Governor Bush I saw at the capitol in Austin in 1999. I asked him where the tough guy had gone. Bush said he was more at ease about his own job and his own political prospects than about his father's. "I saw my dad losing," he remembered. "It was a very difficult time. Ninety-two was a rough year, a difficult year." But an instructive one, he said, with a trace of the old bitterness when he spoke of Republicans—no names—who had been allies in good political times but turned away when the president's reelection prospects began foundering. "I think I learned a lot about Washington loyalty," Bush told me. "Everybody loves a winner. You learn the character of people when things are not so good."

Things were good that spring in Austin. Bush was riding high, the campaign treasury was swelling, and the candidate hadn't said he'd run, hadn't even left town, saying that he had to be on duty as governor until the Texas legislature finished its work. That led to a procession of Republicans to Austin to see him. Party leaders from Congress and his father's Cabinet signed on to advise him. More than half the Republican governors endorsed him before he declared his candidacy. So did more than eighty congressional Republicans. I'd never seen anything like it, probably because there hadn't been anything quite like it since William McKinley won the presidency after staying put in Canton, Ohio, in his front-porch campaign of 1896. Bush's stay-at-home start was part of a campaign strategy shaped even before his runaway reelection as governor in 1998.

In May 1998, a national public opinion poll had shown Bush narrowly preferred over Gore for president in 2000. "I'm mystified," Bush said. He insisted he wasn't going to be distracted by White House talk while he had a job as governor and an election to win in Texas. But the Texas reelection campaign was shaped to flow into a presidential operation, and there was no missing the hints that a reelected Governor Bush would be looking at the White House in 2000. Before he began campaigning for president, he had a carefully constructed Republican bandwagon waiting. Bush was a winner, the party line went. Republican leaders convinced themselves and each other that he represented their best shot at reclaiming the presidency after eight years.

In the party that usually rewarded its veterans by nominating them—Dole, the elder Bush, Reagan—Governor Bush was a relative rookie, just into his second term in his first elective office. But he was the favorite of the party hierarchy before spring training ended and the regular campaign season began. A dozen challengers would surface at one point or another, but most of them didn't get as far as the first presidential primary. Senator John McCain of Arizona overtook Bush and won the opener in New Hampshire, but he couldn't topple the national leader. Bush was too strong, too well financed, the chosen nominee of party powers who didn't want an iconoclast like McCain. So it was going to be Bush. I talked with assorted Republicans and got assorted theories to explain the rise of the second Bush. There was nostalgia for the first among people who remembered his best times and forgot about the fumbling 1992 campaign that led to his political fall. Then, too, there was Clinton fatigue, the feeling that enough was more than enough of the Democrats after the president whose sexual flings and lies had gotten him impeached. George W. began with an advantage over other Republicans—a name people knew. In the earliest preliminaries for a presidential campaign, name recognition is what counts in the polls. Dan Quayle was up there for a while, not because most people wanted him to be elected president in 2000 but because most people knew who he was. For the governor, the Bush family name and his father's legacy of fame were send-off advantages.

Gore's Democratic head start was obvious. Vice presidents who want to be nominated for president almost always are. Still, the office that made Gore the logical nominee in 2000 also came with liabilities. He was vice president to Clinton, a president impeached, acquitted, and still embroiled in scandal, in a party scarred by illicit campaign contributions. Gore's hand showed in the fund-raising excesses of 1996; he was spared the attentions of a special prosecutor, but it was a near thing. Loyalty is part of the vice presidential job description. Gore overdid it when, on the day of Clinton's impeachment, he told a strange rally of congressional Democrats at the White House that history would regard his boss as "one of our greatest presidents." The scene was as bizarre as his fawning praise—Democrats called to the South Lawn to applaud the president on the day of his disgrace. Even if Gore actually believed that he was standing beside one of the greatest presidents, impeachment day was not the day to say so.

Since taking office, Gore had been the man always two steps behind the president at White House proceedings, looking like a courtier or perhaps a caddy. Now he had to campaign to change his image at the same time he took on challenger Bill Bradley, the former senator from New Jersey who'd made his name and the Hall of Fame in professional basketball before making it in politics. And Bradley made Gore nervous. The vice president had intended to ignore the pretender to his presumed nomination, but in the spring of 1999 Bradley was beginning to look like a real candidate who could raise the money and find the support to make a contest of it—a real rival,

not a pushover. Gore had planned on a pushover and wasn't prepared for the challenge.

Gore held a long lead in the polls of Democratic support and an
even wider one in campaign funds. He had the advantages and trappings of his office. He had the endorsements. But he also had a sluggish, top-heavy campaign operation with political aides who too often
competed for influence with his vice presidential staff and advisers,
treating them as a sort of palace guard instead of colleagues in a cause.
There was internal bickering, and there were insider complaints that
the vice president was miring himself in detail work. Bradley was inch-
ing up in the polls and congressional Democrats were restive about
Gore's ability to rally the party behind the 2000 ticket on which they'd
be running, too. Gore did some early campaign remodeling, appointing Tony Coelho, a former congressman and veteran political manager,
to head his political operation. Coelho was a skilled, proven operator,
but he'd quit Congress in 1989 to avoid an investigation of his
finances, which seemed to me to make him an odd choice by a candidate who was trying to explain away his own fund-raising missteps.

When there were rumors that Clinton was worried about the way
things were going in the Gore campaign, the president interceded
with a heavy hand, telephoning the *New York Times* to volunteer
that he wasn't alarmed. Besides, Clinton said, "it's in a lot better
shape now than it was eight weeks ago." Just what Gore needed:
White House intervention to stir a new round of reports that his campaign was a mess. Privately, Gore was irked that Clinton had barged
into print to offer counterproductive public advice. "If he did not
advise me to loosen up, he would be the only person in the United
States who didn't," the vice president told *Newsweek*. He'd been hearing that advice for years and trying to heed it, but he still seemed stiff.
Gore was ridiculed for hiring a fancy image consultant who recommended a new wardrobe. Clothes didn't do it; he appeared as uptight
in earth tone sweaters as he had in dark blue suits. His casual garb
made him look like the cover of a Lands' End catalog. A year later
when Gore changed managers again, Bill Daley, the new chairman,
said one of his goals at the Democratic National Convention would be

to chip away at the stereotype. "Obviously, it would be great for those people who have been convinced for eight years that he's just a boring stiff, an unable-to-speak guy, that he comes through as a real person," Daley told us, describing the image his candidate just couldn't seem to shake. You had to admire the candor. Daley had been raised in the Chicago school of politics of his father the mayor, and blunt talk was part of the curriculum. Even when it involved describing your own candidate's flaws.

By the time Bush ventured out from Austin, the Republican field for the 2000 campaign already had assembled and the odd rites of declaring presidential candidacy were well under way. In that redundant ritual, candidates who already are campaigning for president hire a hall, pack it with backers, and announce in solemn tones, "Today, I announce that I am a candidate for president of the United States." The crowd cheers what they'd known for months, the candidate savors the ovation and gets back to the business of campaigning. I'd been watching these faux announcements for years; the script never changed much, regardless of the candidate or the party. The Announcement is not the real starting point, only a ceremonial confirmation of the obvious. It gets some attention and some television time, even for the long, long shots, most of whom peak on announcement day before being consigned to the list of also-running names. Under the campaign finance laws, candidates have to report their fund-raising and spending whether they are running openly or pretending only to be exploring the possibility. So candidate announcements are playacting, part of the plot line that ends for all but two of them with another, unhappier rite, the Withdrawal, in which losers concede that they are not going to be able to get the nominations. Again, Pat Buchanan was the exception; as a Republican he was getting nowhere, but that didn't mean he'd concede. Instead, he switched to run to a sorry ending as the Reform Party candidate, with even founder Ross Perot opposing him. At least he began with a bang, as usual. "Mount up and ride to the sound of the guns," he exhorted his supporters in a belligerent beginning to his Republican candidacy early in 1999. The rhetorical armament was heavier than when he claimed to be leading peasants with pitchforks, but he was a loser from the day he started. So were a dozen others, with names as familiar as Dan Quayle and as obscure as John Kasich, a congressman from Ohio. Kasich ended his brief campaign by endorsing Bush as his soul brother, an exit line that made you wonder why he had entered. Gary Bauer, a conservative activist who had held minor appointments in the Reagan administration, announced, debated, campaigned, and ran dead last in the New Hampshire primary, at 1 percent of the vote. He quit. "I'm a fighter but I'm not delusional," he said. Delusion is an ailment afflicting politicians who decide for no evident reason that they ought to be president. But Bauer probably got what he wanted; he never pretended that he was going to win the nomination, but campaigning for it enabled him to trumpet his rightist views.

A crowd of Republican rivals was hunting support to take down Bush when the Republican leader debuted as an active campaigner in mid-June 1999. "I know the expectations are high," he said. "As my daughter said, 'Dad, you're not nearly as cool as people think.' " Bush told me he was amazed at his favorite's role after a brief apprenticeship for national politics. He had watched his father go through the Republican chairs for two decades before he was nominated and elected to the White House. George W. was on the fast track. He said he had a "very long and arduous road" ahead of him, but it didn't seem to bother him during a relaxed interview in his Austin statehouse office, beside a wall lined with autographed baseballs, memorabilia of his days as managing partner of the Texas Rangers. He was an easy guy to talk with but also a careful one—when he got a difficult question that might become a political problem, his right-hand woman, Karen Hughes, often interceded and sometimes tried to answer for him. Bush also was a man who did not tolerate cell phones lightly; nothing bugged him more than to be interrupted by that ringing noise in somebody's pocket. My colleague's cell phone sounded while we were interviewing him that day. Bush gave him a bristling, exasperated stare. My partner, Ron Fournier, fumbled with the phone, got it turned it off, and then yanked out the battery to make sure the thing remained silent. Bush smiled, triumphant over wireless technology.

Interview time was up; a church group was waiting to see the governor, and an aide was trying to keep him on schedule. But as we walked toward the door, I asked him whether he thought Major League Baseball would have to do something to keep competitive balance so that the big city moneybags teams wouldn't buy all the talent. He did—he favored revenue sharing among the richer and poorer teams—and he lingered for nearly ten minutes, talking about a favorite topic. In one of the Republican debates in 2000, the candidates were asked to tell the biggest mistake they'd ever made. The others talked solemnly about official and personal slipups, while Bush said his was signing off on the trade of slugger Sammy Sosa in 1989. The Rangers got Harold Baines, a fine ballplayer but not a match for Sosa, who became the home run hero of the Chicago Cubs. One of my AP colleagues bumped into Baines at an airport and asked him what he thought. Baines laughed and said the swap was a major-league mistake by Bush. "I can see why he got out of the business," he joked.

Bush's political takeoff left the other Republicans frustrated on the political runway. I talked with Quayle about it one day in the Washington office of his campaign pollster, a curious setting for his complaints. "They're trying to go with the polls rather than ideas and that is a colossal mistake," the former vice president told me. "You can talk all you want to about polls and all this happy nonsense, who the front-runner is, but you're not going to know until they vote." Quayle quit for lack of support and funds long before Republicans began voting. He had insisted he could dispel the bumbling image of his vice presidential days and get rid of the Dan Quayle jokes, but he didn't have to. His campaign profile didn't get high enough to draw much sniping from the comedians.

Elizabeth Dole, who had served in two Cabinet posts and as president of the American Red Cross, was campaigning for the nomination her husband had gained in 1996. While women had run before, the most prominent of them Senator Margaret Chase Smith of Maine in 1964, Mrs. Dole seemed a more serious contender than those of the past. But she wasn't very good at it. Even the strolling, talk-show-style appearances she'd practiced in 1996 looked stilted and scripted. The speeches sounded like they were coming from the same tape record-ing. "When you feel strongly about something, you have a passion for it," she said, but none showed. She displayed about as much passion as the chaperone at the prom. Her caution and restraint were in marked contrast to Bob Dole's quick wisecracks and ad libs. In one talk with us, she criticized Clinton only after putting her comments off the record. She said Bush would make a fine nominee, an odd com-pliment as she campaigned to keep him from being one. Bob Dole was helping, working to raise money, but in the early going, his most vis-ible role was a gaffe. He said in a *New York Times* interview that he might donate money to John McCain's campaign in order to keep a good man in the Republican field, although he would check with his wife first. "They're buddies from the Senate," Mrs. Dole said. Bob Dole was just talking; he didn't kick in to the McCain treasury, and after Mrs. Dole quit, she endorsed Bush.

When Bush began campaigning that June, you could measure his standing with a look at his opposition. They wanted him to debate them right away. Bob Dole growled on behalf of his wife that Republicans weren't going to stand still for a coronation. The Democratic Party sent out what politicians call a truth squad to track him and dispute him. Their opposition press releases flowed into the Bush pressrooms, crowded with reporters and TV cameras, an entourage more typical for a general election candidate than for the first outing of a man running for the Republican nomination to be awarded nearly fourteen months later. "I'm pleased that the Democrats are paying attention to me," Bush remarked. "They must be worried."

By any reasonable standard, it was early in the game. But not by the calendar that had become the unreasoning, unrelenting standard in presidential campaigns, in which the next one started almost as soon as the last one was over. "You're first in the nation and I'm the last candidate here," Bush said in Manchester, New Hampshire. "I know I'm a late arriver. I'm taking my front porch campaign to every front porch in this state." He'd come with a crowd—three busloads of reporters and TV crews trailed him on that first New Hampshire foray. We didn't learn much. He kept it general, preaching his "compassionate conservative" theme and saying that detailed proposals could wait.

We did learn that he would sidestep questions about whatever he had done in his admittedly reckless youth. "There is a game in Washington, it is called gotcha," he complained. "It's the game where they float a rumor and make the candidate prove a negative, and I'm not playing the game." The questions would persist but the tactic sufficed. Bush admitted that he drank to excess and made unspecified mistakes in his youth, which seemed to have lasted longer for him than for most of us. "I made some mistakes years ago," Bush confessed vaguely. "But I learned from my mistakes." He said he'd quit drinking on his fortieth birthday, July 6, 1986. "All this stuff about George's totally irresponsible past, we never saw it," his father said. There were rumors that he had used illegal drugs, cocaine perhaps, but no evidence ever surfaced. He encountered the drug question in his first campaign for governor in 1994 and replied then much as he did when running for president, that he wasn't going to let people float rumors and get him to reply to them. He did say in 1999 that he hadn't used drugs in at least twenty-five years. Democrats Gore and Bradley both had acknowledged marijuana use in the early 1970s. All the Republican candidates except Bush said they had never used illegal drugs. He fended off the questions and the topic subsided with no penalty in the polls. It was a distraction at the time but I thought it was a break for Bush because the same back-and-forth a year later, after he'd been nominated, would have been far more troublesome. By then it was part of the background, sometimes a sentence in the stories but not the lead. A drug denial covering twenty-five years wouldn't have sufficed for a senior government appointee being vetted for a security clearance, but Bush got by with it.

The youthful mistakes business came back as more than a rumor just before the 2000 election. He'd been arrested for driving under the influence of alcohol in 1976, when he was twenty-eight, near the family summer home in Maine. A Democratic activist got that story disclosed and published four days before the presidential election.

"Dirty politics, last-minute politics," Bush claimed, trying to make an issue of the source rather than the arrest. He said, lamely I thought, that he had kept the episode quiet all those years because he hadn't wanted his daughters to know about it. "It's become clear to America over the course of this campaign that I've made mistakes in my life," Bush repeated, in the line he always used when such personal history matters came up. And, again, "I'm proud to tell you, I've learned from those mistakes." Not enough, I thought, because an old arrest record is a trap waiting to snap on a politician who doesn't disarm it by disclosing it on his own terms and timing. The DUI disclosure certainly cost Bush votes, and while it was impossible to say how many, any ballot lost was a vital one in the dead heat state counts of 2000.

In the summer of '99, the Bush phenomenon was not all about the crowds and the polls; it also was about money. Bush's fund-raising rewrote all the records for a presidential candidate: $100 million-plus in contributions before he got the Republican nomination. By the end of June, the Bush campaign reported raising $36.3 million. Incredibly, that was nine times as much as McCain had raised. The political parlor game that summer was to guess whether Bush, with all that money, would skip the federal matching funds candidates had been getting since 1976 to campaign for presidential nominations because of the restrictions that go with the subsidies. It was a silly game. Of course he was going to decline the money, which would have limited him to spending less than he was raising. And of course his opponents would try to make an issue of it. The only other candidates who had said no to the federal money were running on their personal fortunes, as Steve Forbes did in 1996 and again in 2000. For Bush, accepting government funds would have been a liability, especially with Forbes's ability to spend at will and his track record of doing so in hostile TV campaigns that scarred Republican rivals in 1996.

McCain, who was making campaign reform his trademark issue, said that for Bush to skip the government funding in order to avoid the spending limits breached the intent of the campaign finance law. But no one could argue that Bush was not complying with the law, which set a $1,000 limit on an individual donation to a candidate. His campaign had allies rounding up those individual donors to keep the money coming—"bundling" it was called—but the law didn't restrict that practice. What Bush was raising was called "hard money" in Beltway jargon. McCain and his fellow campaign finance reformers were trying to have Congress limit "soft money," a system under which political parties could raise unlimited funds without disclosing its sources. They were supposed to spend it only for party purposes, not for individual candidates, although the restriction had become transparent fiction. The Democratic fund-raising abuses of 1996, still hanging over Gore in 2000, involved soft money.

No candidate until Bush had built such a bankroll on hard money; his campaign reported that 350,000 people made contributions. There were complaints in rival Republican camps that Bush was trying to buy the nomination and that donors were trying to buy him. Bush denied both and said anybody who thought that a $1,000 contribution was going to buy influence should forget it and vote for somebody else. Bush's unprecedented bankroll drove some of his rivals out of the campaign because there simply wasn't enough Republican money to go around. But campaign cash wasn't enough to carry Bush on a straight line to the nomination, not without stumbles and upsets on the way.

At times the Bush people had more money than common sense. When nine of the Republican candidates competed for a straw vote in Ames, Iowa, in August 1999—a silly exercise validated by all the attention we reporters gave it—the Bush campaign paid $43,500 to rent a site to pitch its tent right outside the hall, the better to attract supporters inside for food and drink, entertainment, and political persuasion. It was a sucker bid in a blind auction. Forbes got the next best tent site for $8,000. A ticket to the Iowa Republican Party dinner cost $25 and included the right to vote in the straw poll. So the candidates bought votes by buying tickets for their supporters. The Bush and Forbes campaigns rented scores of buses to bring in backers. Bush won after spending about $825,000 to get 7,418 votes, at about $111 apiece. Forbes spent at least twice that to come in second. Lamar Alexander was a sorry sixth and quit, saying he didn't have the money to keep running. It gave him one first in more than five years of trying—first presidential candidate forced to concede by a straw vote. John McCain stayed out, saying that before the primary voting began the whole straw show would be forgotten, as it was. Easy for him to say; he was a challenger, not a front-runner.

Bush couldn't pick targets. Bypass a high-profile contest, even a flaky one, and he'd suffer at the hands, or mouths, of the talking heads and columnists. And what if it was only a straw poll—Jimmy Carter used one just like it, in the same Iowa town, to make his first mark in the 1976 Democratic campaign. So Bush stamped his leader's ticket with a win in the only game in town. He was thriving in the public opinion polls. It was starting to look easy, but I'd seen enough leaders go lame to doubt that it would be. The field was dwindling with Alexander out, Quayle out, then Elizabeth Dole, who said "the bottom line is money" and that she couldn't get enough of it. More Republican candidates quit before the primaries than after the voting began.

Among politicians and political reporters, the nearly permanent presidential campaign is a given. Among other people, it is a yawn. "For most people, the election is not going on," Clinton observed from the sidelines. In a poll just after Labor Day 1999, nearly 40 percent couldn't remember the name of a single Republican presidential candidate and half didn't know who was running for the Democrats.

Al Gore was getting increasingly nervous that fall. The brush-off strategy he'd tried to use to quash Bill Bradley's challenge wasn't working. Gore had acted as though a vice president didn't have to bother with a pretender, but Bradley was gaining on him in surveys in the early primary election states. More important, he was proving that Democrats would give him ample funds to campaign against Gore. Gore's campaign headquarters, two blocks from the White House, looked like another branch of the bureaucracy, overstaffed and top-heavy with bosses and underbosses jealous of one another's turf. You got the impression that it had more officers than campaign soldiers. Bradley's base was a cluttered, low-rent shop in West Orange, New

Jersey, where the receptionist sometimes called over the loudspeaker that somebody had a telephone call, which would have been unthinkably informal at Gore headquarters. The Bradley lore was growing—the lanky, casual outsider, jacket draped over his shoulder, against the buttoned-down vice president who still couldn't shake the image that he was a stiff. When I sat down to talk with them, before and after they became presidential rivals, I didn't see that much difference in style. Bradley might be casual, but he also was as cautious a politician as Gore.

With Bradley coming on, Gore suddenly reinvented his campaign for the Democratic nomination, cutting the payroll and moving his headquarters to Nashville, "out of the Beltway." If the tactics of the challenger worked, he'd try them. "I'm going to campaign like the underdog," Gore said. He challenged Bradley to debate him right away, weekly, even twice a week. Bradley said he obviously was making progress, since Gore had been trying to ignore him for ten months. Now there was going to be a new Gore, liberated, the vice president said, not wooden. "You know, Janis Joplin sang, 'Freedom's just another word for nothing left to lose,' " Gore recited as he opened the new campaign shop in Nashville. A strange song for a politician who had everything to lose.

To me, the new Gore looked like the old one in cowboy boots and tan sports shirts. Sounded like him, too. But when he and Bradley got around to debating, in Hanover, New Hampshire, the vice presidential remodeling was on display. In a lull before the television cameras went on, Gore took the role of moderator, inviting questions to pass the time, a ploy that recalled, but did not nearly match, the 1980 debate performance in which Reagan snapped that he was entitled to the microphone because he'd paid for it. After the debate, Bradley shook some hands and left. Gore offered to answer more questions as long as anybody wanted to ask them and did, for an hour and a half, loosening his tie and perching on the edge of the stage. It had the flavor of a campus bull session. It wasn't all that casual a performance; Gore had three members of President Clinton's Cabinet at Dartmouth College that night to praise his debate performance to reporters. "I think people saw the real Al Gore," said Energy Secretary Bill Richardson. I wondered what had taken him so long. Gore had been through five winning campaigns for the House and Senate in Tennessee, and two for vice president. He'd had twenty-five years to get real, yet there were still more makeovers coming.

The Democratic debating got testier when Gore and Bradley met on *Meet the Press* in December. Gore sighed aloud and laughed sardonically when Bradley pushed his proposals. They sat side by side, in blue suits and red patterned ties, arguing in the NBC studio in Washington. Gore challenged Bradley to cancel all broadcast advertising in their campaign and debate him twice a week instead. Gore stuck out his hand to shake on it. "I like that hand," Bradley said, looking at it as though it were a dead fish. "But the answer is no." He said it was a ridiculous ploy by the better-known candidate. A Democratic campaign without TV ads would have been fine for Gore, undermining Bradley's effort to gain name recognition. But the challenge made good TV, and the gimmick gave Gore an opportunity to sound like a reformer.

The Republican field was debating, too, but without the main man. Bush exercised the presumed prerogative of the front-runner and said he wouldn't debate his rivals until January 2000 because people wouldn't be paying attention before the election year began. Wrong. Bush's polls in the first primary state began hinting at trouble: McCain was gaining on him. Suddenly the strategy changed, and Bush found time to debate, pretending it wasn't because of the polls, although none of us believed that. So Bush faced his five remaining rivals in a television studio in Manchester, New Hampshire, on December 2. Nothing dramatic, but the important campaign message from Bush was just being there. There was some sniping but no direct hits, not when Alan Keyes, a black candidate with a fiery, eloquent speech style, accused him of acting like "Massah Bush," nor when Senator Orrin Hatch of Utah got really tough and went to the point of criticizing the Bush campaign Web site. "Yours is not user-friendly," Hatch charged. Take that, W.

McCain was the candidate coming on, and the Bush camp underestimated the challenge. Bush wanted a massive tax cut that McCain opposed as too costly, while flat-tax Forbes was firing at the proposal from the other direction. Bush said he was going one up on his father's 1992 "read my lips" promise against tax increases. "This is not only no new taxes, this is tax cuts, so help me God," he vowed. McCain was scoring with his call for campaign reform. The Bush campaign seemed oblivious. They had their front-running game plan and they were sticking to it. When McCain came under hostile questioning in one of the campaign debates, Bush volunteered, twice, that the Arizona senator was a good man. "I don't know what compelled me to say that about you, Senator," he added, smiling. The genial nice guy vanished after McCain beat him in the first primary. McCain was a full-time campaigner in New Hampshire for the better part of a year, bypassing Iowa, where Bush won the first voting of 2000. McCain wasn't going to squander his campaigning on precinct caucuses that had not foretold a contested New Hampshire outcome since Carter won both in 1976. Good strategy—the pollsters reported him drawing even or ahead of Bush in New Hampshire.

The Bush show wasn't a novelty any longer; it was the same old story. McCain was the new act on stage, different, engaging, creating a contest, which we political reporters always prefer to the predictable. McCain was a hero, a Vietnam POW with a remarkable biography. He had just told his story in a best-selling book, *Faith of My Fathers,* co-written, actually, and you had to like a man who gave credit and royalties to the aide who did the writing. Having survived the Hanoi Hilton and a brush with scandal in a Senate ethics investigation, he made an art form of candor. Sometimes I thought he went looking for things to confess. Adultery? Did it, long ago. Drunken sprees against the rules of Annapolis when he was an underachieving midshipman there? Did that, too. Had his judgment as a senator been affected by campaign donations? Sure, all politicians are corrupted by the campaign finance system, and that's why it has to be reformed. He'd learned what politicians seldom do: that a problem disclosed tends to go away while one concealed is likely to come back and bite. When there was controversy over letters McCain had written to federal agencies on behalf of campaign donors—he said they were entitled to the treatment as constituents—he preempted the issue by releasing stacks of his Senate correspondence, a mountain of paper to bury a problem issue.

Bush had made gentleman's C's at Yale and the *New Yorker* did a piece about it, questioning whether he was smart enough to be president. McCain was fifth from the bottom of his class at Annapolis, almost got expelled for misconduct, and it was written off as youthful exuberance.

Bush's people got testy about McCain's fancy treatment by the political press, and they had a point because feature writers and TV producers were delivering gee-whiz pieces about his style. It looked as though political reporters were so hungry for a candidate who seemed to like their company that they would canonize a guy for riding in a bus with them and answering questions nonstop. McCain played it all like a maestro. He had been among the most accessible of senators and seen it pay PR dividends. Now he was the most accessible of candidates. He was cordial, usually open, unless it was something he did not choose to talk about. "Kill 'em with access," McCain had said. He did, in his rolling interviews aboard his campaign bus, emblazoned with his traveling trademark: "The Straight Talk Express." He'd sit in his swivel captain's chair, sipping coffee, a dozen or so reporters huddled around him. There wasn't room for everyone; reporters had to take turns riding the McCain bus. But McCain had a temper and held a grudge. Reporters from his hometown paper, the *Arizona Republic*, were consigned to the backup bus because McCain had been feuding with the newspaper for years, since the publication of a hostile cartoon about his wife, Cindy, who once had been addicted to prescription painkillers. In a 1999 editorial, the *Republic* said McCain's temper was volcanic and questioned whether he had the temperament to be president. When the temper business came up in campaign debates, he deflected it by joking at the questions. "Now that really makes me mad," he would say, and laugh.

He could afford to laugh. The reform message was working, the crowds were growing, his polling trends were up, and Bush was vulnerable. It was a two-man race despite the free-spending Forbes and the minor entries. Bauer went to a pancake-flipping contest in Manchester, flipped one, backed up to catch it in the pan, and flipped himself off the stage. He fell behind a blue curtain but bounced up like a Kewpie doll, unhurt. Forbes was spending more money than even he had in the bank; he sold some of his shares in *Forbes Magazine* to keep running. Bush was still campaigning for his tax cut, his speech and his tactics set despite the changing challenge. His syntax was still erratic. The reporters who traveled with him regularly had T-shirts emblazoned with the word "They." One night in Iowa he'd given one speech too many and delivered a tongue-bent assessment of the era after the Cold War: "When I was coming up we knew exactly who the they were. It was us versus them, and it was clear who the them was. Today we're not so sure who the they are but we know they're there."

Tormented sentences like that became fodder for critics and commentators who questioned whether Bush was ready to be president. It made an easy column on a dull day. Just add up the slips: He once confused Slovakia with Slovenia (I might have, too), and when a showboating Boston TV reporter asked him on camera to name the leaders of Pakistan, India, Taiwan, and Chechnya, he managed only one. It was a cheap shot question; none of us reporters and probably none of the other candidates could have answered it off the cuff. Bush did make some misstatements about foreign policy, and he did say things like "Is our children learning?" That gave rise to pieces questioning whether Dubya, which was supposed to be Texan for W, was smart enough for the White House. But the taunting commentary didn't stick and never added up to the kind of image problem that had saddled and undone Dan Quayle. "I've said about a million words and ten of them didn't come out right," Bush said late in his campaign. He'd said more words than that and flubbed more lines, but so what. It didn't bother many voters. Not even when Jay Leno asked him on *The Tonight Show* to talk about his most embarrassing incident as a child, and he talked about his brother instead. "Marvin urinated in the steam iron," Bush announced.

Back in New Hampshire, at the end of January, just before the primary, the Bush campaign put on a family show. The former president and Barbara Bush flew in to appear with the candidate at an indoor tennis center in Milford. It was tucked away in the fields on a one-lane road, but nearly two thousand people got through the rural traffic jam for the rally. "This boy, this son of ours, is not going to let you down," the former president said in remarks I timed at nineteen seconds. New Hampshire strategists shuddered; "this boy" was not the image they wanted for their candidate. George W. said the family outing had inspired him "to keep charging in New Hampshire." He chose a strange way to do so—he looked out at the biggest crowd of his primary campaign and spoke for all of seventeen seconds. The people who had come for an afternoon of politicking and country music got only the latter. I thought it was a metaphor for the problem that was dogging Bush. The message seemed to be that there was no message. Name, image, and family fame but not much substance. Just the impression his opponents were trying to promote. By primary day the Bush people knew what was coming: McCain. But they didn't expect the landslide they got: McCain 49 percent, Bush 31 percent. Bush retooled. No more nice guy. People liked reform, so he'd be a reformer. A reformer with results, he said. Not like McCain, who, according to the new Bush, talked reform but played footsie with special interest lobbyists. There were tough TV ads, tough talk, attack tactics on both sides as Bush and McCain campaigned for the South Carolina primary, each blaming the other for going negative. Their differences were about details—how big a tax cut, for example—not basic direction, which made the arguments more personal. "This is probably the nastiest campaign that people have seen in a long time," McCain said and went on, curiously, "but look, I'm enjoying it, this is a great and exhilarating experience." For his campaign, the exhilaration was back in New Hampshire. South Carolina's was a strictly Republican primary. The independents who had boosted his New Hampshire count couldn't vote. He'd win again in Michigan, where Democrats could vote in the Republican primary, and at home in Arizona, but that was it. Bush had the bankroll, the organization, and the Republican establishment on his side, and on March 9 McCain conceded.

From that date, Bush was effectively unopposed, with no major rival for the nomination. Forbes had quit a month before, out another $30 million of his publishing fortune in another hopeless campaign. "We were nosed out by a landslide," he lamented. He was better at withdrawing than at campaigning. I'd spent the last day of his campaign covering him in Delaware, where he came bearing bad news for two generations. He began by telling high school students that they would never see a dime of the Social Security for which some of them already were paying taxes on their part-time earnings. Then he went to an old folks' home and talked about his tax plan. No inheritance tax, he said, and they applauded. You ought to be able to leave this earth unmolested by the Internal Revenue Service. There was less applause. Some of them were in wheelchairs and looked as though they would be leaving soon with or without the IRS. Then a standard Forbes line: "No taxation without respiration." No applause. Too close for comfort, I thought.

The contest between Gore and Bradley turned nasty and personal. Gore said Bradley was too left of center to win the presidency, although the truth was that their basic philosophies weren't diametrically different. Bradley said Gore was too tainted by fund-raising scandals to be elected. He said the vice president was the candidate of special interests, "a thousand promises and a thousand attacks." But Bradley never did as well at the primary polls as he'd done in the 1999 public opinion polls. Gore swamped him in the Iowa caucuses and beat him, narrowly, in the New Hampshire primary. Gore's margin there was only 6,395 votes, and independents who opted to cast Republican ballots for McCain could have been the difference. Or maybe it was waitresses, who certainly outnumbered that margin of defeat in a tourist state. Ron Fournier and I were at the bar of our hotel in Manchester shortly before the primary when Bradley's face appeared on the TV. The blond bartender looked up and frowned. "That dick," she said. We wondered whether we'd heard right, asked, and she repeated it. Bradley, she said, had stayed at the hotel periodically, called for room service, and demanded that his food be at his door almost instantly. When it wasn't, he'd call and snarl at the help.

I asked her what kind of tip he'd added to the bill. No tip, the wait-ress said. He'd just sign the tab with the standard room service fee on it, nothing added. Bradley's reputation as a poor tipper apparently had spread; the *Manchester Union Leader* ran a gossip column piece about it the next day.

After losing eighteen states against Gore, Bradley quit the cam-paign on the same day McCain got out. Bradley said he would sup-port Gore, but he didn't sound enthusiastic, complaining one last time about the "distortions and negativity" the vice president had used against him. "I hope that he'll run a better campaign in the general election."

So the major-party presidential nominees were set, unchallenged, eight months before the presidential election. Bush didn't even have to cope with Buchanan, who had nagged Republicans from the belliger-ent right in two campaigns, because he bolted the party. Buchanan said he wasn't going to accept an "assigned walk-on role" in 2000 and would run as a Reform Party candidate instead. His ideas were alien to that party's positions but he brushed it off, because the Reform nomination was a ticket to campaign all the way to the election, which he'd never get from the Republicans. Even more enticing, the nominee would be entitled to $12.6 million in federal campaign funds, based on Perot's share of the 1996 vote. Buchanan got the nomina-tion, which divided the third party, and he got the money, in September 2000. In the election, he drew less than one-half of 1 per-cent of the vote, far short of the 5 percent required to qualify the Reform Party nominee for future federal funds.

Once Gore's challenger was out of his path and the Democratic nomination was clinched, the vice president didn't seem to know what he wanted to do next. He admitted later there was no real plan for a spring offensive against Bush, who still was favored in the national polls. When Gore urged a campaign finance overhaul, the issue called up echoes of his own 1996 fund-raising excesses. He conceded that he was an "imperfect messenger" for reform and said "I've got the scars to prove it." The Republicans had the videotape to prove it: Gore amid the nuns at the Democratic fund-raiser at the Buddhist temple; Gore trying to defend himself at a news conference by saying repeatedly that "no controlling legal authority" barred the telephone calls he'd made to donors from his office and the White House. At the same time, Gore had to raise more money now that he was the 2000 candidate.

He said jokingly at a fancy Washington dinner that his campaign strategy was to claim credit for the thriving economy while assigning the blame for what went wrong to the departing Clinton. But the balancing routine was not a joke, it was real. Gore was trying to run with and away from Clinton at the same time. That's always a tough act for a vice president trying to take over the top job. The vice president is running to succeed the administration in which he's been the junior partner, and without insulting the boss, he has to convince people that he can do the job better.

Gore certainly could change the worst of the Clinton record—the personal scandal, the lies, and the impeachment. There wasn't going to be any more messing around with White House interns. While Gore had been fulsome to fawning in his postimpeachment praise of Clinton's achievements, he drew the line against the boss's personal conduct. "I understand the disappointment and anger you feel toward President Clinton," Gore replied to the first questioner in his first Democratic campaign debate, although that's not what he was asked. "I felt it myself." Unloading that baggage was a campaign-long mission. When Gore formally announced his candidacy in June 1999, he said that the president's conduct was inexcusable and that too much time had been diverted from real business because of the scandal and impeachment. That line annoyed Clinton, who always seemed to be in something close to denial; he later said that Gore should not suffer politically over "bogus scandals." They were real enough. Gore's choice of his own running mate was part of his antidote. Senator Joseph Lieberman of Connecticut was the first Senate Democrat to publicly denounce Clinton's conduct in the Monica Lewinsky affair, calling it disgraceful and deceitful.

Gore's plus-minus strategy on the Clinton connection reflected the public opinion polls. To the end of the term they indicated majority approval of Clinton's job performance and majority disapproval of him personally. The cliché catchphrase was "Clinton fatigue." When you asked Gore about it, he'd tell you that people were fatigued with all the talk about Clinton fatigue. But it was there, and I suspected the vice president had contracted it himself. He was getting more blame for the downside of the Clinton years than credit for the achievements.

A certain weariness is inevitable near the end of a two-term presidency, a mood deepened in 1999 and 2000 not only by scandal and impeachment but also by the unrelenting glare of twenty-four-hour television news and talk. Watch one White House cast perform for eight years and you're ready to see some different characters. Gore had his questionable fund-raising ventures of 1996 to defend; Bush allies in Congress demanded that a Ken Starr–style sleuthing prosecutor be put on the case, but that wasn't going to happen in a Democratic administration. Add it up, and the issues of trust and ethics were prime targets for Bush and the Republicans.

Gore couldn't find his campaign footing in the spring of 2000. First he said he wanted a campaign of ideas, not insults. Then he called Bush arrogant, smug, inexperienced, irresponsible, and reckless, before another change in tactics, in which he stopped talking about his rival by name. Later, he changed campaign chairmen for a third time. The ship was drifting, and somebody had to steer.

"I don't know how many times you're able to reinvent yourself in the course of a campaign," Bush wondered pointedly, although he'd done it himself. The amiable leader had become a hard-line attack candidate, more conservative than compassionate after losing the first primary. Once the nomination was settled, Bush remodeled again, moving back to the center with a catalog of proposals edging into usually Democratic turf on housing, health care for the poor, education, and the environment. In the Bush campaign, though, the management never changed. Bush was a throwback to the era when friends and longtime loyalists ran presidential campaigns. His high command of Texans had been with him from the Austin statehouse and would stay with him to the White House.

Bush's springtime strategy was to follow the Nixon axiom—play to the conservatives to get nominated, play to the center to try to get elected. A plug from McCain would help, since he'd become the fallen hero of the independents. McCain won a half dozen primaries in states where independents or crossover Democrats could vote on the Republican side. He was their favorite, the reformer, although on almost every other issue he was an orthodox Republican and at least as conservative as Bush. McCain was courteous in conceding, but he was irked at Bush campaign tactics against him, and he did not volunteer an endorsement. After two months, the nominee and the loser finally met for a ninety-minute peace talk in Pittsburgh, after which McCain endorsed Bush. At first he didn't use what his people had come to call "the E word." Asked why he had not offered an outright endorsement, he did, saying, "I endorse Governor Bush" six times over for wry emphasis. He said it was like taking medicine now instead of later. McCain offered the right Republican words at the national convention, saying it was "my time to serve" in order to help Bush win. Joining the Bush campaign on the West Coast in August for a three-day swing, McCain said he would ask his independent supporters to consider Bush but couldn't tell them how to vote because they didn't take instructions on that. "Independents are independents because they are independent," McCain explained.

Then they embarked on the strangest campaign train trip I ever covered—165 miles, an all-day excursion from Salinas up the coast and east toward Sacramento. It was supposed to be a whistle-stop but there was a lot more whistle than stop to it, with rallies at the beginning and the end and a stop at a tiny farm town in between. The Bush campaign explained that they couldn't stop for speeches in cities like San Jose, where there was a crowd at the station and the candidate waved as the train crept through, because they were on the main track and could not disrupt the regular railway traffic. Nice sightseeing, though, a relaxing day's ride in the press cars. The senator and the governor strolled through to answer some questions, then retreated to their compartments at the back of the train. We figured they were back there relaxing together, talking about the campaign, or perhaps chatting. They had nearly six hours. But John Weaver, McCain's top political hand, told me later that they spent little of it together, with each man riding in his own compartment with his own company. Weaver said he thought of it as a sealed train, like the one on which the Germans sent Vladimir Lenin back from exile to Russia to foment revolution in 1917.

Later in the campaign, McCain angered the Bush people by challenging both nominees to voluntarily forgo any use of unregulated political donations in the White House race. Gore accepted. Bush refused, and McCain said that was a mistake. A minor episode, only a ripple in the campaign, but these guys never were going to be best friends. While Bush was circumspect, his campaign aides didn't conceal their McCain fatigue. The senator was a Republican and a declared ally, but they didn't like their allies to be meddlesome.

Gore was still trying to manage the Clinton connection. "We're not going to campaign together because I'm determined to campaign as my own man and present my own vision," Gore said. But the solo rule did not apply in fund-raising; the vice president teamed with the president to raise nearly $40 million for the Democrats. And Clinton wasn't the quiet type. Just before the Democratic National Convention, he delivered his most contrite and candid reflection on the Lewinsky affair, "a terrible mistake I made." He told a convention of clergymen in suburban Chicago that he had learned "the fundamental importance of character and integrity," delivering a ninety-minute confessional and drawing headlines that were no help to Gore in his effort to get past the White House scandal. Clinton had said it all before, Gore claimed, and it was time to look to the future, not the past. At the convention in Los Angeles, Clinton came on like Rocky, his giant image on TV screens above the convention stage as he walked through underground corridors on the way to the platform. He described Gore as the man to "keep this progress and prosperity going," the man who was always there for the tough decisions. Clinton already had said that Gore shouldn't be blamed for his personal mistakes.

After his imperial entrance and farewell address at the Los Angeles convention, Clinton flew to Monroe, Michigan, for a passing of the torch appearance with Gore. He folded the vice president in a bear hug and then left the Democratic stage to Gore. He also left the ethics and trust issues that dogged the Gore campaign. Gore's convention show began with a long, clutching kiss of his wife, Tipper, which made you wonder whether he was ever going to stop and talk. Later, David Letterman suggested to Gore that the Kiss was meant to send a message that this Democrat was happy at home, not a rover like Clinton. "C'mon, c'mon, boo, give me a break," the vice president said. It only looked that way.

Gore's convention address was another declaration of political independence, another attempt to reintroduce himself and shed the wooden image. "I stand here tonight as my own man and I want you to know me for who I truly am," Gore declared in an unintended summation of his image problem. He then hurried through a fifty-one-minute speech, sometimes talking over the applause to get in all the policy details. "I know that sometimes people say I'm too serious, that I talk too much substance and policy. But the presidency is more than a popularity contest." True enough, but popularity gets candidates there.

The Clinton hangover persisted. The day after Gore's nomination, word leaked that the special prosecutor was setting up a new grand jury to hear scandal evidence against Clinton. The White House said the timing "reeks to high heaven." Clinton's own timing and comments were less than perfect. Shortly before the election, the campaign wraps opened a bit, and the president went on get-out-the-vote missions aimed at reliably Democratic minority constituencies. A black radio interviewer in California told Clinton he wished the president could have another term. "You can get the next best thing," Clinton replied, which was not the impression Gore wanted left with voters.

Gore did get a break just after the Democratic convention with word from the Justice Department that there would be no outside investigation of Gore's fund-raising conduct because there was no evidence of lawbreaking. Bush had a pat answer on the topic: He said it was clear that Gore's past conduct raised credibility questions, but that Americans "are sick and tired of all these scandals and investigations" and the best way to end them would be to elect him. No point in risking a backlash with an attack, not when he could take advantage of the issue without one. He played it that way all season; at the Republican convention he said it was time for "a responsibility era" and delivered the make-believe oath of office that would be his finale at campaign rallies. "When I put my hand on the Bible, I will swear not only to uphold the laws of our land, I will swear to uphold the honor and dignity of the office to which I have been elected, so help me God." No mention of the Clinton scandals. None needed. His crowds knew what he was talking about.

The unorthodox selection of Lieberman, an Orthodox Jew, for the vice presidential nomination fit Gore's effort to prove himself an independent operator, not the man a step behind Clinton. The president's men had not forgiven Lieberman's denunciation of Clinton's misconduct in September 1998. That was two months before the Republican House impeached Clinton. In the Senate, Lieberman voted against convicting Clinton and kicking him out of office in 1999, although he wanted the president censured. But his early rebuke of Clinton was what people remembered. His centrist, New Democrat record fit with the campaign position Gore was trying to stake. He joked that he'd campaign 24/6. His orthodox faith would keep him from it on the seventh day, the Sabbath. Lieberman, the first Jew nominated to a major party ticket, said he didn't want people to vote for him to make history but "to forget the history" and think about the future. He made too much of his religion in his early campaigning, quoting Chronicles, by heart, and offering a prayer of thanks when he first appeared with Gore. He talked about his religion and "the dedication of our nation and ourselves to God," prompting a rebuke from an unlikely source, the Jewish Anti-Defamation League, which said that overdoing the religious theme was "inappropriate and even unsettling." He toned it down. Bush, a Methodist, hadn't been reticent about his religion; in a primary campaign debate when the candidates were asked which philosopher or thinker they most admired, Bush replied, "Jesus Christ, because he changed my heart." That prompted some cynical smirks, but Barbara Bush said she wasn't surprised at his answer. "I know that's true," she said. "I mean, George, we go to him as our religious guru."

In choosing Dick Cheney as his running mate, Bush went to the heart of the Republican establishment, to a nominee who had been in Congress, the White House, and his father's Cabinet, a Washington veteran with foreign and defense policy credentials the governor lacked. The wisecrack went that Cheney was there to provide adult supervision, although at fifty-nine he was only five years older than the presidential nominee. He looked like a safe, reassuring choice for the ticket. He'd been known in Washington for a soft-spoken but insistent managerial style and for an ability to work with both parties as White House chief of staff and as secretary of defense. The Democrats were on his case as soon as he was nominated, criticizing his hard-line conservative voting record as a Wyoming congressman, then the multimillion-dollar platinum parachute he was getting from the Dallas oil services conglomerate he left to join the ticket. He'd had three heart attacks, the first when he was thirty-seven, and he had a fourth one, after the 2000 election but before it was settled. His doctor called it so mild as to be trivial.

Bush and his father both denied that the former president had pushed his man Cheney onto the ticket, although they did talk about it. "I love my dad, but I'm going to have my own team," Bush said. Too much of former President Bush would play into the Democrats' contention that Governor Bush was a replay candidate for the White House, without the experience for the job. "Nearest I can tell, the message of the Bush campaign is 'How bad can I be?'" Clinton taunted. "'I've been governor of Texas, my daddy was president, I own a baseball team, they like me down there.'" That made the elder Bush angry, and he said he might just go public with what he really thought about Clinton's personal conduct, but he calmed down and stayed off the stage. Bush and his family wanted to quash the dynasty talk, not risk more of it. There were veterans of the first Bush presidency in the campaign and then in the Cabinet of the second, prompting critics to argue that the new President Bush couldn't find his own crew. The criticism was understandable but so were the carryover appointees. Bush's inner staff was indeed his own, the Texans, but any new president looks to his party's last administration for people with the experience and standing to serve at the top of the new one. In Bush's case, that meant people who had served his father. It wasn't just the family ties. That's simply the way the system works.

The fall campaign between Bush and Gore was not one of breakthroughs or turning points. The polls that showed it close also showed why: Most people considered the campaign uninformative and boring. These guys had been around the block for more than a year and they weren't proposing anything particularly new, let alone inspiring. Bush was for a general income tax cut; a break for the rich according to Gore, who advocated tax reductions at lower income levels to benefit working families. Gore played the populist, saying his programs were aimed at workers and needy Americans. Republicans said he was trying to set class against class. Familiar stuff in familiar rhetoric.

But there were unscripted moments. Bush bumbled by blurting an insult into an open microphone before a rally in Naperville, Illinois, not knowing he'd be heard. "There's Adam Clymer, major-league asshole from the *New York Times*," he told Cheney. "Oh, yeah, bigtime," Cheney replied. Clymer is a skilled, seasoned reporter, and suddenly, if briefly, he was a celebrity, a talk show magnet although he declined the TV invitations. As the saying goes, insult away, just get the name right. Adam had been insulted by experts, major-leaguers, before Bush got into the game. In *The Boys on the Bus*, Tim Crouse called him "a priggish, pear-shaped reporter" who bitched incessantly. Some truth there, then as thirty years later, but who isn't, and who doesn't? Clymer had written pieces raising critical questions about Bush's performance as governor and had sharply questioned Cheney on the benefits he was reaping from his oil company. He said he was disappointed at Bush's language. Bush apparently was not, at least not to the point of apology. His response: "I regret everybody heard what I said." The next time I saw Clymer I told him I didn't think he deserved the major league-slur. Triple A at best.

Gore had his flaps, but none to match that one. He had a problem habit of exaggerating his history and overstating his facts. He said the complaints about it were the exaggerations. Okay, so he hadn't been instrumental in creating the Internet, which dated from 1969, when he was still in college, but he had promoted it after he got to Congress. And maybe he and Tipper weren't really the role models for *Love Story*. And he was only joking when he told a labor crowd that he remembered the union label advertising song as a lullabye from his childhood, which was before it was written. To make a point about the high cost of prescription drugs, he said his mother-in-law was paying $108 a month for arthritis medicine he got for his dog at $37.80. It turned out that the numbers on the arthritis drug came from a Democratic study, not from family experience. Gore said that didn't affect his point, that drug prices were too high.

Gore was still starchy and still trying to break the typecasting. Bush was breezy and promoting the image. Gore was formal but friendly. He knew I planned to retire after the election, and when I asked a question at a campaign news conference, he prefaced his answer by saying he couldn't believe I'd really do it. I did, at sixty-six, after writing the AP account of Bush's inauguration. Gore was being nice; I found it rather awkward.

Bush had a campaign rally at a minor-league ballpark near Appleton, Wisconsin, home of the Wisconsin Timber Rattlers of the Midwest League. They passed out team hats: maroon and black with a big W in front. The next campaign stop was an airport rally on a sunny afternoon, so I wore the ball cap. Bush spotted me as I was getting off the plane. "Hey, Walter, love to see ya in that W hat," he said, spreading his fingers into his W gesture. I told him not to forget that I was a W myself. It didn't register. After the rally, Bush corralled me, threw an arm over my shoulder, and called to the photographers to get a shot of me in the hat and him mugging beside me. "Governor, that's my initial," I said. "I was a W before you were born." Made no difference. He was W. I was Walter.

Bush and Gore debated three times to what I thought was a draw. Advantage Bush, because everybody expected Gore to be better at it. Not even a dogged debate watcher who tuned in to all three plus the vice presidential debate could point to a telling turn of phrase, to a breakthrough, or to a significant blunder. It was like a Broadway musical that left the audience without a tune to hum. No showstoppers, nothing close. Gore accused Bush of favoring big corporate interests and a tax cut for the wealthy. Bush called the vice president a big-spending Democrat who wanted the government to make decisions Americans should be free to make for themselves. That was the daily campaign fare, played in the debates to a national television audience.

Gore didn't do well on style points; he kept changing his approach, not a plus for a candidate who kept saying he wanted people to see him for who he really was but left them with a sort of multiple choice. First time out, in Boston, he offered exasperated sighs and shrugs while Bush was talking. That didn't play well on TV, so in Winston-Salem, North Carolina, he was sedate, even apologetic. But that wasn't quite right, either. In the St. Louis finale he was aggressive, stalking across the stage toward Bush, armed with a microphone. He said later that it was like the porridge in "Goldilocks and the Three Bears," first too hot, then too cold, and then "the third one was just right." The Goldilocks image wasn't one I would have wanted to call up, but that's what he said.

Bush played Bush in all three acts. Same guy, same lines, neither compelling nor commanding but okay, nothing eloquent but free of the twisted words and convoluted sentences that tripped him as a campaigner.

The public opinion polls were getting close, an edge to Bush but not a significant one as the long campaign approached what would be the longest election. It was not that people liked them equally; it was the opposite. There was scant enthusiasm for either candidate except among the partisan cheerleaders on each side. Americans liked Ike long before and long after Dwight D. Eisenhower's presidency. They honored the legend of John Kennedy's Camelot. Even people who opposed Ronald Reagan's politics came to admire his leadership style. But this was an age without political heroes. For all Clinton's political arts, the departing president arrived in national politics with his scars and evasions showing, and his White House misconduct, scandal, and impeachment had heightened cynicism about politicians. The consultant-driven messages, the intrusiveness of the media, and the emphasis on dirty secrets in the lives of politicians all were turnoffs. Nonstop exposure, especially on television, narrowed the distance between the led and the leaders, eroding what remained of the mystique of the men who might be president. None of that was new to the new century, but all of it came together in the so-what mood of the voters in 2000, the year of the dead heat.

The long count began with the quick call that got it wrong. In the news business, there is no pressure greater than that of handling a close election. You want the story first but you have to get it right. Early in my career, I'd learned the human price of an error on election night. In a Republican primary election in Vermont in 1958, a county stringer made a mistake in addition, leading to an AP tabulation so close that the loser demanded a recount. He wouldn't have except for our mistake—he would have conceded because the accurate margin was decisive. He told me afterward that we'd made him look like a poor loser and that he would suffer for it when he tried to make a comeback. That's what happened, a lesson that always put me on the side of caution.

In 2000, we knew going in that Florida would be a crucial state and potentially the decisive one between Bush and Gore. "When Al Gore and George W. Bush look for an early clue to foretell who will celebrate and who will concede their long-locked struggle for the White House, they will check the count in Florida," I wrote the day before the election. "Should the vote be as closely divided as the public opinion polls, Florida also could point to a long ballot count to settle what has been billed as the closest contest in forty years." Given the stakes, and it did not take a genius to see them, I figured that calling Florida for Gore amounted to declaring him president-elect. Without Florida, Bush would have to win an impossible combination of upsets in Democratic states to gain an electoral majority. With it, he finally got 271 electoral votes, only one to spare. But the TV networks and, regrettably, the Associated Press projected a Gore victory in Florida as the polls closed, based on voter interviews outside polling places in selected key precincts. That was the system, and the system ruled. I always clung to a preference for waiting until enough real ballots had been tabulated to test the projections, but that was old-fashioned, not the way it was done anymore. The Gore victory call stood for about two hours, during which Bush and his people protested it as premature and potentially wrong, while Gore's camp worried about the same thing. At 10:13 P.M., Voter News Service retracted the call. The experts had it wrong. The TV stars had to confess the blunder. "If we say somebody's carried a state you can pretty much take it to the bank, book it, that's true," Dan Rather had said in opening CBS election night coverage. The check bounced.

For the first time in the era of election projections based on voter polling, the presidential race was incredibly close in state after state, nowhere so close as in Florida. There, the process and the electoral judgments it requires failed not once but twice because the networks compounded the blunder by declaring Bush the winner shortly after 2:00 A.M., prompting Gore to telephone Bush and concede the election. Temporarily. There were premature headlines in some Wednesday morning newspapers declaring Bush president-elect, overtaken later by accurate accounts saying it was too close to call. Standing against the tide and the pressure in those early morning hours, the AP said it was not calling the election for Bush because Florida was too close to declare him the winner. He was ahead, but by an inconclusive fragment of the votes. The networks backed off, wrong again, and retracted again. The off and on, won or not declarations and reversals on national TV compounded the uncertainty of an uncertain outcome as Florida was recounted, contested, and disputed for five weeks, in more than fifty court challenges by one side or the other. Then the Supreme Court, at five to four as closely divided as the election outcome, ended the Florida recounts.

The election night calls and miscalls were based on the projections and unofficial vote counts by Voter News Service. Since the 1994 elections, VNS had conducted exit interviews outside the polls and projected results based on them and on sample precincts selected to reflect a state at large. The projections were delivered to the networks and the AP, which decided whether and when to make their own election calls. Competitive TV pressure drove those calls; when one network declared a winner the others usually followed quickly. At 2:16 A.M. on

November 8, Fox News Channel declared that Bush had carried Florida and was president-elect. Within minutes, the three broadcast networks and CNN did, too, flashing the report across the screens of anyone who was still watching TV at that hour.

The AP used VNS but also conducted its own, independent tabulation of the votes. In the count of those real ballots, Bush held a rapidly dwindling lead. At 2:37 A.M., with the networks calling him the winner, the AP reported the state still up for grabs. At 3:11 A.M., an AP advisory reported that the Bush edge was shrinking and might not stand. By 4 A.M., the TV calls all had been rescinded, and Florida was back in the undecided column.

But the chorus of television calls for Bush became a sort of reality show. Because of them, Gore telephoned Bush at about 2:30 A.M. Washington time to congratulate him and concede. The vice president was in his motorcade on the way to deliver a concession speech in the rain in Nashville when his campaign strategist got word to him not to do it, that the Florida count was not settled and there would be an automatic recount under state law. An hour or so after conceding, he called Bush again to say that the situation had changed and Florida was too close to call.

"Let me make sure I understand," Bush said testily. "You're calling back to retract that concession?"

"You don't have to get snippy about this," Gore snapped back.

Before the contest was settled, a lot of people were snippy about it. There was no census of all the lawyers who had a hand in all the court challenges, but they certainly outnumbered the 537 ballots by which Bush was certified the winner of Florida's twenty-five electoral votes. The margin had been shaved even finer by partial recounts and court rulings before the Supreme Court told them all to stop. So Bush was president-elect. "It is likely legislative bodies nationwide will examine ways to improve the mechanisms and machinery for voting," Chief Justice William Rehnquist noted in the ruling. But no voting machinery grinds finely enough for certainty in an election as close at Florida's.

The election night and morning after TV blunders didn't count legally, but they had an impact politically. Bush had been winner and president-elect once, Gore had conceded once, and as close he got, within 154 votes under one Florida Supreme Court decision, he never led. That put him on the defensive, casting him as the challenger. Bush was the leader, albeit the shakiest of leaders, and he had to be dislodged. That's the position any politician wants. Let Gore argue that he was trying to preserve democracy with more recounts; the Republicans said he was trying to steal the election.

Bush and Gore each had his own campaign blunders to rue. Bush invested campaign time and money in California, wasting it in a state where he couldn't win instead of spending it where he could. In Florida, for example, where his jeopardy was evident even though his brother Jeb was governor. Gore lost his own state, Tennessee, where winning would have made him president despite the Florida defeat. Clinton loyalists complained all fall that it was time to take the wraps off the president, put him to work in Democratic territory and at home in Arkansas, where Bush also won. Minor candidates seldom make a major difference. They did in Florida. Ralph Nader drained away votes that likely would have been Gore's, and more than enough to have made him the winner. Even Buchanan's otherwise insignificant share was five times the Republican margin. No matter. There had to be a winner and the winner was Bush. And no matter that Gore won the national popular vote by 539,497, because electoral votes choose presidents.

After all the bitter weeks, I thought Gore was a classy loser. He said he strongly disagreed with the Supreme Court ruling but accepted the finality of it and offered his concession "for the sake of our unity as a people and the strength of our democracy." The overtime election had proven both. There was anger but no violence. Nixon wrote that a recount of disputed states in his 1960 loss to Kennedy would have taken months, uncertainty he said could have been devastating in America's foreign relations. There was no such toll in 2000; indeed, while the outcome was in dispute, President Clinton traveled to Vietnam, the first American president to go there since the communist victory. On the way, he told me that he wasn't concerned about lingering partisan bitterness or instability because whoever won, "I think the American people are pretty good about uniting around a president."

"There's nothing to worry about," he told Russian President Vladimir Putin and other leaders at a conference in Brunei.

There wasn't. Gore accepted his greatest disappointment with grace and humor, charms he never quite managed as a candidate. We heard that some of his campaign people were annoyed by his insistence on a self-effacing exit. They knew the game was up, but they were not convinced that he had lost fairly if at all, and they never would be. But Gore said that when he called Bush to concede, "I promised him that I wouldn't call him back this time." His exit line was one he had used from scores of campaign platforms in 1992 against the Republicans, when he prompted the crowds to chant, "It's time for them to go."

"And now, my friends, in a phrase I once addressed to others, it's time for me to go," Gore said on December 13, 2000, after the election was settled at last.

There had been no struggle like it since 1876, when Republicans maneuvered Rutherford B. Hayes to the presidency only two days before he was inaugurated, an outcome forever disputed by the foes who called him "His Fraudulency." Hayes served one term and said nobody ever left the White House with less regret than he did. But Hayes also demonstrated that even a missing mandate does not render a president powerless. He protected the right to vote for black Americans, declared a canal across Panama to be a national goal, and took the first steps toward eliminating the spoils system of filling federal jobs, defying Republicans who had been his sponsors. "He serves his party best who serves his country best," Hayes said when he took his contested office, a line that lasted although the admonition was too often ignored.

President-elect at last, Bush addressed the nation from the crowded chamber of the Texas House of Representatives, saying, "After a difficult election . . . our nation must rise above a house divided . . . I was not elected to serve one party but to serve one nation."

It was only rhetoric and symbolism, from the loser and from the winner, but the ritual was important. In the normal course of election events, the vital transition begins within hours of the poll closings, the transition that makes a campaigning politician into "Mr. President," a leader accepted even by people who did not want him in the White House. One careful step at a time, new presidents prepare for power between election night and inauguration day with overtures to Congress, courtesy messages to world leaders, gestures to their defeated rivals. Half of the ten weeks usually afforded for that process had been spent settling the 2000 election. Bush was the first man elected president despite losing the popular vote since 1888; he said that was because he spent his campaign time where he had a chance, not trying to increase his losing share of the vote in states like New York that were sure to go Democratic. A presidential election is singular, but it really is fifty-one separate elections to award the electoral votes of each state and the District of Columbia to the candidate who wins there, no matter the margin of victory. As a candidate, Bush had said that when he took his proposals to Congress he would tell them that he came with a message from the American people. Forget that; there was no message. The Senate was split, the House narrowly Republican, the presidency settled in court. There was no mandate. But a president defines his own mandate. Political rancor persisted, but the system worked, proven again under stress that would have sent people to the streets or the barricades in some other world capitals.

As vice president, Gore presided when his defeat was certified before Congress with the recording of the electoral votes. It was a ritual but a striking scene. The last vice president to lose the presidential election and then preside over the reporting of electoral votes was Richard Nixon, forty years before. Hubert Humphrey chose to be otherwise occupied rather than take the chair at the joint session that received the electoral votes by which Nixon beat him in 1968. Nixon had said at the 1960 ceremony that "in our campaigns, no matter how hard fought they may be, no matter how close the election may turn out to be, those who lose accept the verdict and support those who win." Now Gore bore the duty in an even closer election. And he bore up, overruling twenty objections raised by black House members who staged final protests against the Bush victory. Representative Jesse Jackson Jr. raised one challenge. "The chair thanks the gentleman from Illinois but, hey," Gore said, grinning. "We did all we could," cried Representative Alcee Hastings of Florida. Gore smiled and said thanks. Then he announced the 271 votes for Bush, the majority plus one, and his own count, 267. "May God bless our new president," Gore said.

I talked with Bush in a spare, dingy airport office in Midland, Texas, his hometown and his last stop on the way to Washington to be inaugurated president. He dismissed as background noise the taunts of his critics that he wasn't smart enough to run the government without a vice president and senior Cabinet officials seasoned in his father's administration. "I am comfortable with who I am, and therefore I can smile when people says he's not smart enough to be the president, and I guess my attitude is that I'm just going to have to show them," Bush said. It was my last interview as a reporter. As it ended, I thanked Bush for the interview. "Thank you for your career," he replied. At Andrews Air Force Base that night, the president-elect was greeted by Cheney and a receiving line of official Washington. I was standing under the wing of the Air Force jetliner, reminiscing about all the campaign flights of all the forty years as Bush shook hands with his official greeters. I half heard a voice calling what sounded like my name. A colleague nudged me and said it was Bush. He had stepped away from the welcomers, and he was waving toward me. "Hey, Walter," he said. "Good luck." "Good luck to you, sir," I called back as Bush waved and returned to the line of VIPs.

I had been writing columns for the AP for twelve years and I had one to go. I interviewed the first President-elect Bush for my first column in 1989 and the second President-elect Bush for my last in 2001. I asked each of them as he began what he would want said of him after his time in the White House.

"I want to give it my best shot," the elder Bush had said on the eve of his inauguration. "The presidency is still the place from which to lead and from which to effect change, hopefully for the better."

Same topic, new president. "I hope people will be able to say he was steady under fire, he was wise enough to listen to counsel and decisive enough to make a decision that made a positive difference," George W. told me.

One final assignment. My last AP byline was on the story of Bush's inauguration:

"George Walker Bush was inaugurated 43rd president of the United States on Saturday, only the second time in American history a son had followed his father to the White House.

"At a cold, drizzly high noon, Bush raised his right hand and swore the oath of the office to which he promised to bring 'civility, courage, compassion and character.' His eyes brimmed with tears at the emotion of the hour. In the pageantry of the transfer of power, George Herbert Walker Bush stood proud witness to his son's inauguration 12 years after his own."

With that final story it was time for me to go. I'd had a front row seat on national politics for forty years. It was exhilarating, exhausting, satisfying, tense, frustrating, and fun—my ticket to see, hear, and write about winners and losers, flaws and failings, in the imperfect American way of nominating and electing presidents.